monty don
The Complete
Gardener

monty don
The Complete
Gardener

LONDON, NEW YORK, MUNICH,
MELBOURNE, DELHI

For Sarah

Project Manager Bella Pringle
Designer Anne-Marie Bulat
Senior Managing Editor Anna Kruger
Senior Managing Art Editor Lee Griffiths
DTP Designer Louise Waller
Production Controller Heather Hughes

2009 EDITION
Managing Art Editor Alison Donovan
Senior Production Editor Luca Frassinetti
Senior Production Controller Mandy Inness

Photography Ari Ashley

First published in Great Britain in 2003

This edition published in 2009
by Dorling Kindersley Limited,
80 Strand, London WC2R 0RL

A Penguin Company

2 4 6 8 10 9 7 5 3 1

ISBN 978 1 4053 4270 4

Reproduced by Colourscan, Singapore
Printed and bound in China by Toppan

See our complete catalogue at
www.dk.com

Contents

Background 8

Being organic 10
Relationship to place, organic horticultural practice, weather, soil, cultivation, tools, compost, manures, mulches, plant propagation, the greenhouse, rainfall and irrigation, weeds, pests and diseases

Structure 88
Planning the design, practical considerations Paths, walls and fences, hedges and laying hedges, trees, the Lime Walk, pleaching limes, the Coppice, topiary

Flowers 132
Spring Garden: spring, summer and winter bulbs
Jewel Garden: annuals and biennials, climbers, grasses and bamboos
Walled Garden: perennials, climbers, shrubs, roses, winter shrubs
Damp Garden: hostas and ferns, willows

Vegetables 238
The vegetable plot, crop rotation
Spring vegetables: asparagus, broccoli, calabrese, salad crops, spring greens, sorrel

Summer vegetables: peas, onions, shallots, artichokes, tomatoes, broad beans, lettuce, carrots, potatoes, beetroot, courgettes, cucumbers, French and climbing beans, radish, spinach
Autumn vegetables: squashes, celery, celeriac, aubergines, peppers, chard, florence fennel, chicory, turnips, swedes, sweetcorn
Winter vegetables: cabbages, cauliflower, leeks, parsnips, winter kale

The Herb Garden 340
Annual and biennial herbs: garlic, basil, coriander, parsley, dill, borage, angelica
Mediterranean herbs: rosemary, thyme, lavender, sage, marjoram, hyssop, bay, lovage, fennel, lemon balm, tarragon, feverfew, mints, comfrey, horseradish, chives, tansy

Fruit 372
The orchard: Orchard fruit: apples, damsons and plums, figs, nuts, quinces, pears
Soft fruit: raspberries, strawberries, gooseberries, blackcurrants, red- and whitecurrants

Index 430

Acknowledgements 440

Background When it comes to gardening I only know what I have learnt in my own gardens, therefore the contents of this book return continually to this garden.

I have gardened since I was a child, although not always willingly. Nevertheless, by the time I was eighteen or so I had a basic grounding, and by nineteen was able to earn money working as a gardener in the South of France. My instinct has always been to cultivate any piece of soil that I have access to and, with my wife Sarah, have done so obsessively for the past 23 years. We made our first garden together in the early 1980s in London and during the six years of creating our garden, I learnt a lot about gardening in a small, urban plot. I loved it, but by 1988 I wanted more space so we swapped our 30m (100ft) back garden for 32 acres (13 hectares) of Herefordshire countryside.

We were forced to sell that house and garden – which I had loved from the first - and moved here in autumn 1991. The house was beautiful but uninhabitable, without sanitation, running water, or electricity and almost everything other than the timber frame had to be replaced or repaired. The two acres of land that came with the house had been uncultivated for a number of years and was a jungle of brambles, tussocky grass, and half-buried building materials. It was a challenge, and a good one. We rented a house nearby and for the first year I did not have a garden. I worked on the house, cleared the site and got to know the lie of the land. This was the best thing I could have done. It gave me a year to try out different garden plans and planting schemes, most of which could be transferred from the drawing board to the site, by marking it out with canes and string. By the

end of the year I had more or less designed the garden as it is now. The only real difference being that a circular lawn occupied the centre of the garden in the space that the Jewel Garden now occupies.

I had learned from our London garden the importance of establishing what lies beneath the surface. In London, we inherited a seemingly neat garden, but when I started to dig, I unearthed skipload after skipload of buried car parts and concrete. It was like a subterranean junkyard and took nearly a year to excavate. This rural site was the opposite. Once I had cut, raked, and cleared the rubbish on the surface I discovered gardening gold. The soil was a wonderful clay loam over gravel. This meant that it was rich, retained moisture and nutrients, but also drained fairly well. In principle, it was almost perfect soil for making a garden.

The site was open – a field really – with just two small trees: a hawthorn and a large hazel. From these bare bones I had to make a garden that would satisfy my desire to create as rich and varied a garden as possible, that included space for my passion for growing fruit and vegetables as well as flowers, topiary, hedged walks, lawns and some kind of water feature. The garden also had to be compatible with the needs of three young children, dogs, a pony, and chickens. And all this had to be done with no money whatsoever. Britain was in the grip of a deep financial recession and with next to no work there was not a spare penny to finance any kind of garden – let alone my expansive dreams.

The first thing to be dropped from my garden plan was the water feature. The combination of the dangers it held for my young children and the proximity of the river to the back door, which flooded expansively into the garden, meant that we had more than enough water.

Initially, most of my energies were put into cultivating the Walled Garden and the Vegetable Garden. The Lime Walk was laid out without its brick path (that came two years later) and, in the first spring, I planted a lot of trees and hedges that I had bought cheaply in a sale. It was a great deal of hard work, but I loved it. I was helped from the first in creating the garden by George Taylor. He was the hardest worker and most decent man I have ever known. Although he would have been the first to admit that he was no gardener, he would try his hand at anything. When things were tough

or a problem seemed insolvable there was the refrain, "George will fix it", and he nearly always did. Later he married and his wife Rose also came to help us and it is not too fanciful to say that their happiness spread out into the garden.

The garden was, and remains, a team effort, but during its creation I spent many, many hours each week outside, often selfishly so. I was obsessed and driven. Making an ambitious garden with little money and limited help is hard work. At times, it was gruelling. But I loved it. It was and still is my element. Nothing gives me such personal satisfaction as the process of making a garden. Sadly, there are only so many opportunities to do this in a lifetime. Gardening organically is not just a question of growing a few healthy vegetables, but a validification of the work and love that has gone into making the garden.

Being organic

Introduction
I often hear people say that they grow their vegetables organically whilst admitting to using the full armoury of herbicides and pesticides on their flowers and lawns.

My organic system depends upon the chickens to provide a supply of manure. The eggs are really just a delicious by-product.

This misses the point. The garden is a whole. To be selectively organic is to misunderstand the concept of holistic gardening.

It is essential to see the whole garden as an irreducible entity. Everything is connected to everything else. It is impossible to have any part of it "organic" if it is not all run along organic lines. How you treat the weeds on your driveway inevitably affects your lettuces. How you tackle the greenfly in the greenhouse is part of the same action as choice of flowers in the border.

For many years gardeners saw nature as something that had to be tamed if the garden was to perform at its best. The heated Victorian greenhouse was the epitome of this, creating an artificial environment to overcome climate and geography through a combination of money, skill and sheer ingenuity. But organic gardening depends upon working with nature – creating a balanced environment that sustains itself. By definition, all gardens are unnatural places and they do not happen independently of the gardener. The gardener is as vital to the garden as the rain or soil.

Organic gardening tries to create a healthy garden. Much of the "sickness" of any garden is a result of forcing it to grow bigger, faster and more intensely than can be naturally sustained. Any top athlete will tell you that when they train hardest they are most prone to viruses. The garden is exactly the same. The intention is to create a healthy garden that heals itself within its own delicate and yet intrinsic system of checks and balances. If you do not use insecticides you will, from time to

All our vegetable waste, from both the garden and kitchen, goes onto the compost heap so that its goodness can be returned to the ground. Nothing is wasted.

time, have outbreaks of destructive insects like aphids that will cause short-term damage. But my own experience is that healthy plants grown without too much fertiliser are less prone to attack and recover well from infestation. Most of the chemicals used by gardeners are wholly unnecessary. My advice is to spend your money on healthy plants instead.

The organic way is not simply a question of passive avoidance. Not doing is not enough. It is important to be proactive. The key words are sustainable and integrated. The garden has to become integrated with your household and your life.

Of course, there is no question of using pesticides, herbicides, fungicides, slug pellets, or chemical fertilizers. I do not purchase any form of peat and aim to gather or buy organic seeds. But this is not quite enough. It slightly misses the point. I do not want just to be seen to be doing the "right" thing. Above all I want to create a healthy garden where every component part, from the smallest microbe in the soil to each plant, bird and human that uses it, contributes to and sustains that overall health.

This book is a personal account of how I manage my own organic garden. It does not set out to be encyclopaedic, and I do not write about plants or vegetables that I have no direct experience of growing. If I am honest I do not have all the answers. I am still constantly searching for solutions, and know that what succeeds in my garden may not work for someone else. Every garden is different and personal. Only the gardener can find the balance that makes it work best.

Relationship to place In a garden, context is everything. This understanding of context goes beyond the garden fence. I have become increasingly aware of the importance of relating

The houses in my area are mainly built of oak because it grows so well on the local soil.

Looking west from my garden out over the fields to the Welsh mountains. This scene is an important part of the garden.

a garden to its surroundings. By this I do not just mean the immediate visual backdrop as this might well be something that the garden tries to get away from. What I think is more relevant is an awareness of the history, geology, climate, and broad plant culture of the area. This will make the garden better and connect the gardener to something more than their own little world.

Some linkage is inevitable. No garden, however vast, has its own weather system. Weather affects the garden more than any single factor other than the soil – and, unlike soil, the weather cannot be improved. The wind here blows mostly from the West. If we want to know what tomorrow's weather is

going to be like – or even what will be upon us in the next half hour – we look to the West. The garden is also situated in a frost pocket and we often have more severe frosts than our friends half a mile across the fields.

Soil type can vary from one part of the garden to another but it is likely to be part of a more general type that is common to the area, influencing the crops that local farmers grow, the trees in the nearest wood or park as well as the plants that grow in your neighbour's gardens. Strongly acidic or alkaline soil will limit and determine much of your garden planting. It is best to work with your soil type rather than fight it.

In my area, the soil is neutral to slightly

acidic, rich and slightly heavy which allows for a huge variety of crops. Grass, wheat, oats, potatoes, apples, blackcurrants and hops all do very well. Trees that thrive in these conditions include oak, ash, willow, and alder, while dogwood, hawthorn, lime, blackthorn, holly and hazel are common in the hedgerows.

There is a downside, however, to producing large yields of a single crop in one region. For example, in our area the ground can produce very heavy potato crops so they are widely grown on a commercial scale. But the negative effect has been that potato blight has become endemic and chronic. The solution would be to rest the soil for a few years until the fungus has died out but the drive to make a profit and the widescale use of fungicides means that

farmers continue growing them. The result is that we are guaranteed to get blight on the potatoes that we grow organically in our vegetable garden. Our tomatoes (being part of the same Solanaceae family as the potato) are also prone to attack by the fungus. There is little we can do about it: it literally comes with the territory.

Whatever I attempt to grow in this garden is part of this pattern and is affected by its relationship with the surrounding landscape. I can try and cheat the natural environment by making artificial pockets of introduced soil or areas especially protected from the wind, but I am convinced that the health and success of an organic garden is heavily influenced by the extent to which it does not try to buck nature.

A fallen crack willow (*Salix fragilis*) rooting in the medieval fishpond at another edge of our garden. The river flows nearby. Water dominates our gardening, both as rain and standing water when this ground floods – which it does often.

15

Organic horticultural practice The most common misconception of organic gardening is that it relates only to the edible produce of the garden and not to the flowers.

I try to create as healthy an environment as possible for all living things to co-exist. If my own micro-ecosystem is working well, then the garden will constantly be healing and balancing itself. All I can do as a gardener is to help that process along – often by simply not obstructing it.

To carefully nurture your cabbages following the strictest organic principles and yet use fungicides on your roses – even if they are at the other end of a huge garden – completely misses the point. The care and cultivation of our flowers should be carried out using exactly the same set of standards as the plants that we grow to eat.

If you grew solely indigenous flowering plants there is no doubt that your garden would be healthier, but one of the problems with the modern flower garden has arisen from the hunger for collecting plant species from around the world. As the British Empire spread, so British gardeners accrued plants from all over the globe. The English herbaceous border became a flowering symbol of British supremacy, filled with a kaleidoscope of flowers from different continents, climate zones and landscapes, from deserts to sub-tropical forests. The organic gardener therefore has to reconcile the inevitable imbalance that is created by introducing such a mixed collection of plants to their garden. A garden is always a highly artificial, man-made creation and obsessive eco-purism that does not allow a varied selection of flowers as possible seems a joyless pursuit.

In our flower gardens, we deal with this potential conflict between the artificial and organic by avoiding plants that do not flourish in our soil and situation. No plant is mollycoddled to enable it to endure the rigours of our climate. This creates quite harsh limitations upon the range of flowers that we can grow but it never fails to astonish me how plants from the other side of the world will adapt and grow completely happily in this garden, cheek by jowl with another plant with supposedly wholly different needs. So, looking out of my window in late summer, I can see dahlias and salvias from the mountains of Central America growing next to crocosmia and leonotis from the grassy plains of South Africa, next to hostas and macleaya from Japan, next to echinacea and asters from North America with sweet peas from Sicily growing on a tripod above them. All are healthy and flourishing in our heavy clay loam.

We grow a lot of herbaceous perennials, quite a few flowering shrubs and bulbs, and not as many climbing plants as I would like, primarily because we have few suitable walls, so most sprawl up tripods or through the branches of trees.

The greatest danger from disease or pests comes when a plant is in poor health. Plants become weak when they are forced too early, grown on too fast, overfed, or overcrowded, especially when young. All these pitfalls are easy to fall into because we are always impatient for flower colour after a grey British winter. Human psychology rather than plant physiology is often the weak point of a successful and healthy garden. Oddly enough, I am coming to the realisation that the more plants you have that offer green structure in the decorative areas of the garden, the better the flowering plants will grow. This is because if the garden maintains a solid green structure throughout winter and spring, rather than looking bare, it will lessen the sense of urgency to grow flowers as fast as possible in spring.

As for overcrowding in this garden, this is a result of two things. The first is our desire to pack in as much as possible. Only experience can control and temper this. The second is the result of our rich, fertile soil which makes everything grow monstrously large, crowding out lesser plants, blocking out light, moisture and air flow. Whilst I love this abundance it has to be controlled and catered for to maintain a healthy balance.

So timing is vital. Put in plants too early and they do not grow strongly, making them prone to pest attack and disease. Too late and we do not get the best of them before the light and heat starts to fall away in late summer. As I stated before, it is all about balance.

Companion planting

It has long been held as a tenet of organic gardening that there is much to be benefitted from specific plant associations. These have tended to be the conjunction of floral and edible plants or herbs and vegetables or fruit. Whilst I do practise this to a certain extent and there can certainly be no harm in it, I believe that there is a deal of pseudo-science written and spoken about companion planting.

As I repeat throughout this book, the least healthy system of gardening or agriculture is monoculture. In the field that abuts onto our orchard, not a single weed was ever visible because it is regularly sprayed with herbicide. It is ploughed to within inches of the hedge, so there is no headland of any kind. Because of the lack of weeds and variety of plants that would be found on a headland, there are few insects to prey on the handful of insects that feed on the crops, so it also has to be sprayed regularly with pesticides. Had they allowed some weeds and a decent headland, they would have had a much more balanced insect life that would have helped create a predatory balance. So in this case, weeds, grasses and wild flowers would have been constructive companion planting.

This, I think, is the only really important lesson about companion planting. Avoid monoculture where possible. A series of small beds planted with different species naturally help this. Interplanting different vegetables is also a form of companion planting. Not only does this attract a mix of insects but it also confuses some of the more specialist destroyers such as carrot fly or the cabbage white butterfly. It will never rid you of attack but it will help.

So I always edge the carrot bed with a hedge of chives. I also regularly crop this to the ground – throwing the vast majority onto the compost heap unused – because the growing chives are much more confusing to the carrot fly than the mature plants.

I also plant basil with my tomatoes to help ward off whitefly. I have never had whitefly on my tomatoes. Is it down to the basil? Who knows.

Garlic does seem to help keep aphids from roses, with the rose systemically absorbing enough garlic odour to ward off the visiting insect.

I let fennel seed itself all over the garden because it attracts hoverflies and parasitic wasps which will eat aphids and larvae of cabbage white caterpillars.

You probably need a greater quantity of the "companion" than the plant that it is protecting if it is to have any measurable effect. I think that the secret is not to measure. Keep your planting interwoven and varied within the demands of healthy crop rotation. And, unlike the monoculture of chemical farmers, nurture a few weeds at the edges of the garden.

Weather As I write this on a bright January morning in the West of England, the weather forecast promises rain by lunchtime.

The sky is a journal of the weather. It shows what is to come and records what happened and the good gardener learns to read it fluently.

I like weather. Weather is change.

But to a gardener, it implies a whole range of things. Will I be able to get outside for an hour or so this afternoon and finish weeding the Spring Garden? Should I stop writing now and spend the rest of the morning barrowing the pile of muck whilst the ground is still dry? Did I remember to put the cloche back over the thyme – which will overwinter quite happily as long as it remains bone-dry? The weather is immediately translated from a broad notion to something that is intimately personal to me and my awareness of the world.

The variety sharpens your experience of the world both seasonally and from day to day. One of the great virtues of modern gardens, in an age when most experience is passive or vicarious and people pay to go on holiday under a dome, is that it brings you back again and again to the irrefutable actuality of the weather. The weather, fair or foul, in countryside or in city, humanizes us all.

As an organic gardener, the trick is to harness this and let the weather work for you. It is an immutable fact of natural life, and it is a complete waste of time and energy to fight it. I have learnt this through bitter and futile experience. Over the years, I have wasted days braving the elements, trying to wheel a barrow through mud lapping about the axle, digging soil when more was sticking to my boots than to the spade or, on one embarrassingly memorable weekend, bullying houseguests to help me plant

a long beech hedge in constant torrential, icy rain.

As with every aspect of the garden, you have to learn every detail and sign of your own personal weather. In this garden, a dirty day can often clear towards evening and reach a patch of beautiful weather for an hour or so before sunset. I know that when the wind is westerly – which is more often than not – whatever is in the other three-quarters of the sky is irrelevant because whatever is filling the western sky is inevitably coming our way. It can be much more local than this. There is a patch of path on a crossroads in our Jewel Garden where, on a cool, damp evening, the grass suddenly becomes crunchy and the torchlight picks up the white rime of frost. This is a sure precursor of frost that will creep into the rest of the garden over the next hour or so. The odd thing about it is that it is in the middle of the garden, neither particularly low or high and exposed. But the evidence is irrefutable.

Of course, just weather alone is half the story. The effect of weather is what matters and that can vary enormously from garden to garden. The nature of your soil, the extent of shelter, your altitude, aspect, and whether your garden is in a valley, on a slope or on an open plain, will all interact to create your own micro-environment.

Other than our own perception of the weather and how it affects what we do and wear from day to day, there are a number of things that the gardener can

do to harness the good of the weather and mitigate the effects of the bad.

The influence of the sun Do you know exactly where the sun hits your garden for every half-hour section of the day throughout the year? You should. For any gardener, managing the sun is an important skill. As the sun rises, climbs to its midday peak, and then slowly falls, the effects of light and heat are quite different and all planting should reflect and use this variation.

There is an enormous variation between the sun's positions in winter and summer. In this garden, even on the clearest day, the midwinter sun never gets high enough to cast light onto our herb garden or back yard. It also sets right in one corner of our boundary, almost before it gets round to shine across the Jewel Garden from the west. But by April, it is setting halfway across the field to our west and filling the tulips with evening light, and in midsummer it goes down behind the church on the horizon almost to our north and the herb garden is the best place to sit and enjoy a preprandial evening drink.

A summer downpour is never bad for the garden and it can be a pleasurable experience for the saturated gardener! Incidentally, here I am carrying copper piping to act as a slug barrier around recently planted-out seedlings. It seems to work.

Plants for dry conditions

TREES
Acacia (Wattle)
Eucalyptus (Gum)
Ficus (Fig)
Gleditsia
Quercus (Oak)
Robinia pseudoacacia

SHRUBS
Artemisia (Wormwood)
Brachyglottis 'Sunshine'
Buddleia davidii (Butterfly bush)
Cotinus coggyria (Smoke bush)
Cotoneaster
Elaeagnus
Euonymus (evergreen varieties)
Genista (Broom)
Hebe (Veronica)
Hypericum
Lavandula (Lavender)
Perovskia (Russian sage)
Philadelphus (Mock orange)
Potentilla fruticosa
Ruta graveolens (Rue)
Santolina (Cotton lavender)

Whatever the season, morning sun is thin and clear. Looking through it is like pressing your cheek against a cool pane of glass. Colours float and change inside it, strength exposed as vulgarity and intensity transformed into brashness. The delicacy of morning light is best suited to soft colours and all the pastels, yellows, and whites, as well as the cooler blues, look at their best planted so that they catch the morning sun.

East-facing walls are generally cold and the worst place in the garden to put any tender or fragile plants. This is because if the weather freezes, they will have been cooling since midday, when they enter total shade, and the early morning sunshine strikes the frozen plants and thaws them rapidly, bursting the cellular structure. Plants on a west- or south-facing wall, that might have been frozen just as hard, have plenty of time to thaw slowly in the warming air before the sun hits them.

It doesn't take much gardening knowledge to know that as the sun rises into the sky it gets hotter. But the influence of this on your garden design and habits can be quite subtle. It will certainly affect where you sit and eat outside. Generally speaking, it is unpleasant to eat lunch under the full glare of the sun. It melts the butter. You need either artificial or natural shade. Colours bleach out in full sunlight and the depth and texture that shadows bring is lost. But you must make sure that your plants that need maximum sunshine to flower or ripen must not be shaded. By the same token, you must make sure that

plants like lettuce or spinach are sheltered from the full blast of midsummer sun. When dealing with crop rotation this can cause an extra level of complexity which must be negotiated.

By the late afternoon when the sun has moved round to the west, the sun is still hot but the light is richer and more sympathetic to the eye. Strong colours seem to absorb this quality and reflect it so that oranges, purples, and deep crimsons become evening sun the best. Wherever possible I would design a North European garden to have its main summer flower borders facing west, and to have a place to sit and enjoy all the softened warmth of the early evening sunshine whilst sheltered from any cool breezes.

Plants and rain Despite the effect of the oceans and mountains, most rain is caused by plants transpiring and sending water up into the atmosphere. As rain falls, some evaporates directly, but most of it goes into the soil and is drawn up through the plant by the roots and is then released into the atmosphere again from the open pores in the leaves. Three-quarters of all rain that falls on a densely planted area – such as a garden – is recycled in this way. A large oak in midsummer can send upwards of four hundred gallons of water a day into the atmosphere. In winter, there are less leaves to evaporate straight off and to recycle the water, so a much higher proportion of winter rain is stored in the soil – which is why winter drought can be a real problem for the subsequent summer and why snow following a long cold spell can be a vital source of water.

Here in the West of England, the rain is heavy and our gardens grow lush and fat. In fact we would get a whole lot more rain if we were not in the rain shadow of the Welsh mountains. Micro-climates lurk in every garden, however small. Each wall and building has its rain shadow and the easterly lee of every house is a dry zone.

The ideal rain for most gardens would be 2.5cm (1in) a week, all falling steadily between 10pm and 5am at night, so that it sinks deeply into the soil with no sun to evaporate it off the leaves. If you water lightly, often no great volume of water ever penetrates the soil, merely sinking in 2.5cm (1in) or so, so the feeding roots all stay near the surface to get at it. Cut off that water supply for a few days and the reserves are quickly used up. Meanwhile the plant has not developed any deeper roots to hunt for moisture, which, when there is an interruption in supply, spells disaster because there are no reserves of water in the soil and no root system to tap into it anyway. Even plants adapted to the most arid of deserts are merely those that have evolved to adapt their growing and reproductive functions to the brief periods of rainfall that there are. If a plant loses a sufficient level of water, then its pores start to close – stopping up completely in drought. This is a self-defence mechanism to stop it losing water, but it also stops it receiving carbon dioxide from the air and thus halts photosynthesis. Big trouble all round. In essence the secret is not to let any plant ever get to that emergency shut-down stage.

The lower the average rainfall, the more important it is to dig the soil deeply and to add lots and lots of organic matter. This will encourage the water to drain deeply and to remain accessible to roots that also delve down to find it. If this deep-rooted supply and demand system is working well, surface conditions are hardly going to be noticed by the plants.

But you can have too much of a good thing. If soil does not have sufficient drainage and becomes waterlogged, most plants can drown. Too much moisture in the soil will leave no room for oxygen, which is essential. As water drains through soil, it leaves just a film of water around each grain of soil and the cavities through which it drained are filled with oxygen. As ever, the secret is to know your soil conditions intimately.

Heavy rain compacts the soil just as surely as clumping footsteps will. The lighter the soil, the more quickly this will happen. Again, adding lots of organic material will bulk it up to make it better able to withstand the hammering of a million rain-blows. A light soil "slumps" very readily under heavy rain, whereas heavy clay retains its structure better but forms puddles as it drains reluctantly.

If we had our ideal 2.5cm (1in) of rain per week on sandy soil, the top 45cm (18in) would be dry by the night of the next rainfall. But on clay only the top 15cm (6in) would be dry.

Rainfall and temperature The combination of rainfall and temperature dictates how our plants grow as well as the soil that they grow in. The more rain you have, the greater the temperature you need to maintain fertility until you arrive at

Plants for dry conditions

BORDER PLANTS
Acanthus (Bear's breeches)
Achillea (Yarrow)
Agapanthus (African blue lily)
Alstroemeria
Artemisia (Wormwood)
Dianthus
Echinops (Globe thistle)
Eryngium (Sea holly)
Euphorbia (Spurge)
Geranium (Cranesbill)
Kniphofia (Red hot poker)
Nepeta x *faassenii* (Catmint)
Oenothera (Evening primrose)
Papaver orientale (Oriental poppy)
Penstemon
Verbasum (Mullein)

BEDDING PLANTS
Brachyscome iberidifolia (Swan river daisy)
Dianthus barbatus (Sweet William)
Erysimum (Wallflower)
Iberis umbellata (Annual candytuft)
Limnanthes douglasii (Poached egg plant)
Malcolmia maritima (Virginian stock)
Nicotiana alata (Tobacco plant)
Verbena

the rank profusion of the rainforest. High heat and low rain equals dusty desert. Lots of cold rain results in a soil with a very high organic content because there are fewer bacteria to digest it – but very low fertility. But every soil has a balance that the gardener must learn and work with, and every soil can be enriched by constant addition of compost. The rain comes from the earth and the type of earth we cultivate is the rain's primary harvest.

Rain can be the harvest that we have carelessly sown. Acid rain falls like a retribution. It is simply any rain with a pH lower than 5.6 and is essentially sulphuric and nitric acids showering down on us from fossil-fuel emissions. (It is worth bearing in mind that the pH scale is logarithmic: which means that a pH of 6 is ten times more acidic than a pH of 7, and a pH of 5 is a 100 times more acidic than pH 7.) What goes up must come down. We are all familiar with northern pine forests stripped of their needles, which seems to be a combination of reduced photosynthesis and a lack of nutrients because the sulphuric acid washes away nutrients in the soil. But I have read that all rain now contains a level of nitrogen equivalent to 10kg per acre per year. This is tiny compared to the tons piled on by chemical farmers, but nitrogen notoriously leaches from the soil into waterways, and if you have a pond in your garden the build-up of algae will be worsened by nitrogen from the rain.

There is little that you can do about rain, although most people underestimate the extent to which summer rain hits foliage and evaporates before it reaches the soil. I have often noticed how dry the ground is at the end of what has been a "wet" summer. On the other hand, in winter, when the leaves have all fallen, it takes very little rain to have an effect on the ground. This is where the nature of your soil will show its true colours. In my garden, twenty minutes heavy rain early in the morning can make the ground unworkable for the rest of the day. Whereas I know people who garden on limestone who can push a barrow across the lawn and work on the soil within an hour of rainfall because their drainage is so good.

Despite my own surplus of rainwater, I am aware that most of the world suffers, for some of the year at least, a general shortfall. The most effective thing that a gardener can do to both make the most of all rainfall, and simultaneously to create good drainage, is to dig in lots of organic material and mulch thickly every year to both supply humus and to stop evaporation from the soil. You should also plant, or make, good windbreaks because wind will dry the soil and leaves faster than the sun.

It is a good idea to have a number of water butts catching rain from the house and any outbuildings, to provide rainwater for watering container plants and as an emergency supply for general irrigation.

Frost in the garden In general, frost is much more of a friend than an enemy to the organic gardener. It kills lingering bugs and diseases, and knocks back the slug and snail population as well as rats and mice. It looks beautiful – a mature garden is as lovely on a frosty morning as in high summer. Frost is to November and December what sunshine is to May and June. It belongs to the season and yet it always arrives as a treat to be relished. Frost kills the caterpillars and slugs, scours through the fungal diseases and infections in the soil and crevices of bark, and washes the wind. It breaks down the soil, gives a few hours hard ground so barrows can be wheeled, and lawns are not sludgy. It is the organic gardener's firm ally. And of course it is beautiful.

So a healthy garden needs some cold weather in winter. By "cold", we tend to think of a visual image of frost, and that is ideal for the three winter months of December, January, and February, but the significant temperature is 5°C (41°F). Few things actively grow below 5°C (41°F). The most obvious example is grass, which needs a temperature of more than 5°C (41°F) to start growing, and for most gardeners grass growing in midwinter is a potent signal of mildness.

Frost acts as a landing stage from which you can get onto the garden – it is the best time for making paths or any kind of earth moving. Traditionally you try and get ground for next spring's sowing roughly dug before the frost arrives so that it can break the soil down for you. Great if you can manage it, but the first light frosts are a good time to dig. After Christmas, frosts can become too hard to get the spade in the ground, and it is amazing how that level of cold will turn intractable slabs of soil into crumbly tilth.

Went outside at first light and everything coated in white frost. The fennel heads extraordinary – worth keeping – in fact, worth growing them – just for this effect, even if it is only one day in the autumn. There seemed to be a lot of rustling of birds, but in fact it was leaves constantly falling off the trees. Thousands upon thousands of leaves all falling at once although there was not a breath of wind. It was as though they had all lost their balance and were slipping off, bouncing on the branches, knocking more free as they passed, rocking and zig-zagging down to the ground.

FROM MY JOURNAL:
16.11.2001

The herb garden on a frosty February morning. Winter frost is the organic gardener's friend, as it it kills off viruses, fungi, and pests such as slugs and aphids, as well as breaking down the soil better than any machine.

Very hardy plants

TREES

Acer (Maple)

Betula (Birch)

Crataegus (Hawthorn)

Fagus (Beech)

Fraxinus (Ash)

Ginkgo biloba (Maidenhair tree)

Ilex (Holly)

Picea abies (Norway spruce)

Pinus nigra (Black pine)

Quercus (Oak)

Salix (Willow)

Sorbus

Thuja occidentalis (White cedar)

Tilia (Lime)

SHRUBS

All Alba, Gallica, and species
  roses (other than spring-
  flowering ones)

Buddleia davidii (Butterfly bush)

Calluna vulgaris (acid soils only)

Euonymus

Jasminum nudiflorum (Winter
  jasmine)

Kerria japonica

Mahonia

Philadelphus (Mock orange)

Spiraea thunbergii

Viburnum, many species

HERBACEOUS PERENNIALS

Ajuga reptans (Bugle)

Echinops ritro (Globe thistle)

Geranium endressii (Cranesbill)

Geranium sanguineum
  (Cranesbill)

Helleborus

Iris sibirica

Lamium maculatum (Dead
  nettle)

Primula vulgaris (Primrose)

Pulmonaria saccharata
  (Lungwort)

Of course frost in spring is another matter altogether and can wreak havoc. We always have some frost in April and often in early May. We even had frost on the night of June 8th 1999, which killed all my pumpkins and squashes that had been planted out for some two weeks. The worst weather combination is a period of warmth in early spring, with clear nights which can mean the temperature will plummet, killing off buds and the very tender new growth.

Whole fruit crops can be lost like this and I have seen our box hedges look as though they have all been sprayed with a herbicide, because all the new growth has been burnt brown by one night's frost. There is not much that you can do about this, other than shelter individual trees and shrubs and rows of vegetables with horticultural fleece which will keep off the effects of any spring frost.

Plant hardiness The semi-tender plants that most of us grow in our borders, like salvias, penstemons, cardoons, melianthus, jasmines, camellias, and bay, will all suffer if the temperature falls much below -5°C (23°F). But other plants, from as diverse a range as garlic to primroses – need a cold period in order to trigger their spring growth or germination. Most temperate garden plants have adapted effective means to counter cold. Deciduous trees and shrubs drop their leaves and stop all but small root growth; herbaceous plants have evolved their annual die-back precisely to counter frozen temperatures and will survive frozen ground perfectly happily because they have shut down all

growth and gone into a state of hibernation. Annuals die as plants but leave a mass of seeds that will survive the cold and grow in spring. Biennials establish enough of a plant to overwinter before growing properly the following spring. Evergreens are the most vulnerable because they hardly stop at all. These might seem the hardiest of all plants simply because they seem to maintain equal vigour in winter, but very cold, dry weather can kill many evergreens. The really important thing is to know your garden in all its weathers and not to try and force it to grow plants that run contrary to its natural local climate.

- **Hardy plants** can manage cold, often down to extreme temperatures such as -15°C (5°F) and can sustain cold for weeks or months of about -5°C (23°F).

- **Half-hardy plants** do not, as a rule, tolerate any temperatures below freezing, but can withstand the no-man's-land of between 5°C (41°F), when growth stops, and freezing 0°C (32°F).

- **Tender plants** do not survive below the magical temperature of 5°C (41°F), which is the arbiter of the "growing season".

Most plants prepare for winter cold. Autumn and spring wean plants into dormancy and then growth. This is why sudden frost in spring or autumn can have such disastrous effects – especially in spring. A plant that might withstand a month of bitter sub-zero temperatures can have half its growth killed by a few degrees of sudden frost in May. The new growth is not expecting it and although the plant might be conditioned to withstand cold, the new shoots have not had time to put this conditioning into practice.

This means new wood and seed ripening over the summer and autumn and hardening off by winter. Timing is everything. Ripen too late and there will not be time to harden, with new wood turning from green to brown, before winter frosts. Grow too early and the same thing happens again – but more so – in the inevitable frosts of spring. This is one powerful argument for growing plants that are local and indigenous to the area you live in. Plants evolve to adapt to the general climate of a region. But many gardens are filled with plants in an entirely foreign territory which, in evolutionary terms, there has been no time to adapt to. Often plants from a zone much colder than a temperate garden can suffer as much as those from one much warmer. The cold-weather plants are conditioned to start rapid growth as soon as any warm weather appears in order to make the most of a very short growing period. But we often get days and weeks at a time above 5°C (41°F) in the middle of winter, followed by frosts which duly kill back all the urgent new growth.

What determines a plant's ability to survive cold are the levels of sugar and proteins in the cell sap and the permeability of the membrane enclosing the cytoplasm of each cell. The higher the level of sugar and protein, the lower the temperature at which the cell sap freezes. If the membrane is highly permeable, the pure water moves out through the cell walls and freezes between the cells.

In consequence, the interior solution concentrates and needs an even lower temperature to freeze at. The hardiest plants prepare for this process through the combination of hot days and cold nights – precisely the weather you might get in late summer and autumn. This means that they continue to lose water through transpiration throughout the day, thereby concentrating the cell sap, and yet need minimum respiration in the cold nights. The result is accumulated carbohydrates in their tissues, which is exactly the best protection against extreme cold. Thus a plant such as a sugar maple can literally freeze solid and survive perfectly well because its cytoplasm is protected by such a high concentrate of the sugars and proteins in the cell sap.

The reverse process is just as important. Too rapid a thaw will kill a plant as effectively as too rapid a freeze. There must be time for the frozen water around the cells to permeate slowly back, otherwise the cell walls will be ruptured. Hence the dire warnings of placing tender plants against an east wall or the disaster of a really late frost, when the early sun hits the frozen tissue and warms it up fast before the air temperature has gradually risen and thawed it slowly.

The effect of altitude One of the chief determinates of cold is altitude. As a rule of thumb the temperature drops 1.8°C (1°F) for every 100m (330ft) rise in altitude. Thus a garden on top of a steep, east-facing hill is much more vulnerable to frost damage than another garden half a mile away on lower ground.

If you garden in a particularly cold spot,

Very hardy plants

CLIMBERS
Clematis viticella
Hydrangea petiolaris
Lonicera periclymenum
  (Honeysuckle)
Wisteria floribunda

ANNUALS AND BIENNIALS
Agrostemma (Corn cockle)
Centaurea cyanus (Cornflower)
Hesperis matronalis (Sweet
  rocket)
Nigella (Love-in-a-mist)
Papaver rhoeas Shirley Series
  (Shirley poppy)

BULBS
Crocus
Eranthis hyemalis (Winter
  aconite)
Galanthus (Snowdrop)
Iris unguicularis
Lilium regale
Muscari (Grape hyacinth)
Scilla (Squill)

try and leave planting of new plants and moving of existing ones until spring. This will discourage early new growth. Also leave your winter pruning until the end of March or even into April so that new shoots develop later. They will soon catch up.

Snow on snow Snow looks good, upping the ante on a hoar frost, but it is a nuisance to the gardener. I consider it a downpour waiting to happen, because when it thaws it leaves a sodden wake. The plus side of this is that in areas of low rainfall, it is a very good way of getting a lot of water down into the soil.

It is also heavy. If you have hedges or topiary, quickly take some pictures of the garden in full snowy rig and then go round with a cane knocking the snow off all lateral branches before they break.

Wind power Wind is usually the biggest single influence on how a garden grows. One of the first things you should do when you take over a garden is to map the wind in your head. Get to know exactly what the relationship is between your plot of ground and the prevailing winds.

The shape of the wind is as important as the direction and strength of it. A mild breeze can be funnelled down alleys and the gaps between houses and, in the process, become a rapier, bayonetting a few choice (and usually slightly tender) plants. A wind flowing as straight as an arrow will tumble over walls and fences, crushing and flattening plants like a boisterous wave. We have all seen the

wind pick up a pile of leaves in the garden and swirl them around like a spoon in a cup of tea. Wind bounces and rebounds off solid surfaces like a ball, hitting crazy angles and causing weirdly unguessable microclimates. One of the most common effects of this is the damage that wind causes at the base of a wall, because the force is directed down just as strongly as it is pushed up over the top.

If you know exactly how the wind behaves as it passes you and your garden, then you can start to protect the site. A filter is much more effective than a solid barrier, that only provides a shelter zone of an area reaching a distance that is the same as roughly twice the height of the wall. Beyond that, the wind often comes down harder than ever.

The best and most usual filter is a hedge. An evergreen one is more solid, but a thick, deciduous one is often most effective of all in filtering the wind, absorbing and gently diluting its force. In a large garden, hedged divisions will create a web of barriers so that there are pockets of very protected areas within a larger, generally protected space. Hedges don't have to be tall – a low box, lavender, or santolina hedge will make a real difference to a herb garden, for instance. Shrubs and trees are also very effective. Windbreaks do not need to be permanent. Jerusalem artichokes or runner beans can be used to great effect at the edge of a vegetable garden as a windbreak during the growing season. I have seen wheat used in a garden as a temporary windbreak. I don't know how effective it was, but it looked great.

I have found that woven hurdles make the best temporary shelter, especially along a newly planted hedge. Hazel ones are best but willow is a reasonable substitute. Trellis also works well, especially if the spaces are small. Even more temporary, but very effective, is netting.

Wind is not all bad. A south wind is wonderfully effective at drying up soggy ground, and a north or east wind scours the garden like a dose of salts. Not pleasant, but you (the garden) come out from it generally healthier. And the rare times when there is no wind at all are fine for a day, if it is sunny, but then the air gets as stagnant and rank as a scummy pond. If there is no real wind, then fungal diseases proliferate and air pollutants linger. Good ventilation is essential for plants, especially woody trees and shrubs like apples and roses, and half of all pruning is to establish a good airflow through the branches. But to make that effective you need flowing air. A gentle, ruffling breeze is always lovely on a hot day, although it can make a mild day cool. Wherever you sit, you must have shelter from the wind, otherwise, no matter how perfect it is in every other respect, you will not use it fully.

There are times when the lack of wind is disastrous to the gardener. If your garden is on a slope with a building or wall at the bottom, cold air will flow down the hill, meet the wall, and eddy back up – collecting as a frosty pool of air – exactly like water. Wind would help disperse that cold air. So if your garden is at the bottom of a slope or in a natural basin, then it is essential to let the wind flow through and get out again.

Wind cools the air around plants as they grow, and in spring will often be sufficient to drop an otherwise mild day below the critical growing point of 5°C (41°F). This is most evident in England in April, when a cold wind can stop all growth for weeks at a time, despite otherwise sunny, mild weather. If a plant is constantly exposed to wind, it will grow lopsided, like trees on top of a cliff where the wind slows the growth dramatically on the exposed side whilst at the same time is absorbed by the tree so that the sheltered side grows normally.

Wind and plant stress Wind can and does put a powerful stress on growing plants and it is extraordinary how sensitive their growth patterns are as a result, even in relatively sheltered sites. But the biggest problem from wind for the gardener is its drying effect. Leaves dry exactly like a row of shirts on a washing line, and the stronger the wind the more plants dry out. Evergreens are particularly vulnerable to damage from wind in winter because they are constantly transpiring and losing water. If there is a cold, dry wind blowing, that water will not be replaced, and it is not uncommon for otherwise quite hardy plants, like box or holly, to die of winter drought, especially on roof gardens. This can happen very rapidly if the soil that they are in is frozen because the roots will not be able to take up any water at all. One of the best solutions in very cold, dry weather is to spray the plants with water, which then freezes and forms a protective film around the leaves.

Soil It is important for the organic gardener to understand that soil is much more than just a medium in which to grow plants.

It has been calculated that one teaspoon of soil can contain a billion microscopic organisms of more than ten thousand different species. We know almost nothing about them, despite the fact that they are essential to maintaining healthy human life.

Healthy soil is a complex living entity made up of countless living organisms. All this subterranean activity is as sophisticated and interdependent as life above ground. It is also – and this is at the heart of the whole organic way of thinking – inextricably linked to all living processes.

This enormous variety of life below the ground works primarily to break down complex organic matter so that it is easily accessible to plants. This starts with the small, visible creatures like slugs, worms, beetles, and woodlice digesting large pieces of waste material. The result of this is that the organic material is reduced to much smaller particles with a corresponding larger surface area. This is also mixed in with the bacteria, fungi, and minerals that are already in the soil and taken down below the surface. Once it is there it gets digested again, at a microbiological level, mainly by bacteria in the soil.

There are many different kinds of bacteria in the soil that contribute some highly specialized parts of the process of making the contents of organic matter best available to growing plants. Some secrete an enzyme that binds soil particles together – making them able to form clumps and have structure. Some will break down molecules so they become more readily accessible to a wider range of plants. Protozoa feed off bacteria and fungi and release nitrogen into the soil as they in turn excrete waste material. When the fungi and bacteria die, they in turn decay and add their own contribution – by releasing the minerals that they have ingested into the soil.

Every aspect of the garden is inter-

dependent. By destroying one so-called "pest" – even if it is a microscopically small bacterium – we diminish the entire balance of the living world.

As farmers are finding across the western world, replacing organic matter with artificial fertilizers means that the complex natural balance is thrown and the soil can become lifeless, acting as hardly more than an inert growing medium. Most of the vast diversity of micro-organisms are killed, which means that the soil loses its ability to recycle organic matter and release the nutrients from it. As a result, crops get smaller and less able to resist disease and more and more chemicals have to be used, making a bad situation worse. So we must value and cherish our soil with all the attention and care that we have at our disposal.

Layers of soil Subsoil is the basic type of soil that you garden on. It forms a layer above the underlying rock which might be a few centimetres, in the case of chalk, or many metres deep. Whilst it does contain water and nutrients for plants, these are often not easily available and plants grown in subsoil will be stunted and unhealthy. The addition of air, organic material, and micro-organic activity can gradually convert subsoil into topsoil.

Topsoil is the layer of soil that has been enriched by the constant addition of organic material and the resulting humus is incorporated into the soil to make loam. Loam is soil that is both rich in organic matter, and light and open. Regardless of the basic type of soil, loam will be created if you grow lots of plants and mulch or dig in plenty of organic goodness each year.

The deeper the topsoil, the easier it will be for roots to grow and take up nutrients, the better it will both drain and retain water, and – not least – the easier it will be for the gardener to work. In an old garden that has been cultivated for hundreds of years, the topsoil can be up to 1m (3ft) deep. In new gardens on uncultivated ground, it can scarcely exist and has to be made or imported. But it is never too late to begin improving the loam that you plant into.

Soil structure As well as the nutrients in the ground, the structure of the soil is vital. You can test the soil structure simply by picking up a handful of loose, dry soil. Squeeze it tight in your hand. Ideally, it will make a firm shape that holds together but which breaks up when you drop it back to the ground. If the soil is light and thin, it will not hold its shape at all. If it is dense and sticky, it will not crumble when it falls.

Nothing helps the structure of any soil more than the addition of organic matter, particularly well-made garden compost. But adding any organic material, from fallen leaves to thick layers of straw will dramatically help create a richly "living" soil as micro-organisms work to convert the material into nutrients.

Improving soil structure Whilst we cannot change the type of soil that we have, we can to a large degree improve its suitability for growing plants that are adapted to that soil type. But the only practical relationship of the gardener with the soil is one of co-operation. I am very uncomfortable with any significant attempt to "change" the soil type. You must get to know your own ground sufficiently well to go along with it. Learn to get the best from it. This might mean having smaller, less vigorous, or productive plants than convention tells you are standard. Don't worry. A healthy plant will make the most of what the soil provides and will limit both its rate and ultimate size of growth to achieve that end.

As you dig, you can feel the nature of the soil: does the soil lift out in great slabs that hold to the face of a spade indicating clay, or in loose shovelfuls, as on a sandy soil?

Exploring your soil

Whilst most garden soil is predominantly one of four geological types – chalk, sand, clay, or peat – how this manifests itself can vary from area to area of the same garden, let alone from garden to garden. It is essential that we each know the soil of our own garden intimately. This begins with finding out exactly what your soil is like. The only way to do this is to dig, feel, and smell it.

Take a spoonful of your garden and shake it up in a jar of water. After an hour it should have settled into mini geological strata. Any sand will sit at the bottom of the jar, with a

layer of silt over it and whatever clay there might be on the top. Having done this, dig a hole 1m (3ft) deep in different parts of the garden. Just the process of doing this will get you very well acquainted with your own ground. Notice the different layers of soil, any compaction, the depth of topsoil, the stoniness, and the depth of any roots that you come across. Are there plenty of worms, and how deep down are you finding them?

Pour a bucket of water into each hole. See how long the water takes to drain away completely. More than an hour means that you have a heavy, slow-draining soil, less than ten minutes and it is very fast-draining. This is as scientific as you need to get. The point is that you cannot do much with the soil that lies below the top 50cm (20in). At a full metre (3ft) down, you are dealing with essential, unalterable conditions that you must learn to garden with.

Clay soil is the most naturally fertile of all soils. Treat it right and you can grow almost anything. Technically any soil that has more than 25 percent clay particles is a clay soil. Clay particles are tiny, less than .002mm ($\frac{1}{16000}$in) in diameter. To put that in context, particles of sand are a thousand times bigger. These tiny bits of clay pack tightly together, leaving little space between them for air and micro-organisms and roots to move through them. It therefore needs lots of organic material added to it to open it out. But it also means that nutrients will not wash through the soil and there is a large surface area for the roots of plants to come into contact with to absorb the goodness, ensuring high fertility.

Testing soil If you are not sure whether you have clay soil or not, pick up a dry handful and squeeze it. If it holds together, it has clay in it.

The downside of clay soil is that if you do not work it at the right moment, it can become baked into unworkable, brick-like clumps as it dries or equally unworkable, sticky putty as it gets wet. You must also add as much organic matter as possible every year. The best way to do this is with a thick mulch in autumn and spring. Garden compost is ideal. Horse manure is better at lightening the soil than cow manure. Mushroom compost is best of all because the high lime content helps break down the clay particles.

You can also add horticultural grit or sharp sand to increase the size of the soil particles and open out the soil structure, improving drainage and root-run. You need to fork in a layer 5–10cm (1–2in) deep. This is incredibly effective and to all intents and purposes permanent, so only needs doing once. But you need a lot and grit is expensive.

Chalky soil is fast-draining, which makes it fast to warm up in spring, and easy to work. Because it is so light and because the high lime content breaks down humus very fast, it is best to mulch any ground to be dug as thickly as possible in autumn, digging it in early spring just before you start sowing. Occasionally chalk lies above a belt of clay. The result is that although the chalk drains quickly, the water sits on top of the clay and makes the chalk above it into a white, sticky paste. There is one singular bonus to gardening on chalky clay: it is the ideal medium for earthworms which can reach a population of 300 per square metre (yard).

Chalky soil is very alkaline. It is not possible to make alkaline soil significantly more acid, so the only practical response to a garden with chalky soil is to eliminate entirely all acid-loving plants such as heathers, rhododendrons, azaleas, many camellias, lupins, and most lilies, and to make the most of the huge range of plants, especially flowering shrubs, that relish it. It is, for example, clematis heaven and chalk provides exactly the right balance between good drainage and hot, stony resilience for Mediterranean herbs like rosemary, lavender, and thyme. Yew and box are in their ideal environment.

Sandy soil is always described as "hungry", meaning that it takes and demands huge amounts of added organic matter to create a good soil structure. But years of such soil conditioning will produce a rich, sandy loam which is great stuff to garden in. It still will have the problem of being rather light and free-draining but, coming from one who has had to cope with heavy clay for years, this seems to me to be the least of a gardener's worries. Sandy soil is ridiculously easy to dig, warms up quickly, and never becomes waterlogged. These are huge advantages.

Because sand particles are so big, there are relatively few of them with little total surface area compared to the tiny particles of clay. Gravity quickly takes water down between the grains of sand, wetting the humus, and leaving a film of moisture on each grain. Nitrogen and other nutrients are dissolved by the water and carried down to the water table. This is what is meant by "leaching". The leaching effect also means that calcium is washed away and calcium is what makes a soil alkaline (pure chalk, for example is all calcium), so that sandy soil has a tendency to get increasingly acidic as it leaches. Acidic soil can be made more alkaline by adding lime, so mushroom compost is very suitable.

Peat soil You find peat soil where the ground is constantly wet and all lime and nitrogen are washed away. Vegetation fails to decompose and builds up in an acidic layer. This occurs on high moorland, and on the low "wetlands". The latter tend to be less acidic and, when drained, very fertile.

Whether wet or dry, high or low, peat is always acidic, which means that it has a pH of below 6.5 and it can fall down to as low as 3.5. Below pH 6.0, phosphates begin to be bound up in the soil and potassium, magnesium, calcium, and trace elements can leach out. When the pH of soil drops as low as 5.0, phosphates are largely unavailable, so roots are short and stunted. By the time you get down to pH 4.0, most flowering plants will not grow, bacteria do not flourish, and most mineral nutrients are washed out.

But some plants are surprisingly tolerant of these acidic conditions, and there are others that only really come into their own when wallowing in it. These are the Erica family, which includes heathers, pieris, sorrel trees, gaultheria, bilberries, clethra, and most of all, rhododendrons.

A very peaty soil can be "sweetened" with an application of lime. This only has a short-term effect, but is beneficial and necessary when growing vegetables on peat soil. Sprinkle either calcium carbonate or quicklime onto the bare soil at least one month before the vegetable plot is to be planted or sown. Do not add manure at the same time as the lime reacts with the manure, releasing ammonia which uses up nitrogen. Mushroom compost is alkaline, especially when fresh, and if it is generously mixed into the plot it will certainly help.

Cultivation The important thing is to know your soil and growing patterns well enough to apply the best form of cultivation for the end that you are trying to achieve.

The strategy of cultivation depends on a number of variables. Do you like digging? (I do.) And do you have the time and physical resources to do it when it should be done? (I don't.) What sort of plants are you putting in? A site being planted up with trees and shrubs does not need extensive cultivation in preparation: a well-dug planting hole and subsequent mulching will be sufficient.

But if you are preparing a flower border or vegetable patch for cultivation, you should dig it as well as possible before beginning planting. This will give you a chance to add compost well below the surface layer, to allow air into the compacted ground, and break up any dense clods or hard pan below the surface. It will aid the plants' root growth and ensure good drainage. Soil that has good drainage and is not too compacted also has a much higher level of bacterial activity.

If you dig properly you will find it hard work but enjoyable and deeply satisfying. If it hurts your back, then you are probably not doing it properly. But very few gardens need more than a day or two of digging a year.

Only dig when the ground is reasonably dry. If the soil is sticking to your boots then it is probably too wet. Hold the spade upright so that the blade chops into the ground vertically. It helps to imagine that you are cutting the straight side of a trench. This action converts most of the energy into the ground, and puts less strain on the back. It is also more efficient, taking up the most soil with least effort. Bend your knees, not your back, as you dig.

Use a good spade, preferably of stainless

steel. This will cost more but saves a lot of effort and should last a lifetime. My own spade is well-worn from fifteen years of almost daily use and is on its third handle now. A good spade should be comfortable to use and cut easily into any soil, lifting it out in thick slabs or loose blocks according to its composition. Use a fork only if the ground has been dug previously with a spade and you wish to break it up. Nine times out of ten, a spade is better. Keep the soil in as large clods as you can, to get more air into it. The clods can easily be broken down later by you or the weather.

Be suitably shod. If it is too muddy to wear anything but wellington boots, then it is certainly too muddy to be digging. Wear stout footwear so that you can use your feet and legs to dig the spade into the ground, further reducing the strain on your back.

There are two basic types of digging: single digging (*see facing page*), which is all you regularly need to do, and double digging (*see page 34*), used when preparing new ground.

Digging up grassland When digging up turf to make newly cultivated areas, strip off the turf cleanly in rows from the plot before you begin. There are three ways in which you can use it. One option is to make a turfstack for a future supply of excellent loam. Stack the turves grass-face to grass-face in a square block. If left for a year, this will rot to a wonderfully rich cake of soil that you can cut vertically with a spade and use in home-made potting compost. Alternatively, the turf could be relaid elsewhere in the garden, or put into

Single digging

This method is an efficient and systematic way of digging your plot. If you do this once a year well before cultivation, the ground will be in good shape for planting or sowing.

1 (*see right*) At the edge of the plot, dig a trench – one spade blade deep (known as a "spit") and a spade blade wide – across the width of the plot, cleaning out the "crumbs" or loose soil, but trying not to mix topsoil and subsoil.

2 (*see far right*) Put the soil in a barrow and take it to the far end of the piece of ground you are digging. Tip the soil in a line along the edge of the plot. This will be used to fill in the last trench that you dig.

3 (*above*) Spread a good layer of whatever well-rotted organic material you have in the first trench.

4 (*above right*) Move back – the width of a spade – and dig the next trench, throwing the soil from it to fill the first trench. The soil will fall into the first trench at an angle, sloping away from you at 45 degrees.

5 (*left*) Repeat the process along the length of the plot. Once you have dug the last trench, fill it with the soil from the first trench. Inevitably, the soil level will have been raised above the surrounding area, but do not be alarmed by this – it will gently subside whilst retaining its new, light structure.

Double digging This is hard work. But if you are preparing a new border or if you are making a new garden in soil that has been compacted, it is worth the trouble. It is a complete waste of time if it is not done properly.

Do a little double digging at a time, making sure that it is really well done.

1 (*see right*) Dig a trench one spit deep and three spade-widths wide across *half* the width of the plot to be dug. Remove the soil to one side or keep it in a spare wheelbarrow, ready to fill in the last trench. As always, try to avoid mixing topsoil and subsoil.

2 (*see far right*) With a fork, dig over the bottom of the trench into the subsoil, to the depth of another spit, breaking up the soil into small clods as you go. Work backwards and do not tread on the soil after you have dug it.

3 Fork plenty of manure into the newly dug bottom of the trench.

4 (*see left*) Move backwards and dig the next trench, putting the soil into the trench that you have just dug and manured. You will find it easiest and most logical to do this in three "mini-trenches", starting farthest away from the previously dug trench, so that the third "mini-trench" is like a wall of soil between the two dug areas.

5 (*see bottom, far left*) When you reach the end of the plot, turn round and start to work back in the other direction, digging the other half of the plot.

6 (*see bottom, left*) Move steadily backwards until you come back in line with your starting point. Use the soil that you had put aside from your first trench to fill the last one. You will find that the soil is enormously raised by this process but, as with single digging, do not be alarmed. This is a sign that you have done it properly and the soil will settle soon enough.

the ground during single or double digging.

If the grassland has been uncultivated for a number of years, and there is a good growth of grass or mixed weeds and wildflowers, the soil beneath will be rich and balanced. You will not need to add any extra compost or manure to the newly dug soil. Dig grassland as for single digging (*see page 33*), but instead of adding compost, lay the turves, grass-side down, along the bottoms of the trenches. Some people say they should be chopped up, but I just leave them to decompose slowly. After planting into this virgin ground, use a thick mulch of compost to start the process of ensuring sustained natural cultivation.

Raised beds If you do not want, or are unable, to dig, then you must make raised beds that can be easily reached from either side so you never have to tread on the soil and compact it. This is a very effective way of growing vegetables. However, although raised beds will not need digging regularly, they do require double digging to create them. Thereafter, raised beds need only mulching once or twice a year.

Clear the whole site of any weeds. Do this carefully and properly, taking out every scrap of root, particularly from the perennial weeds like couch-grass, bindweed or ground elder. Then lightly dig over the entire site to one spade blade's depth to break up the soil. If you do this in autumn, leave it in large clods for the weather to break down. Otherwise, wait until the ground is dry enough to walk on without any soil sticking to your boots and rotovate it. At this stage, it should look like a well-cultivated patch of ground, ready for sowing or planting.

Mark out your raised beds with string or make whatever permanent edging materials you wish. Do not use treated timber if the beds are to be used for vegetables. Some of my raised beds are simple raised mounds without any edging at all. Make the raised beds no more than 1.5m (5ft) wide and 3m (10ft) long, otherwise they are awkward to get round. Leave paths between the beds wide enough to take a wheelbarrow – at least 60cm (2ft) and preferably 90cm (3ft). Double dig each bed, adding plenty of compost and rotovating or forking it to an even consistency. This is the last time you will dig or stand on it. When the bed is dug, shovel the loose topsoil from the paths between the beds onto the beds themselves. This lowers the paths as well as raising the beds, allowing room to lay a hard surface if you wish. Finish each bed by spreading a surface mulch of well-rotted compost 5–8cm (2–3in) thick. This will suppress any weeds in the soil. Plant through the mulch into the soil. You will find that after you have been to all this toil, it will be easy to remember not to tread on them!

Preparing a tilth My aim is always to prepare the soil so that I can sow and plant out seedlings using my hands. If you have light soil that you have dug in autumn and left in large clods, it may just need a vigorous raking over in spring. I find that with my heavy soil I have to fork or rotovate it to break it down sufficiently before raking. I use a very small, mechanized rotary tiller which is light and can be lifted to cultivate small areas. If working a large site, I hire a larger machine. But a fork can do the job perfectly well, especially for small areas. Lastly, rake the soil (*see top right*) into a fine tilth.

For a fine tilth, rake the soil well in one direction and again at right angles. Get the soil level and smooth and remove all surface stones or large, hard clods of earth.

Tools

I am writing this in my converted hopkiln workroom and below me is the toolshed where the tools wait in the dark, all roughly in their right places.

They are not as clean or recently oiled as they might be, but ready. The machinery is kept under lock and key in another shed which does not have any of the romance of this shrine to hand tools. I could go down and check them, but I know them all by heart. I know their places, and can walk in there in the dark, reach out, and know exactly where to find every one of them. I have used every one of them and know how they all feel in the hand. This is the main thing about any kind of hand tool – it has to feel right in the hand. You can have ten identical spades or trowels, but only one will feel right.

Spades I have accrued spades across the years with a compulsion verging on obsession. I love them. There is a stainless-steel border spade, small and precise, and useful for moving plants in a busy border. I have digging spades with wide treads and long straps extending halfway up the handle; trenching, or Irish, spades with extra long handles and tapering blades; spades with YD grips, T-handles, or straight handles beautifully shaped to bulb out slightly at the end so that the hand instinctively seeks and finds the most comfortable, ergonomic position. I have spades practically unused because they look fine, but just feel wrong, and spades worn by many generations of gardeners to lop-sided shavings of their original selves.

All have ash handles, although American hickory is good. Most have YD handles, where the ash is split and steamed to hold the shape of an open fork, which is closed by a tubular ash bar. I would not dream of using a spade with a plastic handle, partly because wood, worn shiny smooth with use, feels so much nicer, but also because plastic will give you blisters much faster. How many people, when buying a spade from a garden centre, ask what wood the handle is from? But you should. It makes all the difference. Would you buy a kitchen knife with a superb blade and a cheap plastic handle? No. Any hand tool works from the hand outwards. The point of contact has to be right or else the whole thing is wrong.

All these spades are sufficiently different to get an outing every now and then, but only one spade has my heart. This is stainless steel and was made at the Wigan foundry of Bulldog Tools. It weighs exactly 2.2kg (5lb) and it balances perfectly cradled on my index finger. The blade, set on a swan neck of forged steel drawn from the same ingot as the blade is pressed from, is gently curved in cross-section, the curve diminishing as it opens towards the edge. That edge is sharp enough to cut string and chop through tree roots like a chisel. It is after all, no more than a blade. But it is a miracle of sophisticated design, as perfectly evolved for its function as a wheel is for revolving. Its angles are subtle and yet precise.

It cost about £90 in 1988 and I regard it as one of the best buys I ever made. It is now on its third handle and I would not exchange it for any other spade in the world. I let no one else use it. There is no negotiation on this – there are spades enough for that and good ones too. Just not this one. This is a spade taken very seriously.

My favourite spade I use this for all and every kind of digging work.

Garden tools I confess that my fork spends at least half its time outside in the vegetable garden (*below left*), stuck in the ground, where it does most of its work, lifting vegetables and breaking up the ground. A spring-tined rake doubles as a grass scratcher and leaf collector (*below centre*) and is also very good on soil for getting a fine seedbed. There are only two things that matter about a Dutch hoe (*below right*): keep it sharp and keep it small. It is a big mistake to try to save time by using a big-bladed hoe. A small one is twice as useful.

But every gardener should take their tools seriously, just as a chef will take his knives seriously or a musician his instrument. Good tools don't make a good gardener, but they do add enormously to the pleasure of gardening. Every single time I use my spade I enjoy the experience, be it lifting an errant hazel seedling to move to a better spot or double-digging. It introduces a pure, aesthetic element to a task above and beyond its success. Digging a rich loam becomes one of life's great sensual pleasures. Good soil plus good spade equals good time. It goes without saying that I like hand tools best, and simple, refined combinations of steel and wood best of all. Most modern attempts at

improving or redesigning garden tools look as though they have fallen out of a cracker. For all that I love the hundreds of gardening tools I own, you actually need very few to garden well.

Forks You also need a fork. I have one that is a companion to my spade and similarly admired, although it is hard to love a fork. I have others too, of various curvature and shape of tine. I prefer square tines (as opposed to round or flat), not too long, not too curved, and of stainless steel.

We have smaller border forks but, unlike their spade counterparts, they seem to be fiddly rather than compact. It is also useful to have an extra-strong digging fork for going through subsoil or stones. This will have a reinforced handle and thicker tines. The only other fork that I use a lot, and would recommend, is a long-handled manure fork, which is ideal for turning compost and transferring it from heap to barrow and again from barrow to soil. That too lives permanently outside, stuck into the current compost heap.

Rakes You need a rake. One will do, but five is ideal. For general preparation of a seedbed, a round-tined flathead rake is best. It does not want to be too big, just wide enough to do the job but narrow enough to get between rows. A spring-tined rake is essential for leaves and seedbeds (*see facing page*). Rubber rakes are invaluable for gathering up leaves from borders without damaging plants and seedlings. An area of long grass is an excuse to buy a proper hayrake. This is made entirely from ash, with 28 wooden pegs for teeth and a handle up to 1.8m (6ft) long. They are a joy to use, collecting long grass in great rolls. I also have a landscape rake, long of handle but light of head as it is made from aluminium. This is used for dragging and spreading soil to shape rather than to a finished surface.

Hoes However much you mulch and hand-weed – and any organic gardener is going to do a great deal of both – if you grow vegetables you must have a hoe. There are dozens of different kinds, but all are fundamentally a blade on a stick, and hoeing is based upon the principle of cutting weeds off just below the surface of the soil. The design of a hoe depends upon whether you push the cutting edge through the soil or pull it back towards you. I think that for smaller, annual weeds, it is best to push. A Dutch hoe is unbeatable for this.

If you are dealing with bigger weeds you need to chop them. Some kind of mattock or draw hoe is needed for this, with its blade at right angles to the handle. Increasingly, I find a mattock useful for earthing up, and even turning, the soil as well as rough weeding.

Although it does not fit comfortably into the category of a hand tool, I also use a flame gun. This is powered by paraffin and, despite its name and the roar of flame that it throws out, works by heat rather than flame – bursting the cells at the base of the plant causing it to wither and die. It is useful for paths and paving as well as killing off seedlings from a piece of ground about to be sown. I also use it to sterilize the soil after an attack of blight.

Kirpi I also have begun to use this multipurpose hand tool from India. It has a curved blade that is serrated on the inside to saw through tough stuff, partially sharpened on the outside edge to hoe with, and a point that will get in-between bricks and paving slabs. I find it by far the most useful hand-weeder that I have ever come across. Half of the profit from their sale goes to the Jatan trust in Gujarat, India, where they come from. The Jatan trust is an organic farming movement in India which has been set up as a counter movement against the government imposition of chemical farming. A good cause and a good tool.

Machete I keep mine permanently at the compost heaps for chopping up any tough stems or unshredded vegetables, to increase their surface area and make them compost faster.

Trowels I own six trowels. They have accumulated over the years, but I only feel that I own two of them and it is one of these, the large or small one according to the job, that I will hunt for even though the other four are to hand. They fit my hand. They have balance. They are called Jeckyll trowels and I only bought them as a pair a couple of years ago and had great doubts because cost a fortune. I suspected that they were intended to be displayed more than used, but whatever the intention, they are superbly useful and worth every penny.

Small cutting tools You must have secateurs and a penknife. I have been given about a dozen various freebie secateurs across the years, but have ended up buying, at full retail whack, three or four pairs of Felco ones. They are the best. I like No.2 and No.8. Always get bypass-cut secateurs and keep them very sharp. I use two knives: a small, straight-bladed one, for cutting string and soft plant tissue, and an Opinel pruning knife, which has a big curved blade with a lock but which is light in the pocket and brilliant for pruning sappy growth from trees and shrubs or acting as a mini-sickle, cutting heads of lettuce and such-like.

Cutting tools for long grass Scythes are a particular favourite of mine. When I was a boy there was a beautiful scythe hung from the wall of the toolshed with a curving handle of silvery ash and a metre (yard) long oiled blade thrillingly sharp to touch. It certainly a quarter of a century old when I first knew it, 40 years ago, and for the past decade I have used it annually to mow a certain piece of long grass. The cutting

movement is a slow side-to-side swing with each pace forward, drawing it back as the right leg leads, and cutting with the left. It should look lazy and yet metronomically efficient, the cut grass flopping aside against the sinuous curve of the handle that perfectly wraps around your body whilst the great blade twists on its wider curve.

At first a scythe seems an awkward thing. It will not stand alone on the ground, will not lie balanced on the floor. But take it in your hands and hold it as intended and immediately it falls into balanced place. The curving snaithe, or handle, has been steamed into shape from lengths of ash, cleft down the grain for strength, allowing exactly for the twist of the body as the hands swing, the blade almost parallel to the ground, tilting slightly forward on the down-swing, and up and away as it crosses the legs. It is a tool perfectly evolved, and the various modern versions that I have seen and tried are futile reductions. It would be like redesigning a shark.

Although its use should look effortless, it is hard work. I am fit and experienced, yet an hour exhausts me. In the pre-tractor age, mowers would work for 12 hours a day for weeks at a time during haymaking. All this was done with skill and as a natural part of their day for a wage of around 75 pence a week – perhaps £20 in modern money. It reduces the preening gym culture to effete inadequacy.

If you can sharpen it and are prepared to sweat, a scythe is wonderfully efficient at cutting the long dried grass of high summer. And if you don't use one, what else will do the job? Wildflower meadows are all very well, but to make them perform at all the grass must be cut in high summer when it is least amenable to cutting. A rotary mower has to be enormously powerful to tackle dried, tall grasses and most ordinary garden versions are not equipped for this. If they will cut the grass at all – and most dribble to a halt within yards – they soon clog. However the advantage that a rotary mower does have is that it chops the grass up and thus renders it compostable, whereas the long strands of scythed grass take years to rot down. After many years of looking and trying various makes and types, I have come across a machine, a Honda UM616, that will cut almost anything – including all our compost, reducing it to fine shreddings much quicker than any shredder I have used. It is marvellous, but not cheap. You could buy an awful lot of scythes for the price of one. However if you only use a machine like this a few times a year, the answer is to hire one.

A strimmer is pretty essential in any reasonably sized plot. We use ours for cutting under hedges and trees (although we are *very* careful about not cutting the trees as the nylon thread can wrap around a young tree and kill it in a second) and on all the hard surfaces to keep weeds from seeding. With a blade attached it can cut fairly long and tough grass, although it is no faster than a scythe and much noisier. I use a hook (rip-, swap-, sickle-, grass-, or brush hook – there are many names and many variations on this particular cutting theme) for cutting the grass in the coppice and getting in under trees.

Cutting tools for short grass
I like mowing grass. I like the easy pace of it – inevitably the mower moves slower than I naturally do – and I like the way that it crisps the garden up – as though it is all scrubbed and spruced for a special occasion. But we are not at all obsessive about grass cutting. It gets done once a week, which takes four hours and that is it, however much it grows during those seven days. The grass itself is mainly coarse and full of weeds. As long as they are green this does not bother me at all. We use a petrol-powered rotary mower with a roller that will cope with grass from 5cm (2in) long down to 1cm (½in) – which is quite short enough.

All our grass is always collected and composted. I do not believe in leaving a blade of grass on the ground as it is far more valuable as part of the compost heap than enriching the growing grass – which is all that ungathered grass cuttings do. Because we have so much grass to collect, I always have a bale of straw to mix with it on a 50:50 basis to keep the compost heap balanced with the right ratio of carbon and nitrogen.

Mechanical tools
We use a tiller to mix in compost and to break up soil that has been previously dug. We never use a rotovator as this only cultivates the ground a few inches deep and creates a hard pan unless the ground has been well dug first. I have found it better to have a small machine that can be lifted on and off raised beds rather than a bigger, heavier one that is a struggle to move around the place. In the end a machine is only as useful as the ease with which it can be handled. Otherwise it will not get used.

We use electrical and mechanical hedge cutters. Electrical ones have the advantage of being light, quiet and easier to control whilst petrol-driven hedgetrimmers can tackle the heavier work and can also be safely used in damp weather and away from a power source. But they are tiring to use and make a horrible racket.

Compost
The compost heap is the manifestation of the principle of organics, recycling waste and returning it to the soil to enrich future plant growth, which in turn will provide for future compost.

I use three-sided bays to make my compost. The materials used to make the bays are not that important. In my time I have used old pallets, chestnut paling, pig wire and straw bales and all have worked equally well.

It follows that the organic garden can never have too much organic waste or too much compost. In practice, most gardens will always have too little. This poses two questions – how to make as much as possible from the available materials in your garden, and how to best use the compost that you do make.

The question of how much compost you can make needs to be put into perspective. It has been estimated that you need at least twice the area of land producing compostable material as the area of ground to be composted. My own two-acre garden produces between five and eight tons of compost a year. To be self-sufficient for our mulching and organic material for digging into the soil we need between three and four times that amount.

The only rational response to this, beyond reducing the cultivated area of the garden to no more than a third and devoting the balance to intensive compost production or buying up the neighbouring gardens and using them to provide material for the compost heap, is to recycle every scrap of available material, to learn to convert this into really good compost, and to then value it like gold dust.

First of all, let me define what I regard as "good" compost. I only regard my compost as ready for the garden when the following criteria are met: it smells pleasantly of rich loam, and it is dry enough to crumble in my hand, with a loose texture that can be shovelled, rather than cutting it like cake or forking it like manure.

Compost bins I make my compost in three-sided bays made from chicken wire supported by a strong post in each corner. The material is

It is important to make the bins, or open heaps, as large as possible because they will then heat up quicker, reach a higher temperature and hold their heat for longer. This accelerates decomposition and kills seeds and pathogens. I would say that the smallest viable size for a compost heap is a one metre cube.

not that important, but whatever you use it is better to have clear soil for the base. Ignore any advice to put twigs, drainage bricks or anything else down. These make shovelling or forking the compost a nightmare and are wholly unnecessary. Bare soil also means that the worms and bacteria in the ground can easily start work on the heap.

Compost worms The worms that will be essential for converting your assorted waste into rich compost are not ordinary earthworms but distinctive, crimson worms called brandlings (*Eisenia foetida*). It is extraordinary how they seem to materialize from nowhere and set to work on a well-made compost heap. In fact, their presence and the amount of them to be seen is as good an indicator as any of whether you are making your compost right. They can only survive and multiply if it is not too wet, not too dry, has air, enough carbon in the shape of straw, cardboard or any dry material, and is warm enough.

Turning the heap Each bay is added to until it can hold no more and then left for at least four weeks (but usually at least twice as long as that) before being turned into the next one. In summer it may need turning only once before being ready to use for mulching or digging in, but in winter, and if we want to use it for potting compost, it will need turning at least twice and leaving for a total of at least six months. On average we use our compost between six months and a year after putting the raw material into the heap.

Turning compost mixes it all up thoroughly, gets more air into the heap and speeds up the aerobic activity, which heats it up and dramatically increases the rate of decomposition.

It is clearly a good thing to do – but it is not necessary. You can simply make a large heap (with a large surface area) and leave it for at least a year and let it gradually convert into good compost.

All our garden compost material, including hedge trimmings, the chicken muck and annual weeds, but excluding grass mowings, is spread on the ground in the orchard and then "mown" by the powerful rotary mower that we use for the long grass. This chops it all up to a uniform texture more effectively than a shredder as well as thoroughly mixing all the different ingredients. This mixing is important. If you build it in layers you will find that some layers will be squashed flat and oxygen will not get to them, so that they form a hard wedge. Cutting it all up first also reduces it in bulk by about a fifth or less. We then mow this with the lawn mower, gathering it all up in the collector. This takes perhaps an hour a week and the result speeds up the composting process by as much as six months. Lawn mowings are added to the heap and mixed, a barrow at a time, with straw, aiming at a 50:50 mix. You will find various different brands of "activator" for sale that promise to be the secret of good compost. This is not true. If you have a well-made heap set upon healthy bare soil any kind of activator is entirely unnecessary.

We keep the long orchard grass separate because the grass has a lot of seed in it and we have found that it needs a full 12 months before all of these are killed.

All perennial weeds and odd bits of turf (good turf is stacked for loam) go in a separate long-term heap which is slowly added to. The outside and top is therefore always weedy and uncomposted but after about three years the

Brandlings, or compost worms, cease their composting activity and breeding if the temperature falls below 5°C (41°F) and die if they freeze – which is highly unlikely in the heart of a compost heap. They also need an alkaline environment, and so I remove highly acidic material like citrus waste.

Compost heap ingredients

Comfrey flowers

Organic straw

Such an important part of the garden deserves the right tools and I always keep two forks at the compost heap, one long-handled one for spreading the additions to the heap as they go on and one short-handled one, which is for turning it.

interior makes wonderfully rich compost. The roots of bindweed, couch grass, and creeping buttercup are burnt and then the ashes added to the main heap.

The ingredients I have said that anything living *can* go on a compost heap and I know of gardeners that happily add dog and cat faeces, dead rats and, on one occasion, a dead python! But I do not add any meat, dairy or fat scraps because these inevitably bring vermin which then live in the heaps. I also do not add animal faeces because of the diseases that these can spread to humans when uncomposted.

Having said this, as well as obvious garden vegetation, I do add all cardboard that is not printed with coloured inks, a great deal of shredded newspaper, all the manure from our chickens, fresh straw, and all annual weeds.

All kitchen waste is put into a bucket that is emptied daily onto the heap, including tea bags, coffee grains, and kitchen towels that have been used to wipe spilt liquid. All cooked dairy and meat waste goes to the chickens and eventually finds its way onto the compost heap via their manure from the chicken shed. I keep any old lime plaster we have (I live in an old house and all the walls are plastered with lime rather than gypsum) and sprinkle this on every time I add the kitchen compost bin. The lime is obviously alkaline and neutralizes the acidic effect of the kitchen mix.

The ideal mix If there is a single secret of good compost it is here in the mix of ingredients. You must try and establish a high ratio of carbon to nitrogen. Straw, dried flower stems, bracken or paper are very high in carbon and fresh grass cuttings, kitchen waste and neat animal manure is high in nitrogen.

The smaller the household, the less carbon there is likely to be available because the compost will be mainly derived from kitchen waste and grass clippings. Grass clippings have half the carbon to nitrogen ratio needed to make good compost. If you then liberally lace the resulting compost heap with an activator – also high in nitrogen – the result will not be compost but a cross between an evil-smelling sludge and silage.

So the secret is to constantly add carbon-rich bulk to the heap. The perfect ingredient for this is straw. Mix grass clippings with an equal volume of straw and they rot down together beautifully. However, an organic farmer needs every scrap of straw they can make because everything not needed for consumption goes back into the land. So organic straw is hard to get hold of.

But cardboard and waste paper is similar to straw – being essentially partly digested cellulose – and available to every household in ridiculous quantities. We all fill our bin bags with huge quantities of paper and cardboard packaging every week – as much as 40 percent of all landfill matter – from empty cereal packets and envelopes to kitchen towels. Put it all on the compost heap instead and not only will it rot down to provide good compost for the garden but also dramatically reduce the amount of landfill.

It is important that the paper is mixed in with the vegetable waste rather than placed in lasagne-like layers. You can flatten very large cartons and use them to cover completed heaps to stop them getting too wet. The cardboard is largely converted into compost via the digestive tracts of brandlings, beetles, nematodes, centipedes, woodlice, and slugs, all of which adore a diet of moist cardboard.

Green manure

saves not just on artificial fertilizers but also on precious garden manure – of which no one ever has enough. It has many virtues and practically no drawbacks, but has never really caught on.

Which is odd. The principle is that instead of leaving ground bare you sow a "crop", the primary harvest of which is the enrichment and improvement of the soil. Green manures work in a number of ways at the same time. They cover the ground and occupy it, which means that weeds have no room or light to get in, which they surely would do otherwise. On that basis alone, the sowing and cutting of a green manure is less work than weeding. Their green foliage also photosynthesizes light and takes carbon dioxide from the atmosphere which it then converts into starches and sugars which, when they are incorporated into the soil, provide food for future crops.

Individual green manures also have specific nutrients that they can leave behind in the soil, either through their ability to trap nutrients and "fix" them in their roots, or through digging in the top-growth and roots and their subsequent decomposition in the ground. The most obvious example of this is the legumes, which fix nitrogen from the air via nodules on their roots and pass it into the soil where it can easily be taken up by growing plants.

Green manures also provide a large amount of organic material for the soil's micro-organisms to work on which improves the structure of the soil, completely bypassing the whole composting process. All you need is a packet of seed and the work of turning the soil over some months later – which you would have had to do anyway.

On this basis, any growth can be treated as a green manure, including annual weeds, but it is essential to cut and dig them in before any seeds are produced, which can be very difficult to time across a range of weeds.

If there is a good reason why I do not use green manures more than I do – and I am not sure that there is – it is because they need some clear planning and careful timing to get the best from them and therefore they do not always fit easily into the chaotic, snatched lives that many of us lead.

The green manure that I do use regularly, and is perhaps the easiest of them all to accommodate, is Hungarian grazing rye, which is best sown on a piece of ground after a summer crop has been cleared. It grows fast and strong, looking like coarse grass or young wheat and leaving no chance for any weeds to grow. It is very hardy and will survive any kind of British winter weather. In spring, I cut it with a scythe and take the mowings to the compost heap. I wait another few days for any foliage on the ground to wilt and then dig the plot over. This has to be done quite deeply to bury the plants, which are quite robust by now. The white roots are very extensive and fibrous and very effective at opening out and loosening heavy, compacted soil. The ground should be left for three or four weeks before you sow or plant into the plot, so that the young plants are not robbed of nitrogen by the decomposition process. Then dig it over again and sow as normal, without adding any manure or compost. I find it best to precede a crop. But if you leave it too long – more than a month – the goodness will start to be lost. As I say, timing is important in getting the best from a green manure.

HARDY GREEN MANURES FOR OVERWINTERING
Alfalfa (*Medicago sativa*)
Alsike clover (*Trifolium hybridum*)
Essex red clover (*Trifolium pratense*)
Field beans (*Vicia faba*)
Hungarian grazing rye (*Secale cereale*)
Ryegrass (*Lolium italicum*)
Vetches and tares (*Vicia sativa*)

FAST-GROWING GREEN MANURES FOR SUMMER GAPS
Buckwheat (*Fagopyrum esculentum*)
Crimson clover (*Trifolium incarnatum*)
Fenugreek (*Trigonella foenum graecum*)
Mustard (*Sinapis alba*)
Phacelia (*Phacelia tanacetifolia*)

Before sowing Hungarian grazing rye, some time between late summer and mid-autumn, I simply fork and rake the ground over and broadcast the seed onto the surface of the soil. It is ready for scything in spring.

Animal manure The combination of an organic bedding material and animal manure has been used since time immemorial to fertilize the soil for growing crops.

The bedding material is invariably a product of one of the crops – such as straw from wheat or barley, or a material that can easily be scavenged, like bracken. Nowadays wood chips are often used. The point is that all manure is recycled from the combination of animal and vegetable waste products to produce an invaluable resource for the farmer and gardener, so wherever possible the organic gardener should try and use as much animal manure as they can get hold of.

In an ideal world this would come in the form of a load of manure delivered each spring, when the sheds that the animals overwintered in were cleaned out. This would then compost down in a corner of the garden that was accessible but out of the way, ready for use over the following winter and subsequent spring. But supplies of manure are getting increasingly hard to come by, especially if you live in a town.

The organic gardener also has the problem of getting hold of "clean" manure. On a conventional farm antibiotics, pesticides from worming mixtures and hormones to promote growth and milk production are passed through the animals into their faeces. These remain in the manure for many months and can enter and pollute your carefully created organic garden. So ideally you should get any manure from an organic farm. But any organic system, be it a small back garden or a farm of thousands of acres, is based around the principle of creating a growing environment that is fully integrated. Therefore you can only support so many animals on any given acreage, which, in turn, will only give you so much manure. This is all needed to go back into the ground. If you get exceptional growth and find you can feed more animals – and therefore get more manure – this "excess" will also be needed to replace the loss of nutrients that the extra harvest has brought. In other words, you simply cannot have excess manure on an organic farm any more than the gardener can make too much compost. The upshot is that you are unlikely to find a supply of organic animal manure unless the farmer is doing you a favour or can trade it.

The best solution is to keep some stock yourself and use your own bedding to create your own organic manure. Most people could keep some stock, even if it is only a couple of hens, but creating the bedding is more tricky, although organic sawdust or chippings are obtainable. Failing that you can try and trade some manure from a friendly stock-owner for some produce that you grow yourself. The final alternative is to buy non-organic manure from a non-intensive farmer and compost it well before using it.

Farmyard manure, which comes from cattle and straw, needs to be well composted whatever the source. I made the mistake, some years back, of mulching new borders with uncomposted cattle manure. I put barrowloads of it down as a mulch about 15cm (6in) thick, thinking that within a few months it would have been worked into the soil, which was heavy and a bit wet, to create a rich loam. The principle was right but the time-scale was hopelessly ambitious. For the first year the

One of our remarkably tame Australorp hens (*facing page, top*). The hens roost and lay in the chicken house (*see bottom left*), which protects them from the weather and the constant threat of foxes. It is completely cleaned once a month and the contents put onto the compost heap (*bottom right*). In this case it is wood shavings but I often use straw.

The value of the nutrients in manure is secondary to the way that it restructures soil and provides organic material for the incredible range of life going on below the soil's surface.

combination of fresh manure and heavy soil made a sticky, slippery dough, which was almost impossible to plant into or even tread upon without ending up on my backside. Two years later this had indeed become a black, crumbly loam, but I could have achieved that effect twice as quickly if I had composted the manure for a year before using it.

Apart from the impracticality of putting fresh manure onto a bed that you wish to plant into, it will also scorch any soft tissue on growing plants and rob the soil of nitrogen as it composts down. Only use fresh manure, if you have no alternative, around woody plants or on ground that you intend to leave for at least six months. Otherwise always compost it first.

There are two ways to compost manure of any kind. Either make a heap next to your compost heaps and mix some in with the rest of your waste material every time you add it. This makes wonderful compost very quickly because the manure acts as an activator, speeding up the whole process, and within six months is absorbed indistinguishably into the finished compost.

The other way is simply to stack it up where it can be left. If it is very strawy and dry give it a good soak with the hosepipe, then cover the top, not so much to keep it dry but to stop the nutrients washing away into the soil beneath the stack, and leave it alone for six to twelve months. At the end of this period the exterior will look largely unchanged, but the inside will have gone from a rather obvious mix of straw and poo to a dark, rich but not rank manure.

The main disadvantage of farmyard manure is that it invariably contains lots of annual weed seeds that often survive the slow composting process (which is a good reason

to mix it up with the rest of your compost as this is much more likely to kill the seeds). These then grow lustily once you spread the manure. Fat hen is the classic manure weed, each plant of which carries an astonishing number of seeds. For this reason alone, I would use it mainly to dig into the ground rather than as a mulch.

Cattle manure is often referred to as farmyard manure or even, in an unnecessary abbreviation, as FYM. It has the great virtue of being produced in huge bulk so you are likely to be able to get quite large amounts cheaply. I have mentioned the dangers of residues in the manure, and this is particularly true if your supply comes from a non-organic dairy farm.

It is important not to overvalue the nutritional virtues of farmyard manure. It varies, of course, but the goodness in an average load of manure consists of no more than 0.5 percent nitrogen, 0.25 percent phosphates, and 0.5 percent potash. The potash comes mainly from the urine and the nitrogen and phosphorus from the solids. If the heap stands uncovered for any length of time most of this will dissolve and leach into the soil directly beneath the manure heap itself.

Although it has limited nutritional value, it is a wonderful soil conditioner, particularly on light soils, adding substance to help retain moisture and create a good, open structure. It encourages a high rate of micro-activity in the soil, and whereas compost is best applied quite sparingly to get its best effect, manure can be added at a high volume and therefore each addition makes a dramatic difference to the soil.

Animal manure tends to be slightly acidic

and I have seen instances where it has been used as a mulch year after year around the same roses where the soil has become measurably more acidic, so it is best to only use it one year in three on any one location.

Horse manure For many people horses are a more likely source of manure than cattle. Riding schools and stables tend to be situated on the edge of towns and are often only too happy to give away their manure. The last house we lived in had been a riding school before we bought it and I inherited an enormous pile of horse manure. It was wonderful. The top and outside, where the most recent stuff had been thrown, were strawy, but inside the pile was about 50 tons of the most fabulous black garden gold, every ounce of which I used carefully in making the garden.

Horse manure is ideal for heavy soil, lightening it and opening it out better than anything else. It is a little higher in nitrogen than farmyard manure, but a little lower in phosphate and potash.

Some of the best garden compost I have ever made was when we had a Shetland pony. He was a bad-tempered bully and hated children, which slightly limited his role as my children's introduction to riding, but he did produce a lot of manure, and I used to muck out his stable directly onto the compost heap. The result was gold-medal stuff, which increased the heat of the heap hugely and the consequent rate of composting and destruction of weeds.

Chicken manure Whilst there are other, obvious, benefits from keeping your own hens, I would say that the manure that they produce was a good enough reason in its own right. It is exceptionally high in nitrogen and phosphates and also provides sulphur, magnesium and lime. To put it into context the average chicken manure has four times as much nitrogen and three times as much of both phosphorus and potash as farmyard manure. I use both straw and sawdust as bedding, which gets changed about once a month, and I always add it to the compost heap rather than use it as a separate manure. In this way our dozen hens add between half a ton and a ton of exceptionally rich compost to the garden.

Keeping poultry Any good organic garden needs a supply of manure and preferably an organic one at that. Garden compost and an intelligent use of green manure go a long way to supplement this, but keeping some form of livestock and recycling the manure that they produce is the best possible solution. For most people cattle, sheep, pigs, or goats are not a practical option, nor that desirable for the average gardener. We want a nice garden, not a farm. But keeping poultry is viable in even a tiny garden and completes the livestock circle.

I also feel very strongly about modern intensive egg production. Intensive animal "farming" of any kind is a disgusting business but intensive chicken factories are really repulsive and infinitely crueller than any kind of hunting. Battery hens live in tiny cages and are treated like a slot machine: just enough food and water is put in to produce an egg as cheaply as possible. Neither the quality of the egg nor the life of the hen is of any consideration at all. If you like eggs then you either buy free-range organic eggs or you keep chickens yourself. It is as simple as that.

Well, almost. Chickens can be beautiful, charming and good to eat, both as egg and meat. But they are also cruel and stupid, have hideous bottoms, cost a fortune and, worst of all, destroy gardens. But I would not be without them. I have kept them all my life, except for one period in London. I even kept chickens in the tiny backyard of my rented digs (they roosted in the outside lavatory) as a student and used to take the cockerel to parties where he had temperedly pecked people and shit on the floor. The reason, of course, for enduring their repulsive habits is the eggs that they produce. Fresh eggs – by which I mean eggs eaten within a day or so of laying – are incomparably nicer than ones that have been through the supermarket food chain, even if they are free range and organic. It is the difference between a strawberry eaten warm from the soil on a midsummer's evening or a chilled out-of-season travesty, or mackerel straight out of the sea and a supermarket ready dinner. One version is memorably delicious and the other a caricature of the real thing.

For the past ten years we have kept a mix of types of hen, with numbers varying from a minimum of six and an all-time high of 33, and found that a dozen mixed bantams and full sized birds (with Buff Rocks, English Game, Barnevelders, Australorps, and Wyandottes being favourite) can supply our family of five with more than enough eggs for over half the year. For the organic gardener, chickens are almost a necessity, although put a chicken in a flower border and it will scratch up every seed, seedling, and piece of mulch, and eat every piece of juicy green growth. It will also find a beautifully prepared seedbed, wait until every last seed is sown, and then and use it as a dustbath. So you must have a chicken run both to protect the garden from the hens and to protect the hens from foxes. Foxes are the number one enemy. Not only do they pick off individual birds but a fox in a henhouse will kill the lot. Over the years I have lost almost every bird I have owned – including ducks and guinea fowl – to foxes.

But assuming that they are fox-proof, the birds are really good at cleaning up a piece of ground before it is cultivated. Ideally, they have a movable coop or ark that can be put on a patch of soil where the birds will scratch around eating every pest, and most of the weeds, as well as fertilizing it. They can also be put into fruit cages after the fruit has been gathered, and into greenhouses and tunnels in autumn to give the place a good going over before it is prepared for spring. We let ours out into the orchard so that they can scratch around under the trees and eat the pests. The really important thing about chickens is to give them access to fresh grass. The birds love this and the flavour of the eggs is dramatically improved. The best method for a small garden is to have a few in a movable hutch and to move it around the lawn every day. This, plus some organic grain, pretty much guarantees a steady supply of eggs from February to October.

Hens are very efficient recyclers of household waste, turning all the really nasty scraps, like fatty things that would block the drains and meaty things that would attract rats to the compost heap, into enough free-range organic eggs for a small family. We feed our hens all the waste from the kitchen that will not go onto the compost heap, such as any fat, dairy produce, meat scraps, bread, rice, pasta, and cooked vegetables.

Laying hens need protein, and meat and dairy scraps are an excellent source of this. We give them these first thing in the morning so that nothing is left lying around after dark, otherwise it will inevitably attract vermin. It is worth remembering that the morning feed becomes the following day's eggs, so make sure that this includes some protein. The organic grain is given in the late afternoon at least an hour before dusk, so that they roost with a full crop and stay warm overnight. I make sure to scatter the grain so that they keep busy looking for it. Hens get bored just like any captive animal. Hens need grit to help digest food and either oyster shells or crushed eggshells will do this. Hens must have fresh, clean water and a dozen birds can drink up to a gallon (5 litres) a day.

If your egg supply suddenly drops, or even stops, the reason is likely to have been three days earlier. Any change can cause this – in food, water, weather, or even people around them.

I would like to let the hens have the run of the orchard, but they stray beyond its boundaries and scratch and nibble destructively. They are particularly disastrous in a greenhouse, gouging great holes in tomatoes, reducing young lettuces to rags, and making great dust wallows as they bath in the dry soil. They also take huge delight in spreading the mulch around a series of young hedges. I must have raked it up and replaced it a dozen times. So I restrict them by clipping their wings and keeping them within a movable fold of metre-high chicken-wire fencing, held up by bamboo canes. A dozen birds are given an area about ten by ten metres (ten by ten yards). The fencing takes half an hour to dismantle and move every few weeks, keeps the birds in and all but the most determined fox out.

Clipping hens' wings is a painless and quick thing to do. Wait until dusk, when they are roosting and completely acquiescent, and

From henhouse to compost heap

We mainly use straw or sawdust as bedding for the hens. The advantage of straw is that the resulting manure is exceptionally good for the compost heap. Chicken manure is very high in nitrogen and is too rich to be used directly on the soil, unless very well rotted. Ours goes onto the compost heap where it is a powerful activator and the straw helps bulk out and improve the texture of the final compost. This, I think, is the real satisfaction of keeping hens. They integrate perfectly into the organic system of gardening.

simply hold each bird, opening out one wing fully and cutting off the first 5–8cm (2–3in) of the primary feathers with a sharp pair of scissors. This does not stop them getting up to roost but makes flight uneven and too difficult for such a heavy bird. The feathers grow back fully within a month or two.

Every hen will have an annual moult, usually between late summer and autumn, lasting from six to eight weeks. They will not lay during this period and will look decidedly scruffy. My birds usually stop laying by mid-October and resume again just after Christmas, as the days lengthen. By March they are in full production.

Rats are drawn to hens like bees to honey. The only solution is to clear any scraps of uneaten food at the end of the day, move the henhouse about so that they cannot burrow under it, and to take action at the very first hint of rat activity.

We mainly use straw as bedding for the hens, although sawdust is cleaner and often easier to get hold of. The main advantage of straw is that the resulting chicken manure is exceptionally good for the compost heap, especially when mixed well with household waste or grass clippings. Chicken manure is very high in nitrogen and is too rich to be used directly on the soil unless it is very well rotted, so every couple of months ours goes straight onto the compost heap where it is a powerful activator and the straw helps bulk out and improve the texture of the final compost. This, I think, is the real satisfaction of keeping hens. On the one hand we get the best eggs you could eat. But they also integrate perfectly into the organic system of gardening. Nothing is wasted. Even the eggshells go either into the compost heap to provide calcium, which encourages worm activity, or to the hens, which helps keep their eggshells thick.

The henhouse must be dry, well ventilated, and have a wooden bar with rounded edges for the birds to perch on. This must be at least 60cm (2ft) off the ground with at least 60cm (2ft) headspace above. Allow 30cm (1ft) of perch per bird, and nesting boxes with clean nesting material. The perch needs to be removable so that the house can be thoroughly cleaned. They do not need a floor if the ground is dry and even and the henhouse is to be frequently moved.

If you do not have a cockerel – and there is no need if you do not intend to rear your own chicks – the hens will still get broody. During this period they are not laying but sit determinedly on a clutch of eggs – often stealing them from other hens – for days or even weeks at a time. The secret is not to let them settle and to cool the hens and the eggs down. I simply pull them off the nest by the tail and turf them outside, removing any eggs. The broody period usually lasts about a fortnight. If you do have a cockerel and want to rear chicks, it is best to have a separate broody coop with a short run, and to provide the broody bird with a little grain and water, although she will be living mainly on her reserves. The coop should be placed directly on the ground and the eggs either directly on the grass or on a thin nest of straw (the moisture from the earth is good for them). The eggs will hatch after 19–21 days – there may be a couple of days between the first and last. Any egg that has not hatched after 22 days will not be viable.

Chicks should have access to very short grass, chick crumbs and some water (in a shallow container so they do not drown), and should remain within the protection of the run for at least a fortnight. They will grow very fast but they are very vulnerable to predators, especially cats, crows, and magpies. The brood will return to its own coop for a while until the chicks are big enough to join the other birds in the henhouse.

It is likely that the majority of your chicks will be male and these will start to fight when they reach a couple of months old. It is best to get rid of them as soon as they are old enough to sex (an expert can do this on hatching, but I wait until they look like cockerels, which is between 8 and 12 weeks). Males have much thicker legs, their combs are redder and bigger, and their spurs are larger. The most sensible thing to do is to segregate them from the female chicks, fatten them up for a couple of weeks and then wring their necks and eat them. I always feed the carcasses of birds that have been eaten and then made into stock back to the hens. The squeamish will object, but the hens like it and it is the least wasteful way to go about it.

Ducks and guinea fowl I have kept ducks and guinea fowl and both birds produce delicious eggs. Ducks are charming birds and very easy to keep, requiring only some water to dabble in (this need not be a pond – a sunken bucket will do, although something a little bigger is better). Whatever you use it must be big enough for the birds to submerge their heads and be kept topped up with water. They will nest happily with the hens, bedding down on the floor of the henhouse. They do not like jumping, so make sure there is a ramp up to the entrance.

They lay punctually first thing in the morning and munch up any slug they come across. But they do make a mess, both with their feet and their copious, very liquid excretions. They like grain and bread with anything else that gets given to the chickens. If you are raising ducklings for the table, kill them when they are between 10 and 12 weeks old, when they will be fully grown and tender. Apparently, I am afraid that I have a very soft spot for ducks and could no more eat them than I could my dogs. But I am a sentimental fool.

I have no such emotional attachment to guinea fowl. They are funny-looking birds, like an unholy cross between a turkey and a pheasant. But they are terribly easy to keep, eating up caterpillars, leatherjackets, and any other bugs. They lay well (their eggs are the size of a medium hen's egg, with one very pointed end, and slightly richer than a hen's) and make very good eating, the taste having the best qualities of chicken and pheasant. They hardly need any housing, being happiest roosting in a tree or large shrub, although they do like some cover if it is wet.

So much for their virtues. But they are bullies and aggressive to ducks and hens if they are all mixed together and I have known them kill both birds. The males can also be aggressive to children and are consequently not suitable for a household with a young family. But this natural aggression coupled with extreme alertness makes them very good watchdogs. They will make their distinctive creaking cackle if they sense any kind of disturbance, day or night. They like to wander in a group, ranging quite far if they have the chance, but always returning home to roost.

Mulches A mulch is any layer of material laid upon bare soil. It has a number of purposes and depending on what you are trying to achieve, different materials have different virtues.

The best time to mulch your borders is in early spring, as the soil is warming up but before too many plants have begun to get growing. For me this is some time between the middle of March and the middle of April. But, as with everything in gardening, a good time is when you have the materials to hand and the time and inclination to do the job. If you have plenty of material to mulch with, it can be very beneficial to mulch again in autumn, after borders have been cleared of any annuals or dead foliage.

Most shrubs, fruit trees, perennial vegetables, and plants in containers also do well with a mulch each spring, just before they start their major growth period. If in doubt, do it and do it thickly. Finish any pruning, weed thoroughly, and spread the mulch around each plant, being careful not to cover any existing leaves or the crown. Any bulbs will easily push through the mulch, however thick, but seedlings, both of weeds or treasured plants,

will be killed. The reasons for mulching are:
• To supply the soil with humus and nutrients.
• To create a barrier dense enough to stop light reaching the soil, thereby stopping any weed seeds germinating.
• To create a permeable layer that will let all water go through it and reach the roots in the soil but to simultaneously slow down evaporation, thereby making more efficient use of all available moisture.
• To create an insulating blanket for the soil, so that it warms up quicker and cools down slower.
• To stop soil erosion in very exposed, dry sites.
• To provide an inhospitable surface against specific pests such as slugs.

I use garden compost, mushroom compost, cocoa shells, and leafmould to mulch my borders. All have different virtues and some limitations.

Garden compost is the richest in goodness and therefore ideal as a mulch to feed the soil. Given a sufficient supply I would use nothing else but I never have enough, so it has to be rationed. It is important to resist the temptation of making your mulch go further by putting it down in a thin layer. Better to put down a decent thickness of at least 5cm (2in) every other year than a scant 2.5cm (1in) annually. I ration mine by putting it on different parts of the garden in a three-year rotation. It can also be slightly acidic so is unsuitable for certain lime-loving plants.

Artificial mulches, such as the polypropylene layer that I use around my blackcurrants, are very effective, cheap, and easy to lay, but ugly. However, they can be covered by wood chips, which looks better.

Mushroom compost is very good for lightening our heavy soil, is available very cheaply in unlimited quantities, especially if you can get a bulk delivery, and is pleasant and easy to handle. I must have put nearly 100 tons of it on this garden over the past ten years and have found it worth every penny, especially in the first five years of making the garden when waste organic material of any kind was in short supply. Obviously, as the garden has matured it has produced more vegetation and therefore more composting material. But mushroom compost has two slight drawbacks (other than the cost). The first is that it is hard to find a supply of organic mushroom compost. I get round this by insisting on stuff that is very well rotted and taking delivery three to six months before I need it so that any residual pathogens can compost out of it. The other potential disadvantage is that it is alkaline so is not suitable for use around ericaceous plants or even certain fruits like raspberries.

Leafmould This is special stuff. There is no gardening substance so evocative, so clean or sensuous to the touch. It is a rich brown, with a crumbly texture, and smells sweetly of fungi and autumn. We make it with almost fanatical zeal, gathering as many leaves as we can, not so much to tidy the place – although that is a useful by-process of the operation – as to use their potential. They are swept and raked onto a suitable path – grass if it is dry and brick if wet – and then mown using a rotary mower (*see overleaf*) to help speed up the composting process. The bulk of our leaves come from the pleached limes and hornbeam hedges, with a good deal of hazel and Field maple thrown in. They then go into a large chicken-wire container and are kept wet. If they never dry out, the leaves will convert into useable leafmould within six months and fine potting compost within 11 months, when the bin is emptied so that the next fall of leaves can take their place.

I use the leafmould as a mulch in our Spring Garden, which is filled with mainly woodland plants and therefore adapted to taking most of its nourishment via leaf-fall, and as part of our home-made potting compost. It is especially useful when potting bulbs. But however many deciduous trees you have in your garden, you are unlikely to have enough material to do more than supply a small proportion of your needs for a nutritional mulch.

Cocoa shells I have also used cocoa shells over the past few years. These have the advantage of being very light and clean to handle and easy to pour into place around plants, of lasting a long time, of working extremely effectively in lightening wet and heavy soil, and also of being very effective in retaining surface water. So they are very useful. Their disadvantage is that they are expensive and are not produced organically. In itself this does not stop them being part of a non-commercial organic garden, but it is not ideal. The timing of using them as a mulch is also critical. I have found that they are best used in late autumn or early spring, as the ground is warming up but whilst the air temperature is low. If you use them when it is warmer they quickly form a crust that is hard and dry on top (ideal for stopping weeds) but warm and slimy on the underside and provides the ideal breeding and resting ground for slugs. So they have to be in place and past this early decomposition process by early summer.

When making leafmould, it is surprising how good a rainproof layer a layer of leaves can be so, to prevent them from drying out, it is important to stir the pile up from time to time.

Cocoa-shell mulch

To make our leafmould we sweep or rake the leaves into a suitable area, then pass the rotary mower over them, chopping and collecting them up in one go. This speeds up the composting process by months, reduces the bulk of dry leaves and makes for more surface area that can be wetted.

Gravel and pebbles As well as playing the vital role of feeding the soil, all of the above will stop annual weeds and smother even the toughest perennials, making them much easier to pull out. They all warm the soil and preserve moisture. But, because they are all organic, they all disappear into the ground within at least a year, when you have to repeat the process to have the same effect. There are times when you want a longer lasting mulch, particularly when its prime role is to preserve moisture or keep down weeds. Gravel or pebbles work extremely well for this. Almost anything can grow through a thick layer of gravel and it is ideal for plants that are adapted for growing in harsh conditions, such as alpines or plants from hot plains. Pebbles are very good for putting round established climbers that do not need feeding, especially against a wall where a lot of rain is absorbed. But of course if you do put down a stone mulch you have to clear it every time you want to plant or add compost to the ground.

Shreddings We keep all our woody deciduous prunings, adding them to a pile that grows for about six months until we get round to hiring a shredder. What deciduous prunings we have get burnt and the ashes added to the compost heap.

There is some debate about the ecological merits of using a shredder or chipper. The argument against it is that it uses much energy in the form of diesel and pollutes the social air with its noise. These evils are set against the relative merit of leaving the pile of prunings to gently rot in a corner of the garden so that they form a refuge for insects, birds, and small mammals, thereby enriching the garden's ecosystem.

I think that I agree with this case when applied to a small garden, although shredded stalks and prunings can be a useful carbon-rich addition to the compost heap as well as a mulch in their own right.

In our two-acre garden the arguments against shredding do not hold water. We do it once a year, for one day only, using far less fuel and making less noise than the average grass cutter does in a week. The pile is there for many months and provides cover throughout the winter, when it is most needed. Also the addition of perhaps a ton of extra organic mulch every year reduces the demands upon our garden compost, so it is doubly useful.

It is important to use a shredder that is powerful enough to cope with the largest item you have to chew up. Anything smaller can make very heavy work of quite small prunings and takes ages to get through them all. It is always surprising how the great twiggy mass that has built up over the winter months reduces down to quite a small heap of chippings. We leave these to rot down for at least three months before using them. This is because fresh chippings initially use up a lot of nitrogen from the soil as they compost. When they are ready, we use our chippings to mulch the hedges, primarily to suppress weed growth.

Artificial mulches You can buy great rolls of man-made polypropylene fabrics in many different guises, although most share the same characteristic of letting moisture through whilst blocking weeds from coming up or light from getting to the ground. The net effect is that nothing can grow beneath them. They are cheap, very easy to lay, and superb at stopping weeds, and they have the great advantage that they can be trodden on without being damaged. But again they add nothing to the soil and they are not beautiful, although you can cover them with a layer of chippings to some aesthetic effect. You have to decide what is the primary purpose of the mulch and see what is available and use it to best effect.

Natural fertilizers

According to my desire to keep everything in the garden as simple as possible, I instinctively do not like using a lot of fertilizers of any kind. I also adhere strongly to the principle of feeding the soil and not the plant.

It is wrong to try and boost either the growth rate or ultimate size of a plant. This will lead to a weakened plant and sappy growth that will attract predators such as aphids or fungal diseases. Because the plant is weakened by the extra growth it will be less able to resist attack. This will boost the predatory population and stimulate a cycle of unhealthy imbalance in your garden. It is far better to have small plants growing healthily and utilizing all available nutrients from your soil than to have big, lush unhealthy growth.

But there are circumstances, particularly when you are growing a succession of crops, where you are taking more out of the soil than can be replaced or where natural limitations – such as plants grown in containers – restrict the plant's access to a full range of nutrition. In these situations I do use fertilizers very sparingly. To summarize, I use them for:

• Young seedlings raised in containers, to encourage a healthy start.
• All perennial plants and shrubs in containers.

One of the blights of organic gardening over the years has been the use of old carpet and underfelt as mulches. They might work, but they have one irredeemable flaw: they are ugly. Everything in a garden should be at least handsome if not beautiful, so only use them if, hand on heart, you think that they are the most desirable option. Ha!

• Ground that is very light, where nutrients are easily leached out.
• Ground which for good reasons is being used very intensively to raise the maximum amount of crops (such as in a greenhouse or tunnel or in a very small garden).

There are three main plant foods nitrogen, phosphorus and potash, and any fertilizer will primarily provide these three in various proportions.

Nitrogen is the most essential plant nutrient and is responsible for green growth. It is created almost entirely by decaying organic material, although legumes (peas, beans, clovers, lupins) draw nitrogen from the air and transfer it to the soil via nodules on their roots. Too little nitrogen and a plant will be stunted, yellowing, and slow to grow. Too much and you will have lush, sappy shoots and foliage at the expense of flowers or fruits. Nitrogen leaches out of soil quite quickly, so needs constant replacement, but because it acts very fast there is a temptation to apply too much too often – as in conventional farming. By far the best source of nitrogen is from organic material like compost or manures, added to the soil rather than the plant. This will also make the soil much better able to hold

Wood ash is used to feed the gooseberries and currant bushes, which are hungry for potash. I also sprinkle it directly around growing members of the allium family – onions, garlic, shallots, and leeks – which respond well to this treatment.

moisture and store nitrogen for longer. Adding very fresh organic material like strawy manure, freshly chipped woody stuff, or fresh grass cuttings will actually deplete the soil of nitrogen because they will use nitrogen as part of the process of composting.

Phosphorus supplies phosphates to plants, which they need to develop strong roots and to promote germination. It is needed in much smaller quantities than nitrogen but the effects of phosphate deficiency can be very similar to those of nitrogen deficiency. However a blue-green tinge to mature leaves, with a tendency to drop early, is a good sign. It is much more prevalent in acidic soils than alkaline ones and adding lime to an acidic soil will help enormously. But if the soil is rich in organic material and has a moderate pH, this should not be a problem.

Potassium in the form of potash is essential for all plants but particularly for fruiting crops, potatoes, tomatoes, and alliums. In a soil with very low potash levels plants may show a brown fringe on their leaves looking like scorching, a yellowing of the veins of leaves, and general stunting and die-back. Fruits fail to ripen and potatoes will turn black when cooked. Potash is released from well-made compost and on a good loam with plenty of organic material incorporated into it there should not be a problem. But a deficiency is much more likely in very sandy soils that leach quickly. Wood ash, comfrey, and seaweed are good sources of potassium.

Other elements There are other nutrients that plants need, but in very much smaller quantities and, as I keep stressing, well-made

compost regularly added to the soil should supply all of these without the need for any extra doses.

Calcium is necessary for the plant's cellular structure and the lack of it can be the cause of scorched, ragged edges to leaves. It can cause bitter pit in apples, clubroot in brassicas, and blossom end rot in tomatoes. Sometimes sufficient calcium is present in the soil but is "locked up" by too much nitrogen or potassium which blocks the plant's ability to take up enough calcium. The more acidic the soil, the less calcium there will be. Ground limestone, gypsum, mushroom compost, and comfrey will all add extra calcium to the soil.

Magnesium is needed by plants to enable them to take in nutrients and in particular in the formation of chlorophyll, which makes them green. Consequently, severe yellowing of the leaves (often with the veins remaining green) is one of the main signs of a magnesium deficiency. Dolomitic limestone and seaweed will help cure the problem.

A lack of trace elements such as iron, zinc, or boron is sometimes the cause of plant problems but not very often and personally this is not something that I worry about. It is, in my opinion, much more important to create a healthy, well-balanced soil than to worry about very small details that could possibly be a problem. Certainly you should never add specific trace elements to the soil. Seaweed meal is nearly always enough to redress any imbalances – which are more often than not caused by the addition of excess nutrients such as nitrogen.

There is an argument, much promoted by the anti-organic lobby, that all chemicals are the same, whether man-made or synthesized from natural sources. In other words, there are no such things as "organic" chemicals. I am happy to go along with this, because it completely misses the point of organic gardening. As I hope this book makes completely clear, organic living is about working with nature rather than totting up Brownie points from some higher moral judge. There are dozens of aspects of organic gardening where the individual must decide what is the right or wrong (that is, inorganic) thing to do in a particular instance. But it is the overall approach to how we treat this planet that is important. Therefore it seems, on balance, better to me to use nutrients that are derived directly from a plant source where possible. There are practical benefits to be had from this. Most of the problems that arise from using extra fertilizers and feeds in your garden come as a result of imbalance and that is more likely to be caused by using too much of one particular nutrient than too little of another. When you use proprietary, prepared feeds you are more likely to overfeed than if you prepare your own. By the same token, if you have to go to the trouble of collecting and making your own fertilizers, particularly liquid ones, rather than simply opening a packet or bottle, you are likely to apply them much less often. Again, less is better.

Providing nutrients Nutrients come in two forms, those you buy and those you make yourself. This is a brief summary of the most common ones that organic gardeners use.

• **Bonemeal** acts as a supply of slow-release phosphates, being about 20 percent calcium phosphate and 3 percent nitrogen. Because it only breaks down slowly the plant can use the phosphate – which it needs to develop strong root growth – as it grows.

• **Dried blood** is a fast-acting source of nitrogen which is easy to sprinkle directly onto the soil.

Until the BSE crisis of 1995, I regularly used dried blood as a top-dressing for evergreens in spring (it is very good with yew hedges) and as an activator in the compost heap. I also used bonemeal as a slow-release fertilizer every time I planted a tree or shrubby plant and as a top-dressing in spring around my roses. But I investigated the subject and was unhappy with the lack of controls over the production of bonemeal and came to a revaluation of my approach to the fertilization of my garden, which I now consider to be entirely unnecessary beyond the maintenance of a healthy soil. All bonemeal and dried blood comes from beef, almost all of which is imported. Bovine tissue was only banned from horticultural products in 1993, although bonemeal has always been the ground residue of bones, after removal of the gelatine or fats by steaming. There has long been a potential risk of anthrax and salmonella from bonemeal and one has always been recommended to wear gloves to use it. There is no serious question of the prion protein or a BSE virus being passed in the bones. The only safety question might be that if the steaming process was inadequate minute residues of tissue would remain, which could contain BSE. Heat alone – the sterilizing process – would not necessarily destroy the virus or the prion protein. (There is doubt which of these is the infective agent. There is doubt about every aspect of this disease.) But, the consensus is that this is a very, very remote chance and simply not worth worrying about, either in the general scheme of things or in the paranoid world of Creutzfeldt-Jakob anxiety.

• **Blood, fish, and bone** is a form of using waste products from the meat industry. I have no problem with this beyond one of safety and need, and it is a good source of very fast-acting nitrogen and phosphates.

• **Hoof and horn** is a slow-release source of nitrogen, so can be added in autumn or early spring as a general boost if you have no source of compost or manure.

• **Seaweed** is a marvellous fertilizer with nitrogen, phosphates, and a high level of potassium, as well as magnesium and other trace elements and plant growth hormones. It is the one "outside" fertilizer that I still use. All island societies have used it, and on the Aran Islands, off the west coast of Ireland, almost all the soil is man-made from a combination seaweed and sand laid directly onto the bare limestone ground. This produces excellent crops.

If you live by the sea it is worth going to some trouble to gather your own supply, which is best added to the compost heap. Otherwise you can buy it as seaweed meal, which can be forked into the soil before final cultivation or used as a top-dressing for container plants, or as a liquid feed. Mixed very dilute, this is an excellent foliar feed for tomatoes, all young trees and shrubs, or any plant that is looking unwell.

• **Rock dusts** are a form of fertilizer that I have used very little and are generally not very common in the UK. However, they are much used by organic growers in the United States and have the advantage of adding natural, long-lasting elements to help the creation of a balanced fertility rather than promoting a quick-fix. They are generally obtained from waste from quarrying and mining and are therefore environmentally attractive. Rock dusts are ground very fine and do not easily dissolve with water but must be applied to wet soil on a windless day. Rain will wash the dusts in and enough extraction of nutrients will take place for plants to access them. They are also eaten by the creatures in the soil and the nutrients are made available to roots in this way. You can also sprinkle them onto your compost heap where the bacteria can digest them. The point is that they add a slow, steady supply of nutrient to create a long-term balance to the soil fertility in response to what your crops are taking out.

On the whole clay soils do not need rock dusts other than perhaps some lime if they are very heavy. But sandy soils can benefit greatly from them.

• **Lime** is perhaps the most common form of rock dust and is used widely to raise the pH of soils and to add calcium. The underground activity of bacteria, worms, and nematodes increases if the soil is slightly alkaline so lime will assist the integration of organic material into an acidic soil. Garden lime is ground chalk and unlike builder's lime, is safe to skin and eyes. Dolomitic lime is ground from rocks and has the extra advantage of containing magnesium. But the best source of lime is probably calcified seaweed, which has all the virtues of seaweed and lime combined and is particularly useful for ground used for brassicas and legumes and if added to the compost heap.

Potash and Potassium are available in ground rock form, but I confess that I have never used them.

I have read great things about the power of ground basalt and granite, which have a wide range of trace minerals and will stimulate the micro-activity in the soil.

Wood ash Of the home-made fertilizers, I use wood ash a great deal in the garden. This comes entirely from the ash from our fireplaces which I take out to the garden by the wheelbarrow load. The advantage of having stone floors throughout the house is that the barrow and shovel come right into the kitchen and sitting room without the bother of worrying about carpets or lugging buckets. It gets used directly around the gooseberries and currant bushes, and also onions, garlic, shallots, and leeks. It is important to keep the ash dry as the potassium is easily washed out – which is fine once it is in position, neatly arranged in a powdery fashion around the neatly pruned leg of a gooseberry bush, but less than useless if left puddling in a barrow.

Liquid feeds Other than for tomatoes, I do not use liquid feeds on any plants growing in the soil. This is as much because my plants seem to thrive without any extra feeding as because I have come to the considered conclusion that it is not necessary. By definition, a soluble feed will quickly drain away making itself available to the plant for a limited period of time, so it is a very inefficient way of providing nutrients to plants unless you are prepared to do it often or if they are visibly ailing. However, for plants in containers that have a severely restricted access to nutrition, liquid feeds are essential. If possible, I prefer to apply them as a foliar spray.

• **Comfrey** makes a good liquid fertilizer. An easy way to make it is to loosely fill a bucket with cut leaves – tearing them up as necessary – and top it up with water, pressing the leaves down firmly as they absorb the liquid until you can add no more. You might feel the urge to add some pee as an activator. You might not.

Cover it up and leave for a couple of weeks to stew. It will look and smell horrible but the resulting deep brown liquid can be diluted and used as a very potassium-rich spray that is exceptionally good for tomatoes, onions, gooseberries, beans, and all potash-hungry crops. As with all fertilizers, it is better to make a mixture that is too dilute than too rich.

Comfrey has entered organic mythology due to the proselytizing work of Lawrence Hills, the founder of the Henry Doubleday Research Association, who devoted all his early work to research and experimentation with comfrey. It is certainly an essential plant in any organic garden as it has an unmatched ability to absorb trace minerals from its very deep roots and is an excellent accumulator of potassium, all of which is transferred to the leaves. I grow a permanent bed of a couple of dozen plants that I cut to the ground for their leaves three or even four times a year. I make a feed from them but also add them neat to the compost heap where they add fertility as well as acting as an activator. I also use the leaves directly as a mulch under rose bushes, tomatoes, and gooseberries.

• **Borage** is beautiful but becomes an invasive annual weed in this garden from July onwards, popping up all over the area where I first planted it ten years ago. But this apparent nuisance can be harvested and made into a liquid feed, very high in nitrogen, which is useful for the greediest summer vegetables like marrows, squashes, and melons.

• **Nettles** may be a weed with a painful sting but they have many virtues. They act as an activator in the compost heap and a liquid feed made from them will act as a tonic to otherwise fragile or ailing plants, making the plants more resistant to disease.

Patch of nettles

Plant propagation

I am always happy to be in my potting shed. It is, in fact, the ground floor of one of our two converted hopkilns, so is spacious and solidly built, but it has the feel of a shed.

Like any decent shed, it is a retreat from the cares of the world and yet a place for quiet, concentrated work. From this brick-floored room I produce thousands of plants each year. The only problem with it is that I feel that I should only be working in there if the weather is bad and I cannot get on outside, whereas often seeds and seedlings will not wait for a rainy day!

I have organized it so that one wall is taken up with racks for different pots and seed trays – supposedly kept strictly in sizes, but needing a sort-out every couple of months. The dirty pots are kept outside and washed in the yard by the back door and only brought back in clean. That way there is less confusion. Another wall has a bench against it where the dry supply of loam, compost, and coir is spread in different bays, with differently sized sieves to hand. The opposite side has a long bench with two built-in wooden trays filled with different potting mixes – one for seeds and the other for potting on or up. Seed, labels, and pens and pencils for marking are stored on that side. Just round the corner is a large sink and tap. There is a radio on the shelf. There is no chair as the surfaces are all fixed at a comfortable height for standing. The centre of the room and the access is spacious enough to wheel in barrows of compost, loam, potatoes, or washed pots.

It is my ideal set-up. Yes, the only window is small, and faces north, and has no glass across its bars so in winter the wind is icy, but it is also pleasantly cool in summer. Yes, it is a little walk to the greenhouse, but that is only through the tool shed and workshop and a few paces across the yard and yes, it has to share space with stored onions, garlic, and potatoes but this hardly feels a problem.

The peat issue Peat is not just a type of soil, it is an issue. Man has been digging peat for fuel from moor and wetland since pre-history. But as long as he just used a spade and dug only for personal consumption, the peat was used at a sustainable level – and still is used as fuel in many parts of Great Britain. But as soon as bulldozers hit the wetlands and means of transporting large quantities around the country became viable, then an environmental disaster began. This began in the 1960s, and until the invention of the garden centre in the early 1970s supplied only nurseries or keen gardeners. But in the last 25 years, peat has been sold to the mass gardening public neat and as the chief component of general purpose "loamless" compost, which is three parts peat and one part sand. Such large-scale mechanical extraction that operates solely for the profits of a few huge companies has made a mockery of the delicate relationship between man and this particular kind of landscape. Take away the peat of moorlands and especially wetlands and you change their entire ecology. The layers just a few feet below the surface are often many hundreds of years old. Once the peat is stripped, it will take millions of years and specific climatic conditions to renew. Digging this up is on a par with ripping out ancient hedgerows solely to make sawdust.

I keep all my seed packets in the potting shed (*top left*) along with pencil and paper to keep a record of what is sown. *Top right*: plugs and seed trays ready for washing. Anything decorative is planted into a terracotta pot. *Bottom*: sunflower seedlings. The lower leaves are the "seed leaves" that appear before the "true leaves" above them.

63

Around 95 per cent of British peat bogs have been lost this century. This is partly because there is a demand for peat, but mainly because that demand has been created and fed by the peat dealers. For a supplier, it has everything going for it. You can imagine the peat producers' pitch: it is light, compactable, lasts several millennium, smells good, is cheap to extract from the ground where it is just lying around doing nothing, and can be sold at a huge profit whilst undercutting any alternative.

In fact the main apologist for peat in the horticultural world has been the trade, especially the nurserymen. These fall into two distinct camps. There are the small, dedicated, fantastically knowledgeable nursery owners, producing astonishing ranges of plants from modest set-ups. They are unsung national treasures. They are their own men and women and deal with the customer as an individual. Then there are the vast plant factories. These are dominated by a handful that produce plants wholesale for the trade, supplying garden centres across the country.

Both types, hero and villain alike, have used peat by the millions of tons, because it is inert, cheap and reliable. The former cannot afford to gamble and the latter doesn't give a damn about anything beyond the next quarterly profits. Which is why almost all containerized plants for sale come in peat. This has led the amateur gardener to believe that this is the best – the professional – way to go about things.

And as far as gardeners are concerned, peat is cosmetically very attractive. It smells good, is pleasant to handle, is light enough to buy in large bags, and has a satisfyingly rich, dark brown colour. It retains moisture well yet drains freely. It is "open" so that young plants can easily establish good root systems. It is pretty much sterile so can be safely used without fear of diseases being spread by it. Peat feels good and therefore, is presumed to do good. In fact, peat has practically no nutrients in it. So commercial growers can control plant food by adding it rather than guessing the compost's own nutritional qualities.

It is not good enough for commercial growers to say that peat makes their work easier and saves them money. I am sure that child labour would have the same net effect, but it does not justify it. If our plants have to cost more as a result of a total boycott on peat, then that seems to me to be a reasonable price to pay. To strip peat in order to make gardens is no more justifiable than it is to dig up rare plants from the wild in order to adorn your garden. In effect, peat is a finite resource and stocks are running low. It is the nature of man to do nothing about this until it is too late. The only way to preserve peat wetlands is to stop buying peat in any form. If the demand dries up so too will the supply. There are alternatives, such as coir and wood-based composts that are almost as good and, in this case, "almost" is certainly good enough.

No gardener should buy peat-based compost. Every time you use a peat-based compost in the garden you are deliberately participating in the destruction of a non-renewable environment that sustains some of our most beautiful plant and animal life. No garden on this earth is worth that.

Compost mixes The idea of any seed compost is to provide a medium that will hold some moisture without readily becoming too wet and provide an easy root-run for the initial frail roots. Seeds will germinate in a completely sterile medium like vermiculite or sand, but unless the seedlings are to be pricked out when very young, the medium should also have some nutrition – but not too much otherwise you will get very lush growth that will attract disease and predators.

Potting compost on the other hand wants to have a little more goodness in it, sufficient to provide the growing plant with its needs to develop a really healthy, extensive root system. The medium must be open and free-draining so the roots grow easily through it.

If the plant is to live in a container – such as our pelargoniums, lilies, peppers, or cucumbers – it must have a potting compost that suits its special needs and which has the ability to provide and store nutrients.

Coir – pros and cons I use a lot of coir, which I buy as compressed "bricks" and soak to expand into a loose, fibrous potting medium. It is a waste product from coconuts and as such is a form of recycling, although there are a lot of energy miles attached to it. But it is a growing medium which produces good root structures, holds water well, and is a good base for mixing your own compost. I spoke to Wessex, who were one of the first companies to introduce coir to this country ten years ago, shipping it from Sri Lanka. I asked how sales of coir were going. They said that in Holland it has been taken up commercially as a preferable growing medium to peat but compost sales in the UK were mainly price-driven. This meant that the companies owning their own peat bogs could wage a price war against any alternatives – like coir. When I taxed them about the energy miles involved in shipping it from Sri Lanka they pointed out

that it was compressed to a sixth of its loose consistency for transportation and that all peat had to be driven by huge lorries or shipped from Ireland or Russia. And that coir was a genuine waste product that would use energy to dispose of. Interestingly, it is not given Soil Association approval, so cannot be sold as organic, but anything grown in it organically is classified as organic.

I certainly feel very happy using it. If you use coir, do not over-water. The surface of the container will dry out but it holds water very well at root level. You do not need to add anything to coir if you are using it purely to raise seedlings, but I like to add loam for anything that is to be eventually grown in the soil. It means that the roots are established in the complex micro-ecology of our particular soil from the very outset. Pure coir is also not ideal for anything other than fast-growing seedlings.

Coir-7s I also have recently been experimenting with coir-7s, which are compressed disks of coir about the size of a draughts piece contained in a biodegradable mesh bag. When soaked in water, they expand to make a plug about 2.5cm (1in) high into which you sow individual seeds. The advantage of them is that each seedling needs no transplanting or disturbance of any kind, the coir plug being transplanted directly into the soil or container. It also creates a healthy rootball because the roots tend to stop growing at the edge of the plug and therefore become compact without being restricted by any kind of container. The disadvantages are that the plugs must be kept slightly moist – although not wringing wet – and that any slow-growing seedlings need more nutrition than pure coir can give them.

Filling a modular seed tray

Seedlings in coir-7s

Soil blocks The home-made alternative to coir-7s are soil blocks. In principle, these are wonderful, although in practice they can take a little experience to get right. You need to buy soil blockers which stamp out the blocks from your compost mix. The trick is to make the mix distinctly wet so that it is sticky and muddy. The principle of them is exactly the same as coir-7s, but they have the great advantage of allowing you to create whatever mix you desire for each batch of seeds. You can include loam and compost so the seeds grow from the first in the complex medium that the plant will mature in, although they do need a significant proportion of coir (about 50 percent) to keep them bound together. They are also more tricky to handle, although I find that a large label works well as a spatula. Last, but by no means least, they involve no pot washing and are very, very cheap!

Bark and garden-waste composts

Crushed bark is another source of compost although "crushed bark" is a slight misnomer because in fact they use "forest residues" which means wood fibres as well as bark. Only softwood is available in sufficient quantity to meet the demands of the market and within softwood there are two extremes, with pine at one end providing a very chunky bark that has been used for years to mix with peat and make it more durable – peat tends to "slump" after a while - and spruce at the other end, which is very thin and soft. This will be composted for at least three months and makes a very peat-like compost. The advantages of bark seem to be peat-like too, in that it has a low pH and is almost without nutrients so is a "blank canvas". This is fine for the commercial grower wishing to produce a standard, uniform product, but not so good for the organic gardener wishing to enrich the growing plant with as broad a range as possible of micro-activity around its roots.

Various firms are now making organic potting and seed composts from recycled waste and many local councils make very good garden compost which can be delivered at a nominal charge. I know growers that simply use sieved garden compost mixed only with perlite or sharp sand with very good results, both privately and commercially. My own opinion is that soil-based composts are not only more environmentally friendly but more useful to the gardener.

Sowing seed There is no mystery to seed sowing, although I do have a routine that has evolved through habit rather than careful research. If I am sowing in plugs or seed trays, I fill the container very loosely, shake it down, and level the top off with piece of wood that I keep for that purpose. I then place the container in a large sink with 5cm (2in) of water for a few minutes, then drain it so that the base of the compost is thoroughly wet but not dripping.

I always pour a comfortable amount of seeds into the palm of my left hand, dipping into it to pinch an individual seed or cluster of seeds at a time. It is worth taking whatever time it takes to sow the seeds as thinly as you can – preferably a single seed per block or module. If the seeds are very small, I use my penknife dipped into water to pick up as few as possible at a time and then place these on the compost. I then sieve vermiculite or coir over the surface (vermiculite is best as it does not cap or dry out or in any way impede the growth of the emerging seedling), water it again, and put it into the greenhouse for germination.

For small seeds that will transplant happily – such as all lettuces, the chicories, celery and celeriac, I broadcast them thinly in a seed tray and then transplant them into large plugs. Although this involves a little more handling, I find that it is not only quicker but that I can also choose the biggest and healthiest seedlings at this early stage. Before transplanting, I water the seed trays of seedlings very thoroughly so they are very wet when I move them and then, once planted, water them in well.

For very large seeds – such as peas, beans, and the cucurbit family – I sow directly into 8cm (3in) pots, sowing two and sometimes three seeds to a pot and thinning out the weakest after germination.

I *always* label every container, with the species, variety, and date before it leaves the potting shed. Pencil is easiest and best. This is absolutely vital as it is amazing how often varieties or even species of seeds get mixed up.

Most seedlings go either onto the mist propagating bench or onto the heated mat. The danger is usually of overheating and overwatering so I set the thermostat for 18°C (65°F) for most seeds and 21°C (70°F) for ones like melon, aubergine, French beans, or all the squashes. I also try to resist the temptation to overwater which can encourage damping off – a fungal disease that can wipe out a whole batch of seedlings.

If they are in plugs or soil blocks, most seedlings do not need any handling before planting out, so I transfer them to the cold frames as soon as they have two true leaves and harden them off on an outdoor bench for at least a week, and ideally two, before planting out. I also brush trays of growing seedlings with my hand. This has a hardening-off effect.

Taking cuttings Many seeds do not come true so the best way of propagating from a much-loved tree, bush, shrub, or perennial is by taking cuttings. The principle is that the amputated piece of plant will grow fresh roots if placed in a suitable growing medium. But from the second that it is separated from the parent plant it is dying. Therefore the process is a race between the expiration of the cut stem and its ability to grow new, life-giving roots. With some plants, like willow, the roots win almost every time. I have known sawn willow logs, unloaded from a trailer and left on a lawn for a month, to grow roots. Box will often take if merely stuck into the nearest bit of soil. Others, like the new growth of most herbaceous plants, are much more likely to wilt before rooting.

When taking cuttings of any kind there are a few helpful rules:

• Use a very sharp knife or secateurs.
• Put the cutting material immediately into a plastic bag and keep it there until you are ready to pot it up.
• Take cuttings from strong, healthy, non-flowering shoots.
• Where appropriate, I always like to include a tear of stem (heel) at the base of the cutting.
• Morning is the best time to take cuttings as the plant has more moisture in its cells.
• Use a very free-draining compost with at least 50 percent perlite or sharp sand.
• Remove all but two or three leaves from the cut material and if the leaves are large, cut them in half to reduce the rate of moisture loss.

Different types of cutting

Softwood cuttings are taken from the current season's new growth. These root very fast, but wilt even faster, so need to have an artificially

Basic seed mix
3 parts coir
2 parts fine perlite or sharp sand
1 part finely sieved garden compost
1 part sieved loam (preferably molehills but also from stacked turves)

Medium for cuttings
1 part coir
1 part perlite

Medium for pricking out or potting on
2 parts coir
2 part perlite or sharp sand
1 part sieved garden compost
1 part loam

General mix I use for container plants (although this will vary)
2 parts coir
2 parts perlite or sharp sand
2 parts sieved compost

Potted bulb compost
2 parts coir
2 parts perlite or sharp sand
2 parts sieved leafmould

Trays of box cuttings These are taken in September from semi-ripe wood, root very easily, and will be ready to plant out a year later.

Hardwood cuttings are very slow to make roots, but because they are taken from ripened wood in autumn, or even winter, the leaves will have fallen and therefore they are very slow to dry out and die. They are usually used for deciduous trees, shrubs like roses, and fruit such as currants.

I also take cuttings from dahlias and delphiniums from the new shoots that emerge from the plant crown in early spring, taking a section of root at the base of each cutting.

I never use a hormone rooting powder, not through any real principle but because it is one less thing to fiddle with and I have never needed it. However, I do have a mist propagator and it really comes into its own for cuttings as the fine mist radically reduces the rate at which any cutting will wilt and the gentle heat of the bench increases the chance and speed of roots growing. If you have need for a good number of plants, then a mist propagator will earn its keep in the extra plants it produces in a year or two.

humid atmosphere. Most deciduous shrubs and climbers are suitable for softwood cuttings.

Semi-ripe cuttings are taken from midsummer to autumn from the current season's new growth that has begun to harden off. They are treated like softwood cuttings but are generally more robust.

Greenhouse

Possessing a greenhouse is one of the things that sorts out the committed gardener from the person with a garden. A greenhouse, however small, implies a level of involvement that is a stage beyond mowing the lawn and planting out a tray of pansies. They are also seen as an expense that many find hard to justify, but a small greenhouse is at least as good an investment as a good lawnmower, which costs about the same, although the price of a mid-range ride-on mower will buy you two commercial-size greenhouses. A small set up, perhaps 3m (10ft) by 1.5m (5ft) would cost a few hundred pounds and be big enough to

propagate seeds and cuttings and to grow some tomato plants as well as store tender plants in winter and would last at least ten years. It will also be a peaceful place to go, a glass shed, warm, protective, and filled with light and a musky, sexy fragrance. Without the protection of a greenhouse, gardening here would be very much harder and more limited. As it is we have two greenhouses, a large polytunnel, and six cold frames. If this seems excessive, let me say that if space and finance allowed I would have another polytunnel and double the cold frames.

In many ways, the heart of the garden is the

yard with the propagating greenhouse and cold frames. Almost all our seeds are propagated in this greenhouse and the seedlings are grown on in the cold frames. All cuttings root in there and we use it from the middle of summer to grow cucumbers (in pots in the mist-propagating section) and peppers (also in pots, with a little bottom heat). In winter, any tender plants (although we have very few) are kept in there, including brugmansia, citrus, cacti, and salvias as it is the only greenhouse that we heat, but only sufficiently to keep the temperature above freezing.

The top greenhouse used to be our sole one and, what is more, it used to be the bottom greenhouse until one day we took the panes of glass out and picked it up and six of us walked it to its current home. It served well in the early years for seedlings and tomatoes, although in those days I grew many more seedlings outside. The onset of global warming has meant a huge increase in overwintering slugs and snails: this has made it much harder to grow seeds sown direct. So now I grow as much as possible in seed trays, plugs, and soil blocks in the much more controllable environment of a greenhouse.

The second greenhouse is unheated and is now used for tomatoes in the summer and salad crops from the new year until late spring, all of which is grown in raised beds. There is a separate compartment, that can be closed off, which we use for the tenderest or earliest crops. We have followed the same regime for the past five years or so, which seems to work well. In

In spring, this greenhouse becomes a plant factory producing thousands of seedlings.

October, the tomatoes are pulled up and the greenhouse is thoroughly washed with a very dilute solution of disinfectant. It is then left wide open until the new year so the frost and chickens can get into it to respectively kill and eat the fungi and bugs. In the new year, the top 15cm (6in) of soil is removed and replaced with a mixture of loam and compost. This is then covered with fleece and the greenhouse closed so that it can warm up. In February and March, it is planted up with early salad crops such as rocket, mizuna, mibuna, various types of lettuce, endive and land cress, which we will harvest from the end of March through to the end of May, when the tomatoes are planted out. There is no water or electricity to this greenhouse although we collect the rainwater in two butts.

The tunnel The tunnel is run on similar lines, although it is twice the size of the greenhouse and has four large raised beds. We have a tap inside it although no electricity. In principal anything can be grown in here although so far we use it mainly for tomatoes and basil in summer and salad crops in winter and spring. We have only had it for a few years and are still experimenting with it, but it has made a wonderful difference, stretching the seasons by weeks at either end. On a cold winter's day, with the wind cutting through from the north, the tunnel is my favourite place, sheltered from the wind and with the slightly translucent light of a tent. Unlike a greenhouse, which always feels like a glorified glass shed, a tunnel feels like a huge cloche, a vast protective carapace put down over a piece of the garden and consequently working inside it feels like gardening outside – only inside.

There are two main choices when it comes

to buying a greenhouse, aluminium or wood. Wooden greenhouses are slower to heat up but hold their heat longer than aluminium. They are softer to the eye but almost all modern timber greenhouses are made from cedar, which is not, in my opinion, beautiful. However it needs little attention, whereas a painted wooden one will need repainting regularly.

Aluminium greenhouses are light so can buckle in very high winds. However, the weight of the glass is usually enough to stop this. My two have survived terrific storms without damage. The aluminium framing collects condensation, so needs extra ventilation.

If you have a south-facing wall that is 3m (10ft) or more high, it will always be better to have a lean-to greenhouse built against it. Otherwise a freestanding one will give more options. Always get the biggest you can possibly afford and fit into your garden. You

Watering young lettuce plants in the top greenhouse in early spring. These will be cleared later to make room for tomatoes.

The top greenhouse after early lettuces have been cleared and replaced by young tomato plants and basil (*top left*). *Top right*: tying tomatoes in the tunnel. *Bottom*: the cold frames are invaluable, especially in spring. The tops are glazed with polycarbon which is lighter and safer than glass, and in winter the inside is lined with polystyrene insulating sheets.

71

will find that every inch will be used.

When I was a child, we had a greenhouse built in the 1870s and heated by a rusty boiler in the potting shed that was tacked onto the end of it. Like most of the Victorian greenhouses I have seen, it had huge pipes to heat it and a water tank that had as much sunk below ground as above. I wish I had thought about it when installing my own current greenhouses, as a submerged tank keeps the water temperature constant, is easy to dip watering cans into (much quicker than filling from a tap), and takes up little space.

Ventilation is vital. The combination of warmth and water is an ideal breeding ground for fungal growth which, once established, is tricky to get rid of. Good ventilation will stop it developing. Most greenhouses now come with automatic hydraulic window vents which I would consider an absolute necessity. Always open the doors wide except on the coldest days and fit as many side vents as the manufacturer can supply. In winter, it is a good idea to close up the doors a few hours before sundown – by three o'clock here in midwinter – so the warm air inside the greenhouse does not cool down.

It is a good idea to insulate the greenhouse in autumn with a layer of bubble-wrap taped or tacked to the inside of the frame. This is a fiddle but worth the trouble and is sufficient protection against frost for all but the tenderest of plants. Overheating in summer is as much a problem as cold in winter and I know people who leave the bubble-wrap on all year to insulate against heat as well as cold. A wash of distemper will do the job well and can be washed off, or you can get shading nets. But when you put your greenhouse up make provision for access and fixing.

Finally, do have a water and electricity supply laid on when you put the greenhouse in. The water you will need from day one and a tap inside the house is best, although, as I have said, the addition of a submerged tank is ideal. The electricity is for under-soil cables, a mist propagator, electric fan heating, and lights, all of which are highly desirable extras which you may acquire at a later date.

Cold frames In some ways, cold frames are more useful than a greenhouse. Mine are home-made from brick, built against a west-facing wall and glazed with polycarbon glass lights that are propped open by pieces of roofing baton. The bases are made from thick layers of crushed scalpings. Everything that is propagated in the greenhouse goes into the cold frames as part of the hardening-off process and between October and March they are jammed full of overwintering plants like agapanthus, salvias, geraniums, melianthus, and of course, the annual batch of hundreds of box cuttings. By mid April, there is a log-jam as seedlings come out of the greenhouse but half the contents of the frames are not ready to go out. Somehow everything is squeezed in and space is made as things are planted out.

One of the beauties of cold frames is that you can regulate their levels of protection from almost total exposure – good for hardening off on warm days – to extreme insulation. In winter, I insulate the inside with thick polystyrene sheets and in the coldest weather I unroll thick bubble-wrap over the closed lids, held down with bricks. Inside, it is a snug as a bug in a rug and even the tenderest seedling is unharmed by our -14°C (3°F) frosts.

Rainfall and irrigation
We have a high annual rainfall, so drought and irrigation are not major considerations. As I write, in autumn 2002, we have not had any rain for three weeks.

This is exceptional and it is far more usual to have some rain at least every three days!

However, the greenhouses and tunnel need year-round watering and I do water everything when it is planted. Certain vegetables like squashes, celeriac, or Florence fennel need as much water as possible and all vegetables will be watered at critical stages of their growth such as at flowering for legumes or a week before harvesting for lettuces. Watering is a daily necessity, especially for seedlings and young plants in the greenhouse and cold frames. So we have half a dozen standpipes dotted around the garden, another two in the propagating greenhouse, and one in the tunnel. We also have a huge rainwater tank near the propagating greenhouse, another large one near the tunnel, and two more to supply the top greenhouse, so all our inside watering can be done from rainwater if we choose.

There is a well in the backyard which supplied all household water until we moved in. However, one of the drawbacks to our site is that it is effectively perfectly flat – which means that any collected rainwater supply must be either pumped from a subterranean tank or else stored in an elevated tank. The former is expensive and needs a power supply and the latter is ugly. Nevertheless, I very

A young aubergine plant with a seep hose in operation. Seep hoses are a very good way of getting a steady supply of water directly to the roots, and save a great deal of time.

much regret not putting in a large underwater tank when we were initially putting in the services and the resulting mess would not have been quite so significant.

Whatever the source of water, it has long been established that plants are best watered at their roots and that sprinklers and sprays are only really suitable for areas of grass. This is because most of the water lands on the foliage and either evaporates before it reaches the ground or else falls at the edge of each plant's canopy, failing to provide enough moisture to the entire root system. So any watering must be directed at the base of the plant, whether it is a tree or a lettuce. This is where an irrigation system is very effective.

I use porous pipes made from recycled tyres in the tunnel, having them lying on the surface so that they leak water directly onto the roots of the tomatoes. The other advantage of an irrigation system like porous or "leaky" pipes is that the water is delivered gently and slowly. This means that it slowly soaks into the soil without compacting it, running off it, or splashing it – all things that almost inevitably happen when watering with a hosepipe.

However, an irrigation system is out of the question for the garden at large as, indeed, is daily watering. Rather than spend hours watering every day or even every week, it is better to invest time in creating a soil structure that holds water without becoming waterlogged so that roots can access a water supply even in sustained dry weather.

It always amazes me how plants like hostas or ligularias, which generally are happiest in very damp ground, will survive healthily for weeks in a time of drought because their roots have grown deep and spread to access moisture that is not apparent when you dig

down. But this only happens if the soil is well-fed and in good heart.

It is far better to water very thoroughly once a week than to give plants a shower every day. In fact daily, light watering can reduce water uptake, especially in hot weather, because the water does not penetrate deeply into the soil and encourages the roots to grow to the surface to get available moisture. The roots are therefore prone to drying out fast in between showers and will suffer dehydration much more rapidly when you cannot water.

Mulching thickly will stop evaporation and is one of the best ways of cutting back on watering, *but* it can act as a barrier between water and soil, and a light shower will not penetrate it before it evaporates, so when you do water, be sure to give a good soak.

Many people underestimate the desiccating effect of wind, which will dry plants out quicker than all but the fiercest sun. I have known box plants in large pots, which are pretty hardy and drought-resistant, die from drought in the middle of winter as a result of icy winds. Any plant in a container of any kind should be kept out of wind, and hedges, fences, and trees will reduce the need to water thirsty plants like vegetables or annual flowers.

Roof gardens will always need much more watering than a terrestrial garden exposed to the same rainfall and wind levels. An irrigation system is an extremely good idea and a tap out on the roof is certainly a must, but the activity of watering and the way that it forces a daily inspection of each plant is part of the nurturing process that all gardeners love. The downside is that when the gardener is away, it still needs watering.

Weeds are a problem in every garden. *Any* unwanted plant will compete with your carefully nurtured, chosen plants for water and nutrients.

The nature of all prolific weeds is that they are extremely good at grabbing all available goodness, and in the process can choke out any less robust plants that would rob them of nutrients. This is why they are survivors. Obviously there are places where this competition is less harmful – around mature trees and shrubs or along the bottom of a fully grown hedge. But hedges can be the last resort of perennial weeds in an otherwise weed-free garden. We have bindweed, greater celandine, creeping buttercup, and couch grass all firmly entrenched in our hornbeam hedges and only removal of the hedge would get rid of them.

The weedkiller question Weeds are manageable and need not become a disaster. There was a time when although otherwise organic, I would use glyphosate, a systemic herbicide, to clear new ground and along the bases of hedges and around trees. It was expensive, unpleasant, and there were only ever a few days a year that were suitable for spraying, but the effects were undoubtedly effective. The truth is that I miss using weedkiller in the same way that a vegetarian misses bacon.

I know that it is wrong and don't really want to use it, but I would be a liar if I did not admit that at some point every year, when the weeds are getting on top of me, the temptation does enter into my mind. After all, who would know? ... Well, I would. Throughout this book, I keep referring to an organic garden being a balanced, holistic

entity, and using a systemic weedkiller is entirely against the spirit of that. We know that it seems harmless to the soil and subsequent growth seems to be unaffected, but there is too much that we do not know about the infinitely complex and delicate world of the soil and its role in the food chain as it is, without throwing in potentially poisonous cocktails of chemicals for short-term weed clearance.

I have often had people claim that they never use weedkillers in the vegetable garden, or that they "only use herbicides on the paths", as though this meant that they were really organic after all. Not so. The garden is a body and whatever you do to one part inevitably affects the whole. This means that your methods of weed control should share the same principles on the drive as in amongst the lettuces.

What is a weed? It is a well-rehearsed axiom that a weed is merely a plant in the wrong place. I often find rampantly healthy tomato seedlings growing in the borders where they have seeded themselves via the spring mulch from the previous autumn's compost heap, but on the whole we all know what weeds are. They are plants that we do not want that ruin the intended aesthetic and make the plants that we do want to grow less. However, differentiating a weed from a seedling, particularly in spring, can be confusing.

All over this garden I have creeping buttercup, burdock, greater and lesser celandine, couch grass, bindweed, dock, and nettles, and those are just the perennials. I can also count on annual weeds, showing up year after year, like the great rafts of goosegrass, wavy bittercress, shepherd's purse, caper spurge, dead nettle, groundsel, sowthistle, and chickweed.

The advantages of weeds

If not amongst the vegetables or flower borders, weeds do have a useful place in the organic garden. Many weed flowers are important as food sources for predators such as wasps and hoverflies, that in turn feed off pests such as aphids. Vast tracts of agricultural land are now plagued by insects that would have otherwise been naturally controlled by predators – simply because so many weedkillers have been used for so long that there are not the host plants to attract the predators. This inevitably promotes a vicious circle whereby there is an increase in the insecticides used. The same crazy loss of balance is created in the garden when you use weedkillers. A healthy garden has a number of flowering weeds as an important part of its self-sustaining biodiversity.

The greater fecundity of your weed population, the healthier and better conditioned is your soil. So if you take on a new garden and it is filled with weeds, be thankful. The soil that they are growing in is good. Secondly, the greater the diversity and range of weed types that you have growing uninvited, the greater the range of plants of your choice that you will eventually be able to grow.

The type and limitations of the weeds growing are a useful indicator of the nature and condition of your soil. Very acidic soil will produce lots of sorrel and plantain, but no charlock or poppy which thrive on lime. Chickweed is a good indicator of a neutral pH. Nettles, ground elder, fat hen, and chickweed point to a soil high in nitrogen. Silverweed and greater plantain will grow on very compacted soil where other plants will not penetrate. Creeping buttercup, horsetail, and silverweed (again) point to a wet soil with poor drainage.

Some weeds are very good to eat. I like nettle soup very much, using just the freshest new growth, which makes a very good substitute for spinach and is equally rich in iron. Dandelion leaves are a very good addition to a salad; ground elder was originally grown as a vegetable crop; wild sorrel makes a good sauce; and horseradish, which can be one of the most intrusive and difficult of all weeds, is as essential to a rib of beef as marmalade is to breakfast toast.

Lastly, some deep-rooted weeds have extremely effective abilities to accumulate minerals. If you harvest their leaves and add them to the compost heap you will, in time, recycle these minerals back into the soil via the compost heap. Most gardeners know that comfrey leaves contain high levels of potassium, but nettles and horsetail contain silica; chickweed contains copper, iron, manganese, nitrogen, and potassium; dandelion leaves are high in nitrogen, calcium and copper; fat hen has calcium, iron, nitrogen, phosphorus. and potassium. If you cannot remove these weeds you might be able to keep cutting them back to stop them seeding, and adding the leaves and stems to your compost heap.

Weeds invariably grow in awkward nooks and crannies and sometimes the only answer is slow, painstaking weeding.

ANNUAL WEEDS
(Never let them seed!)

Caper spurge (*Euphorbia lathyrus*)
Charlock (*Sinapis arvensis*)
Chickweed (*Stellaria media*)
Fat hen (*Chenopodium album*)
Goosegrass (*Galium aparine*)
Groundsel (*Senecio vulgaris*)
Herb Robert (*Geranium robertanium*)
Himalayan balsam (*Impatiens glandulifera*)
Knotgrass (*Polygonum aviculare*)
Petty spurge (*Euphorbia peplus*)
Prickly sowthistle (*Sonchus asper*)
Shepherd's needle (*Scandix pecten-veneris*)
Shepherd's purse (*Capsella bursa-pastoris*)

In practical terms there are two types of weed for the gardener: annual and perennial:

Annual weeds grow from seed and survive for only one growing season. On the whole, a thick crop of annual weeds are no problem and can even be seen as a good thing as they indicate that the soil is fertile. They are easy to pull up and add to the compost heap.

If you cannot pull them up completely, hoeing or cutting them before they seed will stop them spreading. It is very common for a mulch of manure to be followed by a rash of annual weeds, the seeds of which have passed through the animal responsible and have been quietly waiting in the manure until light triggers germination.

The most common annual weeds you are likely to have in your garden are groundsel, chickweed, fat hen, and annual meadow grass.

When sowing any new crop from a new lawn to a row of radish, it is always a good idea to prepare the ground and then leave it fallow for a few weeks. Inevitably annual seeds in the ground will germinate. These can be hoed off and raked away, leaving the field clear for your sown seeds to germinate and establish without competition for water and nutrients.

Perennial weeds survive for more than two growing seasons – sometimes for very much longer. Dock seeds can apparently lie dormant for up to 90 years, waiting for the soil to be disturbed before germinating. I like the thought that there are docks emerging from a century-old sleep, conceived in an age before aeroplanes, televisions, and computers. Other common perennial weeds are nettles, ground elder, bindweed, couch grass, and thistle.

There is only one sure-fire method of dealing with a perennial weed: remove the plant before it seeds, dig every last scrap of root from the ground and burn the lot. But there are also weeds like horsetail, horseradish, and Japanese knotweed with roots of enormous depth and resilience. Horsetail roots can go down 2.5m (8ft) and those of knotweed can be as tough as steel hawsers.

Certain weeds like ground elder, bindweed, and couch grass have a habit of winding in amongst the roots of plants you wish to keep, so have a safe haven from the most diligent weeding. the way to deal with this is to dig up the infested plant and wash the roots thoroughly under a tap or power hose, blasting out every scrap of weed root. Before you replant it, dig over the planting site with obsessive meticulousness to remove every tiny scrap of weed root.

Using a flame-gun to weed the path in the Lime Walk. This is also a very useful way of dealing with slippery moss and algae on paths.

Weed control There is

no one easy solution, but a combination of the following should get your garden under control. Focus your mulch and hand-weeding in areas like mixed borders where weeds are hardest to eradicate, and use a hoe regularly on open soil, as in the vegetable garden.

Using a mulch Cover every piece of bare soil with a light-excluding, but moisture-permeable layer. I use a lot of mushroom and garden compost and cocoa shells. Well-rotted horse or cattle manure is good, but cattle manure can include a lot of weed seeds if it is not very well rotted. If you are prepared to forgo aesthetics (which I am

PERENNIAL WEEDS

Very difficult to control
(will take long-term strategy or inspired acceptance)

Horsetail (*Equisetum arvense*)

Japanese knotweed (*Polygonum cuspidatum*)

To take very seriously
(dig up every scrap of root and burn; do not compost the roots)

Bindweed (*Convolvulus arvensis* and *Calystegia sepium*)

Couch grass (*Elymus repens*)

Ground elder (*Aegopodium podagraria*)

Creeping buttercup (*Ranunculus repens*)

Lesser celandine (*Ranunculus ficaria*)

To work at
(dig up as and when you can)

Broad-leaved dock (*Rumex obtusifolius*)

Burdock (*Arctium lappa*)

Creeping thistle (*Cirsium arvense*)

Stinging nettle (*Urtica dioica*)

Spear thistle (*Cirsium vulgare*)

Handsome but intrusive

Alkanet (*Pentaglottis sempervirens*)

Comfrey (*Symphytum species*)

Daisy (*Bellis perennis*)

Dandelion (*Taraxacum officinale*)

Deadnettle (*Lamium species*)

Feverfew (*Tanacetum parthenium*)

Greater celandine (*Chelidonium majus*)

Hogweed (*Heracleum spondylium*)

Mallow (*Malva sylvestris*)

Plantain (*Plantago major*)

Selfheal (*Prunella vulgaris*)

Silverweed (*Potentilla anserina*)

Rosebay willowherb (*Epilobium angustifolium*)

Teasel (*Dipsacus fullonum*)

not), anything will do the job, including straw, hay, shredded bark, permeable plastic, old carpet, or rolls of white paper mulch.

If you are using an organic mulch (that is, one that will rot down into the soil), place it at least 5cm (2in) thick. Four is better. This will completely suppress annual weeds and although it will not stop existing perennial weeds growing through, it will make them much easier to pull up. Obviously an organic mulch that will increase the fertility and improve the structure of the soil, as well as suppress weeds, is infinitely preferably to one that works as a weed suppressant alone, but I do use a water-permeable, proprietary black plastic mulch for some paths. This is not beautiful but extremely effective, especially as a temporary measure.

Weeding with a hoe There are lots of hoes available, but there are only two basic principles; either you push or you pull. I find I use a Dutch hoe most of the time which, if kept sharp, slices through the roots of any weeds just below the surface of the soil. I have one very old one that is much smaller than most and can get right in amongst young plants without damaging them. The secret of hoeing – like all weeding – is to do it little and often. Old gardeners used to say that if you could see that it was time to hoe, then you had left it too late.

If you have a very weed-infested bit of ground you want to cultivate (and remember weed-infestation implies good, healthy soil) and they have not yet gone to seed, then a good tip is to hoe the weeds off with a mattock, or large draw or field hoe, let the weeds wilt for a day in the sun, and then dig the whole thing over, weeds and all. This will

not get rid of the perennial weeds, but will increase the fertility and allow you to grow a crop of fast-growing and weed-suppressing vegetables like potatoes, beans, or squashes.

Weeding by hand Hand-weeding means getting down on your knees and carefully removing every scrap of weed with your fingers and a handfork. But, unlikely as it initially may seem, hand-weeding is one of the most enjoyable aspects of gardening. I love it, especially in early spring just as everything is starting to grow and the weeds have not become depressingly rampant. You really get to know your soil, your plants, the seedlings, and herbaceous perennials coming through and you improve an area dramatically without major surgery. It is deeply satisfying work.

The importance of timing It is essential to try and stop weeds of any kind spreading their seed. Cut, hoe, mow, or strim them, but do not let them go forth and multiply. There is a saying that "One year's seeding is seven years' weeding", and there is a lot of truth in this, in that trials have shown that even if all subsequent growth is removed before seeding, it takes about seven years for all of one season's crop of seeds to stop germinating.

Integration A few years ago, I visited the wonderful Irish garden, Mount Usher, south of Dublin, which is gardened organically. Their philosophy is that if you cannot lose the weed then you must use it. This strikes me as being the best practical approach. It means that you weed wherever you can, but if the weeds are beyond digging then accept them, go with their form and timetable, and plant along with them.

Mount Usher has a large bank invaded with horsetail which likes wet, heavy soil and extremely long, brittle roots. It is a nightmare to get rid of organically. They have planted fritillaries, grasses, bluebells, and umbellifers that mix well with its wispy fronds. An invader is thus channelled into being decorative. We all know how beautiful a field of dandelions can be, both in flower or as seedheads, and bindweed would be carefully nurtured to produce its white twists of flower if only it was not such an impossibly intrusive beast. Even nettles have their moments when young and flushed with green.

However, if you have an area of ground that is full of really tough weeds like Japanese knotweed, brambles, horsetail,

bindweed, or horseradish you may find that it is an unequal struggle trying to share it with plants you do want. Another organic solution is to cut them back and lightly rotovate them into the ground before sowing with rye grass seed. The grass will be swamped with weeds, but a weekly mowing will gradually weaken the weeds and in time the grass will take over. The turf can then be lifted, the ground dug over (removing all and any roots), and planted up. I prefer this to the often recommended advice to mulch with black plastic, which looks horrible.

I have compiled a list of my own worst weeds (*see p.76 and facing page*). It is not inclusive. We all have our own horrors. But if you have any of the weeds listed, it is worth doing what you can to get rid of them.

A Dutch hoe, kept sharp, is invaluable, especially in the vegetable garden. I prefer to use a small one, so I can get in between plants.

Mulching the Jewel Garden with mushroom compost in early spring. A 5cm (2in) layer stops all but the strongest weeds and will greatly improve the soil.

Pests

If a weed is no more than a plant in the wrong place, then a pest is only an animal eating the wrong food. Your garden – any garden – is just an intensively cultivated piece of landscape.

A range of animals (and for the health of your garden, this range wants to be as diverse as possible) want to live off and in your plot. The extent to which they can healthily do this will be determined by the food supply and the levels of predation. These two factors are inextricably linked. In the natural scheme of things, the food supply will fluctuate according to season and the amount of mouths it is feeding. Where there are seasonal gluts of food, the breeding cycle will be one of boom and bust as the population will multiply rapidly and then eat itself out of house and home. At this point, they will move on to another source of the same food supply, eat something else, or die. Part of the "dying" process involves a rapid reduction in breeding in an effort to ration the available food.

Where you have a boom of one predator, you will inevitably have a parallel increase in the creatures that predate on them, and so it will go right up the food chain. By definition it is self-limiting. When the food supply is abundant, numbers increase right up the line. When it falls, everyone goes hungry. It is often the case that gardeners react immediately to a sudden increase in pests but their actions are rarely very successful, although it does satisfy the sense of doing something about it. It is often better to wait a while and let the natural predatory balance assert itself without human interference – and whilst it might look disastrous for a few days, my experience is that surprisingly little damage is done to plants. A case in point is blackfly (the black aphid, *Aphis fabae*) on broad beans, which looks bad,

but does little or nothing to reduce the crop, and provides a meal for the aphid-eating population.

Every well-stocked garden adds the unnatural element of a constantly renewed food supply each year, in the shape of carefully grown plants. This means that as long as you, the gardener, are willing to keep replacing the lettuces, cabbages, roses – or whatever – that have been eaten, then to an extent you are merely nourishing the predators.

A small example of this in my own garden is that we are blessed with a large population of blackbirds and thrushes. This means that we have fabulous birdsong between March and September. They can sustain a relatively high population because we have a much larger density of insects, earthworms and snails than the surrounding countryside. But the crops that provide insects and snails, and the rich earth filled with earthworms, also support sparrowhawks which we often see hunting in the garden catching the songbirds. This simple food chain is held together by a few, very intensively cultivated acres set amongst hundreds of acres of meadow.

So any garden will always invite in animals of one kind or another to prey upon the plants that we grow. All things being equal (which they never are), this is inevitable. Song thrushes eat snails; ground beetles eat the eggs of root flies; rove beetles eat aphids; as do ladybirds, hoverfly and lacewing larvae. Damsel bugs eat caterpillars. The numbers will reach saturation point within a year or two and then fluctuate according to weather and the type of plants you grow. A predatory balance will be established. Now I can live with this as the status quo. It means that I lose some plants but the garden is essentially healthy, rich with a diverse chain of animals ranging from bacteria in the soil and tiny insects to birds of prey and large mammals like foxes and badgers. As I discuss below, healthy plants will cope with this very well. I think of this like the minor cuts and abrasions and viruses that the human body is constantly fighting and recovering from. It is the ability to resist disease and heal your wounds that indicates health – not the absence of such problems.

Occasionally there is a plague of pests where, either because of circumstances beyond the garden, like exceptional rain or drought, or because of the life-cycle of a particular animal, like that of the field vole, there can be a huge increase in one particular problem. Beyond short-term expediency, I tend not to take this personally and accept that it is beyond my control.

Maintaining a healthy garden To have this degree of *sang-froid* about predators, there are certain rules that every organic gardener should follow to ensure a healthy set-up.

• **Do everything you can** to grow healthy plants. A robust plant will not be weakened by the odd nibble by a slug or caterpillar, or having sap sucked by an aphid. It will heal itself faster than the predator can cause permanent damage.

This does not mean, however, that you should load every plant with fertilizers. Never force any plant into quick growth. This is disastrous as it causes fast, sappy growth that is both choice food and too weak to recover.

That is why plants like lettuce, that is naturally fast-growing and sappy, are the first to be attacked. Feed the soil, not the plant. If your soil is in good heart, the plant will grow at the rate it can cope with. So on poorer soil it will grow smaller and slower than on rich soil but potentially be just as healthy.

• **Keep your housekeeping** up to scratch. By this I mean basic horticultural practices such as:

Pruning properly at the right time so that there is good ventilation.

Gathering up debris so slugs and insects cannot hide amongst it.

Tieing climbers securely so that they do not get weakened by rocking and fraying against other branches.

Not leaving anything too long in a container so that it gets root-bound and grows weakly.

Keeping on top of the watering and weeding – so plants receive a steady supply of liquid and are not having to compete with weeds for nutrition – and removing any diseased or weakened plant that will attract predators.

This is all common sense but makes a big contribution to a healthy garden.

• **Avoid monoculture** wherever possible. The greater the variety of plants, the less chance of a visiting pest finding a host. In a small garden, this is not so much of a problem, particularly if you have neighbours on either side with their own diverse mix of plants, but even within small areas of the garden, it is a good idea to break up blocks of plants. Alternate rows of unrelated vegetables and use annual companion plants amongst soft fruit.

• **Use companion plants** to attract predators. My vegetable garden is full of self-seeded poppies, forget-me-nots, evening primroses, and violas. Because they attract hoverflies whose larvae eat aphids, I only remove them – individually – if they are competing too closely with a vegetable. And they look good. All umbellifers (dill, fennel, cow parsley) attract hoverflies and I always have some dill growing in the vegetable garden as well as the herb garden.

• **Never force** anything to grow where it does not want to. You could argue that much of all horticulture over the past two hundred years has been the process of doing just that, but it is not, to my mind, good gardening. Accept the limitations of your soil, climate, and aspect. There is a cultural belief that it is somehow "better" to have as wide a variety of plants as possible, but this makes a garden hard to keep healthy. Grow as many indigenous plants as possible. These will have evolved defence mechanisms against local pests as well as being an integral part of the local micro-food chain.

• **Never rush** the season. It is a temptation to push right up against the edge of hardiness in a plant in spring, putting it outside as soon as possible so that it will flower or crop a few weeks early, but this never pays off. We often have very cold nights in April and May and over the years, I have found that all but the hardiest plants are better sown or planted only when the nights have warmed up. Extreme fluctuations in temperature – which we can have in May with daytime figures of 25°C (77°F) dropping to 0°C (32°F) at night – will weaken any young plant and make it more susceptible to damage by predation. Be patient. It is a long game.

Particular pests I can only write about the particular pests that we cope with in this garden, but the list is plenty long enough for me!

Slugs and snails are the biggest problem that I have to contend with in my own garden. In gardening terms they are one and the same animal, with the only real difference being that slugs mainly live in the soil and snails spend the day in a dry, dark resting place. This tends to mean that snails are more prevalent in town gardens and slugs in the country. The combination of global warming (which means that many more survive the winter), high rainfall, a densely planted garden, very rich soil with a high level of decomposing organic material, and plenty of dry branches and walls for the snails to hide in, mean that we sustain a huge population of both animals. There are four main garden slugs:

The grey field slug (*Deroceras reticulatus*) will eat anything and will produce three generations a year.

The garden slug, (*Arion hortensis*) is shiny black, with an orange belly. It is also omnivorous, but its party trick is to eat off bean plants at ground level and riddle potatoes with holes.

The keeled slug (*Milax* species) is black, with a thin orange line down the centre of its back. It spends almost all its life underground, feeding off root crops.

The black slug (*Arion ater*) which is usually black, but can come in almost any colour, is differentiated from all others by its size which can reach 20cm (8in) long. Despite its size it is the least harmful of all garden slugs.

Slugs and snails feed on seedlings and young growth of herbaceous plants, and are especially fond of the squash family, celery, French beans, hostas, delphiniums, cardoons, and, of course, lettuces. They do not eat everything. I notice that they do not touch the allium family, so all onions, shallots, leeks, and garlic are fine, as are young carrots, parsnips (although they will eat them as they get older). The chicories in their various forms are not too troubled and – surprisingly – spinach is spared too once it gets past a certain age. Early potatoes tend to be spared because they have such a high sugar content, which is thought to be repellent to slugs. However, as they ripen, the sugar that makes new potatoes so delicious to humans turns into starch, which the slugs love.

After years of trying every method of slug control, I now concentrate on keeping vital parts of the garden slug- and snail-free and don't worry too much about the rest. So I pick over the propagating greenhouse every night, checking under every pot with a torch. I take everything out of the cold frames once a week and check for small snails and slugs. The younger the plant, the more susceptible it is to slug attack, and I have had whole rows of emerging seedlings eaten overnight.

So now anything that can be grown in a soil block, module, or plug is done so and only transplanted outside when it is strong enough to grow away faster than the slugs can eat it. I find that this is completely successful and allows the slugs and snails and us humans to co-exist quite happily.

Even if the organic gardener could use slug pellets – which you can't because you are adding a poisonous chemical to the food chain – they are only effective very locally and it has been estimated that at best pellets will kill only ten percent of any slug population.

It makes sense to encourage natural predators. Beetles eat slugs, but the trouble is that for their predations to be effective you have to create a beetle-friendly garden. Beetles like cover, so leave dead wood and leaves around for them.

Hedgehogs eat beetles, but prefer juicy slugs. They are to be encouraged in the garden. Toads eat young slugs and thrushes eat snails. The law of supply and demand says that in order to get these attractive additions to the garden there has to be a supply of food – so no snails, no thrushes. No slugs – no hedgehogs, toads, or beetles. Ducks love slugs and will gobble them up from duck-friendly areas of the garden – which unfortunately does not include flower or vegetable borders.

In the short term, the best way to deal with slugs or snails is physically to get between them and the object of their hunger. Any form of barrier will do, although gravel or grit is probably the most effective. Spread this as a mulch around hostas, delphiniums, and all other susceptible plants, and the slugs and snails will avoid crawling over the abrasive surface.

Most slugs live in the soil, coming out to pillage after dark. Go out into the garden on a warm, damp evening and shine a torch around. The chances are that the garden will be slowly writhing with slimy bodies. In one experiment, 27,500 slugs were taken from one small garden without making any noticeable difference to slug activity. Densities of 200 slugs per square metre (yard) are moderate.

In a small garden, beer traps work quite well, by sinking a carton half-filled with beer into the ground so that the slug, attracted to it, falls in, and cannot get out. But in a large garden this is a waste of time. It is a good idea to rotovate the soil just before planting – especially in very dry weather – which will chop up the slugs hiding below the surface.

A cabbage white butterfly finds the mustard in brassicas irresistible (*see top left*).
Top right: a tray of seedlings big enough to plant out and grow faster than the slugs can eat them.
Bottom right: fine netting protects young chicory from snails (but not slugs).
Bottom left: collecting leaves and debris that house slugs.

Anti-cabbage white butterfly netting

Common garden snail (*Helix aspera*)

You can put individual lettuces in makeshift cloches made from sawn-off plastic bottles which are a fairly effective, but aesthetically ugly, barrier.

I have used the nematodes *Phasmarhabditis hermaphrodita*, which you apply in a water solution onto warm, wet soil. They then penetrate the slugs' bodies and release bacteria which cause a fatal disease. Nice work if you can get it. I found it too limited within the context of a two-acre garden, but they are very useful in a small area. One application will work for six weeks.

Caterpillars There are only two caterpillars that cause me any problems at all, but both do their best every year to strip all my brassica crops bare. There are two species of butterfly that do the damage, the large white and the small white. These butterflies have the curious ability to taste the quantity of mustard in a plant, the principle being the stronger the taste, the better the host for their eggs. The curiosity factor in this is that the plant developed the mustard taste as a defence against insects rather than as an attraction. The butterflies take on the mustard taste in their own tissues, which works effectively against predation by birds.

The large white lays its eggs on the leaves and the yellow and black caterpillars cover them by the hundred, stripping the young plants to a skeleton. The small white lays deeper into the plant and its wonderfully camouflaged green caterpillars do their work less conspicuously but to just as noxious effect.

There is a microbial spray called *Bacillus thuringiensis* which only kills caterpillars when they eat it via the leaves. Spray it on in the evening because bright sunshine will kill the bacterium. This is preferable to pyrethrum or derris, which are both organically acceptable but not selective in their killing. We pick them off by hand and spray the plants with salt water.

Netting with holes of less than 1cm (⅜in) put over brassica crops (cauliflowers, cabbages, turnips) plus nasturtiums and mignonettes will stop the cabbage white butterfly landing to lay its eggs. Cover the plants from the day that they go outside (including in a cold frame) to mid-October.

Sawflies The larvae of sawflies – which look just like little caterpillars – are a great problem on my gooseberries and redcurrants. There are three species of sawfly, but all behave in the same despicable manner. The fly lays its eggs in spring on the undersides of leaves down in the heart of the bush and when the larvae hatch they eat up and outwards until they have totally defoliated the entire bush – which they frequently do. This means that you do not necessarily notice them at work until it is too late.

The solution is to prune each bush severely so that it is an open goblet with no closed centre and lots of room for ventilation – which the fly does not like. It is also a good idea to establish a "leg" – a single, branchless stem about 23cm (9in) tall – for each bush, to raise it off the ground and let air flow underneath it.

If you find an infestation, as a last resort, use derris powder (which is organically acceptable) to kill the larvae. But be careful as it will also kill other beneficial insects that it comes into contact with. Certainly prevention is better than cure.

Moles cause huge amounts of damage here. They leave great molehills everywhere, tunnel just below the surface of the grass causing it to

subside in great grooves and runnels, and pop up under roots and herbaceous plants to disastrous effect. But I like moles. I think that they are beautiful. I always hate it when the cats catch them – which they do every few months – because they seem such harmless, special animals – in the same category as otters, badgers, or field mice. We have so many moles here because over the past ten years the soil has been improved so much that we now have a huge earthworm population. Moles eat worms and are consequentially coming in for dinner from miles around. No worms, no moles.

Folklore is full of tips like sticking a twig of elder or a clove of garlic down the run, or growing caper spurge as a deterrent. The best thing about moles in the garden is that molehills make good potting soil. I collect the molehills on a frosty day and make up potting compost with one-third molehill, one-third sharp sand, and one-third sieved garden compost. It works especially well for shrubs in pots.

However great the desecration and however vast the amount of soil erupting onto your lawn, it is usually the work of one solitary animal in any one area. It is only in spring, at mating time, that they get together. Otherwise they are solitary animals.

If you want to trap them, the mole traps should be set in the run a foot or so away from a fresh molehill. However, I refuse to trap them, although I can think of no direct benefit that they offer the gardener and I hate what they do to my garden. I think the only solution is to live and let tunnel.

Rats and mice Rats are disgusting but by no means the biggest pest in the garden. They were more of a nuisance when vegetables were stored outside in clamps and apples in sheds. Mice are a bigger problem because, unlike rats, they burrow into the soil and eat seed. Mice can be particularly destructive, with the absence of other food sending them to crocus corms that you have tediously and carefully planted and to the early broad beans. In spring, they eat early sowings of peas and apparently have a taste for sweetcorn seeds. You can tell if mice are the problem because any top-growth will be ignored and only the seed eaten.

"Mice" is a catch-all term that covers a range of rodents including the wood mouse (*Apodemus sylvaticus*) which eats all our hazel nuts, the lovely yellow-necked field mouse (*Apodemus flavicollis*) as well as the shrews and voles that cause more damage by burrowing just below the surface than by what they eat.

There are two voles I get here: *Microtus agrestis* and *Clethrionomys glareolus*. They both undermine everything that I do in the garden. Literally. The cats catch them by the dozen, bite their heads off, and leave them on the path outside the front door. Owls love them. But owls and cats cannot contain them. They should not be hard to catch as they hardly move more than a few yards from their base camp. All they do is eat and breed. Given a well-stocked garden to browse they will eat their own weight in dry food every week, and in the process pass over 1,000 droppings a day. I suppose I should be grateful for the manure.

The worst thing about voles is not the damage done to roots, not the fact that they nibble at bark and shoots causing death and destruction to beloved plants, not that the ground gives way beneath one's feet causing a twisted ankle, but that they prompt our terrier to spend hours digging for them – causing twice as much damage in her wake.

The best thing about mice and voles in your garden is that they are part of the food chain that includes owls, whose local population responds very quickly to theirs. I will willingly put up with my broad beans being nicked in return for a pair of owls in the garden.

Whitefly Whitefly can do to conservatory or greenhouse plants what caterpillars do to a good-looking cabbage, although in a different way. The flies are sap-sucking and live on the underside of the leaves. You might notice a stickiness on the tops of leaves, perhaps with a black mould, before you see the tiny winged insects themselves. This "honeydew" is excreted by them and drops down onto the leaves below. They can be successfully treated with a minute parasitical wasp, *Encarsia formosa*, which lays its eggs inside the nymphs. When the eggs hatch they feed off their hosts, killing them and eventually hatching out from their redundant bodies like a bad dream.

As with most pests, an understanding of their life-cycles is necessary if you are to successfully control them. The whitefly eggs hatch into nymphs or larvae that have the same limpet-like profile as scale insects. The adult whitefly population must first be reduced with a soap solution or else they will outbreed the wasps. The temperature must not be allowed to fall below 15°C (59°F) after encarsias have been released. The adults live for about two weeks and should lay around 100 eggs each.

The wasp is bought as a living insect and can be ordered from a garden centre. It will be sent to you at your home and must be used within 18 hours of delivery. You attach a cardboard tab low down on each plant and a batch of the tiny wasps eat their way free before getting at the whitefly nymphs.

Carrot fly The tiny fly, *Psila rosae*, lays its eggs in the soil next to growing members of the carrot family (carrot, parsnip, celery, and parsley) and when these hatch, the maggots eat the roots, causing tunnels just under the surface which tend to collapse and roots rot.

The fly has an astonishingly acute sense of smell and can apparently smell one whiff of carrot (as when the plants are thinned) from up to half a mile away. Sowing carrots in amongst members of the allium family will mask this smell to a certain extent, and I always surround the carrot and parsnip beds with chives for that reason. But the best defence is to screen the carrots with a fly-proof barrier a 60cm (2ft) tall, such as fleece, plastic, cardboard, or very fine mesh. The fly travels very low to the ground and will not go over the top of the barrier. The problem with this, of course, is that it can look pretty unappealing. Another way round the problem is to cover the crop with fleece immediately after sowing and to leave it in place until the roots are finally cleared, lifting one side as necessary to harvest the carrots.

I have found that it is a good idea to keep celery and parsley well away from carrots to stop easy spread of the flies, which will hatch and lay eggs of three generations each season. The timing of the crop can also be important. A late sowing in spring tends to miss the first wave of flies and carrots harvested by the end of July will miss the second generation.

Structure

Planning the design I imagined and dreamt the garden for many months before doing anything, so that when I did finally start to lay it out it felt familiar.

The way that I have designed my garden is, as a friend of mine only half-jokingly described it, "like a series of allotments". It means that there are a number of different areas, all quite separate and usually hidden from the rest. I make no apologies for this and enjoy the surprises and sense of enclosure that it brings.

Inevitably this means that different sections of the garden (which we tend to call "gardens" such as the Vegetable Garden, the Spring Garden or the Jewel Garden) have their own character. We also try to treat each separate area as though it were the only garden that we had. This means that each section has to stand up to the strictest scrutiny and aesthetic standards. Having said this, one of the reasons for having many different compartments to a garden is that whilst it is very hard, if not impossible, to make an entire garden look wonderful

the year round, it is much more achievable to have at least one section looking good at any given time. By the same token, some of the different "rooms" can rest for part of the year or even shut down completely for a while. This gives the opportunity to indulge in favourites that might have a short flowering season or a group of plants that share the same conditions but which are at odds with much of the rest of the garden.

The gardens I like all have two distinct qualities above all else. The first is a strong sense of ownership. Gardens are a human construct and do not just happen, so I like to see the hands of their maker on everything. This gives the garden character, which is more important than any horticultural aspect.

The second is a good use of space. It is the spaces between plants and objects that make a garden interesting,

not just the plants themselves. This can be quite a hard concept to grasp for the organised western mind but in truth it is simplicity itself. I think of it (slightly pretentiously) as "sculpting air". In practice, it means getting the proportions right with the space available, using paths, walls, hedges, trees and every kind of plant that one wishes to grow so that they make beautiful spaces.

These spaces do not have to be formal or geometrical but they must be considered. Sometimes they create themselves by accident – but if they are recognised then they can be included and relished. It might just be the way that a tree is pruned or the curve of a path is cut into the long grass or the grouping of pots by a doorway – there is no recipe other than a constant awareness of the shape of the spaces between things. I can be just as pleased by a length of grass path between flanking green hedges as a complex flower border. The box pebbles of the hopkiln yard never fail to give me pleasure, even though I have walked through them thousands of times.

Knowing how to keep it simple is probably the most important part of any garden.

In practice this has translated itself to this garden by a grid of straight lines marked out by hedges, paths and pleached trees. That has created blocks which have been filled by a variety of gardens. In summer, when everything is lush and fulsome the grid softens and becomes subordinate to the planting within it. In winter it provides a structural framework for what is otherwise a very grey and brown formless scene.

There is a tendency to only visualise a garden in its summer pomp. The unhappy truth is that for half the year it is either waxing or waning and here at Ivington, halfway up Britain, it is more often cloudy than clear, more often wet than dry and the winter days are at best cold and short and more often positively drab. The most effective way to counter this is with crisp edges and shapes and strong colours. Too much fuzzy planting simply becomes absorbed in the general haze. This is fine on a soft summer's evening but disastrous on a wet November afternoon.

Practical considerations Over and above any aesthetic considerations there is a mass of practical problems that has to be solved or dealt with when designing a garden.

All gardens start at the building to which they are attached. The first thing to do is to establish a "platform" around the house that is the direct link between building and garden. The size of this will be determined by the house and not the garden and, I think, so should the materials.

Every door and window should relate to the garden both from the view looking out and looking back to the house. One of the first things that we did here was to make the Lime Walk path that leads from a door in the Hall ...

The view from the house past the herb garden and on down the Lime Walk in midsummer. It is important to provide clear sight-lines connecting the garden to the house so that both share the same footprint.

only for years after the path was made the door just led to a narrow passage. But I knew that one day it would become an important link between house and garden so the path had to be in place ready for that time.

For the first four years our only access to the vast majority of the garden was either through the house or via a field that was often flooded or at least very muddy. The gate to this field was right up at the other end of the garden yet became our main service point and the orchard was planned entirely around its accessibility. Anything that could not be carried or wheeled easily through the house had to go round there when conditions made it possible and then wheeled to where it was needed in the garden. This meant that paths had to link the end of the garden back to the house rather than vice versa.

It is important to get the practical infrastructure in before any planting begins because it inevitably makes a mess and disruption, and hard paths provide dry access for wheelbarrows, rotovators and even small diggers.

I had the good sense to put a water pipe in the ground when the digger was putting in the septic tank, before the garden began. We now have over half a dozen standpipes dotted around – but I wish I had thought this through a little more carefully before planting began.

It is a good idea to get as much structural planting in as soon as possible. With a new garden you can easily cut into grass to make beds and borders at any stage but the hedges and trees need time to establish. I was lucky

A view through the vegetable garden to the hopkiln yard (*left*). The combination of box and hornbeam hedges, espaliered pears, pleached limes, grass and brick paths and woven fences all make a complex but harmonious structure within which the plants are contained. The door frame at the end of the Lime Walk (*above*) invites you down although, in fact, it only opens onto our boundary fence.

to buy a whole load of trees in one afternoon from a clearance sale by a tree nursery. This included many hedging plants and kick-started the framework of the planting, turning ideas on a page into three-dimensional reality.

A large ball of heavy duty twine and a bundle of canes are the best design tools in the garden. All the plans are drawn accurately or sketched out on paper but until they are transferred to the ground they remain ideas. Marking everything out with string and canes gets a feel of the spaces and their volumes. I have often found that a convenient "paper" measurement – usually rounded up or down to the nearest foot – is not best on the ground. As a general rule borders can always be bigger and lawns smaller. Hedges take a metre of ground themselves and affect whatever is growing at their base for a further metre by taking moisture and light. Do you want a path to hurry the walker along – in which case make it straight and narrow – or a place to meander and chat? If the latter it needs to be

at least 1.5m (5ft) wide. Wheelbarrows have to get round corners so need a turning area that is wider than the path. Remember that people do not like to go round things to reach what they can see: either block off the line of sight or make access easier and quicker. All these things can be tested on the ground with the help of some string and sticks.

Once I have marked my lines of borders, hedges or paths so that they seem to be exactly where I want them. I have often used hurdles, temporary staked, to represent hedges to increase the stagecraft. I always live with the strings and canes for at least a week before taking any further action. It is better to live with the rough idea of something for a while before committing yourself than to rush in and then regret it later.

Then, when you do plant your hedges, make your paths and dig your borders, I have learnt – often painfully – that no amount of preparation or time spent doing the job properly is ever wasted.

93

Paths, walls and fences It is a mistake to think of a path as a gap between the things that it leads to, a kind of horticultural no man's land.

A grass path leading from the Jewel Garden to the orchard. This was made by mowing the original field grass. It was free and looks good in summer but is very wet in winter.

Initially I made hazel fences to define and protect borders and hedges (*top left*). But they look fine – although these in the vegetable garden are ready for replacement. Brick paths (*top right*) always work well as a backdrop for soft plant colours. This old door from the back yard into the Spring Garden (*bottom*) was salvaged from a bonfire along with its original frame.

Paths

It is almost impossible to imagine any kind of garden existing without a planned system of paths. They are where you look at the garden from and the channels along which the philosophy and perception of the garden is established.

Nothing connects a garden so clearly to the building it belongs to than the paths leading from the house. If they line up with the doors and windows they immediately impose a symmetry and proportion onto the design dictated by the house. I think that this is often highly desirable, but you can just as easily make use of paths to free the garden from the potential restrictions of the house.

The first law of any garden path is to get you from a to b. If it is the main route to the compost heap, herb bed, or greenhouse, then it wants to be as direct as possible. It is an absolute rule that people will eventually work out the quickest route and use it, even if it means ignoring a beautifully made, dry path to slice diagonally across a muddy lawn or step through a flower bed. If you want to take the path indirectly to its goal you must block off the alternatives with impenetrable planting or a more solid barrier. It is not just humans that this applies to; our dogs rather weirdly leave the straight path down to the front door and do a little curving diversion onto the grass, making a worn doggy groove in winter.

It is always a mistake to have a path like a runway taking you down to a point that is visible throughout the whole journey. It must lead to places you cannot see without going to the very end. People who are more interested in plants than gardens tend to assume that one's eyes will be cast down looking intently at the plants, treating a path rather like a gangway at a flower show. This is nonsense. If you can see everything without having to move along the path then the incentive to continue down it is greatly reduced, however rare the plants along the way. Either the path must curve you round and away from the goal so that you are drawn back to it or else you must take the path through at least one entrance. This might just be a gap in the hedge and the hedge might be there solely to provide the said gap, but some kind of screen there must be.

Grass paths It is not enough just to have paths looking good. They must work if they are to be used. When we first moved in eight years ago, I believed that we could simply cut beds from the grass of the field, mow the bits in between and call them paths. It is not a bad policy if you have limited funds, and half our paths are still just mown field and need only a pass with a mower once a week to keep them that way. I especially like the paths made by cutting the orchard grass at different lengths with the mown, gently curving strip fringed by the meadow grasses. Dead simple, but dead lovely.

We do not have lawns as such, although the central path that runs right through the middle of the garden does open out into a section some 8m (25ft) wide and 40m (130ft) long which we have used as a cricket net for the

The box balls in the hopkiln yard are set in a grid of cobbles. These look like paths but are for access only and cobbles make an uncomfortable surface for the feet.

The path to the front door was made from odd pieces of stone and the gaps filled with cobbles. The slight slope is dealt with by making a feature of a small step half way along.

past five years. But it was not made as a lawn and is still no more than the mown field.

The truth is that I have no great interest in raising immaculate grass. If it is green, reasonably flat and the length that I wish it then I am satisfied. Where I have sown new grass (as on our mound) I have used a rye and timothy mix which allows for children playing and yet is not too coarse.

To achieve good grass – be it for a path, playing cricket or a sweep of lawn – drainage is the most important factor. Unless the ground is naturally free-draining I would always add 50 percent sharp sand to the topsoil as well as putting in drainage pipes.

But grass on our undrained, heavy soil is useless in the rainy season, which, with the unstoppable roll of global warming, is at least six months of the year. You can scarcely walk on it without creating muddy puddles in your wake like an oar dipping into water. If you try and push a barrow full of compost it simply sinks up to the axle in the mud and gets stuck. Even in summer, every time you set foot on the path, let alone wheel a heavy barrow on it, you are compacting the soil down, worsening the drainage and increasing the subsequent winter quagmire. In this garden by mid-October going outside to get a sprig of rosemary or to shut up the chickens means taking off your shoes and putting on wellington boots. Only frost brings sufficient hard dryness to walk unprotected. If a path is to be any use for most of the year it must be made of almost anything except grass.

So over the years, as money and time have allowed, we have been converting our paths from grass to hard surfaces. The luxury of walking dry shod is worth the work and expense. It also opens up a whole range of colours, textures and structure to the garden.

A grass path can hardly be called structural, whereas a brick path is a wall on edge.

Brick and stone paths It is important to use local, natural materials wherever possible. We have tried to recycle any stone that has been dug up as the garden was made, or stone left over from building work. When we have bought stone flags they have all come from locally reclaimed buildings. There was a brickworks in Leominster, our local town, that closed in the mid-nineteenth century, which made especially dense, large bricks. These were used for most of the brick parts of the house and are ideal for paths and wherever possible we have sought these out and used them. Choosing bricks that relate to those of the house or any existing walls is the most important aspect of any brick path. It is laid basket-weave fashion and I love it, although the shadiest bit gets incredibly slippery. Using reclaimed and local materials has the obvious advantage of reusing existing resources and reducing travel but it also maintains the connection to local identity and place, connecting the garden to its surroundings.

The first hard paths we made were from stone and cobbles. They were intended to be all stone but after the first few yards it became apparent that we did not have enough stone and started mixing in cobbles to fill the gaps and make the stone go further. It worked very well, despite the fact that cobbles are too knobbly and slippery to walk on with ease. But if you have sufficient stone they are fine. Cobbles are reasonably cheap to buy as dredgings from a nearby quarry and we have dug up loads and used them to edge paths and as a surface barrier in areas where we do not want people to walk.

We then made what I think is our best path. It is very narrow and curves through the Spring Garden and is made entirely from all the leftover bits and pieces of the first phase of building work. The only consistent materials are concrete blocks which are laid sideways a block's-length apart. The gap between them is infilled with anything that could be used. This includes quarry tiles, cobbles, bricks, paving stones. The only brief was that no two sections should be alike.

In the vegetable garden we now have brick pavers. These are like bricks but baked much harder so that they take more wear and tear and, crucially, will not break up or split when they freeze. The down-side is that they are very brittle and prone to cracking when you lay them and they look very new. I don't mind the latter but we had to choose from scores of variations before finding a paver that worked in with the existing brick paths.

Pavers are not cheap so we then used them as narrow "paths-within-a-path" down the centre of some of the grass paths. This is both handsome and practical as you can mow over them and yet walk and wheel a barrow down the centre in the slushiest of weather. The plan is to continue this throughout the garden. Beneath them is what amounts to a trench 30–45cm (12–18in) deep, half of which is filled with hardcore, then a generous layer of scalpings tamped down very hard, then a thick layer of sand on which the pavers are laid. (Scalpings, the waste product from quarrying, are used

Brick and paver paths in the vegetable garden make access easy whatever the weather or season and are very hardwearing. They also induce a certain formality in the planting which is very practical for vegetables – in this case a bed of chicory and red lettuce and climbing beans surrounded by red cabbage.

beneath every yard of road in this country. They are a mixture of stone and dust and will compact to a porous, hard layer – ideal for putting under gravel.) If you have very well-drained soil you won't need such elaborate measures to ensure drainage, but for us it is essential.

We have a few short paths that are made from stone flags. These are always handsome and often beautiful but invariably expensive. They are often priced by weight and the thicker – and therefore heavier – they are the better the path sits. However, laying a stone flag (and most of ours are made from a Welsh sandstone and not the ubiquitous York stone, which is beautiful but involves heavy travel, financial and environmental costs) is no more difficult or different from laying a concrete slab.

Other path materials Our final paths, in the Jewel Garden, are topped with a material called "Redgra" which comes from a quarry in the Forest of Dean some 48km (30 miles) south of us. This is a kind of pink sand with an element of clay that binds it solid when laid. You prepare the path with hardcore and

a layer of scalpings, then spread a thin layer of this binding surface which you bang in with a whacker plate. It goes on almost as sand but after 24 hours it is pretty solid. It is much cheaper and easier to lay than paving or brick, but if it doesn't have really sharp drainage it can get almost muddy in very wet weather.

Our latest path is the simplest. It is a long ribbon of concrete running from the propagation greenhouse yard up to the top greenhouse and compost heaps. It is 45cm (18in) wide which is fine for a single pair of feet and the front wheel of a wheelbarrow and guarantees a dry service path in all weathers. It is not beautiful but entirely functional and the wider path it runs down has always been a service corridor to the garden rather than part of it. So it works well in that situation.

I hope that there will be more hard paths as money and time allow. But whatever they are made from, in the end a garden path has to work. Feet and wheels must find them easy the year round. What materials you use will influence the way your garden looks as much as the surrounding planting, so choose well.

Walls are a great luxury in a garden.

They provide one of the best surfaces for raising a wide variety of flowering and fruiting plants, look wonderful in their own right, provide shelter from the wind and reflected heat from the sun. But they are very expensive to build. One of my regrets is that we have so few walls in this garden that are suitable for growing against. A brick-walled vegetable garden is one of the great gardening delights.

We have, however, built a few stone walls in this garden, using the huge amount of building stone that was in the Walled Garden

when we arrived. It is all a fairly soft local red sandstone which is the bedrock beneath our soil. We also have a few brick walls, and have tried hard to either use bricks that match the ones used in the house as well as the paths. As with the house, there is no cement used in the mortar, just lime and sand from the local quarry.

I find the form and colours of the stone and brick an enormously important part of the garden and much more than just a foil for plants. As a rule of thumb, if a wall is not sufficiently handsome unadorned by planting then there is something wrong with it. By the same token any plants must work with the wall rather than merely lean against it.

It is important that the organic gardener is sensitive to building materials, always using local materials and binding them with the softest possible material. It is worth remembering the basic rule that the more weather-prone a surface is, the softer it should be. So, for example, you should never repoint a brick wall with a mortar that is more durable than the bricks themselves. This goes against much modern building wisdom but means that you do not get the situation where the pointing remains untouched whilst the bricks are worn away.

Gardeners need to also remember that whereas a hedge or open fence will absorb and sieve the wind, walls block it and then throw much of it over the top so that it lands with extra force on the other side of the wall up to a distance of about twice the height of the wall. The result is that anything growing on or directly against the wall is very sheltered but plants in the "wind-shadow" may be very buffeted.

The Lime Walk path mirrors the brick wall flanking it (*left*). The wall separating the box balls and the propagating greenhouse (*below*) faces east, but the other, warmer side shelters the cold frames.

The outside face of a hurdle woven from split hazel. This is held entirely without nails or any other binding and yet is solid enough to withstand any kind of wind for years.

Fences
I have only used two types of fence in this garden and both are variations on a single theme. One is fixed fencing made from coppice hazel and coppice chestnut and the other hazel panels made entirely from coppice hazel.

This is a very exposed, wind-swept site and when we arrived in 1992 there was no protection at all. So one of the first things that I did when I had marked out the design for the garden was to build fixed fencing made from hazel and ash woven through Sweet chestnut stakes. The result was an instant three dimensional layout of my plan. This type of fencing has been used by humans since the Iron Age for walls of buildings and boundaries and is enormously strong as well as a tremendously effective windbreak, combining man-made structure with organic materials. I then planted my hedges on the sheltered side of each fence. The fences provided shelter until the hedges grew and meant that the hedges themselves grew much faster because they were also protected from the wind.

The problem with fixed fencing is that the posts have to be very firmly banged in every 45cm (18in) or so – which with 2.5m (8ft) posts is hugely laborious – and the hazel, if thick enough to do the job, can be heavy work to weave. If you want to be more flexible or if the ground is not suitable for so much post work then split hazel panels are the answer.

I bought split hazel hurdles for marking the boundaries with neighbours and the track and later to provide shelter for the raised beds until their hedges grew.

Hazel hurdles are beautiful and curiously satisfying objects. Everything about them, from their texture, scale (all are 1.8m/6ft long and can be made from 90cm-1.8m/3-6ft high) and even their smell is friendly and harmonious. They are entirely man-made, and untreated, and use an endlessly renewable resource. They use 7–10-year-old wood, (large enough to split but young enough to be supple) which is the ideal timescale for sustaining hazel coppice (*see page 113*). They have been used for centuries – if not millennia – as sheepfolds, providing protection for the lambing flock

The newly-made raised beds have a hawthorn hedge around them which will shelter them in time, but woven hazel hurdles provide the necessary protection until the hedge has grown.

Chestnut stakes stacked up ready for use. Sweet chestnut (*Castanea sativa*) makes very good fencing stakes because it splits very easily and yet is very strong and slow to rot when sitting in damp soil. As well as making one of the most ancient and splendid large trees, it is also ideal for coppicing as long as the soil is not heavy clay or chalk.

as well as containing them. Shepherds used them by the thousand on the South Downs near to where I was brought up. They are light to carry, very strong, perfect for filtering the wind and easy to make by the skilled hurdler. All they need is a post between each hurdle and strong string or wire to fix them so that they will withstand a gale.

Therein lies the rub. There is great skill in making hazel hurdles. The skill lies not in weaving the split hazel between the upright hazel "sails" but in the splitting. A hurdler will do this fast and true every time, hacking his curved and pointed bill hook into the hazel near the top so that it cuts exactly halfway through it (itself tremendously difficult) and then twisting the handle as he bears down on it, easing the stem apart. Try it. If you can get the knack then you can make anything from buildings, to seats, to fences. If, like me, you find it very difficult, you are restricted to the heavy labour of fixed fencing.

Willow hurdles are a poor substitute for hazel and only suitable if you live in an area where "withies" are grown. Whereas a hazel hurdle erected along the wind will last ten years, a willow one is lucky to survive intact for half that period.

Trees

Any garden that has a large tree is blessed with a scale that transcends the domestic and if it is a small garden it can revolve entirely around this one plant.

A large deciduous tree provides an enormous boost to the range of wildlife that can live in the garden. It is said that a mature English Oak (*Quercus robur*) can support up to 500 different species of invertebrate and insect life as well many birds and mammals. It follows that the greater the variety and range of animals of all kinds living as part of the garden's eco-system, the healthier it will be.

Evergreen trees such as pines, cedars, hollies and yews are very important to add structure and colour in winter as well as providing cover for birds and insects. Personally I find that there are far too many evergreens planted in gardens – particularly the range of false cypresses – at the expense of deciduous alternatives, but every garden should have some.

However trees take time to grow to maturity and we are in an age of impatient gardening. We want everything done fast, and the healthy growth of an oak is not dramatic enough for many people. This is wrong headed and also plain wrong, as trees grow extraordinarily fast and I get as much pleasure from seeing a young sapling develop year by year as I do from one that is fully mature.

In this garden I have planted hundreds of trees, many of which are pruned each year but some are now beginning to reach real size after just nine years. Once the roots have got established and start to grow, a young oak or ash can put on as much as 1m (3ft) every year. My own experience in this garden is that a 1.8m (6ft) sapling can become 6m (20ft) tall in seven or eight years. This transforms the garden more than any other factor. One of the less celebrated pleasures in life is to climb up into the top branches of a tree that you have planted as a 1.2m (4ft) sapling.

There is another important aspect of growing trees, which is that it puts the garden into a much bigger perspective. When you plant an oak you are potentially taking a role in the next 500 years. Even an ornamental cherry or *Sorbus* will outlive you and perhaps your children. This makes tree planting an act of faith in a future that we wish to share and lifts us beyond the petty concerns of our own immediate lives.

The perspective is not just chronological. Trees also put the garden into a different scale. They add height and size that balances buildings and creates the right set of proportions. Far too many gardens are arbitrarily capped off by lack of height in their planting.

Deciduous trees provide leaves for leafmould, shelter from wind, shade for the range of lovely woodland flowers as well as for the hot gardener, and in this garden have the unexpected effect of soaking up lots of excess moisture which, as they grow, is becoming increasingly useful on this very wet ground.

We all know that trees are vital to maintaining the balance between oxygen and carbon dioxide. Without the excess carbon dioxide in the atmosphere being absorbed by trees and oxygen being released, human life would cease to be viable. I like the notion that gardeners take responsibility for the broader

Deciduous trees provide a harvest of leaves for leafmould (*above*). The river next to us (*opposite top*) is fringed with pollarded willows. All the trees in my garden are less than ten years old but are growing at different rates. So the field maples (*opposite, bottom left*) are twice the size of the apples, and the wild cherry (*opposite, bottom right*) blossoming in late April, has grown even faster.

103

The autumnal colouration of leaves is dependent upon two different processes, one leading to yellows, the other to reds. Yellow caratenoid pigments are always present in leaves but are usually masked by chlorophyll. When the temperature begins to drop and the daylight hours get shorter the chlorophyll is not renewed and the yellow pigments become visible.

But red pigmentation of leaves is made anew each autumn. It is closely related to carbohydrates and is made most on warm, sunny days followed by cool nights. The sugars go back down the tree as sap via the phloem to feed new wood cells. But in late summer and early autumn the transportation of sugars from the leaves is restricted by the cold nights, leading to the concentration of red pigmentation in the leaves. So the intensity of our autumn colour is determined by the weather in August and in September.

issues of the planet from within their own back yard. By planting one tree you are making a positive act of sustaining human life. This does not even need the process of planting. By nurturing one of the inevitable tree seedlings that emerge in the garden, you are meaningfully countering the depredations of the rain forest. It is not much – but then it does not take much to change the world.

Planting trees The biggest influence that you can have on any tree is to plant it really well. The smaller it is when planted, the faster and healthier it will grow. I planted a number of quite large trees in this garden, but only because they were available very cheaply and I wanted to create some structure on my empty field. But if you are prepared to be patient for the first few years, a sapling 1m (3ft) tall will catch up and overtake one three times that size within a few years and is likely to have developed a much better root system.

Before planting, *always* soak a tree in water for at least 10 minutes. If it is bare-root – and bare-root trees tend to be cheaper and better quality – *never* let the roots dry out for even a minute. I find that a soaked hessian sack is useful to have on hand to cover the roots with whilst digging the hole.

Whatever the size of tree, dig a hole at least 1m (3ft) in diameter or twice the spread of the roots – whichever is the larger. Remove one-spade's depth and break up the next spit with a fork, removing all stones. Add some compost or manure, but not too much. The purpose is to get the plant off to a good start rather than provide any long- or even medium-term nutrition as the tree will extract all that it needs from the soil. I would stress here, as I have throughout this book, that it is better for

any plant to grow slowly and healthily than to be forced into faster growth with extra feeding.

Place the tree in the hole and spread the roots. If it is over 1.2–1.5m (4–5ft) tall it will need staking. Position the stake so that the roots can fit easily around it, remove the tree (keeping the roots moist) and bang the stake in firmly, putting it on the side of the prevailing wind. Then reposition the tree and cover the roots with the topsoil that you removed. When there is a layer of soil completely covering the roots, firm it down well before adding more soil. Repeat this process, leaving a couple of inches below the surface of the surrounding ground. Tie the tree to the stake and then water it very thoroughly. This means adding at least a large bucket of water and if possible leave a hose on it until the water overflows onto the surrounding area. The tree will probably need watering once a month for the first year or so, especially if it is an evergreen.

When the water has fully drained, add a thick mulch of compost. This will stop evaporation and work into the top 15cm (6in) of soil which is where most of any trees feeding roots are. Top up the mulch every spring and keep it scrupulously weed-free for a couple of years.

Then leave it. Let it grow.

Moving a mature tree

We have a single horse chestnut growing as a specimen tree at the end of the central path that runs right down through the middle of the garden. It was originally planted at the edge of the spot where we now have our grassy mound and when the digger came to landscape the mound the tree either had to be ditched or moved. Moving trees, even quite small ones, is a risky and skilled business but we thought we would give it a go, scooping the whole thing up in the bucket of the digger and driving it the 100 yards or so to its new home. The secret of moving a mature tree is to take as large a rootball as possible and to make sure that the tiny feeding roots do not dry out at all in the process and then to work the soil carefully into every nook and cranny amongst the roots. The tree must also be completely supported for at least three years. So far, firmly staked and regularly watered, our chestnut seems to be growing well, but in my experience it takes at least three years for a tree to recover its previous rate of growth after being moved.

Oak

I have planted only two oak trees in this garden, although in my last garden there were a number of magnificent oaks over 200 years old.

Oaks are the archetypal tree of the British landscape, the measure of wealth and security. This was literally the case as land was judged by the size and health of the oak trees that grew on it. In countryside around my garden, oaks grow better than anywhere else in the land. The framework of my house is constructed from oak as are all the barns. As I type these words with the computer on an oaken table, my feet rest on oak floorboards, books on oak bookcases and the doors and windows are made from oak. When oak is "green" or freshly cut it is fairly soft and easy to work. But as it ages and dries it becomes unbreakably hard and strong. I have reused timbers in the fifteenth century part of the

house that are at least 700 years old and they are still superbly strong and undamaged.

Oak has an extraordinary ability to stay alive even though the majority of its branches and trunk might die back. A few miles down the road is an oak tree that is reckoned to be at least a thousand years old and is 11m (34ft) in girth, 1m (3ft) above the ground. It is hollow, has caught fire, but is still living.

Any organic gardener needs no other reason to plant an oak other than its beauty but an oak tree houses more living creatures than any other growing plant in Britain. No other plant contributes more to the sustenance of diversity in our landscape, including gardens.

An oak's health tends to depend upon its access to light and air. It regenerates poorly in woodland whereas it thrives in open ground. Gardeners should bear this in mind and always set it in as much uncluttered space as possible.

Unripe acorns of the common oak (*Quercus robur*).

105

Italian alder (*Alnus cordata*)

Fraxinus angustifolia 'Raywood'

Alder

Alder loves the wet. There has been a fungus quietly killing off the common alder (*Alnus glutinosa*) which, in truth, can be a little dull, but I have a number surviving in the garden, planted specifically to provide shelter from the west wind, which they continue to do in their unassuming way. Much more handsome in every way is the Italian alder (*Alnus cordata*), a fabulous tree with practically evergreen leaves. I planted a row of 45cm (18in) saplings nine years ago where the coppice now grows and the survivors (I have thinned them considerably) are now 10m (30ft) tall and distinctly stately in appearance compared to the slightly scatty, bent-backed habit of the common alder. When I say "nearly" evergreen, I mean that given mild, wet conditions they do not drop their leaves until they are renewed in spring, but they will defoliate at the end of a dry summer or in very cold winter weather. They will eventually reach 25m (80ft) or more.

Alders are the only broadleaved trees to carry cones – the Italian alder's black and the common alder a dirty grey-brown. It is also nitrogen fixing, like legumes, although few plants have a chance to benefit from this increase in fertility around its roots.

Ash

Ash The largest tree in the garden is a 'Raywood' ash (*Fraxinus angustifolia* 'Raywood') that I planted in the spring of 1993 and which now, nine years later, is large enough for me to clamber 6m (20ft) up into its branches. It is a magnificent shape in summer and in autumn the narrow leaves turn a rich plum colour.

I am a great fan of the common ash (*Fraxinus excelsior*) and have a couple of dozen growing in the garden. It is one of the dominant trees of the Herefordshire landscape, and until about 50 years ago huge old ashes were regularly pollarded every 20 years or so over a period of hundreds of years, providing timber for carts, tool handles and fuel as well as being a prime sources of poles for growing hops before the modern wire structures took over. The new growth would emerge beyond the reach of grazing cattle whilst the trunk became gnarled and massively thick through the centuries. Most are now uncut so the 3m (10ft) high trunk is topped by a characteristic mass of thick branches, quite unlike the tall, lean and dead straight trees of woodland. They are often positioned at corners of fields and bends in the road to mark boundaries. Both pollarding and coppicing, increase the life of the tree enormously and ash stools are still coppiced that are over a thousand years old.

There are people who criticise ash because its leaves are one of the last to arrive and amongst the first to fall in autumn. But there is more to ashes than merely summer dress and it is too utilitarian and philistine to measure beauty in terms of longevity. Certainly a mature ash tree in midsummer is a lovely living thing. The pinnate leaves cast a particularly delicate shade so there is always a feathery light filtering through, which makes it suitable for woodland underplanting.

Before they come into leaf the knobbly tips of the branches carry matt black buds, curiously inanimate and almost crustacean before they open out. The male flowers come next, frizzy and strange, like party streamers caught on the end of a stick, and then finally, after the rest of the arboreal world has had foliage out for weeks, the ash leaves emerge, floppy fronds that might be considered exotic on another, less determinedly common a tree.

The outline of a common ash in a field is of a huge blowsy tree with generously sweeping branches. But as a young tree it does not mimic its maturity, starting out spindly and only slowly developing its promise, and this, I think, is why it has never really been taken into the gardening lexicon. But it has real garden potential. One of the most interesting aspects of ashes is the speed with which they regrow after cutting. This willingness to regenerate growth was used in coppicing. Ash wood is straight grained and strong and the ease with which it splits makes it possible to harness that strength along the grain as well as making splitting it for firewood a joy.

Maples (*Acer campestre*) provide

the best autumn colour in our garden, turning a brilliant yellow before flushing to pink and orange. I planted a number of them as trees in the orchard, Spring Garden and along the boundary of the Damp Garden and they have all matured into fine small trees, giving shape and shade onto an otherwise empty field. It seems to me that this is an undervalued indigenous garden plant and rather like hawthorn is still mainly considered as a "wild" tree of the agricultural hedgerow. So it might be, but it is a waste to leave it out of the garden.

There are a few "garden" varieties, none of which I have grown myself. *A. c.* 'Postelense' has pale yellow leaves when young, turning greener as the summer progresses. *A. c.* 'Schwerinii' is a purple-leafed version which could be potentially very useful in a large border, given the acceptance of being regularly hard pruned. I had a Norway maple (*Acer platanoides*) in our previous garden and it was certainly beautiful in autumn, turning lemon yellow before sometimes blushing red.

I suspect that *Acer palmatum* is unmistakably decorative with its low mounds of finely cut leaves glowing with autumn colour. I have not yet worked out why I do not like them but it is certainly for no rational, objective reason. I did try growing *Acer palmatum* 'Dissectum Atropurpureum' in the Jewel Garden and for three years it obstinately refused either to grow or gracefully die.

My favourite Eastern maple is *Acer griseum*, the Paperbark maple from China. The leaves dutifully do their maple bit in autumn, turning rich scarlet in autumn but the bark adds a spectacular sideshow, peeling and flaking to reveal a cinnamon coloured under layer. I would love to grow one here.

The third group of maples comes from America. At their autumnal best the maples of the East Coast are staggering. I flew over New York State in early November and was astonished by the mile upon mile of pink. We inherited a sugar maple, *Acer saccharum* (not to be confused with the confusingly similarly named silver maple, *A. saccharinum*) in our last garden and I hoped that it might give a little mini-performance of East Coast fall, but it only blushed apologetically instead of the expected explosion into crimson. The truth is that it is a very rare year that we can provide a combination of very hot August days and very cool nights that they need to produce that foliar display.

The Lime Walk is the immediate link with the house and the largest part of the garden, stretching away from it like a gangway, and is intended to draw you outside whatever the weather.

That is never much of a problem for a keen gardener but every garden needs some kind of intermediate space connecting indoors and out. The Lime Walk runs 40 of my paces from a door into the medieval hall of the house down to another wooden garden door. As you leave the house there is a seating area in the middle of four small beds, then the Herb Garden, that mirrors this layout, and then this path becomes what we call the Lime Walk, flanked on either side by narrow borders, hornbeam hedges and pleached limes. As the limes were the first things to be planted along its edges they claim nomenclature. It has always been an important artery of the garden and resolves the design problem of having the house tucked right into one corner of the site by taking you from the house and opening into two avenues that run at right angles from it right down through the garden. Initially it was the only hard path and even though half of it is often submerged by floods, it is a reliable firm foothold. Also the limes were relatively mature when I bought them for a song in a tree auction, so it created a glimpse into the future of the garden when all else around it was based upon hope and trust rather than any physical structure.

For a year or so the path was hardcore and gravel but on my 40th birthday, two years after the limes were planted Sarah gave me enough bricks for 40 paces and our long-term helper George expertly laid them. This added another dimension of maturity to the embryonic garden. The hornbeam hedges beneath the limes were planted in the same year and the limes gradually began to grow along the framework of three parallel rows or tiers of hazel rods that I had put up to train them along. In late winter the previous year's growth is all pruned back to the bare bones of this structure which simultaneously restricts the extent of the tree's growth and stimulates vigorous new growth a few months later.

Now the hedges and limes provide solid green walls in summer which in winter changes to a tawny brown, topped by the bright red and green shoots of the limes before pruning.

As the hedges and trees have matured so the planting along the edges of the path has changed. In spring, before the leaves have grown, the first flowers are white tulips. We used to follow these with white foxgloves, *Digitalis purpurea alba*, but the shade from the new lime leaves causes the foxgloves to lean frantically inwards looking for light. We also used to follow the foxgloves with *Nicotiana sylvestris* which cast the most fabulous scent in the night air as you walked down the path – but again it is too shaded now and the growing trees and hedge take too much moisture from the summer soil (in winter there is more than enough water for everything and everyone). So now we follow the tulips with *Alchemilla mollis* which is perfectly happy and will take one or even two hard cut-backs to stimulate fresh foliage and flowers.

But the main aesthetic pleasures of the Lime Walk are architectural and in its various shades and intensities of green. Any flowers that accompany this must be single colour, simple and uncluttered.

The Lime Walk is under-planted with the tulip 'White Triumphator' (*above*).

Pruning the lime trees in February (*opposite top left*). This is one of my favourite jobs. The pruned limes just putting on new leaves in the crystalline light of late April (*opposite top right*). The Lime Walk in high summer (*opposite bottom left*). The tulips have been replaced by *Alchemilla mollis* which spills over the brick path. This will be cut back hard twice during the summer. The leaves are starting to thin in October and the light is fading (*opposite bottom right*).

Pleaching limes
Pleaching is the process whereby a chosen number of parallel stems above a clean trunk are trained horizontally to meet, to form a framework similar to espaliered fruit trees.

Limes are ideal for pleaching because they grow fast, respond enthusiastically to pruning and have very long whippy new stems that are easy to bend and tie into position. The fresh young growth of limes is soft and yet slightly resistant and cuts in a particularly satisfying manner.

We have lime trees in this garden almost by default. I had never grown a lime before we came here at the beginning of the 1990's but in April 1993 I bought dozens of them as

a job lot in a tree sale, smaller ones for as little as 50 pence and 20 trees 5m (15ft) tall for around three pounds each. This was absurdly and irresistably cheap. They were sold to me as *Tilia cordata*, the small-leafed lime. These would have been ideal for my purposes of making a pleached avenue as *T. cordata* do not grow too monstrous and do not drip honeydew from aphids in the summer as other limes, especially the common lime, *Tilia x europaea*, are prone

Pruning pleached limes

The first thing is to reduce all shoots growing at right angles to the line of the pleaching, cutting right back to the base. I then cut back all vertical growth, leaving just spurs with a few healthy buds. On the top row, which receives most sunshine, this can be as much as 1.8m (6ft). When this is done all that should be left are the horizontal shoots between each tree. I have learnt over the years to be absolutely ruthless and to cut away everything other than the three chosen lateral branches. The only exception is if I wish to train in a new lateral to replace an existing one that is broken or unsuitable. What is left is just the skeleton of the trees and looks shockingly reduced. But this harsh pruning stimulates new growth and by April it is sprouting new leaves from each knobbly cut, followed in May by the new stems, which we give a light trim in midsummer. My advice to anyone establishing new pleached limes is to:
• Choose young trees that have a strong leader and are dead straight.
• Put up a really strong supporting framework of wires or sticks. I have found that hazel works well but needs constantly replacing.
• Get the shape right from the outset. There is a temptation to bend and cajole shoots to the framework but it never pays in the medium-, let alone long-, term. Be ruthless about cutting back any shoots that are not right on the supporting framework, even if that means reducing the tree to a stick with buds. The harder you prune the faster they will grow.
• Tie them with tarred twine and *never* with wire or plastic ties.
• Go no higher than you know you can prune.

to do. As it turned out some were *Tilia platyphyllos* 'Rubra' and others *T. p.* 'Aurea' and none *T. cordata*.

T. platyphyllos is the big-leafed lime and these do produce enormous leaves each spring, growing to the size of serving dishes. It also has the advantage of not creating the "forest" of suckers that bristle out from the common lime.

The new shoots of *T .p.* 'Rubra' are bright red, coming into their own after leaf-fall. On a frosty day, against the backdrop of a clean blue sky, they glow like a jewelled aura around the tree. The new growth of *T. p.* 'Aurea' is a sort of olive-green, also rather fetching. Both look very good on their own but when mixed at (unintentional) random they present a slightly rakish harlequin aspect to the winter sun. Never mind. It fairly represents my haphazard approach to gardening, and they are now a distinctive part of this winter garden.

I have a few limes planted in the Spring Garden which, in time will mature as large trees. Limes make one of the best parkland trees, growing upwards as a tower of branches and having real grandeur when mature.

Pruning the pleached limes is one of my favourite winter jobs. Lime cuts better than any other wood so all you need is a sharp pair of secateurs. It takes nearly a week to complete but transforms the garden from a shaggy mass to a pared down bristly framework. For a month or two, the trees become a tightly controlled sculptural grid before the leaves and new branches begin to sprout.

A coppice is crop of wood that is harvested as deliberately as a field of wheat, utilizing some trees' willingness to regrow vigorously as a result of this drastic pruning.

Hazel, Sweet chestnut, ash and oak are the most common coppice trees although many others will respond to this treatment. The regular cycle of coppicing utterly transforms the landscape from dense woodland to almost open field, although a few standards are usually left to mature in every acre of coppice. Unlike a plantation, it is entirely self-renewing and, as a result of the coppicing, the trees have their lives extended to hundreds and even thousands of years. Nothing is wasted, nothing is destroyed and everything is adapted to its best possible use.

This harvest happens every seven or eight years with hazel, 10–20 years with ash and 30 years with oak. If you have more than an acre then you will coppice as much as you can manage every year, and traditionally this is two acres for a full-time woodman. So 24 acres of hazel would, at any one time, have 12 different stages of growth accompanied by 12 different stages of shade, ranging from the wholly open to almost complete summer cover. The net effect of this is to create a finely tuned, varied micro-environment where plants, insects and animals can live in very tightly defined habitats with exactly the right amount of shade and cover that is both sustainable for centuries as well as changing every year.

My favourite form of woodland is the coppice with standards. The "standards" are trees left to grow for timber, usually of a different variety than the coppiced wood and usually oak, ash or beech. So you might have a hazel coppice with beech, ash or oak standards, or an ash coppice with oak standards.

If you can extract those conditions and fit them into the intensive jigsaw of a back garden then you add more than just the sum of its plants. You create a special, beautiful and self-sustaining ecosystem.

As much as anything else, it is a matter of being in tune with a particular association of a group of plants, light, soil and human need. You do not need acres to do this. A corner that you are prepared to give over to this permanent cycle or even a couple of hazels that you cut to the ground every five years will have the required effect

My own coppice is not yet ready for cutting although it soon will be. Until it is, I cut hazel for the garden from a friend's wood in South Wales.

Over the years I have used thousands of hazel rods woven into fixed fences. Wherever there is now a hedge, I first made a woven fence to provide instant shelter for both the garden and the growing hedge. Many of these fences are hidden inside the now mature hedge. I also defined the raised beds of the vegetable garden with low woven fences, although these are being replaced by box hedging.

I also used hazel as the framework for the pleached limes and annually as supports for climbers, both decorative and edible. I use the brushy tops of the hazel as peasticks. When they are too brittle to be used in the garden they become excellent kindling for the fires. Nothing is wasted.

Coppice flowers Primroses, *Primula vulgaris*, are my favourite spring flower, and they take pride of place (*see top right*). The wood anemone, *Anemone nemorosa*, will not flower in shade and so appears early, before the leaves grow. If you come across a large carpet of them you can be sure that the wood is very old, because they spread incredibly slowly – no more than 1.8m (6ft) every 100 years.

Violets may seem more delicate than wood anemones but establish and spread much faster. The common dog violet, *Viola riviniana*, and *V. reichenbachiana*, which is more petite, are both woodland plants which increase enormously the year after coppicing and are doing well in my little patch (*see bottom left*).

Bluebells (*Hyacinthoides non-scripta*) survive the deep shade of the end of the coppice cycle in an attenuated form, flowering modestly and then, when a coppice is cut, the bluebells (*see top left*) go berserk and spread themselves wildly. In the garden, it makes sense to grow bluebells in a situation that mimics coppicing, but it is a hopeless plant for any kind of border as it will completely take over once established.

Hedges

The word "garden" derives from the Old English "geard" which means a hedge or enclosure. A hedge enclosing a space is the exact definition of a garden, just as it defines a field.

I often think about gardening as a substitute for farming and that the English obsession with garden hedges is because really they are psychological remnants of the fields that time and history have made into motorways and shopping centres and are irretrievable. Instead of thinking of the garden as a series of outdoor "rooms" perhaps we should more helpfully see it as a jumble of small fields, enclosed meadows, carved out of the wild wood that are our cities and suburbs and housing estates. "The Countryside" to most Englishmen is a hedged, farmed place, the glorification of what our own gardens would be if they could take wings and fly. Every stupid, greedy farmer that rips out another hedgerow is despised not just because he is doing irreparable damage to the balance of the ecology for short-term gain but because he is clawing at the guts of the landscape and reaching into the viscera of our own gardens.

So instead of connecting the garden to the house by making it into a roofless living room, better to think of it as our piece of land that we tend. We crop contentment, beauty, privacy, some prized bits and pieces of food and maintain that direct link to our own private farmed countryside.

I think that most gardens underdo hedges. Maintaining them is not much work – certainly less that a lawn or border – and even a very small garden can usually be improved by subdivision. Garden hedges do not have to be four-square. A "cloud" hedge looks great and hedges can just as easily snake and bend as march in a straight line. The important thing is to get the height right in relation to the space that the hedge bounds. As a rule most hedges are too low. Just as a high ceiling tends to improve the proportions of a room, so high hedges make a garden seem bigger and more beautiful. And there is the added bonus that the higher and longer your hedges, the more bird life you will have in the garden.

Hedge cutting Straight-sided hedges (as opposed to rounded ones) are best with sides that gently slope out so that the base is wider than the top. This is called a "batter". If you cut the sides dead straight then the top of the hedge will shade out the bottom. A batter lets light get at the bottom half of the hedge which in turn means that it maintains its thickness and density right to the ground.

Topiary of any kind is best done with shears or a light electric hedgecutter. If you are using shears a good tip is to hold one hand still and rather than using both hands like a bellows, work only one side. This gives much more precise control.

Trimming a hedge encourages dense, sprouting growth. Therefore the more you trim the sides of a young hedge, the denser it will grow. Leave the top until it has reached the height you want to keep it at and then trim it off. Try and keep young hedges narrow – it is all too easy to let a hedge become sprawling and not very thick.

If you have a young hedge or an established one that is not very healthy, make sure that it has bare soil running at least 30cm

Collecting hedge trimmings (*top left*). The vast majority of this is soft enough to be shredded and added to the compost heap. The hornbeam hedges (*top right*) keep many of their leaves throughout the winter but at least half fall and I collect them assiduously for making leafmould. The box hedge (*bottom*) in the vegetable garden is *Buxus sempervirens* 'Handsworthiensis', a particularly large-leaved and vigorous variety of common box.

(1ft) either side. Weeds or grass in this area will seriously restrict growth. Mulch this strip with good compost and replace it at least once a year until it has fully grown and make sure that it is well watered.

Hedge cutting is simply a form of mass-pruning and the laws of pruning apply. The implications of this are that cutting a deciduous hedge in winter will stimulate vigorous growth the following spring and summer, whereas trimming it in midsummer (August is the best month in Britain) will restrict vigour but promote bushiness.

Hedge planting

• **Do not cut corners** in preparation. All time, effort or money put into preparing the ground for a hedge will pay dividends in health and speed of growth.

• **In my experience** it is always better to plant deciduous hedges small, ideally between the middle of October and Christmas, but certainly by the end of March. Evergreen hedges are best planted in April in colder areas and September in a mild, sheltered garden.

• **Plant deep enough** to cover the roots, but do not bury too much of the stem. Planting distances vary but in general a single row with adequate spacing will make a stronger hedge than a double row or one planted more thickly. A minimum of 45cm (18in) is a good rule of thumb for beech, hornbeam and holly and 30cm (12in) for hawthorn and box. Yew should be at least 60cm (24in) apart. Never plant *Leylandii*. Firm in really well and water very thoroughly. The watering after planting is as much to move the soil round the roots as to provide moisture.

• **I delay mulching** for a week so that the soil can settle a little and I give the hedge another big soak first. Then mulch thickly. This is important as it will stop weeds competing for moisture and nutrients in the vital first two or three years. Anything will do as long as it is water permeable and thick enough to stop any light getting through but obviously compost or manure will feed as well as smother.

• **Staking each plant** will stop wind rock and help the hedge to grow faster and straighter, so whilst not necessary it is a good idea.

• **There is some debate** as to the merits and extent of cutting a hedge back after planting. Hawthorn definitely grows denser if cut back by 50 per cent immediately after planting and some say that all deciduous hedges should be reduced by about one third. I have found that hornbeam is best left to establish for a couple of years before cutting back by about a third. Do not cut the leaders of evergreen hedges until they have reached their intended height but keep the sides cut well back to encourage thick lateral growth.

• **In the first year,** water the young hedge. Drought is the biggest hindrance to growth.

Cutting the hornbeam hedges with a petrol-powered hedgetrimmer. I only use a petrol machine for the larger hedges and prefer a much lighter electrical cutter for the box hedges and all topiary. We cut the deciduous hedges in summer with a second trim in autumn.

Planting a hedge

There is always a temptation to get a hedge off to a visually impressive start by putting in as large plants as you can afford. But this is nearly always an extravagant mistake.

Young plants recover much faster from the shock of planting and grow very much faster and stronger so that after five years they have invariably caught up plants three times as big – and ten times as expensive. If possible buy bare-root plants direct from a nursery as these will be much cheaper and probably healthier. Before planting give them a good soak in a bucket of water (*right*) and only remove each one at the last moment before placing it into the ground (*below left*). Prepare a generous trench at least 30cm (2ft) wide adding plenty of compost. Carefully place each hedging plant so that the roots are all covered but the stem should not be buried (*below right*).

Do not plant too close – remember that a hedge is effectively a line of trees and wider spacing will mean bigger, bushier plants. Firm the plants in with your foot so the roots are secure and backfill to within an inch of the surface before watering the line of hedging very thoroughly indeed. In the photograph (*left*), I am cutting the young hawthorn plants back by half to encourage bushy growth. Wait a few days for the soil to settle, water the young plants again and then mulch thickly to suppress any weeds and enrich the soil.

Types of hedges

The choice of hedging material, for any particular garden is a personal one. These are the hedges that I like most, and work best, in my own garden.

Hornbeam

One of the formative moments in my gardening life was visiting Het Loo in Holland. This is one of the palaces of William of Orange and his bride Mary, eldest daughter of James II of England. It is remarkable for its Baroque completeness, but what I loved – as opposed to admired – was the bit known as the Queen's Garden. This has a palisade of labyrinthine tunnels and leafy caves made of huge oak trellis work and clothed in hornbeam. From the outside it appeared to be solid hedging, 6m (20ft) tall and clipped to follow the shape of corridors and open hallways like a mini palace, but light streamed in through the leaves in the interior making it a cool, dappled space. The hornbeams were planted very close – perhaps 30cm (1ft) apart and pruned hard back so they were less like a hedge and more like a cordon apple – but of hornbeam.

Consequentially, when I started to make this garden I planted it with hornbeam hedges to provide all the divisions. The odd thing is that hornbeam is not a common hedge. This could be because people don't like it, preferring beech, which it superficially resembles, but in almost every respect hornbeam makes a superior hedge to beech, particularly if you want to pleach or train it. The best – or at least most famous – example of a pleached hornbeam "hedge-on-stilts" is at Hidcote in Gloucestershire, where there are a pair of hedges raised 1.5m (5ft) in the air poised above the "stilts" of their trunks. The result is as perfect a work of art and architecture as well as a living horticulture.

Hornbeam is similar to beech in that if the leaves are clipped in midsummer many will stay on the branches all winter, although they turn a paler, more matt, tawny than beech's auburn. Hornbeam leaves have serrated, edges like little teeth and veins divided by gentle corrugated troughs. In spring they are the freshest most exciting green conceivable and to look at them is to make your eyes dance.

Conventional gardening wisdom has it that beech only grows happily on chalky soil and that hornbeam needs heavy clay to thrive, but beech will grow perfectly well over a clay subsoil and hornbeam, whilst certainly very happy on a rich, clay soil, will also thrive on well-drained sand or gravel soils.

My own empirical observation is that hornbeam grows very fast indeed if it has plenty of moisture, particularly when young and that it responds dramatically to a rich, well dug planting ground. It will also grow well in heavy shade, albeit a little less luxuriantly than in open sunlight. The long and short of it is that I believe hornbeam to be the best deciduous hedging plant available to the gardener.

But a hedge, be it making an outdoor covered walkway, balancing on stilts or merely defining a boundary, is only a line of trees planted closely together. Hornbeam is not a hedge but a tree and a good one. It was usually managed as wood pasture, which meant that the trees were pollarded for timber and cattle grazed around them. The timber is good for firewood and exceptional for charcoal

I have used hornbeam as the main structural hedge in my garden. On our damp, heavy soil it grows quickly into a thick structure and has the great virtue of retaining many of its autumnal, russet leaves in winter until they are replaced by the wonderful flush of new green in spring.

but it is so hard – the hardest wood that we can grow in this country – that in the days before cast iron it was highly valued for things like cog-wheels in mills, piano keys and hammers, pulley blocks – butcher's blocks – anything that needed exceptionally hard-wearing surfaces. What has this to do with gardening? Well, I like the provenance of native plants and making the connection to their uses outside and beyond the garden fence. Bring that knowledge into the back yard and everything is enriched.

BOX hedging is one of my garden essentials. It is aesthetically particularly important in winter, adding green shape and structure to what is otherwise rather a bleak scene for months on end. In summer the low hedging contains but does not dominate or distract from the planting that it frames.

We have planted box hedging around all the beds in the Jewel Garden and the Herb Garden and are in the process of edging all the beds in the vegetable garden and the Walled Garden. This is taking time as it requires thousands of plants, all grown from cuttings. But the result looks great and costs nothing other than a little patience.

The range of possibilities of a box hedge is far greater than any other plant material. No other plant makes such a good job of spanning that ambiguous gap between edging and hedge. For hedging, there are only two types of box to consider; the common box (*Buxus sempervirens*) and the dwarf box (*B. s.* 'Suffruticosa'). The latter grows much more slowly and to much smaller ultimate dimensions. Traditionally it was used as edging for borders, growing to no more than 45cm (18in) tall. It is more expensive and you need more plants to make a hedge as they have to be planted as close as 15cm (6in) spacing. I think that a dwarf form of *Buxus sempervirens* such as 'Latifolia Maculata' (which has very yellow young growth) does the job just as well although when mature it might need clipping twice a year to keep its crisp edge.

Some varieties of *B. sempervirens* can be planted very widely and will grow into a thick hedge 1.8m (6ft) or more tall. There is an amazing example at Powis Castle in Wales that must be 6m (20ft) or more tall. I planted *B. sempervirens* 'Handsworthensis' 60cm (2ft) apart and within three years they had grown into a solid hedge 90cm (3ft) high and 30cm (1ft) thick. This is a particularly vigorous type with much larger leaves than normal, although new growth after clipping has denser, smaller leaves. Variegated box is extremely common, but the variegated effect is minimal with the leaves edged in either cream or yellow. *B.s.* 'Elegantissima' has a compact form with white edging and 'Gold Tip' and 'Aureovariegata' have yellow edging.

Box is much less prone to suffering from urban pollution than yew which makes it ideal for the small town garden. If you have a very small garden it will grow perfectly happily in a container, although beware of the desiccating effect of wind, especially in cold weather. I grew a line of carefully clipped cones in pots on a flat roof in London and lost the lot because they dried out in the wind even though I gave them the same amount of water as other box plants in a more sheltered spot.

Growing box is straightforward enough. It is long lived so should be planted with good preparation which means a trench or hole dug with organic material added for a hedge or single plant accordingly. The roots are shallow and spread laterally and create a "no-grow" area along an established box hedge which can be unappealing if you are using it to frame a bed or border and you want the effect of plants spilling over its frame. But you can chop the roots back with a spade without damaging it at all. I do this every couple of years.

Although box is tough, it responds well to feeding and watering, especially when young. It is also essential to allow a young box hedge plenty of light and air as it can be smothered by rampant growth around it, like that of the nasturtiums in the Jewel Garden.

Taking box cuttings Before the annual trim of the box topiary I always take cuttings from the most vigorous plants.

Nothing strikes as easily as box and they are cripplingly expensive to buy so it seems too wasteful not to do it. Although they root so easily I try and take care to cut just below the point where this year's growth begins, so that there is a "plug" of older wood at the base. This stops them drying out too fast. I don't use hormone rooting powder, just strip off the bottom half of the leaves, cut back any bushy side shoots and stick them in a compost made up of 50 per cent perlite and 50 per cent coir. I have put box cuttings straight into a border, which works well enough but normally I use 7.5cm (3in) pots, with four cuttings to a pot. But this year I partitioned off an end section of the cold frames, lined it with mipex landscaping fabric to stop any weeds growing through the gravel base and put in a 15cm

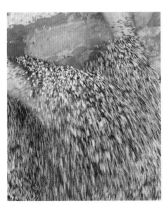

(6in) layer of coir, perlite and vermiculite. Then I put the cuttings directly into this at about 5cm (2in) spacings. The cold frame shelters them from the worst of wet, heat and cold as well as giving them as much fresh air as needed. When you take a cutting it is a race between that stem withering and its ability to create growth by establishing new roots. Ideally you want to minimize moisture loss and maximize the speed of root growth. So take off most of the leaves, leaving just enough to feed the new roots if the do grow. Keep the cutting moist but not wet, or else it will rot. Put it where it will not get too hot or cold and make sure that it has an easy root run.

Old box that has not been cut regularly will get "leggy" which means that all the foliage will be on the top, carried by a few naked stems. If the plant is fairly big, cut it right back, leaving, where practicable, half of the plant unpruned, and new growth will emerge from seemingly bare wood. When this is growing strongly – usually the second or third year after the drastic cut-back – repeat the operation with the other half. Within five years you should have a really dense, good-sized

bush growing to whatever shape you fancy.

The best time to clip an established box hedge is the first week of June, after the last frost has past. It might need another clip before the end of August. A young box hedge should have its sides trimmed in August, leaving the top until it has reached its desired height before trimming. If you cut it later than August there is a danger of an early autumn frost following a warm September burning tender young regrowth.

Yew No other hedge creates a better backdrop for a border or so perfectly defines an outdoor space than yew (*Taxus baccata*). Evergreen, dense, retaining a clipped edge for eight to nine months of the year (it grows vigorously from late spring to late summer) it adds substance to any garden. If they are shaded – and no tree casts a deeper drier shade than a vigorous yew – then they grow scrawny and woody, although perfectly healthy. But if exposed to sunshine – even after hundreds of years in shade – they make a wonderfully dense tree. It is, of course, that density that we exploit by clipping it and making into a hedge.

One of the myths about yew hedges is that they are very slow to grow. This is completely untrue. Given the right conditions of rich, very free-draining soil, plenty of water and sunlight, they will put on a steady 30cm (12in) a year and plants 45cm (18in) tall will make a solid 2.5m (8ft) hedge in 10 years. However, it is true that it slows right down once it reaches maturity and they will reach an incredible age. It is now believed that the largest churchyard yew trees predate the earliest churches by as much as 2,000 years and that the oldest may

be 4,500 years old. In other words churches were built on sites where there were already huge yew trees that had been the oldest and biggest thing around for longer than any cultural memory. No wonder they built churches near them.

The common yew grows best in the "wild" on chalky soil but for garden purposes you can plant it in any type of soil as long as it has good drainage. This drainage is absolutely essential – as I discovered to my cost. I planted yew hedges in the front of our house with yew topiary cones. Everything was planted in a deep trench or hole half-filled with manure or compost and grew well for the first few years, putting on 15–30cm (6–12in) of growth a year. On one side of this front garden the yew hedge flourished but on the other side I lost half a dozen quite large plants and another 20 or so became bronzed and ill.

My theory is that they have grown strongly through the topsoil but then they met the stone foundations of much earlier buildings. Abnormally high levels of autumnal rain saturated the ground, so that the roots have sat in puddles on the subterranean stone and the plants were literally drowning.

I have not planted yew in our wetter back garden and if I had done I think that I would have put a drainage pipe along the bottom of the planting trench. With yew, drainage is everything.

I planted eight Irish yew (*Taxus baccata* 'Fastigiata') in the Jewel Garden to provide winter structure. It grows (very slowly in this garden) to make a slim column for the first twenty or so years of its life and only starts to gradually swell at the base thereafter. Like all yews it can be clipped hard back to the bare wood if need be, so that is the perfect evergreen tree for making a green pillar.

All Irish yews come from one of two female trees found in 1780 on a hillside in County Fermanagh. It is happiest in conditions similar to its original home, and grows taller and straighter in the wet West than the East, so there is hope for it in this wet, western plot.

Hawthorn

Two hundred thousand miles of hawthorn hedges were planted across the agricultural landscape of Britain in the great enclosure periods of the eighteenth and nineteenth centuries. All came from home-grown stock and from parish to parish, county to county within the same climatic zone, they react as if by one prearranged signal.

Nothing is so thrilling as the first realisation on a fine March evening that the hawthorn hedges are starting to dance with leaf. For the first week the new green hovers above the undressed shape of hedge, half memory and half botany. Then it seems to slowly settle down upon each plant, green layering on impossibly bright green.

I have used it in this garden to soften the gradation from formal to informal and from our tightly controlled domesticity to the surrounding agricultural landscape, so all the hedges around the coppice and in the orchard are of hawthorn. It is a wonderful hedging material, suitable for any soil, as tough as anything, will simpler get denser if cut, has vicious spikes and can be laid every 20 years or so to provide an impassably solid barrier. Hence the thousands of miles of it planted about three hundred years ago. But it has never quite made the grade as a garden hedge or tree – mainly, I suspect because it is so common outside the garden and so firmly fixed as an agricultural feature. But don't overlook the humble hawthorn, *Crataegus monogyna*. It will grow in almost any soil or position, has lovely flowers, cuts to any shape, is ideal cover for birds and produces fabulous berries or haws and is about the cheapest tree, that you can buy.

Early June is probably the best time to trim an established thorn hedge. If you want it to flower next spring then do not cut it again. If you want neatness above floriferousness then give it another trim in autumn to reduce the number of mildew spores that overwinter in the outer buds.

Holly

Ilex aquifolium, makes a marvellous hedge, albeit one a little slow to establish. I planted one 10 years ago with plants 1m (3ft) high which I cut back by half to encourage them to be bushy at the base. They bushed out all right but didn't grow up much for the first couple of years although – rather curiously – every four plants or so has thrown up a tall leader twice the height of its neighbours. However, it is now a good 1.8m (6ft) and thickening encouragingly. I am confident that the entire hedge will be evenly thick and tall within a few years and impenetrable to all but the most determined invaders.

Topiary

The essence of topiary is very simple. You plant a healthy specimen and train the leaders in the direction you want growth whilst cutting back hard to stimulate bushy thickness.

The stone pebbles resting on our walls (*above*) were the inspiration for the box topiary that is slowly taking shape in the hopkiln yard (*opposite top right and opposite bottom*).

Topiary is slow sculpture. In many ways it is a paradigm of all gardening. It involves growing a plant so that it is as healthy and vigorous as possible and then controlling that growth to suit the entirely human whim of the grower, especially trying to hold it still at a point of perfection. Plants do not want to do this. It is unnatural. And topiary is often attacked on this ground, with topiarists accused of teasing and twisting poor plants into contortions that are belittling or "unnatural". But this begs the question of what is natural in a garden? Certainly not lawns or clipped hedges or herbaceous plants from scattered Continents all growing healthily cheek by jowl, or robustly healthy vegetables or... nothing at all really. A good garden is a wholly unnatural environment run wholly in tune with the natural world and should be celebrated as such. Which, it seems to me, is precisely what topiary does. It is a concrete celebration of what gardening is all about, the combination of man's desire to control and contain plant life with every plants' uncontrollable process through growth, reproduction and death.

Training and clipping You can tie the leaders to canes or, much more expensively, make "formers" to sit over the bush so that it grows through and then is clipped back to that outline. But there is no need for that degree of expense and elaboration. Anything can be trained and clipped to almost any shape with some patience and a little skill. It is an entirely free form of expression and as such is, I think, entirely wonderful. But the things to remember

about this kind of topiary are that nothing in a garden stands in isolation. The relationship between each shape and outline is as important as the piece itself. In other words, topiary usually looks best en masse and as part of a considered piece of design. This can grow and change organically – indeed it should and almost certainly will – but the overall concept should be there from very early on. This inevitably leads on to the other question of manipulating and understanding the bits that are not there. It is the space between outlines that is often more interesting than the carefully trained and primped plants themselves. I would take this further and say that the best bits of almost every garden are the empty spaces between things. These spaces have to be shaped and maintained just as carefully as the objects that define them.

Winter shape In winter, when there is more space than at any other time of year, the gardening of emptiness is at its hardest. Anyone can make a green path flanked by immaculate tall hedges look good if they are in the full flush of midsummer health, but a grey November day is less forgiving. The eye does not wash over rough grass, straggly branches and floppy evergreens, but sticks at each irritant. Hence the importance of topiary. But topiary does not have to be restricted to cones and spirals. Any kind of training and pruning that is done for effect rather than the health of the plant amounts to topiary. Deciduous plants are perfectly fair game for this. All you have to bear in mind is the basic

principle of pruning which is that if you cut a shoot back, the new growth will be more vigorous. The harder you cut back, the more uninhibited is the subsequent response. So if you have a plant that is intended to be symmetrical and one side is growing weaker than the other, the correct thing to do is to cut the weak side back hard whilst gently pruning the vigorous side. It goes against instinct but not nature.

Holly, yew or box only needs one cut a year. But if you make topiary from hawthorn, privet or *Lonicera nitida* – all of which will make good dense shapes – you will have to cut them at least twice a year to hold their shape cleanly. The box hedges here get cut in June, after the first lovely flush of green has lost its fire and – more prosaically – any risk of frost is well past. But the box topiary, which consists of 64 cobble-shapes in the hopkiln yard and 12 balls in the Walled Garden, is left until late summer along with the yew cones in the front. The holly topiary is all in the Jewel Garden, and this gets trimmed in autumn when the surrounding herbaceous foliage has died down.

By cutting the yew and box in late

Looking across the clipped box cobbles towards the herb garden. The box shapes are surrounded by a grid of stone cobbles which I dug up by the score as I planted each box plant. All but half a dozen of the 64 box shapes came from cuttings and none is more than 10 years old. Each topiarized plant is essentially identical to the individual plants that make up the low box hedge around the herb borders.

summer it means that they stray trim right through until next spring. This is standard practise with yew but a lot of people will cut their box in early summer and again in September but since the box psyllids took up residence in the area that we call the hopkiln yard (because the hopkiln, where I sit writing this, looks directly onto it) which is planted with 64 box pebbles, the growth of this topiary has slowed to a crawl. The psyllids suck the sap of the box from April through till June then fly away, returning to lay eggs in July which hatch and hibernate over winter before sating their appetites the

following spring. This means that the pebbles never attain that bushy growth they used to achieve by late summer. They grow from March to late April then pick up again in late July. So they don't need cutting until late August.

I use an electric hedge-cutter for my topiary. This is fast and light, which is important for control. I have a length of hosepipe running for three metres or so from the trimmer to stop the cable being cut. I have tried using a petrol-powered cutter but it is too heavy and noisy for something that needs concentration. I have done it many

Trimming box balls

There is no mystery to cutting the box cobbles. They are rounded but not spherical, so I resist the temptation to be symmetrical. Each one is different and has its own shape and character. The effect is made by their accumulated and repeated shapes rather than by any single one of them, so there is no need to be precious about it. I simply start at the bottom and cut a line up to the top and move steadily round, always working from bottom to top. I find it easier to keep cutting until it seems to be right, rather than pecking away at it and the less I think about how to do it the better it gets done. The "Zen of Topiary". Actually this bit of the garden, with its apparent rigid grid and formality is all about feeling right without in any way needing analysis or explanation. The only rationalisation I did this year was to undercut them all rather harder than I had done in previous years. There is a tendency for the rounded curves to become domes, tethered to the ground on a wider base than is necessary or aesthetically desirable.

times with shears, which are cheap, effective energy-saving and good for the muscles of your forearms. But they must be very sharp.

The terminal bud of a stem produces a chemical that inhibits the growth of any buds below it. By clipping off these terminal buds – we are stimulating the growth of the buds below them. The harder a stem is cut back, the more vigorous its responding growth will be. So pruning topiary creates a denser shape and more vigorous plant. Therefore if a shape has a hole or weak growth it is best to cut this bit harder than the rest to stimulate more growth.

In the short term removal of leaves reduces the plant's ability to feed itself. So after its annual trim it is a good idea to weed around each plant, feed it with seaweed meal and water it well.

Evergreen trimmings will not compost. Better to burn them and put the ash on the compost heap.

Trimming yew cones

The yew cones are different from the box cobbles in lots of ways. I have to think about cutting these, constantly checking the line of the cones because although each of the 16 are a bit different, they share the same intention. Unlike the box bobbles, they were meant to be identical and only my ineptitude and the way things always slip away mean that they have evolved into separate entities. Cutting them each year is a forlorn attempt to rein them in. In fact it exposes their idiosyncrasies. They look naked and sleek, as though stripped off to go down to the river for a dip. Perhaps this is the great attraction of topiary. We personalize them in a way that no flowering or free-form plant can be personalised. The constancy of topiary is a reassuring thing and we cut them down to size to try and hold time still.

Flowers

The flower gardens

From the outset I knew that this garden was to have a number of smaller areas, or gardens, each with their own character and theme. I wanted to be able to walk around dipping into different areas of colour, shape and light, each little garden being self-contained and distinct from the others and yet there needed to be a progress of sorts so that they were linked as you walked around. But despite this broad aesthetic plan the choice of what to put where was largely dictated by practical considerations.

The first was of soil. Even within a very small garden there can be quite a big variance between soil types, drainage and often buried rubbish or stones. Without digging the whole plot you cannot know or map this out in advance but it was apparent to me that the drainage was worse as the garden stretched away from the house and the soil was heavier in these areas.

The second consideration was light. On the whole flowers need as much light as possible to thrive but there are some that grow in half or even full shade so these were grouped in the areas of heaviest tree and undergrowth planting such as the Spring Garden. It is worth stressing that area has only evolved into the Spring Garden because we have carefully selected plants that will be happy in that location rather than through any inherent quality of the site. Until 1995 it was simply the corner of an open field.

The Jewel Garden grew out of a series of experiments. It is at the very centre of our plot, getting maximum sun and air and was originally the proposed site for the vegetable garden.

It then became a circular lawn, a willow circle and the chicken run! This evolved through various experiments into the current flower garden with many alterations to the layout, including moving and removing hedges, paths and borders in the effort to create the best effect.

The Walled Garden began as an area devoted to my roses and herbs in four large beds filling the space, and this combination remained until a few years ago when the children wanted a small lawn in that area. The changing layout changed the planting with the importance of the morning light influencing our choice of soft, pale colours.

The Damp Garden has had most changes and as I write it is still evolving. Much of this evolution is forced by the maturation of trees and hedges which completely alter the shape and quantity of available light and shelter. It takes great experience to predict exactly the effect that a 4m (12ft) hedge will have when you first plant it as a series of insignificant 45cm (18in) plants.

But each of these areas of the garden here at Ivington has a different atmosphere as well as a different planting scheme. We feel our way into doing what is right for each as much as coldly plan it. In other words each takes on a life and character of its own – and sometimes that is rather different from what had been originally planned or expected.

I wanted to be able to walk around dipping into different areas of colour, shape and light, each little garden being self-contained and distinct from the others and yet there needed to be a progress of sorts so that they were linked as you walked around.

The flower borders
What is common to all our flower borders is the remarkable fertility of our soil. This results in exceptionally vigorous, lush growth.

This is wonderful but brings with it attendant problems. To start with, the weeds grow with the same vigour as our flowers and weeding is a constant labour. We mulch very heavily, which helps a lot but does not eliminate the problem. The soil is also very prone to fungal diseases and everything needs a great deal of staking and support. Some of the problems are unexpected: because we have such a rich soil there is a great deal of worm activity which attracts dozens of blackbirds. These make an enormous mess throughout the summer, spreading the mulch everywhere as they scratch about like a flock of tiny chickens. In a wet season the ground can become waterlogged and in a drought it sets like concrete. If I was making the flower borders again I would have spent more money and time on incorporating more horticultural grit to counter this.

You cannot prepare the soil too thoroughly. All time, energy and most money spent on getting the soil into the best possible condition before you start planting is never wasted. If the soil is basically good then this is no hardship – you dig it over, add some compost, prepare a good tilth and off you go. But if the soil is poor or its structure has been badly damaged (often compacted by heavy machinery if the house is fairly new) then this takes great discipline. But even if you spend a year getting the soil right your garden will quickly catch up and overtake any planting done into less well-prepared ground.

The planting plan On the whole we strive for effect rather than horticultural interest. There are few rare or even unusual plants in our garden. If we like a flower we grow lots of it. And, most importantly, we do not persevere with any plant that does not thrive. A healthy flower garden with a limited range of plants will always look more beautiful than

one crammed with "interesting" flowers struggling to survive.

If you have a border or part of the garden where you bung in any old plant that comes your way it is inevitably going to become a mess. By imposing a theme or brief onto an area you are immediately giving it integrity and coherence. Everything is tied together either by colour, shape, season or provenance. It is important to remember that having made your own planting rules, you are free to break or change them. In fact it is probably vital to do so, otherwise you risk disappearing up your own rigidly controlled horticultural nether regions.

The flower gardens This garden has the Jewel Garden where all the planting is supposed to be either in rich, jewel colours (which we have elected to include oranges, magenta and lime green) or the metallic colours of gold, silver, bronze and copper. There is no white, pinks or pastels of any kind. But in the Walled Garden we have only whites, violets, pinks, soft yellows, lavenders, mauves – all the colours that are not "allowed" in the Jewel Garden. The Spring Garden is determined not by colour but by season and habitat, so it only has woodland flowers and bulbs that perform from the New Year until the beginning of June, by which time the deciduous canopy is blocking out most of the light. It also has the added complexity of flooding at least twice a year – although this does mean that the soil is the best and richest in the whole garden. The coppice carries the woodland pattern to an extreme so that only plants that will thrive in uncultivated ground such as primroses and bluebells at the base of the hazels and standard trees are included and their flowering season is very short – but glorious. The Damp Garden is – you've guessed it – wetter than anywhere else on our patch and therefore hosts those plants that thrive best in wet conditions. In fact the Damp Garden is a complicated area to plant successfully because it is exceptionally wet in autumn, winter and spring, and yet the soil is bone dry and this whole section of garden is blazing hot in summer. But then gardens rarely conform neatly to the patterns that we try and impose on to them.

THE FLOWER BORDERS FLOWERS

The spring garden

The Spring Garden is a triangular slither of garden running from directly opposite the back door down to our closest boundary with the water meadow that skirts the garden.

It is the nearest point to the river and the river regularly takes itself up into the Spring Garden, putting most of it under water. This has clearly happened for a very long time because the soil is deeply enriched by black silt brought in by every flood "tide". This flooding also brings in a rich variety of weed seeds every year which relish the rich soil as much as my planting.

This little garden was made almost by accident and certainly by degrees. The west boundary came first when I planted an avenue of limes that I had bought cheaply at a sale. This created the separate area that had originally all been part of the rough field that the "garden" consisted of when we took it over in autumn 1991. It enclosed the large hazel which was one of only two trees in this field (the other was a hawthorn which is now part of the coppice) and I dug a border that surrounded this hazel, edging it with a low woven hazel fence. I filled the border with the plants that I had found in hazel coppice woodland when I was a child – primroses, violets, bluebells, herb Robert, snowdrops and daffodils – and added hellebores that were going very cheaply at, of all places, the local health food shop. The rest of this slither was grass. Along the boundary with the water meadow I planted a screen of willows, holly,

field maple, damson, alder and ash. In 1993 and '94 when I did this they were all tiny seedlings or even unrooted cuttings. As I write, nine years later, they have become tall trees.

The next phase was to enlarge the circular border around the hazel, which everyone agreed was very pretty, especially in spring. It is a rule of garden-making that when you have a good thing you are almost certain to lose something when you try and make more of it. Enlargement means change rather than merely more of the same thing. However, intending to turn the whole area into a bigger version of this round bed, I lifted the turf, dug the ground over and prepared for planting. Despite the alluvial soil, digging proved to be difficult because this area, particularly the top bit nearest the house, had obviously been used as a midden for years, if not centuries – the ground was full of broken crockery, metal tools, terracotta cooking pots, bricks, and other pieces of archaeology. Every time I planted anything I had to remove a bucket of debris.

Before I started planting we needed to make a path. Because the area flooded this had to be soundly made and durable. Grass would be muddy for half the year and dust for the other half. I wanted the narrowest possible path, simply wide enough for one person to walk pushing a wheelbarrow. It started at the

The Spring Garden starts flowering with snowdrops in January *(top left)*. The hellebores (mostly oriental and largely self-seeded) primroses, pulmonarias come into their own from the end of February until mid-April *(bottom)* and then, the later spring plants like tulips, euphorbias, geraniums and the fabulous early roses *(top right)* make the last – and best – spring display.

Crocus tommasinianus (unknown variety) flowering in February *(top)*. The white tulip **'White Triumphator'** is almost ready to open whilst the fritillaries beneath it are in their prime. A good pale *Helleborus orientalis*. **Cowslips** should not be there really (they do best in grassland) but look good. **Solomon's seal** is part of the late spring display.

139

house end and curved round the line of the original border around the nut tree – because I had been too lazy to take out the retaining fence. This curve is vital to the garden and is – I am slightly ashamed to say – practically the only curve in the entire, grid-like garden. I had a pile of concrete blocks that had been saved from a wall that we demolished and decided to recycle these, laying them flat and spaced by the length of a block. Then I asked George, who had helped us in the house and garden for a number of years, to work down to the end, filling in the spaces between the blocks with all the leftovers from our building work. The only proviso was that no two consecutive filled spaces should be the same. Over a period of a couple of months, in between all the other jobs, George made his path entirely from recycled building materials, using floor tiles, bricks, cobbles, paving blocks and whatever else we had. Since then it has always been known as George's path and is an important part of this piece of garden. George

died in 2001, but I always think of him whenever I step into the Spring Garden – which is several times every day.

Planting was easy. This is a tiny deciduous woodland and therefore all the plants have to be able to grow and flower from mid-winter to spring, before the leaf canopy closes over and excludes the vast majority of light. However there is a huge difference in moisture between the section that regularly floods and the slightly higher piece nearer the house that remains dry, which is also in deep shade.

Helleborus orientalis dominates the garden, mainly because I had bought a couple of dozen so cheaply and these had seeded freely. Over the years I have added named varieties from nearby Ballard's nurseries to these, although the darkest colours have been moved to the Jewel Garden. *H. niger* has not been so prolific and is much more sensitive about soil and situation. I also planted quite a few *H. foetidus* which did well for the first couple of years but have since faded badly on me,

The narrow path in the Spring Garden is made entirely from recycled building materials.

As the leaves emerge in April and May *(left)* the level of light falls dramatically in the Spring Garden and many of the earlier spring flowers become dormant. By July it has changed its character completely, becoming straggly and overgrown without a flower to be seen *(below)*. At this point we clear some of the foliage, weed it thoroughly and practically ignore it for a couple of months.

despite their reputation for growing almost anywhere. I have *H. argutifolius*, *H. viridis* and *H. nigercorse* but the *orientalis* hybrids dominate the garden in early spring, along with snowdrops, crocus, pulmonarias, and primroses. By mid- and late spring all this is replaced by euphorbias, Solomon's Seal, tulips, the roses *Rosa cantabridgiensis* and *R. hugonis*, *Clematis alpina*, forget-me-nots, geraniums, fritillaries, aquilegias, and, last but by no means least, the emerging green leaves of the hornbeams and pleached limes.

But these leaves signal the end of the Spring Garden's flowering year. By the second week of June the garden goes into hibernation and we hardly dip into it for days on end. It gets a thorough weeding and then is left to quietly conserve energy after a hard season. It becomes a dark tunnel.

But at the beginning of August it comes back to life. We weed it again and cut back hard, letting in as much light as possible. This is the best time to move any plants and to add new stock. We dig up the inevitable hazel seedlings and pot them up for replanting

elsewhere. I mulch the garden sometime between autumn and the New Year, ideally with leafmould, but mushroom compost or garden compost are also used. It is important to keep the falling autumn leaves clear of the crowns of the plants so that they do not cause rot, but otherwise the Spring Garden needs very little attention before the first snowdrops appear just after Christmas.

141

Bulbs What differentiates a bulb from a perennial plant is that the nourishment for the flower is stored within the bulb itself. This is why a bulb will begin to shoot whilst still unplanted, abandoned in a shed.

Not only the nourishment but all the memory needed to tell the shoot how big to grow and when to flower is stored within that little dry root. There is something miraculous about the way that a little grenade of dried up tissue can explode into a complete flower.

When the flower has finished, the leaves are greedily converting sunlight and water into the nourishment for next year's flower and they – the leaves – feed from the bulb's roots. That is why you must never cut off the leaves from a bulb after it has flowered. Leave them until they die back of their own accord before tidying them up or else you may find that there will not be enough food stored and the plant will be "blind" in a year's time.

It can be hard to find organically grown bulbs but it is worth looking and asking for them to try and create a demand and therefore increase the supply. When buying bulbs from a

retailer, the bigger the bulb – of its type – the better the quality.

The rule of thumb when planting bulbs is to allow at least twice their own depth of soil above them and to put them "pointy" end up. That's it. Everything else is fine-tuning. However, in practise, the ground is often like rock and the dibber won't dib a proper hole. If you have a bulb planter, which removes a plug of soil that you can put back over the planted bulb, life is made easier, but if your soil is heavy it is a good idea to put a handful of grit or sharpsand into each hole first, as few bulbs react well to sitting in the wet.

Planting in grass is slow and rather repetitive. However, it is worth doing, even if on a modest scale amongst a few trees. Most people will be aware that once you plant bulbs in grass you must never cut the grass until the leaves of the bulbs have started to yellow and die down – which for daffodils is going to be June.

Snowdrops can be a bit tricky to establish when planted as a

dry bulb and do much better if planted "green", immediately after flowering. Tulips should be left until November to avoid tulip fire disease, which can reduce an emerging bulb to a mouldy wreck.

Most bulbs come from mountainous, almost alpine conditions. This means that they have a very short growing season between winter and summer – which accounts for the early flowering – get a summer baking, are very well drained, yet get plenty of water from melting snow in spring. Consequentially cold is rarely a problem but dampness can be, except for *Eranthis* (aconites), fritillaries, snowdrops, *Anemone blanda*, the summer snowflake, *Leucojum*, *Narcissus cyclamineus* and *Tulipa sylvestris*, so choose your plants for the conditions. One way of growing bulbs that prefer dry conditions such as crocus, daffodils, tulips and scillas in ground that is fundamentally wet, is to plant them around the roots of a deciduous tree or shrub which will take up most available moisture in the ground. It will also provide the light, spangled shade.

We tend to call anything that is bulbous a "bulb", whereas there are a number of bulbous roots that have different characteristics. A true bulb is only one of a number of different underground storage organs. All these storage organs share the characteristic of making new plants by division, regardless of sexual activity.

Bulbs are made from concentric layers of fleshy leaves with a protective dry outer layer. Daffodils or tulips are typical of this. However some lilies and fritillaries have no protective skin and the scales are separate. Corms are replaced by new corms every year and are made from the swollen base of the stem. Crocuses, gladioli and colchicums are all corms. Tubers are the swollen roots that are used for food storage – unlike most roots which are solely a medium for conveying food to the plant. Tubers are found in some orchids, in dahlias, anemones, corydalis and in cyclamen species. Rhizomes are swollen underground stems, usually horizontal and the best known examples are irises and lily-of-the-valley.

Although there are bulbs for the whole year round, we grow bulbs for three seasons, winter, spring and summer. There are lovely autumn bulbs to be grown but, for no particularly good reason, they are not – yet – in this garden.

Winter bulbs
As we turn into the New Year the first bulbs start to appear. The worst of the weather might still be to come but these delicate flowers are a powerful harbinger of spring.

Winter aconite

Aconites
(*Eranthis hyemalis*) are rhizomatous tubers that spread very fast once they are established but by seed rather than by bulbous increase. They like damp, light shade to do well and the base of deciduous trees is ideal. The flowers only open up in sunshine, which is perhaps why, as they are always associated with sunlight, we always think of them as being a particularly brilliant yellow. The sunshine can be accompanied by frost and icy snow and still the flowers will open.

If you dig up a patch and plant it as a group it will gradually make its own colony. It is important to plant the rhizomes at the right depth, which is generally rather deeper than one might think, with the top of the roots about 7-10cm (3-4in) below the soil. They prefer an alkaline soil, so if you garden on peat you will need to add plenty of mushroom compost and perhaps a little lime to the site in autumn. The seeds ripen around May and can be gathered and cast to widen the spread, but you will need to check the plants fairly often as the seed is shed whilst the capsule is still green. Use the seed immediately as it loses viability from the moment that it is shed. Where there is an already established group, you can increase the spread by simply strimming the plants when you think the seed is beginning to fall, spreading them as you cut.

Galanthus nivalis

All our snowdrops are in the Spring Garden and flower from the beginning of the year until the middle of February. They will spread slowly by seed but every few years I will speed the process along by lifting and replanting each clump. The time to do this is immediately after flowering.

Snowdrops
We have a little vase, which, since I was a small child, has always been used for snowdrops. The first tiny bunch of nodding flowers in this vase on the kitchen table is a wonderful moment. Snowdrops cut well if you pick them carefully enough to get a longish stalk. They also grow well in pots and can be brought indoors whilst they are flowering then stacked away in a damp, shady corner to regroup their energies for the remaining 10 months of the year. But they are essentially an outdoor plant, and like aconites or bluebells, best appreciated en masse.

It is an oft-repeated piece of advice but if you are new to snowdrops, they are best spread "in the green" which means digging a clump up and dividing it thinly either whilst they are still in flower or just after. They can, of course, be planted as bulbs, but they are very small and fiddly and you will have a much better success rate if you establish them as growing plants. They will increase their spread by seed at the rate of 2.5cm (1in) a year if left to it. If you only start with a few, that is going to mean a steady spread measured across generations. It also depends upon a warm February to provide enough insect activity for pollination and different species or varieties must be growing close together to provide cross-pollination. But you can speed up the colonisation by digging up the clumps every three or four years, splitting up the bunch of bulbs and replanting in smaller, more widely dispersed groups. As with aconites, the time to do that is immediately after, or even during, flowering.

Crocus laevigatus

Crocus popping up amongst the hellebores in the Spring Garden, both catching the weak beams of March sunlight.

Crocus

Crocuses are corms which is really just a short stem stuffed like a hamster cheek with sustenance. Inside the corm the flower is fully formed and the food supply is principally used to develop the roots and leaves and is completely consumed by the process of flowering. The new leaves then store next year's food in a new corm that is built up sitting on top of the old one. It dries out over summer and starts developing new roots sometime in autumn – which is why the best time to plant spring bulbs is at the end of summer, to give these new roots maximum time to get established.

Crocus laevigatus is usually the first to appear, pushing up lilac or white flowers in any mild period from Christmas on. This has two great advantages for the ordinary garden; unlike most crocuses it will grow well in dappled shade (in the lee of a deciduous tree or shrub but not under an evergreen hedge) and it also seeds itself everywhere.

Other than their first wispy presence, crocuses seem to arise from the ground all flower. I think that this is what makes them seem an annual miracle as opposed to the seasonal ritual of daffodils or snowdrops. We planted ours in the orchard by lifting turves and placing them like woody marbles on the ground before covering them back over with the turf. The closer you can make their growing conditions to their original habitat, the happier they will be, and crocuses mainly come from Greece and grow in the hot thin soils of that part of the Mediterranean. They belong to the *Iridaceae*, or Iris, family, that includes, as well as irises and crocuses, gladioli, montbretias and freesias. Give them good drainage and plenty of sunshine and they will not worry too much about the quality of the soil.

Early iris

The tiny *Iris reticulata* can come into flower before Christmas and stay strong until March, its colour varying from the icy blue of the cultivar 'Cantab' to the purple-velvet of the species, both with a splash of gold running down the centre of each petal. All have a delicious – if subtle – fragrance.

Iris 'Cantab' will flower a few weeks earlier than other reticulata iris. They come from the mountains of Iran, Iraq and northern Turkey where winters are harsh, and will flower unconcerned with a collar of freezing snow around their amethyst faces. Perhaps more important is the type of summer and terrain that they get there, which is respectively hot and very well drained. Bear that in mind when you plant *Iris reticulata* by giving it rich soil with plenty of grit thrown in and a site where it will get as much summer sun as possible, although by then the flowers will have long gone. Like all bulbs, resist the temptation to tidy the untidy straggle that the rushy leaves become after flowering and let them die down at their own pace. They do not increase very fast, so plant a few bulbs every September.

The other iris that chooses to flower in the cold is the Algerian iris, *Iris unguicularis*. Less intense in colour than *I. reticulata*, it is bigger and more like the conventional image of a summer iris, with faded purple flowers marked with a stripy feather decoration to guide insects into its pollen-filled heart. They like being very dry so are good for the base of a south-facing wall and dislike being moved. Think carefully about where you want them to be and let them get on with it undisturbed.

If you must transplant them, do so in August which is when their new roots begin to develop. As with any iris, dig them up and divide them with a knife to create new groups.

Iris unguicularis 'Mary Barnard'

Although they flower in winter, early irises are dependent upon hot summer sun to develop good flowers the following year, so plant them in full sun and leave them unshaded all year.

Spring bulbs are the most hopeful of all flowers. Once they arrive, regardless of the weather, everything is possible. They celebrate the present whilst holding an optimistic future in their cupped petals.

Daffodils are the archetypal bulb both in public awareness and in botanical classification. A true bulb is a reduced root stem which grows fresh roots each year. Also, each year a new stem is formed in the centre of the bulb, but the bulb itself lasts for year after year. So that bulb will not just contain a flower coiled within its layers but is equipped to do that trick again and again. Amazing!

Daffodils look best when planted with light-fingered abandon. Of course a lot depends on the species or variety that you choose. *Narcissus minor* or *N. bulbocodium* are both short and pretty and look good in short grass (but which is allowed to grow longer before cutting in summer.) These are modest, stubby-stemmed flowers, adapted to coping with bracing winds and this individual diminution contributes a lot to their massed charm.

There are about 50 different species of narcissi and thousands of cultivars with the flowers ranging from the pure white of *Narcissi* 'Portrush' or *N.* 'Tutankhamun', via the lemon of the eponymous *N.* 'Lemon Glow' to a rude orange of which *N.* 'Rockall' is plucked at random from dozens. There are also differences of form, with the conventional trumpet varying from a most un-daffodil-like starburst in *N.* 'Rip van Winkle', to the funnel-shaped flowers of *N. bulbocodium*. Daffodils can have fragrance too. The deep yellow species, *N. jonquilla* is good as is *N.* 'Trevithian' which will bear up to three flowers a stem and naturalises well. *N.* 'Sweetness' makes a good, highly scented

cut flower when, in truth, you are only really likely to appreciate daffodil fragrance. I grow the two types only, *N. cyclamineus* in the long grass of the orchard and a very delicate and pretty cultivar called *N. cyclamineus* 'Tête-à-Tête' which grows beneath the large hazel in the Spring Garden, flowering alongside the hellebores and pulmonaria. It is probably a little too shaded and dry for them there but they seem to be doing fine. In an ideal garden daffodils like well drained soil with plenty of moisture and a position in full sun or light shade.

You rarely contemplate a daffodil in isolation, any more than you do a snowdrop. A group of simple flowers balanced in form and modest of colour and size will always please. Avoid mixing different species and cultivars, especially when planting in grass as you will still struggle to plant in the same way that wild narcissi spread by seed. Keep the groups thickest at the centre, thinning as they spread out. It helps to focus the planting between bushes or trees.

Plant all daffodils extra deep, 22cm (9in) or more, in a border so they do not get disturbed when moving plants around them. Also, avoid planting them too close to large herbaceous plants – daffodil leaves must get plenty of sun before they die back and a voraciously growing herbaceous plant in May and June will shade out all sunlight. Daffodils work well beneath deciduous shrubs; after they have finished flowering the emerging leaves of the shrub will hide the mess of the daffodil leaves without screening all light from them.

Narcissus 'Tête-à-Tête'

Narcissus bulbocodium

Narcissus cyclamineus (opposite)

Tulipa 'Orange Favourite'

Tulips raise the stakes, suddenly

pitching the garden into the exotic from the more homely virtues of primroses and daffodils.

They come from the scorching hillsides of Turkey and Iran where the drainage is brutally sharp and the winters surprisingly harsh and dry. It is astonishing that they grow so well in our sodden climate and doubly so in my own quagmire of a garden. We have a batch of 'Queen of the Night' in our herb beds where the winter wet and odd bouts of frost regularly kill rosemary bushes and reduce the sage to sorry rags, yet the tulips always come back with a cocky vengeance, albeit a little smaller flowered each year. 'Queen of the Night' if you are not familiar with her, has a satiny purple head with plum-shaded depths balanced on a smoky green stem. In our garden she is juxtaposed with forget-me-nots and the new leaves of lovage and fennel coming through in her last week (she lasts for about two good weeks) and the emerging buds of the hornbeam hedge opening daily behind her. What works best is that there is only one variety of tulip in this area. You are as likely to mix tulips up together successfully as you are to get a good drink by sloshing together half a dozen different great wines.

Most tulips look better against the backdrop of spring green, which is handy, given that they emerge just as the new foliage of spring is at its most brilliant. Fill a tulip flower with sunshine (just leaking out from the rim, translucent, glowing) and back it with euphorbia and intensity is taken as far as it can go whilst still hanging on to delight. In our Spring Garden we have 'Spring Green' a viridflora tulip with ivory petals with what the trade describes as "feathered green", which translates as a soft green blaze along the back

of each petal. There are also some *T. sylvestris* – pure, bright yellow with pointy petals, all clean lines and spring simplicity – and 'West Point' another lily-flowered tulip with primrose-yellow pointed petals.

Lining the Lime Walk is 'White Triumphator' which is a lily-flowered tulip, its simplicity enhanced by the massed effect. Like all white flowers, it looks best in some shade. In the Walled Garden there is 'Carnaval de Nice' which is a white with a raspberry ripple splashed on it and 'Negrita' one of the many varieties of triumph tulips, a plum-coloured flower with rather thin leaves.

But it is the Jewel Garden where most of the tulips flourish. There is 'Queen of Sheba', lily-flowered, a burnished red edged with orange. The other side of the main path is 'Abu Hassan', described in the catalogue as "dark mahogany", which it isn't, but it does evoke that verbal struggle for richness. Like all triumph tulips it is thick stemmed and ideal for cutting, although it is hard to take a single one from the garden. It makes sense to have a cutting area just for that purpose and to leave the border tulips well alone.

Then there are the parrots. The oddest thing about tulips is that they are most treasured for their aberrations. So the tulips that really inspired huge prices were the "broken" ones – offspring of monochromatic tulips that had been infected with a virus spread by aphids, causing streaking and stippling of the petals. So if tulips are a glorious celebration of sex (and they are) then the parrots rejoice in decadence. To me, a parrot tulip often looks as though it has just been hit by a bullet, the petals flayed and ripped on the exit but otherwise scarcely touched. We have 'Blue Parrot', which is not blue at all but the colour

Since the early seventeenth century men have lusted after tulips, paying – and losing – fortunes for single bulbs. Among the most prized aspects were the variations and faults that produced special effects and could be bred into a variety. Here we see the following cultivars: *Tulipa* 'Carnaval de Nice' *(top left)*; *Tulipa* 'Orange Favourite' *(top right)*; *Tulipa* 'Negrita' *(bottom left)* and *Tulipa* 'Black Parrot' *(bottom right)*.

The tulip 'Queen of the Night'
growing in our herb garden.
This is one of the richest, darkest
coloured tulips, it flowers quite
late and looks especially good
against the lime-green of new
spring leaves.

of red paint water with a blue brush dipped in,
and 'Black Parrot', which is not black but the
richest, deepest shade of burgundy. Opened
out it is like a frosted port-wine stain on a
window. 'Rococco' is vermilion corrupted by
a puckered scar of greeny blue and 'Orange
Favourite' which has green blotches and a
yellow base. There are more oranges with
'Prinses Irene' and 'Orange Artist' and 'General
de Wet'. 'Orange Artist' is a member of the
viridiflora group and is amongst my favourite
tulips of all, an orange flower streaked lividly
with purplish, greenish grey, on a thick
chocolate stem. 'General de Wet' is a single
early, uncomplicated bloom that opens out
like a huge orange buttercup on a stalk.

The best time to plant tulips is in late

autumn although I have planted some as late
as February and they have grown and
displayed perfectly well. If they are to stay in
the ground, plant them at three times their
own depth – which is surprisingly deep. But if
you intend to lift and store them then they can
be planted quite shallowly so that the roots
can gain the best of the topsoil. The advantage
of shallow planting is that you can plant the
garden more freely throughout the year
without the risk of damaging dormant bulbs.
Dry the bulbs on a rack or net and keep the
large healthy ones for replanting next year.
Any smaller bulbs can be grown separately
in a special bed and in a couple of years they
will be large enough to flower and can be
planted out.

Fritillaries

No snake's head was ever so beautiful as *Fritillaria meleagris*, the common snakeshead fritillary. Although they do have a kind of sinister, reptilian quality, especially before they open out, with their pointed flowerhead hooked over from the straight stem, and evenly spaced leaves which are hardly more than thin green grooves. Look at the chequered petals closely and you will see how they are a perfect combination of blocked precision and smudged expressionism – perfect because it is not predictable or measurable. I like their folk name of Sulky Ladies – it exactly catches their pouty appeal.

As ever, for the gardener there is a lesson to be learnt from observing how something grows best beyond the garden boundary. The fritillary is a bulbous wild flower that thrives in wet meadows that are allowed to grow for hay under the "Lammas" land regime. The hay is cut and harvested between the 1st July and the 12th August (lammas) and the land is grazed until 12th February. This exactly dovetails with the fritillary's growth pattern. The bulb is dormant after June until August, when it grows new shoots that stop just below the surface. These shoots remain dormant in response to cooler night temperatures, then as soon as the weather warms up in spring, they start to grow fast from this poised position so that they can flower and set seed before the grass gets going. Cowslips spread in the wild under an identical regime in dry, limestone meadows. A harvest of Sulky ladies or cowslips for people to walk in and enjoy before the onset of the hay harvest seems to me a better use of land than chemically forced junk-grass respected only as part of the process of making a hamburger.

The only other fritillary that we grow is the Crown imperial, *F. imperialis*. With a tuft of shiny green "punk" leaf seemingly growing out of the middle of the circlet of hanging orange-yellow bell flowers growing on a thick stem 1m (3ft) high, it is as stridently in-your-face as the snakeshead is shyly beautiful. It stinks of tomcat too. In fact the bulbs – great squashed things that they are – smell almost poisonous in an acrid, chemical way. You plant them on their side, the pointed end horizontal to the ground. We have *F. imperialis* 'Rubra' in the Spring Garden where they are rather louche against all the rest of the seasonal subtlety.

The snakeshead fritillary (*Fritillaria meleagris*) above, is a modest but ravishing wild flower of damp meadows whereas the crown imperial (*Fritillaria imperialis*) below, is a giant exhibitionist 1m (3ft) tall.

Summer bulbs

Most summer bulbs originally come from regions that have dry, cold winters for their dormancy and warm dampish summers in which to grow and flower.

The importance of bulbs in summer can be overlooked, but without them most gardens would be impoverished and they are key components of my summer garden. Spring bulbs tend to want hot dry summers and wetter, milder winters, while summer bulbs want cold winters and damp summers, so the two types of bulb are unlikely to grow successfully in the same patch. The most important thing for a summer-flowering bulb is getting the summer growing conditions right – rich, free-draining soil with plenty of moisture. Normally one reckons to plant summer bulbs at the same time as spring bulbs, in early autumn, but certainly flowers like gladioli, dahlias or crocosmia should be left until spring before planting to avoid the risk of exposing them to late frosts.

Alliums,

in their various forms, take a prominent role in the garden in that lovely period when spring slips fully formed into summer, flowering from the end of May until July.

The first out are the tall drumsticks of *A. aflatuense*, which are about 60cm-1m (2-3ft) tall with lilac flowers fringed with a silvery halo. As they emerge, the colour showing through the thin tissue of sheath, they look like flat-topped thistles but they open out to a cylinder. The leaves hang slightly dejected with a kink in the middle. The same is true of the leaves of its offspring, *Allium* 'Purple Sensation'. But the colour of the flowers is a fabulously rich purple tinged with burgundy, the individual florets of each flower forcing out rather than hanging together within an invisible globe. We have them in the Jewel Garden backed by cardoons and they are pitched perfectly against the grey foliage.

Down the far end of the Jewel Garden, we have *A. sphaerocephalon*, which does not flower until midsummer and, although the Latin name translates as "rounded-headed leek" they are not round at all, more bell-shaped or thimble-headed.

Just a few yards round the corner, but miles away in style and form, are clumps of *Allium schubertii* either side of a path. This has a whopping great flower ball and great fat, wavy leaves. It is a dumpy, bull-necked thing but develops the most astonishing flower head in the garden with spikes exploding from its centre.

Allium giganticum has fantastic blooms with a great round ball of flower on a 1.5m (5ft) spike but it is prone to rotting and must have really good drainage – as I have found to my cost, losing over two dozen bulbs through rot. In the Walled Garden *Allium christophii* has huge, loose flower heads that last longer than any other allium. *A. aflatuense* is on the other side of the same bit of garden. The leaves have little hairs along the edge: a curiously delicate feature on such a robustly constructed plant. *A. christophii* is more open than many other alliums, more dandelion-like and tenuous in flower structure, although the purple stems of the florets within the umbel give it an intensity that glows from within the flower.

Allium 'Purple Sensation' in the Jewel Garden (*top*). This has the deepest and richest colour of all alliums and is early, flowering in May. *Allium schubertii (bottom left)* is one of the most spectacular flowerheads in the garden, exploding out from its centre. It will retain this shape after flowering for months. *Allium sphaerocephalon (bottom right)* does not flower until midsummer but makes a marvellous interwoven tapestry of colour as the flowerheads fade from purple to a violet and tawny shade.

155

Iris sibirica

Summer iris

No other flower sucks in light so voluptuously and returns it with such velvet intensity of pigment as an iris. Unlike the Early irises like *I. reticulata* or *I. histroides*, the bearded irises are rhizomes. I wish that we grew more of them although there are a limited number of locations in this garden where they would receive the baking sun and very good drainage that they need.

If an iris is not to be wet, then it must be very dry. Bearded irises (because they have a bit of "bum-fluff" on the down-curving petal or "fall") want to be in full sun, their rhizomes only half-buried so that the top is above the surface of the soil, which must be well-drained.

Beardless irises are smooth of jaw and the rhizomes are planted just below soil level. They include the Pacific Coast and Siberian irises. The Pacific Coast irises like acidic, sandy soil, have evergreen leaves and tend to have subtler colours and gentler form than the bearded ones. They spread more rapidly than bearded irises and form large clumps, but share the same requirement of good drainage above all else. They will tolerate some shade. There are a whole clutch of named varieties of beardless Siberian iris other than the species

Iris sibirica, *I. chrysographes*, *I. clarkei*, and *I. forestii*. It seems to me that the choice is clear: if you have very heavy, poorly drained soil then the beardless Pacific Coast and Siberian irises will give you the best iridescent hit, but if you have reasonably well drained soil and a sunny site then you must choose bearded irises for the full iris experience.

In an ideal world all irises are best planted in September, but in my experience containerised plants can be put in at any time of year and "dry" rhizomes will fare reasonably well if put in the ground in spring. Just because bearded irises like to be well-drained do not omit to water them until established.

Bearded irises are best dug up every three years and divided with a knife to make three or four new clumps. Set these divisions 15-30cm (6-12in) apart. It is best to throw away the oldest part of the rhizome, which will be much less vigorous. The leaves should be cut back to 15cm (6in) (enough to stop them catching the wind and rocking the plant before new roots have a chance to grow and to stabilise them) and the roots trimmed (to encourage strong, dense new growth) before replanting.

Iris **'Gingerbread Man'** is a standard dwarf bearded variety *(opposite top left)*, *Iris* 'Eternal Waltz' *(opposite top right)*, *Iris* 'Kent Pride' *(opposite bottom left)* and tall bearded iris *(opposite bottom right)*.

Lilium regale

Lilies

The lily family includes tulips, erythroniums, fritillaries, kniphofia (red hot pokers) and colchicums (autumn crocus), although it does not include lily-of-the-valley, or day lillies. But genealogical accuracy misses the point. For the true lily experience you need the *Lilium* species and its hybrids alone. This hardly constricts your choice as about 80 species are recognised by botanists, with many hundreds of hybrids.

You would have thought that such an adaptable and widely spread plant would be more or less easy to grow in the garden, but they can be a little tricky. Most of them have an alpine desire for sharp drainage and plenty of water, but they are essentially woodland plants and need semi-shade, ideally with their flowers in full sun and roots in shade, and a "woodland" soil, namely one that is like leaf-mould – rich, well drained yet moist. They are difficult to store because although proper bulbs, they must not dry out. In fact many of

Lilium 'Red Night'

Foxtail lilies

the Oregon cultivars have been bred specifically to be less demanding and so require less pampering.

L. martagon is one of the easier lilies to grow. If it escapes from the garden, it will naturalise, although it is claimed to be a native in a couple of woods in the Wye Valley, which is just down the road from here. *L. martagon* is not the same, of course, as the hybrid Martagon lily which is bred from this dominant parent. It flowers in July, with up to 50 of the "turks cap" flowerheads on each stem, making fanciful turbans ranging from pure white to dark maroon above the stamens, which hang below like the metal claws of an amusement arcade grabber.

L. regale is a more conventional trumpet shape and for the past 90 years it has been the most popular garden lily and the easiest to grow. The scent from the familiar pink-streaked white trumpets is as overwhelming as an aria and as welcome. It likes dryish soil, good drainage and will need support for its stem when it gets top-heavy with flowers.

Madonna lilies, *L. candidum*, are amongst my favourites but to get the most out of the Madonna Lily you must plant it shallowly in well drained soil in a sunny spot and leave it well alone, as it hates being disturbed. Unlike most other lilies it prefers a dry alkaline soil; in the old cottage gardens where it flourished best, people would traditionally plant it in a hole or trench filled with wood ash. Do not plant too many other kinds of lilies near the Madonna lily either, as it can become cross-infected by them. It should be one of the first lilies to flower.

Growing lilies in pots We have grown lilies in pots for years and they do very well in containers as long as you get the compost mix right.

We use sieved leafmould and grit on a 2:1 ratio and this works fine, although I read that the conventional mix is 1 part grit, 1 part coir or leaf mould and 1 part loam. The key thing about lilies in pots is to give them enough room. Don't try and cram half a dozen bulbs into a small container. Give them plenty of space – about three bulbs for a 5 litre or bigger pot – and then they will grow strongly and produce masses of flowers over a longer period. I plant out all of last year's lilies into the garden about a month after they have finished flowering and pot up fresh ones in their place. This way the garden stock gradually increases and the potted lilies retain their vigour.

Crocosmia 'Lucifer' has become a garden cliché and for the very good reason that it is a marvellous plant, robust and easy to grow and adding an intense red to the high summer borders as well as having a delicate structure to each flower. The herringbone seedheads look good too.

Crocosmia is a very important

part of the high summer garden, although its large, strap-like leaves give body and form for weeks before the flowers emerge.

The dominant crocosmia in the Jewel Garden is 'Lucifer'. It is a hybrid from *C. masonorum*, which is a brilliant orange red flower from South Africa, and *C. paniculata*. The leaves of 'Lucifer' appear like blades from the corms and I support them early on so that they do not flop too much over their neighbours. The flowering stems, rising above the leaves to a good metre high, make incredibly fine splays of pleated bud before they open into an upright row of blooms standing on each spray with orange bases and petals of their familiar devilish red. Well, vermilion actually. The plant is as tough as old

boots and will take any amount of cold and wet in winter and need no feeding or watering in summer (although that might be a reflection of my heavy soil). After it has flowered – it has quite a short season – the seedheads are worth their place, starting out as a row of green peas flanking the flowering spine and turning ochre into autumn.

We also grow 'Emily Mackenzie', which has intense orange flowers and rather darker leaves. In fact, as I write, the dozen or so 'Emily Mackenzies' that we have in the garden are small plants, bunched in groups of three. But crocosmias spread and grow very large and it is a good idea to lift a large clump in early spring and tease the corms apart, replanting them in smaller groups. They will respond with increased vigour and flowers.

159

Gladioli mostly come in bright, even garish, colours and very few are remotely subtle. But they have a cheerful brightness that is uplifting in the late summer border and they make excellent cut flowers.

Gladioli became one of the objects of the hybridization obsession that swept through the Victorian era and still feature at every flower show. These are known as florists' gladioli and need quite a lot of tending to get the best out of them. They must be staked individually, dead-headed, weeded, watered and fed if the "tower of flower" is to be at its best. They are also prone to the gladiolus thrip, which is a tiny black insect that feeds off both foliage and flowers, rasping the leaves and leaving the surfaces a glistening pale grey. The leaves then turn brown and dry out. These insects also nibble at the developing flowers so that the buds wither before they open.

Gladioli need a friable, well-dug site, with plenty of well-rotted compost or manure added the previous autumn. They are members of the iris family and grow from corms which should be planted at the same time as you put dahlia tubers out – about the end of April here. These corms should be dug up after flowering, around the beginning of October at the same time that you dig up your dahlias, dried off immediately and stored in a cool, dark dry place ready for planting next spring – although I often miss corms and many reappear quite happily the following year.

Gladioli grown on wet soil or in a very wet summer are prone to bacterial blight. This will appear as brown spots on the leaf, which then dies. The only way to deal with blight is to pull up the plant and get rid of the corm.

Gladioli can be propagated from "cormels", which are baby corms that grow off the parent and which, unlike seed, come true to the variety of the parent. Leave the corm and its cormels to dry out and the following February they can be teased off the corm. Plant all the cormels (they will vary in size but all are viable) 2.5cm (1in) deep and 2.5cm (1in) apart in a seed tray. When shoots develop, either pot them up or plant in a cold frame. Leave them for a couple of years until they flower, then lift and treat as other corms.

Dahlias bring carnival to the garden and happily sidestep good taste, which is, after all, only ever a stumble away from dullness.

There are few other flowers whose petals cram so much colour into themselves, soaking up hue like a floral sponge. You will not get blue dahlias but they come in reds, purples, mauves, pinks, yellows, magenta, orange, apricot and white. Put a border of dahlias together without giving much consideration to their colour combinations and you have a display of Ascot hats walking through the make-up section of a cheap department store, cackling with laughter as they pass.

The fact that a lot of the colours that they come in are garish and bright does not stop the gardener picking and choosing those that fit into their own colour scheme. As I am a latecomer to dahlias, we only have 'Bishop of Llandaff' and 'Arabian Night' in our garden – both intense crimson, although 'Arabian Night' is much darker and does not have the Bishop's yellow anthers at its centre. But gradually we will grow more.

One of the great advantages of 'Bishop of Llandaff' is its foliage, which is a chocolate shade of purple and finely cut, unlike most dahlia foliage which can be rather overwhelming, in a drab kind of way, unless absorbed into the surrounding flowers. Both these dahlias fade in the sun and we deadhead ours as they begin to fade, which is a bit of a fiddle but keeps the tones very deep and rich. I should acknowledge that 'Bishop of Llandaff' has been hijacked by gardening snobs who would not be seen dead with a decent array of gaudy flowers in their refined gardens. But it is a good plant for all that.

I lift all my dahlia tubers at the beginning of November or after the first hard frost, whichever comes first. On top of the climatic problems, slugs love eating the tubers, but if your garden is reasonably slug-free, is in the sheltered south and has free-draining soil, I think that planting deep and mulching them very well over winter with straw or bracken, should be protection enough.

If you do decide to bring them in, cut them down to within 15cm (6in) of the ground after the first frost blackens them, (not before because the plant will go on making new tubers right up until the first frost) and dig up the tubers carefully, shaking off any excess soil that sticks to them. Put them upside down in a seed tray or cardboard box for a week so that any water can drain out of the hollow stems. When the stems are drained, turn the tubers the right way up and stack them together in a box, with the tubers covered by old potting compost, coir or vermiculite – keeping the crowns uncovered. They must be dry but not left to dry out completely, so check them once a month or so and water them lightly if they are getting too dry. Store the tubers in a dark, dry, frost, and rodent-free place.

One of the advantages of bringing dahlia tubers in over winter is that you can pot them up in early spring – about mid-February – and force them with a little heat and protection. I put mine on a heated propagating mat in the greenhouse, but a windowsill above a radiator would do the trick. The new shoots that grow make very good cuttings, rooting very quickly if cut off at the junction with the tuber when about 7cm (3in) long, and enable you to build up plenty of strong plants that can be grown on over the summer to be planted out in July to fill a gap. The parent plants can be put outside in mid-May, when the risk of frost is past. If you are not going to take cuttings, plant the overwintered tubers out about 15cm (6in) deep in early April in good rich soil in full sunlight. The new shoots appear above ground about a month later.

The biggest pest that preys on dahlias is the earwig, which regards the flower as a great delicacy. This can be quite a problem if you must have perfect specimen plants, but if you deadhead often enough there is such a good supply of new flowers that the earwigs are effectively outnumbered.

It is a good idea to deadhead all dahlias as often as possible because they will then grow new buds without cease right up until they are hit by frost, giving you a flowering season from July until November.

The Long Garden
This is really a long path running parallel to the Lime Walk, dividing the Jewel Garden from the vegetable garden.

Like the Lime Walk, the Long Garden is flanked by pleached limes, although these were planted a few years later and as much smaller trees so they do not have anything like full maturity yet. The path is much narrower than the one in the Lime Walk and consequently the borders are wider. This changes the whole balance of it.

For some years we grew cardoons and artichokes along here with great success. There was a dramatic transformation through spring into summer as the plants – especially the cardoons – went from pale wisps of grey leaf to whopping great giants topped with dramatic thistles. We underplanted these with fabulous *Allium giganteum* that flowered before the cardoons really got into their growing stride so were able to coexist well with them.

But although they looked marvellous, there were problems. The first was that the allium bulbs hated sitting in winter cold and wet and rotted. At a cost of over £5 per bulb this was unsustainable. As the wet weather can continue from October right through until April the obvious solution of lifting the alliums after flowering and replanting, was potentially tricky. Also as the limes matured they excluded more light and the cardoons began to grow etiolated and leaning inwards towards the light in the middle of the path.

So we cleared the whole length of the Long Garden, took the opportunity to weed, dig and manure it properly, adding plenty of sharpsand in the lower, wetter, end and planted this garden with one single wallflower 'Blood Red', grown from seed. This worked very well in spring. We then followed this with 32 tripods of sweet peas, underplanted with squashes.

The scheme has been only a partial success. The concept is great – a deliciously scented walk with height and colour. But – and it is funny how there is always a "but" – the execution has not quite worked out as well as it could.

There are a bundle of reasons, good and bad, for this. For a start, although we chose the varieties for their scent as well as colour, not all the sweet peas are equally scented. So instead of wafting down a path swoony with sweet pea fragrance you dip in and out of it, rather like losing a radio signal. But the biggest problem with our mixed bag of sweet peas is what is happening – or not happening – beneath them. Sweet peas are best growing up or through a support that masks their rather threadbare bases. A really vigorous plant smothered in flower can have a bottom 60-90cm (2-3ft) that looks as though it is about to wither away completely. In the Jewel Garden and Walled Garden (where the sweet peas are all white) this is not a problem at all. They haul up through all kinds of other plants. But in this garden, after the wallflowers were cleared the sweet peas went into completely bare ground. I had hoped that the squashes would quickly provide a lower storey of interest. But because it was cold and miserable in June and early July the squashes and pumpkins grew very slowly. About a third got eaten by slugs in this semi-paralysed state. Eventually some grew as I had intended them to but not until the sweet peas were way past

If you pick sweet pea flowers regularly they will not set seed and keep flowering continuously right into autumn. We have found that cutting all the flowers every 9–10 days produces the best display.

We raise our sweet peas in pots *(opposite top left)*, sowing three seeds to a pot early in the year and weeding out the weakest. We then plant them out in May. We always use wigwams made from hazel sticks to support the sweet peas *(opposite top right)*, planting the contents of a pot at the base of each hazel stick. They are self-supporting to a degree but need tying in every few weeks for the first couple of months. Looking back up the Long Garden in August *(opposite bottom)*.

their best. It highlights one of the great truths of gardening – it matters not so much what you do, or even how you do it, as when you do it.

The truth is that this piece of garden is evolving. It will go on changing until it feels right for a while and then probably change again. I do not mind that at all. The whole point of have a healthy organic garden is to react and adapt to events rather than to try and impose yourself onto nature – and that applies to design as well as cultivation techniques.

The plan for the next year is to change our approach completely. I have begun to edge the path with box and will encourage a 60-90cm (2-3ft) high box hedge all the way down. This will, of course, reduce the available light. But this will not matter because inside this hedge we will train clipped box, holly and yew all the way down, ultimately looking to create a flowing, structural, abstract avenue of permanent green that is impervious to the attacks of slugs and snails, the vagaries of the weather or the shading of the light.

The clipping will require some work but I enjoy this. Amongst this all-season planting we can add tulips that will create the same dramatic monochromatic effect as the wallflowers without anything like the work involved. Wallflowers are wonderful but they are biennials so the seed must be sown in early summer, the best 800 plants pricked out, grown on and then planted out in midsummer to mature – which requires a lot of free space – before transplanting in October. This operation has to be repeated each year for a month's fantastic display. The tulips merely need planting once and adding to each year to maintain the vigour and size of the flowers.

The Long Garden (*opposite top*) at the end of April when the wallflowers were at their best. This kind of monochromatic planting (the wallflower is *Cheiranthus* 'Blood red') looks fantastic for a few triumphant weeks but does involve a lot of work to attain that brief glory. Once they are past their best (*opposite bottom*) – the end of May – they must all be pulled up and taken to the shredder (they have very tough stems). The Long Garden (*below*) photographed the previous year when it was still used for cardoons and artichokes.

The jewel garden

The Jewel Garden

I try and keep my gardening simple on the basis that it is better to do a simple thing well rather than a complex thing badly; but one bit of our garden is openly ambitious.

This is the Jewel Garden. It started out as a slight idea to provide a colour scheme for some new borders we were making and then turned into a good wheeze for a whole area of the garden. For ten years Sarah and I worked as costume jewellers and we wanted to make an area of planting that both reflected this experience and used jewel colours as the theme. In itself this was a modest plan but it has turned out to be the heart of this garden, both geographically and metaphorically. It is certainly as much Sarah's garden as mine and represents thousands of hours of work that we have both spent in making and tending it.

You arrive in the Jewel Garden either by crossing the vegetable garden and the Long Garden or by going down to the end of the Lime Walk and turning left up the grass path flanked by high hornbeam hedges that opens out into the lower end of the Jewel Garden. Now there are eight large borders that should merge into one vast, monstrous flower bed, but it started out smaller, with four quite distinct pairs of borders, bounded by 1.8m (6ft) hornbeam hedges, with each pair planted to fulfill the restrictions of the four palettes of costume jewellery: crystal (white and silver); brights (oranges, magenta, and lime green); pastels (mauve, pink, pale blue) and jewel (ruby, emerald, and sapphire).

In May the laburnum drips gold flowers over the plum and purple globes of *Allium* 'Purple Sensation'. By midsummer *(top right)* the self-sown hardy annuals dominate the garden, with purple orache, marigold and poppies particularly dominant. By late summer *(bottom)* colours are richer and heavier with *Verbena bonariensis*, fennel and the *Dahlia* 'Bishop of Llandaff' prominent.

We planted the garden in spring and summer of 1997. The idea remained good, but it somehow didn't work. For a start, any careful colour scheme is very difficult. Added to this intrinsic trickiness was the plant material we already had which we were loath to chuck out, and what we could afford to buy to add to it was limited. In the end our four pairs of borders almost worked within themselves – certainly worth perservering with – but the whole scheme didn't hang together. So we had a rethink.

The four hedges that divided the four areas came out (which was a major performance; each two-year-old hornbeam already had a very deep root system and took a big excavation to extract. But they have all survived transplantation, which proves that most things can be moved if you take enough of the roots with you.) and the whole area was subdivided into 16 square beds with two crossing central paths and much smaller cruciform access paths. The plan was to make it seem like four huge borders when in mid-summer full sail. We replanted using yellow and gold flowers and foliage to represent gold, and included trees such as robinia and laburnum, as well as achillea, potentillas and thalictrums. Silver was represented by the glaucal foliage of weeping pears, cardoons,

Marigolds and orache *(top)* are allowed to seed themselves freely across the garden although need rigorous thinning. **Echinacea** is grown for its rusty golden seed heads rather than the mauve flowers that we pick off. **Heleniums** have exactly the jewel-like richness of colour of petal and central boss we want. The bright gaudiness of a **Pacific hybrid lily**.

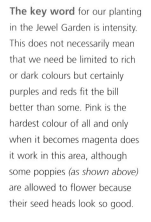

The key word for our planting in the Jewel Garden is intensity. This does not necessarily mean that we need be limited to rich or dark colours but certainly purples and reds fit the bill better than some. Pink is the hardest colour of all and only when it becomes magenta does it work in this area, although some poppies *(as shown above)* are allowed to flower because their seed heads look so good.

macleaya, melianthus, *Stachys byzantina* and grasses such as *Festuca glauca* and *Helictotrichon sempervirens*.

The rich "jewel" colours worked best, with *Penstemon* 'Garnet', *Angelica gigas, Dianthus barbatus*, oriental poppies, the fantastic rich plum colour of opium poppies, salvias (especially *Salvia guaranitica*), *Knautia macedonica*, Chocolate cosmos (*C. atrosanguineus*), alliums, violas, crocosmia, and clematis on tripods such as C. *viticella* 'Purpurea Plena Elegans', *Clematis* 'Jackmanii', *C.* 'Perle d'Azur', and *C.* 'Etoile Violette'. We happened to have lots of *Geum* 'Mrs

Bradshaw', which is a true vermilion and worked superbly in this context. But the major star of this group turned out to be a weed – purple orache, which had seeded itself from the vegetable garden. This type of spinach is a fantastic foil and progresses from a low covering with velvet rich leaves to a tall, seeded filler that anything and everything looks good against. Another indispensable foil that self-seeds everywhere is *Verbena bonariensis*, which provides a backing purple from August through to November (although it can be reduced drastically if you weed over-enthusiastically in spring).

We did all this on the basis that it was year one and we could tinker as we saw how it panned out. It felt a bit like playing 3-D chess and there were days when it looked frankly boring. But there were some sublime moments, usually at sunset when the structure was backlit and the rich oranges, burgundies and purples shone out of the falling light. Then the colours glittered and pulsed and we would feel that excited skip of the heart that accompanies the sense of making something better than you knew you were capable of.

We then extended the space, adding almost half as much again so that it now runs across the whole width of the garden butting up to the water meadows, resulting in a total area of some 800 sq m (8,000 sq ft). With this extra space we also simplified the planting.

The "crystal" planting idea was the first to go. This meant taking out all the white flowers. Then the pastels went. The "jewel" colours and the "brights" remained but were mixed. More bronze, copper and metallic colours were introduced. Now, the only pale colours come from foliage and work mainly as a foil for the richness and intensity of the floral colours. If it is Jewel Garden by name then so must it be properly jewel-like in nature.

That left quite a big hole and posed some tricky questions, such as when is pink not pink? This is where magenta steps in. I love it and the most successful part of the Jewel Garden Mark 1 was the gaudy bit ("brights") with the orange ligularias, tithonias and leonotis, magenta *Lychinis coronaria* and, most strikingly, the almost-red magenta of the rose *Rosa* 'Scharlaglutt' that dominates the whole garden for a couple of weeks at the beginning of June.

We planted more clematis and put up

tripods for sweet peas looking again for structure and height as well as colour. Ideally you should feel as though you are inside the jewel, submerged by intense colour rather than looking on with polite botanical curiosity.

At one end there is a distinctly bronzy tone, with the brown grasses such as the *Carex comans*, *C. flagellifera* and *C. kaloides* mingling with the apricot foxglove, *Digitalis ferruginea*, the poppy, 'Patty's Plum' and the

Poppy our Jack Russell terrier looks down one of the narrow cross-paths that give access to each of the four little sitting areas. This is mid-June.

171

rusty brown heleniums like 'Moerheim Beauty' and the annual sunflowers shot with velvet brown like 'Velvet Queen' as well as bronze fennel and the iris 'Wild Ginger'. We don't grow enough irises yet, and will add their unique intensity of colour to give us the blues, purples and maroons we need.

Blue, as ever is the most precious colour. I have mentioned *Salvia guaranitica*, and we also have *S. patens*, anchusas, cornflowers, delphiniums, nigella, *Aconitum* 'Newry Blue' and *Cerinthe major* 'Purpurascens'.

The borders have been increased in size, swallowing up some of the original paths, although little sitting areas have been made as a focus for the surrounding planting. We have

started planting lots of tulips with that number to be increased over the next year or two.

The beds have all been edged with box hedging with the intention of achieving a jack-in-the-box effect, of colour and vitality spilling out over the framing green edges of each border. The outside of the Jewel Garden is bounded by hornbeam hedges that are clipped once a year and provide essential protection from the wind. On the east side the pleached limes from the Long Garden give even more protection and on the west the coppice shelters it from the prevailing west winds.

To maintain this vigour we mulch very heavily each spring with our own compost,

There comes a point when chickens can be too free-range as they scratch up all the mulch looking for grubs, and nibble at juicy young growth. This lot *(below)* know they are about to be shooed back to the orchard. The bronze fennel on the right adds a wonderful shimmering texture to the border.

mushroom compost, and cocoa shells but feed nothing. All the goodness is a measure of the soil rather than added nourishment.

We have learnt that everything must be planted in large blocks, sometimes with as many as seven plants in a group to get the intensity of effect. In amongst these polished facets of colour one can dot magentas, oranges and lime greens that have the power to survive dissipation without being diminished. The other thing that it is essential to grasp, and this applies to any kind of planting, is that floral colour is only as effective as the foliage that backs the flowers.

So we are trying to use the full range of leaves from the jet straps of *Ophiopogon nigrescens* through all the hundred greens, the bronze and straw-coloured grasses, to the purple and ruby leaves of purple hazel and orache.

The Jewel Garden will never be finished. It has very good moments – even whole days – but leave it untended for a few days and it shows signs of wear and tear. It is fantastically labour intensive and ambitious and can – and often does – look both dull and chaotic. But for Sarah and myself, it is our yardstick. If the Jewel Garden is doing well, then so are we.

Red in its various manifestations across the seasons. *Crocosmia* 'Lucifer' *(main picture).* Small pictures *(clockwise from top right):* the rich crimson veining of ruby chard, a self-sown opium poppy, *Lychnis coronaria, Tulipa* 'Orange Favourite', *Dahlia* 'Bishop of Llandaff', as the golden stamens start to appear, the flowering bracts of *Euphorbia griffithii* 'Fireglow' and the magenta *Geranium* 'Ann Folkard' next to *Dahlia* 'Bishop of Llandaff', when the latter is at its most intense red that only lasts a day.

173

Maintaining the Jewel Garden

In many ways the Jewel Garden is very old-fashioned because it only looks good if it receives a lot of care. Some of this work consists of the big annual tasks, like the mulching in spring, which takes a good week, and in autumn, after the first hard frost, we also have a few days of intensive clearing, cutting back all dead or dying foliage and pulling up any of the remaining annuals.

But it is not these big hits that take the time. It is the daily thinning, staking, tying, and deadheading that really make a difference to the garden. Part of the reason for this is the fertility of our soil. Everything grows with such lushness and abundance that it is more affected by wind and more likely to topple than the same plant on poorer soil. Also the demands of a garden that sets out to be jewel-like are that any dead flowerheads or dying foliage immediately stand out, whereas under a more relaxed regime they would simply merge in – as they do in our Walled Garden.

The major lesson that we have learnt over the years is to be ruthless with thinning and cutting back. This is particularly applicable in midsummer, as the initial flush of spring perennials and early annuals is dying back. We throw away barrowloads of perfectly good annuals and cut back load after load of spring perennials in order that we might give the tender annuals and the later herbaceous plants some light and nutrition to get established.

Everything grows extremely vigorously on our rich soil and we have to be ruthless about thinning and cutting back if the early season vegetation is not to swamp the flowers that appear in midsummer *(top left and bottom right)*. Although we weed out most of the purple orache *(top right)* we still keep a great deal and allow it to mature to its full 3m (10ft) height. Each plant will need staking if it is not to tumble over onto its neighbours. The smaller varieties of sunflower can be supported by a strong cane, but the larger ones like 'Californian' *(bottom left)* have stems that are as thick as my forearm and have to be supported by hardwood staves driven into the ground with a sledgehammer.

Clearing the flower borders

Oriental poppies should be cut back hard immediately after flowering. This does two things. The first is to stop the leaves forming a carapace that can overwhelm and rot the plant and anything growing in its vicinity, and the second is to get light and air to the plant. It will respond by growing fresh leaves and should flower again in late summer, albeit more modestly this second time round.

There is usually an uncomfortably bare week or so around the end of June but this is quickly filled with new growth. We are also constantly checking supports and staking of plants as they grow, not to repair the damage of wind and rain but, wherever possible, to prevent it from happening. We use hundreds of wire supports for this as well as a few canes for taller plants like sunflowers.

Annuals and biennials

For quick results, no flowers do more in less time than fast-growing annuals; but there is no such quick-fix to be had from biennials.

An annual is any plant that germinates, grows, flowers and sets seed in the same growing season – usually between March and October in this country, although some annuals, like field poppies and corn marigolds, can string together a complete lifecycle in around three months. In the wild most annuals grow in cornfields or on dry open slopes. They are rarely found in tightly packed places, interspersed with shrubs, or in damp conditions – both of which are closer to the average back garden than a cornfield.

Modern cultivars tend to be lower, stockier and brighter or more garish than their wild relatives because the flowers are tested in open fields where taller plants would blow over and more subtle colours become lost. However the plants have a very different effect when brought into the restricted, sheltered environment of a back garden.

Hardy annuals withstand frost but need light to grow and flower. They are best sown or planted in March or April and will flower until they have set their seed. Deadheading flowers as they fade will encourage them to flower longer. Opium poppies, nigellas, cornflowers, and corncockles are all hardy annuals.

Half-hardy annuals are frost-tender and should only be planted or sown after the middle of May. The first frosts of autumn will kill them. Cosmos, bells-of-Ireland, zinnias, nicotianas, sunflowers, busy lizzies and snapdragons are all half-hardy annuals.

Half-hardy annuals need a temperature of at least 10°C (50°F) to germinate. They must be hardened off, which means transferring them to a closed cold frame or very sheltered corner at least three weeks before planting out. We rely on half-hardy annuals to spread our flowering season and to add colour to complement permanent planting. We

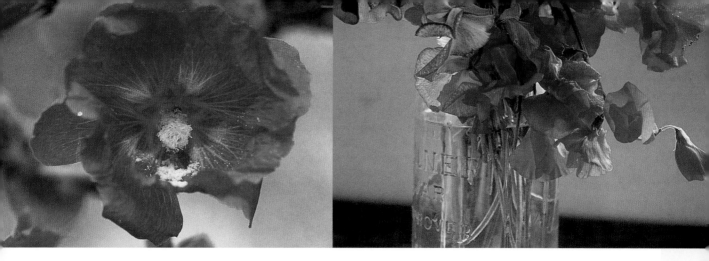

regularly grow, tithonias, leonotis, sweet peas, cosmos, zinnias, nicotiana, verbena, salvias, nasturtiums, sunflowers, helianthus, rudbeckia, snapdragons, and cerinthe and all add vitally to the depth and range of the flowering palette.

Biennials lie in the uncertain ground between annuals and perennials although you will often find them lumped in with annuals as though the difference was a technical nicety, which makes it all the more confusing. To reiterate the difference: annuals germinate, grow, flower, set seed and die all within one growing season, which for hardy annuals is March through to the first hard frosts and half-hardy ones within the frost bracket, which is mid-May to mid-October, where I live. Biennials have the following timetable: you sow them in May/June, plant them in October and they flower the following spring. Biennials, by definition, establish themselves as a plant in their first growing season and flower in the second, producing seed which will start the cycle again. The main thing to take on board is that they will give no kind of display in the summer of their sowing. There is no quick-fix to be had from them. They must be allowed to pass

through the looking-glass of winter and come out the other side before they can justify their existence. But they are all tough (they have to be), easy to grow and growing them is an investment in next year's garden and an act of faith for your own future.

Some biennials set seed so prolifically that once you have them in your garden all you need to do is dig up the young plants and move them to where you want them. Forget-me-nots are an irrepressible promiscuous blue froth every April and May and teazels and the vast silvery thistle, *Onopordum*, spread themselves all over my garden. These latter two plants can be a bit overwhelming if you let all the seedlings mature. Although their readiness to seed removes the job of sowing a new crop ahead of time, you will need to move the self-sown seedlings in autumn. If you leave it until spring they will have developed a tap root and will not move easily.

A less dominant but an even more lovely biennial is the foxglove. I like best the white foxglove, *Digitalis purpurea albiflora*, and no plant looks better under the shade of a deciduous tree. But the seed does not always come true.

Growing annuals and biennials I grow all our annuals in plugs indoors because they are less prone to slug attack that way. It means more handling but guarantees more plants.

I also find that if you have a fairly mature border, annuals grown in pots or plugs can be planted more carefully than any amount of direct seed sowing.

The whole essence of good organic gardening is to raise the healthiest plants possible and to grow them in the healthiest soil you can nurture, and this especially applies to annuals of any kind whether edible or flowering.

It is essential that you get the timing right when growing annuals in containers for planting out. Because their life-cycle is so short, the delay of a couple of weeks can irreparably limit their growth and flowering. I speak from bitter and repeated experience. As a rule it is best to prick them out, pot them on and plant them out as soon as possible, provided that they have a decent root system

at every stage and that they are properly hardened off (*see below*) for at least two weeks before putting out into the border. However rich the potting compost (and it should not be too rich) and however carefully they are watered and tended, miss planting them out by more than 10 days and they will never realise their potential.

How do you know when this is? First by gently easing the plants from their pots. If the root structure holds the soil yet is not pot-bound then it is ready to go out. Second, by checking that it has vigorous, healthy-looking leaves. If it has started to produce flowers or is looking stunted or etiolated then it is a sure sign that it should have been planted out already.

The corollary to this is not to be too eager to sow your seeds. It is no use having a mass of annuals waiting to go outside if the weather

Hardening off

Any plants raised indoors must be hardened off before planting out. I do this in two phases. The first is to transfer them from the propagating benches of the greenhouse to a cold frame, which can be completely protective or opened wide according to the weather. The final phase is to stand the plants outside in their pots for at least a week before planting out. Here we have sunflowers *(near right)* and cosmos *(far right)*, both ready to leave the frames.

and soil is too cold. Annuals will always do better if sown too late than too early.

I raise my annuals under cover because our soil is cold and wet and I have the cover to raise them under, but sowing direct is not a bad thing, especially if you live in a mild area or if your garden is reasonably sheltered and dry. For the new garden or gardener nothing is more satisfying than a few packets of seeds sown into soil that has been dug and raked to a fine tilth. The best way is to sow in zigzags, crosses, circles or lines to differentiate the growing seedlings from the weeds that cultivation will inevitably produce. Annuals grow best in a rich soil but do not feed the soil with extra manure as that will only produce lots of green growth without any extra flowers.

The only hard bit is to sow much more thinly than seems sensible and then be ruthless enough to further thin the seedlings so that each plant has room to enrich itself – as much as 15cm (6in) for most plants. This is another good reason to grow annuals indoors if possible, especially if the seeds are difficult to come by or hard to germinate. But poppies, nigella, cornflowers, helianthus, eschscholzia, phacelia, nasturtiums, calendula or zinnias – amongst others, will all do well sown directly where they are to flower. In an age of instant garden gratification and magic transformation no flowers do more in less time than annuals.

But as well as the annuals that we carefully raise and plant for artfully considered effect, there are also annuals that fill the garden uninvited. All were planted originally, but once here they decided to stay for good. Quite a few annuals have the ability to take up residence against all the odds, the seeds lying dormant in the soil for at least a winter,

untouched by cultivation or weather before germinating in spring.

It is a simple enough miracle, as they go. The ground is bare, looks dull in a pleasant enough, earthy kind of way, and then pow! it is covered in a rash of seedlings that become plants. It never fails to amaze me.

There are three main culprits that we allow to self-seed indiscriminately, purple orache (*Atriplex hortensis*) in the Jewel Garden, poppies (mainly the opium poppy) and marigolds. If we let them, nasturtiums would join the list as well, but whereas the other three grow reasonably upright and therefore do not take too much light or air, nasturtiums can be ruinous in a border, especially if the

Opium poppies and marigolds in the Jewel Garden. Both of these are hardy and although the poppies finish flowering long before the weather turns cold, the marigolds will carry on right into winter. Although we originally sowed both directly into the soil, they now are completely self-sown and come back year after year.

All the pictures were taken in the vegetable garden where I allow nasturtiums *(top left)* opium poppies *(top right)* marigolds *(bottom right)* and purple orache *(bottom left)* to flower as long as they are not directly getting in the way of the vegetables. This is because monoculture of any kind is asking for trouble. I am certain that the more varied and integrated the planting of the garden, the fewer pests and diseases will occur.

Self-sown nasturtiums and poppies weave in amongst the foliage of the Jewel Garden. The delphinium at the back is 'Black Knight' and the magenta flowers in the foreground are the geranium 'Ann Folkhard'. Whilst we encourage these self-sown annuals we also weed them out ruthlessly where necessary. This is especially true of the nasturtiums that tend to smother everything in their path.

soil is rich, falling, trailing and smothering everything else around them, where the slugs and snails love life in the permanent dark damp beneath nasturtium foliage. They are best grown in poor soil where the foliage has to struggle for existence but the flowers are produced as well as ever.

Purple (or sometimes red) orache is by far and away the most promiscuous and virile of our resident guests, the large flat seeds covering the ground like confetti in late summer and early autumn. It is in fact not an ornamental plant at all but a vegetable, best when the young leaves are eaten raw, although it cooks just like spinach. We weed out at least 90 per cent of the resulting seedlings and keep removing plants all through the summer, but are still left with too many. If you let it seed you are likely to have

it with you forever, but that is no hardship, and the seeds fall very locally and are not spread far by the wind, so colonise rather than invade. They overwinter in the soil and will grow up through any thickness of mulch that I have ever put down, appearing as a welcome burgundy rash in April. The velvety leaves, starting plum-coloured and darkening to purple as light and age dulls them, are the perfect foil to the green overkill of May and June. Then by midsummer they are becoming the giants that they want to be and they add not just a foil but structure to the border. By late summer the seedheads are a tan colour, perfectly in tune with the faded tapestry of the season. By the time that we pull up the plants at the end of October the stems that started out as softly edible are like hawsers and have to be shredded.

Gathering organic flower seed

Collecting the seeds of purple orache. We try to keep as much of our own seed as possible, storing it in brown paper envelopes in the fridge, and for plants like opium poppies that hybridize very freely, it is the best way of selecting colours and

forms that you particularly like. It is hard to find a good supply of organic flower seed and when I have to buy non-organic seed I always check to see that it has not been treated with chemicals after harvest to prevent disease or fungus.

Next in startling ubiquity are the opium poppies (*Papaver somniferum*). You can get them in a huge range of colours, from the deepest, darkest of purples (sold as black) as glossy as the skin of an aubergine, to pure white, although bypassing every hint of blue on the way. They are fresh and gay, in exactly the way that a summer frock is. Before they open fully the flowers sit on their stems in a cut-edged semi-circle, looking like a cross between a cocked hat and an ice-cream wafer, as translucent in the evening sun as a butterfly wing. Then the peony-flowered ones, a great mass of ripped petals, are balls of shredded silk. I let these grow in the vegetable garden, only uprooting those that actually interrupt the lines of vegetables, as they add jollity and also attract hoverflies and aphid-eating wasps.

If you want to keep seed of the best poppy colours, pull up the whole plant as soon as the petals begin to drop, root and all, and hang it upside down with the seedheads in a plastic bag. As long as the roots are attached they will ripen like this and all the seeds will fall into the bag. As soon as the seedheads are empty put the seeds into a brown paper envelope and label them. Store them cool (we keep ours in the fridge). You can sow poppies in autumn or spring, the autumn-sown ones flowering some weeks earlier. Always sow annual poppies in situ as they hate being moved except when tiny. Either scatter them and let them grow where they land or sow them thinly in zigzags. If you choose the latter method it is more wasteful of seed as you will have to spend time thinning the seedlings as they appear.

Our marigolds are English or pot marigolds, (*Calendula officinalis*), and although they started life as named varieties, I can't identify them as such now. Their pale green foliage grows inch for inch with the much bluer green of the poppies, the burgundy of the orache making a spring premonition that is balanced between the three, but then the marigolds get swamped and can only perform on the fringes, leaning into gaps and pathways, the flowers peaking out a foot or more below the poppies, chasing every variant of orange and yellow. Like nasturtiums they can smother and harm more valuable, permanent planting, but judicious thinning will control that easily enough. They last much longer than the poppies, and if you deadhead, will go on into late summer, looking great against the strong reds of dahlia, crocosmia and helianthus.

'Ladybird' *(top left)* an annual poppy with black markings on the centre of each petal. 'Patty's Plum' *(top right)* an oriental poppy. This is a perennial and not an annual. Two variations on opium poppies *(middle row)* that have hybridised and self-seeded. Opium poppies *(bottom)* in the vegetable garden where they attract hoverflies that in turn eat aphids. The fabulous shredded petals of peony-flowered poppies *(large picture)*.

Choosing annuals and biennials

Although these include some of the easiest and cheapest flowers to grow in the garden, choose them with care so that they will flourish.

As ever, this means not fighting the conditions or soil and choosing annuals and biennials that are adapted to thrive in the situation that you place them. This will result in better flowers and a much healthier garden. Whatever the details of soil and aspect, it is worth preparing the ground as well as possible so that the plant roots can grow fast and gain all the nutrients possible. But do not over fertilise the

soil as you will end up with very vigorous plants with lots of leaves – but few flowers.

It is also important to select the right places for the annuals that you do grow so that they integrate with your more permanent planting and with each other. In other words it is better to put very tall plants at the back or middle of borders and make sure that those that must have sunlight are not shaded by surrounding plants.

Calendula officinalis

Forget-me-not

ANNUALS FOR DAMP SOIL

Mimulus sp

Poached egg plant
    (Limnanthes douglasii)

Purple orache *(Atriplex
    hortensis)*

Pot marigold *(Calendula
    officinalis)*

Teasel *(Dipsacus* sp)

Annuals and biennials for damp soil

Most annuals do not grow well in wet sites and many thrive in what amounts to drought – as long as the soil is in good heart. But there are some that will make the best of the damp. Poached egg plants, (*Limnanthes douglasii*), which will grow anywhere, wet or dry, can be broadcast on almost any soil surface, *Mimulus* grows best in wet, and pot marigolds like moist soil. Sweet peas are a must for really rich, damp soil and sunflowers do surprisingly well in the wet. I tend to associate them with sun and heat and therefore dryness but this is not so. Do remember to stake them much more securely than you possibly imagine being necessary, otherwise by late summer they blow all over the place. Evening primrose is not conventionally a moisture lover but it grows freely in the wettest parts of our garden. It is not very fashionable to like it but I am very fond of it and love the way it seeds itself so promiscuously. Finally, another biennial that spreads itself all over our garden, making the most of the endemic wetness – is the teasel, (*Dipsacus sativus*). Like evening primrose, it is

a sort of weed really, but welcome all the same and adds a double display for its money – the first in spring when it flowers and then again in late summer and autumn when the seed heads acquire their familiar bristly silhouette.

Tall annuals and biennials

Any annual growing over 1.2m (4ft) will need some kind of support. But they can be very useful at the back of a border to stagger the height of flowering.

Hollyhock (*Alcea rosea*) will reach 2.5m (8ft) and is excellent for a softer, cottage-garden feel. Sunflowers (*Helianthus annuus*) can produce the tallest (*H.a* 'Russian Giant') of the lot, reaching up to 6m (20ft) tall. In fact there are few borders that can accommodate this without it becoming a freak show and it is often better to go for some of the smaller varieties. *H.a* 'Velvet Queen' (*below, bottom right*) is a glorious russet and *H.a* 'Lemon Queen' is, unsurprisingly, lemon. Both grow to about 1.8m (6ft).

Cosmos bipinnatis (*below, top right*) is a tall, delicately branched plant with beautifully elegant flowers. They need deadheading daily to prolong flowering. Try the white 'Purity'.

Black-eyed Susan (*Rudbeckia fulgia*) will grow to 3m (10ft) and has striking yellow or orange flowers with chocolate centres.

One of the best tall annuals that we grow is *Leonotis* (*below left*) which makes minarets 3m (10ft) tall with whorls of bright orange flowers set in tiers all round the stem.

TALL ANNUALS AND BIENNIALS

Hollyhocks

Leonotis

Onopordum
  (*Onopordum acanthium*)

Sunflower (*Helianthus annuus*)

Teasels

Lathyrus odoratus 'Ruffled mauve Spencer'

T. peregrinum 'Canary creeper'

Ipomoea tricolor

Climbing annuals *Ipomoea tricolor* (morning glory) is easy if it is raised in warm, humid conditions and then planted in a very sunny spot. The canary creeper *(Tropaeolum peregrinum)* grows as fast as anything, with a mass of tiny yellow flowers.

Climbing annuals

Sweet peas (*Lathyrus odoratus*) are the best of all the annual climbers. There is no point in growing a sweet pea that does not smell sweetly, so avoid most modern varieties and stick to reliably scented plants like those in the Spencer group.

Sweet peas grow very well up trellis, netting, or in a pot up a wigwam of canes. If planted at the base of a wall they will need lots of water. They also like the richest soil possible. If you keep picking the flowers they will flower on into August.

They are the only climbing annual that we grow here, but we grow a lot of them and I love them so they fulfill my needs in this department. The scent of a bunch of sweet peas is as haunting as the sound of woodpidgeons at dawn. Given their fabulous depth of fragrance it seems extraordinary that plant breeders should have deliberately developed a range of sweet peas that have no scent at all. I go out of my way to buy older varieties that have their full depth of delicious scent.

Although sweet peas inspire a fanaticism amongst a band of growers, we grow them here enthusiastically but lazily, although well enough for us to enjoy them, which is all we ask. Traditionally you sow sweet peas in October. They germinate and then spend the winter in a cold frame developing good roots and a hardy, bushy top growth. When they get planted out after the worst of the frosts – they are hardy to about -5°C (23°F) – they are like athletes taking to the track after winter training and romp away. But our frosts, global warming and all, are fierce and can and do happen well into May. So on the two years that we sowed in autumn the sweet peas sat in their pots for the best part of six months and

grew potbound and lank, and I certainly do not have time nor inclination, let alone compost and pots, to pot them all on. This year of writing (2002) we have grown 53 separate wigwams supporting sweet peas in various parts of the garden, each planted with eight plants. I dig a pit under each wigwam and fill it with mushroom compost and try to give the plants as much water as time will allow. It is never enough. They are greedy plants.

Simply by being late every season I have discovered that what works best for me is to sow the seeds in a rich but well-drained potting compost in late February. They are ready to plant out by mid-May and will grow away strongly. It might mean that we do not get flowers until midsummer, but that does not bother me at all. What comes late stays late and they are still going strong well into October. We pinch out the growing tips when the young plants are about 15cm (6in) tall and still in pots, which thickens them up, making bushier growth. As they grow they all have to be tied to the hazel rods. It is laborious, fiddly work, done with a mouthful of cut green twine and hopefully a good radio programme, and has to be done three or four times before they cling unaided. It is part of the summer ritual, like shelling peas or deadheading.

To keep the plants flowering you have to keep picking them, because they quickly go to seed as the weather warms up. We try and pick every single flower about once every 8-10 days, filling buckets and baskets of them. A pint glass is a perfect vase and the house becomes filled with them. I once came home from a filming trip and Sarah had put ten vases filled with white sweet peas on the bedroom floor. I have never seen or smelt anything so beautiful.

Scented annuals and biennials

Because they are so desperate for pollination, scent is often an important part of the annual's armoury. Use it.

The best place to plant or sow strongly scented annuals is where you sit – which tends to be in the evening, so plants like nicotiana, which has my favourite scent of all plants, or night-scented stock whose fragrance is much stronger at night, are ideal for this. Another good trick is to plant them by an entrance or gap in a hedge so that as you go through you catch a whiff of their fragrance. We use wallflowers for this and they are one of my favourite scented plants of all, seeming to take all the warmth of the sun on an April day and process it into fragrance, creating a scent of hot dry earth out of a chill spring afternoon.

Oenothera biennis

SCENTED ANNUALS AND BIENNIALS
Sweet rocket *(Hesperis matrionalis)*
Lemon verbena *(Lippia citriodora)*
Night-scented stock *(Matthiola incana)*–warm, spicy scent
Tobacco plant *(Nicotiana elata)*
Evening primrose *(Oenothera biennis)*–night scent strongest

Annuals and biennials for shade

Although most annuals really need as much sun as possible, some have adapted to grow in shade.

My favourite is the white foxglove, *Digitalis purpurea* f. *albiflora* which will gracefully grow in almost complete shade and, like night-scented stock, dry shade at that, which is rare. We use foxgloves in the Lime Walk, beneath the shade of the limes which increases steadily from spring through to late summer as the trees grow dramatically. But because they are propagated by bees that indiscriminately visit purple as well as white foxgloves, new seed is likely to be purple, and they have to be replaced every year.

Tobacco plants all grow in shade (but do not necessarily prefer it). The monkey flower, *Mimulus*, however, is completely happy without direct light.

Viola tricolor

ANNUALS AND BIENNIALS FOR SHADE
Forget-me-not *(Myosotis species)*
Foxgloves *(Digitalis purpurea)*
Honesty *(Lunaria annua)*
Impatiens *(Impatiens species)*
Monkey flower *(Mimulus species)*
Viola *(Viola species)*

Grasses Sarah often describes our Jewel Garden as a "Mad Meadow", by which she means it sometimes looks like a monstrous, surreal field of wildflowers amongst grasses.

Any such planting is not remotely like a real meadow of course, any more than tropical plants in the garden are like a "real" jungle. The grasses in the Jewel Garden are not field grass but border grasses that we use quite extensively. Actually, I came to border grasses late in my gardening life and am still relishing the novelty of range of texture and form that they add to the flower garden. The use of grasses as border plants was brought to this country from Germany, where they had been using them on a large scale for low-maintenance public planting schemes, amongst others. This hardly makes them seem romantic, but I love them – and they have all the romance and beauty of most flowers.

Grasses add a lightness of touch when allied to fuller, voluminous border flowers. Also, our Jewel Garden looks best in the low, slanting light of evening and grasses pick up that light almost better than any other plant, holding it in the flowerheads and panicles like gentle torches. A real meadow depends on soil with low enough fertility to discourage the grass and encourage the flowers to put all their energy into flowering fast rather than bushy foliage so that they can produce seed before running out of nutrients or water. Too much fertility is always the element that ruins the amateur gardener's wildflower aspirations and our soil is fat with fertility. But make a parody of that inside the literal framework of a border and you can get the best of both worlds with the fullness of a perennial border and the lightness and airiness of an unsprayed hayfield in June. Any spikes or spires of flowers look

good in this "tameflower" set-up, be they mulleins, *Verbena bonariensis*, kniphofias, monardas, salvias, lythrums, and *Digitalis ferruginea*. Ordinary foxgloves would look wonderful too, but their pale colours are banished from this bit of the garden. We shall have to take grasses to them instead. The delphiniums, when they were in flower, looked just right as do the hollyhocks, heleniums and echinaceas as well as the gentler sprawlings of the geranium 'Ann Folkard', the tangles of *Clematis viticella* and even the roses. The grasses add veils and layers and constantly move, transcending the slightly stuffy heaviness that a mixed border can arrive at in mid- and late summer.

Stipas, if you have the space for them, make wonderful border grasses because they add a grand scale whilst the light gets through and around them and they do not hog the eye and block out their neighbours. The Pheasant grass, *Stipa arundinacea*, has wonderful fluffy foliage with rusty fringes that get redder as summer creeps into autumn. We have quite a few *S. gigantea*, which are stupendous, majestical plants with golden oaten flowerheads on 2.5m (8ft) stalks. These must be planted to catch the evening light as the flowerheads will catch the low sunlight and glow like slow-motion sparklers. The initial plant is surprisingly modest for something with such a dramatic maturity, only developing its flower spike in the second season, but if you plant in the autumn it will work ok next summer. Stipas are prone to being bashed by

Stipa gigantea

Stipa gigantea catching the evening light in its seed heads like a golden sparkler (*top left*). One of the great advantages of stipas is that they do not create a barrier, so here the flowers of *Verbena bonariensis* (*top right*) can be seen through the golden seed heads. The very slight, almost fragile, straw flowerheads and stalks of the Switch grass, *Panicum virgatum* (*bottom*), exactly match the colour of the chair. Pure chance.

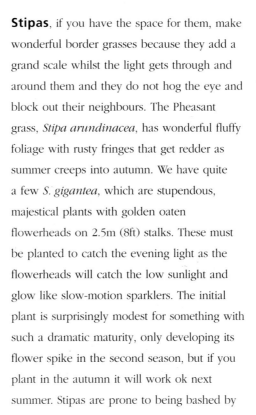

189

Ophiopogon planiscapus 'Nigrescens'

Carex comans 'Bronze Form'

The great thing about grasses is that they add such a variety of texture to a border as well as adding "body" that is such an essential foil to the more dramatically colourful plants. The following are shown here: *Miscanthus var. purpurascens (top left)*, *Stipa arundinacea*, commonly known as Pheasant grass *(top right)*, *Miscanthus sinensis 'Silberfeder' (bottom left)*, and *M. sinensis 'Zebrinus' (bottom right)*.

the wind and are difficult to support as they are too fragile, so should not be in an exposed spot. It is difficult to know whether to plant them in a relatively open position – to enjoy their leaves as well as the extraordinary leaping tracer of flower – or to have them appearing out of a welter of flower at their base. Both look good and both is what we do.

One thinks of grasses being fundamentally green but both these stipas rely on gold or russet, and if you look at any summer meadow it is actually hardly green at all – more every shade of fawn. It means that the green foliage of your flowers does not disappear into the grassiness but works with and against it.

I know that there are people who find the brown grasses to be "dead" looking and therefore offputting, but I think the bronze form of *Carex comans* is terrific. Any sense of deadness is belied by its obvious vigour and health and it spills out of itself like a demented Pekinese; if given half-decent drainage it needs no attention and lasts practically all year round. Add to that *C. buchananii*, which is similar but has charming wiggly bits to the ends of its leaves, and *C. flagellifera*, and you have a really useful extra bronze foil for the border which works spectacularly well with all the various glaucous leaves, such as cardoons, thalictrums, melianthus, macleayas, and onopordums as well as other grasses like Lyme grass, *Leymus arenarius* with its great flowing straps of leaf, and the steely blue of *Festuca glauca*. By no means all the carex are brown – we have a variegated one called *C. hachijoensis* 'Evergold', which has a pale golden stripe down its leaf.

The brown carex look dry to the touch. As a contrast this is fine, but the incredible tactility of some of the grasses comes as a

welcome relief. *Deschampsia flexuosa* is called Wavy hair grass as much for the way that it feels as for its looks, and we have some near enough to the edge to ruffle as you pass, but the most sensually tactile of all is *Stipa tenuissima* (sometimes labelled *S. tenuifolia*). If you plant it in groups of about five the upright clumps are like the finest, softest handfuls of hair.

Imperata cylindrica 'Rubra' is a mouthful of a name that rather solemnly describes one of the best grasses of all for a mixed border. It starts out modestly, not growing very enthusiastically at all in early spring, and when it does get going the tips of the leaves are flushed blood red. This spreads down the whole leaf as summer progresses, providing a fantastic foil for yellows and blues and the surrounding greens. It loves our rich, rather damp soil and prefers not to be in full sun.

We have put in various miscanthuses to get height and volume (whereas the *Stipa gigantea*, for all its size, seems to float above the border), including *Miscanthus sinensis* 'Strictus', which has horizontal yellow bands. *M. sinensis malpartus* has plum-pink flowers, and *M. sinensis* 'Silberfeder' has silver-pink ones. We also have *M. sinensis* 'Goldfeder', but that is less dramatic. The taller *M. sinensis* 'Zebrinus' has lateral cream stripes across its green leaves. *M. nepalensis* produces rich, tawny gold plumes like strands of golden thread. The rather taller, blue-green, thin leaves of *M. sinensis* 'Morning Light' are fabulously even more delicate and graceful, curving out of the air in a perpetual falling trajectory. This wants to be planted somewhere you can appreciate its all-round form rather than in a wodge of surrounding plants.

Imperata cylindrica 'Rubra'

Looking down the path leading from the Jewel Garden into the vegetable garden. These two larger areas are separated by the Long Garden. The new edge of box plants in the foreground of the Jewel Garden will eventually attain the crispness of the box hedging in the distance. While it looks good now, this hard edge will make the leaning golden strands of *Stipa gigantea* look even better.

We have the delicate Fountain grass, *Pennisetum alopecuroides* 'Hameln', which has flower tufts like giant hairy caterpillars. The effect is too fluffy to be as horrific as it might sound. It is smaller than the perennial grasses I have mentioned so far but makes a clump of gracefully spaced arching leaves about 60 x 90cm (2 x 3ft). A grass that has very slight, almost fragile, straw flowerheads and stalks is the Switch grass, *Panicum virgatum*. We have the form 'Hänse Hermes'.

Melica altissima 'Atropurpurea' was grown from seed and they have deep purply brown panicles with black seeds. *Panicum miliaceum* 'Violaceum', which is better (and more simply) known as millet, was also grown from seed. They are slow to get going but by midsummer develop fly-swat flowers, which in turn become purplish seed heads. They can spread very freely but are easy enough to weed out.

I think that the pale, steely blue *Festuca glauca*, which is so often used as an architectural plant to mark a corner or in a pot, works exceptionally well struggling to claim space among crowding competitors. We have the form 'Blue Fox', which is very vigorous.

Growing grasses Grasses are all undemanding plants to grow. As a general rule, they all like soil with good drainage and some sunshine. Sedges and rushes are the exception to this, thriving in damp and even wet soil. I do not feed our grasses at all or add any extra compost to the planting hole, although they have all gone into well-dug, well-manured ground. However, I do add grit to the soil of each plant to encourage a free root run and better drainage.

Bamboos are true grasses with

large, woody culms or stems. I have always wanted to grow bamboos so that we could be self-sufficient in canes. So about five years ago I bought a couple of bamboos, nurtured and cajoled them with tender loving care, and so far I have cut – one cane. It is a start.

Admittedly, I have moved both bamboos twice, which will not have done their productivity much good, although they are now finally in the right place, in the back of the Damp Garden. One is the golden *Phyllostachys aureosulcata* and the other *P. nigra*, the black-stemmed bamboo with culms that acquire an ebony sheen as beautiful and odd as any plant in the garden. I want both to eventually spread and provide a thicket, although they are being very modest about this so far. With bamboos only too much is enough. Of course, there are some that will take this literally and really run riot, like the *Sasa* bamboos, which are very vigorous and not really suitable for anything other than a large garden, and *Pleioblastus gauntlettii* and *P. pygmaeus* both spread very vigorously but both are very short and therefore can be used as quickly establishing ground cover –

although once in it can be almost impossible to get rid of.

The very vigorous ones can still be grown in a small garden, in a container. You find instructions in lots of books to contain the spread of bamboos by sinking a barrier around the roots, thereby creating a kind of containerised safety zone, but I find that pretty nonsensical. Either grow the thing in a pot or choose a plant that will not need restraining.

And it is wrong to demystify the vigour of bamboos. Their astonishing growth is half of their charm. I would love a plant that grows 1.5cm (½ in) an hour like the *Phyllostachys bambusoides* in the Moss Garden at Kyoto that reaches 15m (50ft) inside a couple of months.

If I had really just wanted bamboos for their canes (and I don't – they are extremely beautiful plants, especially in early spring), it would have been better to have chosen the Arrow bamboo, *Arundinaria japonica*. A lot of bamboos get ragged in the wind and much prefer shelter but this one makes an ideal windbreak. I had also got the idea rooted in my ignorance that all bamboos needed wet to flourish, but this is not the case. They like plenty of rainfall but most dislike boggy conditions. However, the Arrow bamboo is also an exception in that it will grow well in the wet. The only problem with it is that it tends to flower vigorously, which causes dieback of the stems.

Unlike other grasses, bamboos like lots of feeding. They seem to relish mushroom compost above all else. When planting put lots in the hole, water them very well, and mulch very thickly with more. For the first season, the plants should be watered once a week but thereafter can be treated like any normal plant as long as they are given an annual mulch.

Phyllostachys nigra

Phyllostachys aureosulcata

The Walled Garden

The Walled Garden

We always eat in the Walled Garden. Before we moved here it WAS the garden. Everything else was farm.

I have an old photograph of vegetables growing in anonymous rows, with cattle in the yard the other side of the wall. To be honest, it is a bit pretentious calling it the Walled Garden, if not untrue. The wall curves around two sides only, west and north, but giving us a good south-facing stone suntrap. To the south is a rough hedge with overgrown damsons that screens us from the track in summer and I enclosed the area with a yew hedge planted nine years ago, which is now a foursquare and ageless green wall.

Because it had that sunny wall we used it as our outside eating area from the first, and while the rest of the garden was still a field pretending to be a garden, it had identity. It belonged to the household in a way that a brand-new garden never can. I divided it into four square beds into which we planted the collection of some 40 different old roses that we had brought with us when we moved, accompanied by herbs. Roses and herbs always go well together, and there was enough vigour in both parties to complete the sense of maturity and permanence. Given that the house was a building site and the rest of the garden effectively a ploughed field, this gave a valuable sense of putting down roots. It was outdoor nest-building.

We made a terrace laid with sandstone flags and a table from planks and trestles. We eat out there as often as we can – which, given the vagaries of the British weather, is never often enough. This is a place where sitting feels right.

Everything in the Walled Garden is soft and pale. No hard colours at all, unless you count white as hard. It is the only bit of the garden where I am comfortable with pink, which is just as well as it is full of every pink we can muster, as well as blues, yellows, greys, and whites. In spring, when the *Clematis macropetala* is in full pomp and the rosemary flowers are still out, and forget-me-nots are a pale blue crowd jostling into every nook and cranny, it has a freshess that no other piece of the garden provides. Then, in May and June, when the alliums, roses, eremurus, nepetas, crambes, and lilies are at their best, it has a voluptuousness that is still light and soft. In later summer it goes past its best, although the acanthus is very good and the fennel shimmers better here than anywhere else in the garden. We cut back hard and there is a second flush of growth and flowering in September.

For a long while, we had the trampoline in here and the place came into its own. Most of my measures of real happiness have been

Two views of the Walled Garden, looking north towards the house. These are our only south-facing walls, and are ideal for growing figs. The small orange trees in pots (*top*) are moved from the greenhouse into this sunny spot for spring and summer, and borage (*bottom*) is allowed to self-seed freely among the poppies and foliage of the newly planted *Cosmos* 'Purity'.

Five of the flowers in the Walled Garden shown here (*from top to bottom*): the white umbel of an **agapanthus**; the steely blue of *Echinops ritro*; the yellow flowers of a **mullein** emerging among the white coating of down; the white flowers of *Cosmos* **'Purity'**; and a pink **opium poppy**.

197

The flower buds of onopordum *(top left)*. This self-sown biennial will reach 3–4m (10–12ft) by midsummer. The flowers of *Acanthus spinosa (top right)* flanking a sweet pea. Bees love acanthus. *Lilium regale (bottom right)* is perhaps the easiest of all lilies to grow as long as the plants have a sheltered, well-drained site. Lovage is an excellent foil for the Alba rose 'Königin von Dänemark' *(bottom left)*. The terrace *(right)* is a sun trap in the morning and completely sheltered from the wind, so is an ideal place for elevenses.

Looking south from the terrace in the Walled Garden. The newly planted tree is *Prunus* 'Taihaiku' and has since been moved again and the grass re-seeded.

established here – good food eaten outside, good company, good bouncing, and good midsummer flowers.

But, for all that, it was not quite right. The proportions felt too open and the borders too peripheral, even though they were 3m (10ft) deep. I had edged them with a woven hazel fence, which never quite transcended the restrictive. So we removed the fencing, widened the back bed, and made two new beds that enclosed the grass, save for an entry path, so the lawn in the middle was now a square with the round trampoline in the centre of that. I moved three roses – for about the fourth time, poor things, but they seem to be all right. I lost the labels of all my roses years ago and always forget what is there until they flower. This is where keeping a photographic record helps. One is certainly 'Alba Semiplena', one is 'Cardinal Richelieu', and I won't have a

clue what the other is until it flowers. But I do not possess a rose that I do not love, so this does not bother me in the slightest.

Then the trampoline was moved out and I planted a cherry – *Prunus* 'Taihaiku' – in the middle of the lawn. This is the most decorative of all flowering cherries, with a bundle of huge white blossom, hanging, like delicate explosions caught and frozen in mid-air, from the end of each spindly shoot in April. It looks forlorn at the moment because it has lived too long in a pot. But it will recover and thrive.

In late summer, the plums and damsons ripen and our dining table is accompanied by the angry buzzing of wasps; but it is worth it because the fruit makes wonderful jam. In a good summer, the figs on the south wall will ripen and provide a few Mediterranean moments, although not in the year of writing, which has not been hot enough.

Perennials

Every colour, leaf type, size, and shape is to be found under the broad heading of perennials. The possibilities of combining them are endless and I cannot imagine a garden without them.

Perennials are defined primarily by having no woody growth or permanent structure. Herbaceous perennials have top-growth that dies back completely at the end of the season, while the roots remain perfectly healthy, if largely dormant, below ground. They put on vigorous new growth in spring – sometimes, as in a cardoon, to a phenomenal extent. This is a device that the plant has evolved to protect itself in its natural habitat, which, in the main, has hot summers and cold winters. The dead growth from the summer acts as insulation against the cold and rots down to provide nourishment. Because its season is so short, the plant has to grow with tremendous vigour in order to flower and set seed before autumn. Hence the dramatic transformation in the herbaceous border in the months from April to the end of June.

The vast majority of herbaceous plants that are now growing in millions of gardens across England originate from an eclectic scatter right across the globe. Well, not so eclectic when you start to plot it, because a great many herbaceous plants come from long-surrendered strongholds of the British Empire, such as South Africa, New Zealand, and India, as well as trophies snatched from countries that resisted domination, like China, Japan, and America. Either you see in this a smug domestication of all this rich, wild diversity into a very English version of nature, or the particularly English genius of assimilating cultures. But it would be fascinating to trace the provenance of our most familiar herbaceous plants through the remnants of the Empire.

Given its links to the Empire, it is not surprising to find that the history of the herbaceous border is a recent one. It stems from William Robinson's revolution against the tyranny of bedding plants. By the era of high Victoriana, which can roughly be dated from 1850 to 1883, when Robinson

published *The English Flower Garden*, herbaceous plants were not included in any decorative flower schemes other than in cottage gardens. They were relegated to the kitchen garden and used partly for cutting and partly as a second-division entertainment (because the owners of Big Houses rarely visited the kitchen garden). The notion of making a border in a prominent place filled with herbaceous plants was radical but quickly caught on. By the end of the nineteenth century it was mainstream and for the first two-thirds of last century an horticultural convention.

There are some perennials that maintain their foliage – such as bamboos or hellebores – with new growth adding to it. In principle, a perennial goes on living from year to year but in practice there is a huge range of life expectancy, from three or four years for the average lupin to a minimum of 20 years for a healthy peony. However long-lived, most are extremely tolerant of being dug up, split, moved around, and generally manhandled. This is what makes them so invaluable to any gardener.

In the wild, perennials have adapted to every different type of environment and climate as a means of competing with trees and shrubs and grazing animals. Spring perennials tend to originate from woodland and open and flower before the leaf canopy shades them out. In summer they are dormant and they start growing again in early autumn as the leaves begin to fall. Some will grow high on mountain sides, where trees and shrubs cannot survive, and are adapted well to summer drought. Others come from grass plains and avoid being grazed through their spines or unpalatability.

The great beauty of an herbaceous plant is the never-failing element of surprise that comes with its renewal each spring. It adds electricity to a mixed border and the lushness that can only come with rapid growth. So however old-fashioned the true herbaceous border is, dying back to a bleak emptiness in winter, herbaceous plants will always be part of any garden. There is always something wonderful about the sheer volume of growth an herbaceous plant can make in a season, and in the wonder-stakes size counts for a lot. Even a very small garden can use them to make the most of this short season.

Growing perennials Because perennials come from all over the globe there are plants adapted to grow in every possible situation. That is the good news.

Mulching between the early perennials in the Spring Garden. I use leafmould to help replicate the woodland conditions that these plants like.

Helenium *'Moerheim Beauty'* *(top left)*, which flowers from July until mid-autumn. *Euphorbia polychroma* in the Spring Garden *(top right)*. The vivid lime-green flowering bracts are at their best in April and May. *Echinacea purpurea* *(bottom right)* is a late summer perennial that we grow for its bronze central bosses. *Aster novi-belgii (bottom left)* flowers in autumn.

However, to get the best out of them it is a good idea to make your soil as good as it can be, and because herbaceous plants live a long time and grow so fast, they need a lot of nourishment. This starts with the soil, and the better the soil, the better the plants will thrive.

Good soil means digging deeply and adding lots of organic matter. It is best to do this in autumn and winter, but it is not too late at any time. Every ounce of effort and drop of sweat that you put into this will repay dividends from the first year. There is no bucking it. It is a once-only job and the single most important aspect of creating a good border. A good tip is to start covering the proposed site of a border with organic material over the months or even years before you start digging. Anything will do: compost, weeds, straw, or vegetable thinnings. They do not even have to be composted. Just chuck them on the ground "raw" and they will rot down and be incorporated into the soil over the months in exactly the same way as a more conventional mulch will. It is not so much fertility that you are after – although that will help – but a decent soil structure.

If you have a new garden with a new house, you are very likely to have compacted soil as a result of the builders driving over and over it with fork-lift trucks. In this case, you MUST break through that compaction and dig the soil to at least a spade's depth. There is no easy solution to this and it will be horribly hard work. Don't whinge. Get stuck in. Better still, persuade someone else to stick in for you. Either way, what you want is soil that has

enough body to retain moisture but also enough drainage to stop it from becoming waterlogged.

The traditional method of maintaining a good soil fertility and structure, despite the demands being made on it by closely planted, hungry herbaceous plants, was to lift all the plants in an herbaceous border every three years and double dig it before splitting the plants and repositioning them. Few people have the time or inclination (or border devoted exclusively to herbaceous plants) to do this, so a thick mulch of well-rotted organic material each March suffices. I always plan to add another mulch in autumn but somehow never get round to it.

It is still a good idea to split herbaceous plants every few years. We dig up and replant a good section of our herbaceous plants in the Jewel and Walled Gardens every spring, before we mulch. Quite a few of the larger herbaceous plants grow outwards from the centre, which means that the youngest and most vigorous part is on the outer edges while the centre section produces very few flowers. The best thing to do is to take healthy sections from the outside, cutting them with a sharp spade, or tease the roots apart if they are fibrous, and ditch the interior. This regenerates the plant, gives you a chance to get any weeds out of the roots, and also provides more healthy plants. It also means that you can redesign the borders periodically.

It is vital that you do not just plonk the plants down at random. A border must be composed with all the care of a picture, paying attention to colour, shape, height, and texture.

Red, our very black dog, in one of her favourite shady corners in the Jewel Garden. Behind her is growing *Echinacea purpurea*, which has had most of its petals removed to accentuate the bronze central bosses.

Alchemilla mollis

Sedum spectabile

You need height at the back, using plants such as *Macleayea cordata*, rudbeckias, filipendulas, and inulas to give the border a sense of scale. These tall plants need to be planted in groups so that they do not look too spindly.

Oriental poppies, lupins, phlox, and plants with bare stems should go in the middle of the border, so the plants in front of them will hide their naked nether regions but not obscure their flowers. Plants such as sedums and *Alchemilla mollis* are ideal for the front, spilling over onto a path or lawn. And always plant in blocks and clumps rather than individual dots. This takes great discipline in a small garden as the temptation is to collect more and more different plants, but you must decide whether you want a beautiful garden or an impressive collection. It takes great

expertise to make the two compatible.

Because they grow so fast, herbaceous plants are very soft and will bend, buckle, and break in bad weather. They must be supported. The secret is to provide support before they need it, and not as a salvage job after a storm. You can use bamboos (which are effective but ugly), proprietary metal supports (which are pricey), string stretched between inconspicuous uprights and around each clump of plants, or (best of all) twigs and branches cut specially for the job the previous winter. These are stuck into the ground all around each clump and become hidden as the plants grow.

If you are starting anew, either with a border or a whole garden, buy your herbaceous perennials small and in bulk. This is much cheaper than large specimens from a garden centre and enables you to plant the whole area at once. The nature of herbaceous plants is to grow very fast, giving you a mature border in a couple of years. Also, because they do not mind being moved, you can rearrange them over the course of the coming few years in the light of their maturity.

There are a lot of perennials that do well in mild, moist conditions, feeding the need for fast, lush growth. In a normal year a border is too dry for them, except in the heaviest of ground, and by August they are looking as exhausted and dehydrated as a runner crossing the marathon finish line. Of course, there is a fine line between true bog plants –

like gunneras and *Lysichiton americanus* – and plants that merely do well when the ground is wetter than normal. If it is bog plants you are after, then you must create an environment which never dries out. A bog is really permanent mud and while it certainly feels that way here for weeks on end, by the end of summer the ground may well be very dry indeed. So the perennials that are likely to adapt best to the climatic shift towards wet winters and dry summers must be those that are happiest with a substantial amount of wet locked into the soil but able to cope with a couple of months of real dryness each summer.

A corner of the Jewel Garden in mid-June. Delphiniums 'Black Knight', to the right, and 'King Arthur', in the centre with a white eye. They are backed by the grey leaves of a weeping pear *Pyrus salicifolia* 'Pendula'.

Choosing perennials One of the great virtues of perennials is that whatever your soil, climate, or aspect, there will be a wide range of plants to choose from for every season.

LARGE PERENNIALS FOR WETTER CONDITIONS

Astilbe rivularis
Campanula lactiflora
Eupatorium purpureum
Filipendula rubra
Inula magnifica
Ligularia dentata,
L. przewalskii (below)
Lythrum salicaria
Phormium tenax
Rheum palmatum
Rodgersia
Rudbeckia
Thalictrum delavayi
Thalictrum speciosissimum

MEDIUM-SIZED PERENNIALS FOR MOIST SOIL

Astilbe
Astrantia major
Cirsium rivulare
Euphorbia palustris
Helenium
Hemerocallis
Heuchera
Hosta
Knautia macedonica
Lobelia
Lychnis chalcedonica
Lysimachia
Lythrum
Rudbeckia fulgida
Trollius

SMALL PERENNIALS FOR MOIST SOIL

Ajuga reptans
Bellis perennis
Erigeron
Gentiana
Geum 'Borisii'
Primula
Viola

It therefore makes sense to choose plants that are adapted to your particular soil and conditions. Here are some lists of plants that will grow best in particular conditions. That is not to say that they cannot be grown in very different circumstances, and for every rule there are numerous exceptions.

Most disease and pest predation comes when plants are forced to grow too fast or in conditions to which they are not best suited. Put your plants where they will be happiest (which is not always where you would like them to be), prepare the soil well, and they should grow healthily and flourish.

Perennials for wet conditions

There is a real distinction between bog plants that will tolerate sitting in water and plants that like moisture.

If the soil in your garden is very wet and heavy it is important to add lots of organic material to improve drainage and perhaps dig in horticultural grit before

planting. If you wish to grow any of these plants and have light soil, also add plenty of organic material and plant them in the shade. Wind dries leaves exactly like washing on a line, so make sure that drought-susceptible plants have protection from the wind.

Perennials for dry soil

There are certain outward signs that indicate that a plant is likely to cope well with drought. The first is a silvery colour. This comes from a coating of fine hairs on the leaf surface, giving a felted or woolly texture as with *Stachys byzantina*, or Lambs' ears, or *Artemisia schmidtiana*. The coating reflects light and reduces moisture loss through transpiration. A bluish tinge to the leaf is often caused by a waxy protective coating, such as found in rue or artemisia. Another obvious clue as to the ability to withstand drought is the size of the leaves. As a rule, the bigger the leaf the more water it needs. But even plants that survive drought well need watering when planted and benefit greatly from a well-dug soil with lots of added organic material. For most of these plants, it is not dryness that they require but drainage. All hate sitting in water, especially when it is cold, so good drainage is essential.

PERENNIALS FOR DRY SOIL

Achillea
Alstroemeria
Anthemis
Artemisia
Bidens
Cynara cardunculus
Echinops
Eryngium
Euphorbia characias
Foeniculum
Kniphofia
Sedum
Stachys
Verbena bonariensis

Perennials for shade

The combination of shade cast by leaves and evolution has seen to it that many plants have adapted and learnt to love the gloom. And of course there is shade and shade. There is dry shade, which is tricky and has fewest plants that actually fit in this category, and wet shade, which produces a wide range of invariably lush, leafy plants.

The amount of light that makes up shade varies from a haze of cloud to total gloom. So the daylong dark in the lee of a high, north-facing wall is altogether a different class of shade from the dappled pebbles of shadow that a deciduous tree drops from its leaves in mid-spring.

The timing of shade, both during the diurnal cycle and the annual one, is very relevant to the type of plant that will make best use of it. Deciduous woodland plants have learnt to flower early, before the canopy of the trees shades out all light, and to put on healthy growth despite the shade overhead. They are ideal for a garden that only gets early morning sun. From late spring through to leaf-fall, plants such as primroses, violets, and bluebells are under an umbrella of leaves and they hibernate throughout what is for them a long summer's night. These plants have also learnt to love what they cannot avoid and that is an annual dressing of falling leaves which rot down to create a soil that is almost pure leafmould. This is the perfect growing medium for all woodland plants and if at all possible you should collect leaves from your garden, the street, or the park and bag them up in bin-liners. Make sure that they stay moist all winter, and use the mould as a sweet-smelling mulch the following spring.

PERENNIALS FOR SHADE

Ajuga
Alchemilla mollis
Anemone x hybrida
Aquilegia vulgaris
Astrantia
Brunnera
Dicentra spectabilis
Digitalis
Euphorbia robbiae
Geranium phaeum
Helleborus corsicus, H. foetidus, H. orientalis
Hosta (below)
Lamium
Lysimachia
Pulmonaria

Climbers

This garden is noticeably devoid of climbers against any of our walls. Of the very limited range of climbers that we do grow here, clematis and sweet peas dominate.

We do have a couple of climbing roses ('Souvenir du Docteur Jamain' and the rambler 'Paul's Himalayan Musk') and a handful of honeysuckles. And the bindweed climbs anything and everything that it can entwine itself around!

This lack of climbers against the walls was not planned. In fact, the very first thing that I did when we moved in was to start to dig a piece of ground in front of the house to plant a climbing rose to clamber over its south-facing walls. But within five minutes of digging, it became apparent that there was no soil at all to be dug. In the front, the house stands on the site of a Norman building, which must not be disturbed, and in the back it is built on an outcrop of stone. Thus, any planting directly against the house must be in containers.

The Walled Garden is the only place that has walls backing onto soil, and we have figs growing against the south-facing section and plums, gages, and cherries against the east-facing part. As I write this, I feel that it is time for a change. The figs will stay but the east-facing wall will be used for more decorative purposes – especially as the plums and gages are not very productive.

But we do grow plenty of clematis and sweet peas scrambling through trees, shrubs, and especially up wigwams made from hazel sticks. This gives us instant height and structure in the borders, both from the wigwams themselves, which are a very satisfying shape and size, and from the plant as it grows.

Caring for climbers Climbers are simple to care for. Whatever climber you choose, plant it with the same care, size of hole, and amount of goodness as if it were a tree. The extra 20 minutes that this takes will transform the performance of the plant and prolong its life by years.

Plant any climber as far from the wall as you have the space to do so, up to 1m (3ft) if possible. This gives the plant a chance to establish without competing with the wall for moisture and allows rain to reach the roots.

Most climbers will need support to hold them against a wall. This is best either via a series of wires attached tautly to hooks at 30cm (1ft) spacing, or on a trellis screwed onto wooden blocks that hold it well away from the surface of the wall or fence so that the plant has room to grow without being crammed.

Do not use plastic-coated wire ties for anything other than annuals or growth that is to be pruned away at the end of the season, as although they are very convenient they cut into the plant tissue. Always use soft twine.

All climbers need lots of feeding, so mulch heavily in spring and summer with well-rotted compost, and feed them in April with potash-rich fertilizer, which will help production of flowers. A proprietary tomato fertilizer will do very well. They also need to be fed with seaweed meal or foliar spray monthly during the growing season.

Be careful where you weed. Most feeding roots for climbers are near the surface, so do not get too energetic with a fork near the base of the plant.

Clematis alpina growing up inside a wigwam support of hazel sticks and thick hop-twine. They grow very well like this but the wigwams need replacing every few years.

Clematis 'Niobe' in the Jewel Garden (*opposite top*). This is pruned back to the ground each March. Tying hop-twine around a hazel wigwam over a new *Clematis viticella* in May (*opposite bottom right*). This will produce a mass of new growth that will all be cut back the following spring. Honeysuckle growing against a north-facing wall of the house (*opposite bottom left*).

209

Choosing climbers
Vertical surfaces are important in any garden but for many people the wall and fence space can amount to as much as the ground area available for plants. So climbers are vital.

SOUTH-FACING WALLS
EVERGREEN
Ceanothus impressus
Clematis armandii
Magnolia grandiflora

SPRING-FLOWERING
Clematis armandii
Jasminum beesianum
Rosa banksiae 'Lutea'

SUMMER-FLOWERING
Ficus
Rosa 'Souvenir de la
  Malmaison'
Wisteria sinensis

AUTUMN-FLOWERING
Ceanothus 'Autumnal Blue'
Eccremocarpus scaber
Jasminum officinale

WINTER-FLOWERING
Chimonanthus praecox
  'Luteus'
Clematis cirrhosa

WEST-FACING WALLS
EVERGREEN
Camellia
Escallonia 'Iveyi'
Magnolia

SPRING-FLOWERING
Ceanothus
Clematis armandii
Lonicera periclymenum
  'Belgica'

SUMMER-FLOWERING
Clematis 'Jackmanii'
Rosa (all)

AUTUMN-FLOWERING
Clematis 'Madame Julia
  Correvon'
Lonicera periclymenum
  'Serotina'

WINTER-FLOWERING
Chimonanthus praecox
Clematis cirrhosa
Jasminum polyanthum
Lonicera fragrantissima

It is important to know which direction your walls and fences face. Plants measure their lives by sunlight and you must become as intimate with the movement of the sun across the patch of sky over your garden as they are. A south-facing fence or wall will support a range of plants that would hate a north-facing one. If you have four clearly orientated vertical surfaces then you can be slightly more sophisticated and choreograph your planting to grow as wide a range of plants as possible within their varying shades and shelters. Every vertical surface above 1.5m (5ft) tall has two functions in a garden: it can support and sustain a climber of some sort, as well as providing shade and shelter for plants planted at its base.

The first thing to take into account when planting against a wall or fence is its aspect. A north-facing wall will be cold and shady, an east one only gets morning light and will also be cool, a south-facing wall will get very hot and be dry, and a west-facing wall will be sunny, particularly in the evening, and get more rain than any other wall.

When choosing a plant for a wall it is essential to consider how it will react to these different conditions. In general, climbers cope with shade better than many people imagine, and lack of moisture is a bigger problem than lack of sun.

Although we do not grow any plants up walls in this garden, other than the rose 'Souvenir du Docteur Jamain (on the north-facing wall outside the back door) and the honeysuckle *Lonicera periclymenum* (also on the north wall), here are some suggestions for growing plants to make the most of them.

South- and west-facing walls

A south-facing wall will get the most of available sun (although not a lot more than a west-facing wall) and is the hottest and driest wall. Therefore, it is ideal for the tenderest climbers, especially if it is well sheltered. Mulch all climbers on a south-facing wall especially well as they will dry out the fastest.

A west-facing wall is ideal for most plants. It is not too cold and never gets scorchingly hot, and has some shade in the morning but plenty of light after midday, when the air will have warmed up. It is also likely to get the maximum amount of moisture available as rain normally comes from the west in Britain.

Hydrangea petiolaris (above) and
Pyrancantha coccinea (left).

North- and east-facing walls

A north-facing wall gets just a little weak sun at dusk in the middle of summer and absolutely none all winter. Not only is it dark, but its brand of shade is cold and dry. But there are enough plants that relish these unlikely conditions to make it interesting, as well as a surprising amount that will tolerate it. The biggest problem – lack of water – can easily be rectified by watering and enriching the soil with lots of compost and manure.

A few plants, all suitable for a north-facing wall, need no support. The most important are ivy, *Hydrangea petiolaris*, *Euonymus fortunei* var. *radicans*, and Virginia creeper, *Parthenocissus quinquefolia* (although the latter will give better autumn colour if given some sun). Of these, the hydrangea is the most handsome, with white flowers in mid- to late summer. It can be slow to get established but have patience and it will make good ground (or wall) after two or three years.

You could do much worse than plant the one fruit tree that will feel fully at home against a north-facing wall, give you flowers in spring, and delicious fruits in the summer, namely the Morello cherry.

The type of sunlight that an east-facing wall receives is thin, and looking through it is like pressing your cheek against a cool pane of glass. Colours float and change in it: strength is exposed as vulgarity and intensity transformed into brashness. The delicacy of morning light is best suited to soft colours, and all the pastels, yellows, and whites, as well as the cooler blues, look their best planted so that they catch the morning sun.

NORTH-FACING WALLS
WINTER
Hedera
Jasminum nudiflorum
Lonicera fragrantissima

SPRING
Clematis macropetala
Clematis montana
Clematis 'Moonlight'

SUMMER
Hydrangea petiolaris
Lonicera x americana
Rosa 'Souvenir du Docteur
 Jamain'

AUTUMN
Cotoneaster
Pyracantha coccinea
Vitis coignetiae

EAST-FACING WALLS
SPRING-FLOWERING
Chaenomeles
Clematis macropetala
Forsythia suspensa

SUMMER-FLOWERING
Lathyrus latifolius
Lonicera x tellmanniana
Pyracantha

AUTUMN-FLOWERING
Lonicera periclymenum
 'Graham Thomas'

WINTER-FLOWERING
Garrya elliptica
Jasminum nudiflorum
Lonicera fragrantissima

An east wind is usually dry and invariably cold, and anything that will grow on a north-facing wall will grow on an east one. But let's be more sophisticated than that and relish the subtle variations of aspect. An east-facing wall changes its character throughout the year. In the middle of winter, it is in shade almost all day, while in summer it is potentially bright from 5am until after lunch. Its post-prandial shade is a soothing coolness and suits plants like clematis or roses perfectly well. Actually, both types of plant are, in my experience, pretty damn tough and will cope with a huge variety of positions.

It is a general rule that an east-facing wall is not a good place for any delicate early-flowering climbers. Camellias, for example, should not be planted on an east-facing wall except in the mildest areas, even though they will flower very well on it. The reason for this is that in cold spring weather the east wall will have been in shade since early morning, will have been cooling rapidly since midday, and is therefore prone to any frost that is about. The frost itself will not damage hardy flowers but a cold spring night means clear skies so is usually followed by a sunny morning, when the heat from the sun quickly melts ice that has formed between the flower cells. Water then flows back into the cells, bursting them. By the time the much hotter sun reaches the west wall – which might have been just as frosty – the ice between the cells will have melted gradually and no damage will be done.

Clematis

There is something generous and easy-going about the way that clematis grow vigorously without getting out of control and flower freely without losing subtlety as they climb any wall or fence.

Early-flowering clematis The first clematis to flower here are the *C. alpina*, which come into flower in this garden around the very beginning of April, just when the pear blossom is beginning to break. We have one 'Pamela Jackman' growing up a hawthorn in the Spring Garden, and two more on wigwams in the Jewel Garden. These flowers are made up of single petals that hang down like psychedelic goats' ears, growing directly from the leaf axils of the previous year's growth (which is why they should not be pruned, except for tidiness and then only immediately after flowering). The leaves are the freshest green imaginable, a green you only find in April and May lit by that clear, almost cold, clear light of a British spring. We also have *C. macropetala* on a wigwam in the Walled Garden, its sky blue flowers accompanying the forget-me-nots at its base.

Blue is always at a premium in the garden at any season, and goes particularly well with the primrose-yellows of spring, so I have no real desire to vary from alpina's natural inclination to be blue, but you can get varieties of *C. alpina* in plum-red like 'Ruby', a pink like 'Constance' or 'Jacqueline du Pré', or white as in 'Albiflora' or 'Burford White'. Whatever the colour of the flower, the seedheads all resolve as a wispy call that lasts prettily right through winter, as dry as the seemingly dead brown stems that will miraculously break into hundreds of pointed buds by the beginning of March.

A little later, *C. montana* var *rubens* 'Elizabeth' comes into flower. It is a gentle pink and scrambles over a hawthorn in the coppice, flowering about the same time as its host.

Late-flowering clematis Then there is a gap until the later-flowering clematis start to break into bloom in the Jewel Garden at the beginning of July. These late clematis define part of the year. They flower in the school holidays, in the long, slow season of butterflies, dusty soil, mucking about, morning dew, and the gentle withdrawal of light, and all with their colours soaked into the deep velvet of the sepals and all in shades of violet, purple, and maroon. They are among the few plants that manage to be intense and cheerful at the same time. It is quite a trick. Some, like 'Honora', change colour as they go along. It starts out a twisted funnel of intense adolescent plum and matures into a cheerful, gappy purple flower. 'Gypsy Queen' holds its purple Romany depths until it drops, and *C.* 'Jackmanii Superba' has streaks or ridges of claret-like scarification lines running down each sepal. 'Perle d'Azur' makes a serious attempt to be blue and another – name and label long forgotten – is a burgundy violet with a big central boss.

The late clematis flower on the current season's growth (unlike early clematis like *C. alpina* or *C. montana*), so they are ideal for growing in a border because they will not smother early flowers and can be supported on a tripod or left to scramble through a woody shrub. They should be pruned hard every spring, clearing away all but 15cm (6in)

Clematis macropetala

We grow nearly all our clematis up tripods made from hazel. In early spring, *Clematis alpina* has green foliage while all around it the Jewel Garden is still in its winter clothes.

Clematis 'Jackmanii Superba'

Clematis 'Niobe'

Although we have clematis growing in every part of the garden, they are perhaps most important in the Jewel Garden, where their flowers add months of rich colour. Here, *Clematis* 'Honora' is planted to contrast with the magenta flowers of *Rosa* 'Scharlachglut', although the clematis will go on flowering long after the rose has finished.

or so of the top-growth. Hard pruning will stimulate very vigorous growth, which in turn will mean lots of flowers appearing from the base of the plant to the very top. If these plants are not pruned every year, they gradually develop very bare lower stems with a scattering of flowers right at the top.

C. viticella was introduced from central Europe in the sixteenth century, and has since been bred to produce many well-known cultivars such as 'Madame Julia Correvon' and 'Etoile Violette', but the best is 'Purpurea Plena Elegans'. This is a mouthful for a flower that is delicate in a fumbly sort of way, flowering against the backdrop of its foliage like jewels on an Elizabethan dress. This is not a fanciful image as it has been grown in English gardens since Elizabethan times.

Planting clematis Soak the plant (in its pot) for 10 minutes in a bucket of water while you are preparing the planting hole. Clematis like to have their roots in the shade in rich, well-watered soil. Prepare a hole at least twice the size of the plant's container, and add a bucket of compost.

Like roses, clematis need to be planted deep. Take the plant carefully out of the pot, being careful not to disturb the root ball but gently freeing a few of the roots growing in ringlets at the base of the pot, and place it so that the soil level of the container is at least 2.5cm (1in) below the soil level of your hole. Fill back the topsoil to the junction of the plant and the potted compost and give it a good bucket of water. When this has drained, top up with a thick mulch of more compost.

Clematis are woodland plants that like to have cool, shaded roots and their flowers in sun. If the base of the clematis is in the sun it is a good idea to put large pebbles or a tile or two around the roots to keep them cool and moist. After planting, give it a full bucket of water once a week for the first few weeks and repeat if the weather is dry. If you are planting a clematis to climb an established tree you will have to water more frequently.

Whatever the type of clematis, once you have planted it, be bold and prune it down to a strong bud about 30cm (1ft) off the ground. This might seem drastic but it will ensure a strong, healthy framework to establish the plant and more flowers in subsequent years.

Clematis wilt can reduce a perfectly healthy specimen to brown tatters in less than 48 hours. It only attacks large-flowered cultivars, leaving species and small-flowered cultivars (such as *C. viticella* types) alone. It is caused by a fungus called *Phoma clematidina* and attacks the plant just above soil level, usually through a point that has been slightly damaged. The fungus grows, killing cells of the stem, and stops the sap reaching any point above the point of infection, causing the plant to turn black and collapse. Sometimes only one or two stems are affected but all damaged stems should be cut right back to ground level. If you have planted the clematis, 5–8cm (2–3in) below soil level, it should regrow without any problem.

If the same plant gets hit by wilt every year, cut it back and move it to another site in the garden, replacing it with a *C. viticella* cultivar. Some varieties of *C.* 'Jackmanii' have a tendency for their lower leaves to brown and seemingly wilt in summer, but don't cut the stems back. It does this because these lower leaves have done their stuff and their job is taken over by the newer leaves further up nearer the sun.

215

Shrubs are, by definition, woody, multi-stemmed perennials. · They can be evergreen or deciduous, and many produce wonderful flowers while some are distinguished mainly by their berries.

There was a time in my childhood when there was a trend to grow shrubs as a labour-saving device. All over England, in gardens larger than average, borders and vegetable gardens were put down to grass. It was a kind of inverted reduction of a border, scattering individual specimens across a grassed area that had formerly contained a number of intensely planted flower beds. In its own quiet way it was the beginning of a gardening revolution.

However, I didn't like it then and I don't like it now. Shrubs are often useful and sometimes beautiful but are best grown in a border, where they can create mass, using their twiggy substance as a virtue to block out areas just as a painter blocks out colour on a large canvas before working in the detail. I like borders that have a front and back, where shrubs can add height, texture, and mass against the backdrop of a hedge or wall. This contains the looseness of the shrubs within a formal framework based upon straight lines. Shrubs in backed borders share – with the rest of the planting – the quality of light in each border and one adjusts the planting accordingly. Obviously, there are more shrubs that prefer full south-facing sun, but there are also plenty to choose from for each aspect of the compass.

Remember that pruning provokes growth, so if you have a lopsided shrub, prune the weaker side back hard and leave the well-developed side alone. This will balance the shrub out. I know that people can get into a muddle about pruning shrubs, as though there was anything to be muddled about. The first rule of all pruning is when in doubt, don't. The second rule is to always cut back to something, be it a leaf, bud, or branch, and the third is that winter pruning promotes vigorous spring regrowth. So resist the evidence of your eyes and cut the existing weak growth back hardest.

Notice if the flowers are produced on the current year's fresh growth or on the previous year's. If the former, it is best to prune in early spring, as with buddleja, and if the latter, the time to do it is immediately after flowering – as with flowering currants. When you plant shrubs, prune any weak growth hard to encourage good strong shoots from the base of the plant next spring. If you are growing a shrub for its leaves, as I do with a cut-leaf golden elder (*Sambucus*), cut it back hard in spring and the new leaves will be both bigger and better coloured than if it is left unpruned.

The white flowers of *Viburnum plicatum* flowering in the Damp Garden in May, *(opposite top)*. The mass of *Hydrangea macrophylla* 'Lanarth White' flower buds *(opposite bottom right)* are tinged pink before the white flowers open. It also has fine purple leaves in autumn. The rose 'Scharlachglut' *(opposite bottom left)*, flowering in the Jewel Garden. This is an exceptionally tough shrub rose. The elder, *Sambucus racemosa* 'Sutherland Gold' *(right)* has been purned hard in spring to encourage bright new growth.

SHRUBS FOR SHADE
Bamboo
Camellia
Choisya ternata
Daphne laureola
Elaeagnus
Fatsia
Garrya elliptica
Hypericum
Kerria japonica
Mahonia
Osmanthus decorus
Pyracantha
Ribes alpinum
Skimmia
Viburnum davidii

SCENTED FLOWERS
Buddleja
Ceanothus 'Gloire de Versailles'
Choisya ternata
Corylopsis
Daphne
Elaeagnus
Hamamelis mollis
Lonicera
Magnolia
Osmanthus
Rosa
Syringa
Viburnum

WINTER FLOWERS
Daphne mezereum
Garrya elliptica
Hamamelis
Jasminum nudiflorum
Lonicera fragrantissima
Mahonia japonica
Viburnum x bodnantense, V. farreri, V. tinus

FOR SMALL GARDENS
Buddleja
Cornus
Corylus avellana
Fuchsia (hardy types)
Rubus cockburnianus
Sambucus
Salix daphnoides
Weigela

217

Roses No garden is complete without roses. Of all the shrubs, they are the best known and evoke the most passionate response to their exquisite flowers.

And yet I came to roses late, not really knowing anything about them other than their obvious and conventional status as an icon of beauty. I then assumed the rigour and rigid parameters of the newly converted, affecting to love only "old" roses and publicly despising all Hybrid teas, Floribundas, and China roses. This was as silly as limiting yourself to only liking rap music or pre-1750 cantatas. If a flower is lovely, who cares if it belongs to a Gallica, Centifolia, Floribunda, or rambler? None of those labels affect its loveliness.

Yet as I learn a little more about roses, historically, botanically and, through direct experience, horticulturally, I do tend to get more pleasure from shrub roses than Hybrid Teas, and more from the older shrubs, like the rugosas, Bourbons, Damasks, or Albas than modern shrub roses. I particularly like the combination of delicacy and opulence, the way that none are designed (literally) to be labour-saving, fast, long-lasting, thornless, small, or whatever attribute is thought to be desirable for the modern gardener.

The flowers vary enormously but tend to have better colours, ranging from the pure white of *R. rugosa* 'Alba' to the incredible deep red of 'Souvenir du Docteur Jamain', 'Charles De Mills', or 'Tuscany', without any of the weirdly ersatz, almost chemical shades you see on so many Hybrid Teas. Also, most shrub roses follow my 60/40 rule, which is that you need at least 60 per cent foliage to 40 per cent flower – and usually more – if the flower is to look good. This puts an onus on the foliage to have qualities of its own, and means that

plants are never chosen for their flowers alone, which is the only justification for many Hybrid Teas.

Unlike many of the Hybrid Teas or Floribunda roses, the point of shrub roses is never solely a flower, leaf, or hip; the entire plant contributes to its attraction. In fact, it is very rare for a shrub rose not to have a number of flowers that are mouldy or spoilt or healthily rotting at the same time as many more are at their best. The plant is not just a vehicle for the flower, however stunning that may be. I firmly believe that every plant must earn its keep in the context of the garden rather than just as a specimen. This means that the real skill and pleasure of growing plants is not judged by the success of them as individual performers but their relationship to one another, the season, and the whole range of factors, such as soil, aspect, climate, and structure. It never fails to astonish me that a single rose that you can cup in the palm of your hand can look, feel, and smell so wonderful and yet at the same time the whole shrub – up to 4 x 4m (12 x 12ft) in the case of a large Alba – has exactly the same effect within the context of the garden.

One of the confusing aspects of gardening that muddies the waters is that enthusiasm for horticulture can evince itself in fanatical love of a plant, with lives literally devoted to their cultivation, amassing extraordinary depth of knowledge and yet without any development of aesthetic judgment. I think that is why I always return to writing about this garden. In the end, every judgment and decision is

One of the greatest pleasures of my gardening year is to go out into the Walled Garden and pick a basket full of roses and then arrange them in jam jars to put around the house *(opposite top)*. The Moss rose 'Chapeau de Napoleon' *(opposite bottom right)*, so-named because of its extraordinary tricorn-like bud. The simple flower of the modern shrub rose 'Nevada' *(opposite bottom left)* which is one of the first to flower and continues on and off all summer.

Left The roses featured are as follows: *top row left to right:* 'Céleste', 'Souvenir du Docteur Jamain'; 'Tuscany Superb'; *middle row left to right:* 'Charles de Mills'; 'Cantabrigiensis'; 'Chapeau de Napoleon'; *bottom row left to right:* 'Nevada', 'Cardinal de Richelieu', *R. moyesii.*

subjective and bound inextricably in with taste and preferences. To abstract any garden plant from the garden where it has most meaning to you is to diminish it. Context is everything.

I can categorize the roses in this garden into three groups: the early ones, midsummer roses, and the species roses.

Early roses The first roses in spring are harbingers, like the first swallow or cuckoo, wonderful both in themselves and all that they promise in their wake. *R. cantabrigiensis* will undoubtedly be the first to bloom in this garden, its little snouts of primrose flowers breaking along the length of its branches against the fern-like leaves. This makes me extraordinarily happy when it happens. A rich day.

The spring-flowering roses must therefore be seen as spring flowers first and roses second. Their value is as much due to when they come as how they do so. Spring light is usually delicate and clear, and yellow dominates, both as a flower colour – think of the daffodils, primroses – and the new growth of euphorbias. The first roses have a combination of delicate leaves and yellow flowers that epitomizes the spirit of May.

I grow *R. hugonis*, which is as tough as old boots and has lovely single, primrose-coloured flowers that start to bloom at the end of April and eventually smother the length of the bristly, brownish stems. It looks best in the light shade of deciduous tree cover of the Spring Garden rather than in full sun. The leaves bronze rather nattily in the autumn too.

A chance seedling between *R. hugonis* and *R. sericea* was found in Cambridge botanic gardens in 1931, resulting in *R. cantabrigiensis,* which has pale, primrose-yellow flowers that

follow soon after *R. hugonis* so that by mid-May both are resplendently covered in knots of pale yellow flowers. The foliage is unusually long and fern-like, also turning bronze in autumn. The delicacy of the leaves is at the heart of their grace.

I do have a similar (ish) but altogether more lusty specimen of 'Frühlingsgold' – or is it 'Frühlingsanfang'? Same sort of idea. There are other kin of this German offshoot of the *pimpinellifolia* family, all prefixed with "Frühling". They may not be delicate but are great in a golden floral romp each spring, rather like a good-natured labrador puppy, and need no horticultural attention whatsoever. They are mostly single-flowered, but the Scotch burnet rose, *R. pimpinellifolia* 'Double Yellow' is, as its name describes, double. The flowers are small and bright yellow, becoming hips that are a wonderful black. There are millions of pimpinellifolias or Scotch roses, with the doubles being essential traditional elements of any self-respecting cottage garden. All are very hardy and will grow in almost any soil, but for the purposes of our spring display, *R. pimpinellifolia* 'Glory of Edzell' is very early and a note of pink in an otherwise yellow palette; the species itself, *R. pimpinellifolia,* which has single creamy flowers, is also early.

A modern rose which might come from *pimpinellifolia* stock, or might be a *R. moyesii* hybrid, is 'Nevada'. It has white flowers fading to yellowy-pink, with a first flush in May, scatterings and smatterings throughout high summer, and another proper go at it in later summer. The stems are chocolate-brown and it grows with the toughness of a buddleja on a building site. Every garden should have one, even if just to count spring in.

221

Midsummer roses There is a point around the end of June – just a week or so – when the Walled Garden is perfect. The ruffled, bouffoned complexity of Albas, Gallicas, Centifolias, Damasks, Mosses, Hybrid Perpetuals, and Bourbons hold sway. This is their time. There is a sense of profligacy, of beauty so abundant that it can be utterly careless without any sense of waste.

The colours range from the slatey crimson of the Gallica 'Cardinal Richelieu', via the velvet red of 'Tuscany Superb' with its yellow core, through the extraordinary delicate pink of 'Cuisse de Nymphe', which illuminates the petals exactly, like folds of richest silk, to the clear white of 'Alba Semiplena'. Fragrance rises up from them like dawn light.

Their flowering may be limited to a couple of months for most varieties but all are tough and healthy plants. Roses can send non-

organic growers scurrying after sprays and lotions like a hypochondriac singer. But most old garden roses are as tough as brambles. That is one of the reasons that they have survived in gardens, in many cases unaltered for hundreds of years. Albas are perhaps the hardiest of the lot and are a good starting point, being easy to grow and seemingly indifferent to soil or shade. All Albas have wonderful scent and are pale in colour. My favourite is 'Alba Semiplena' – white, multi-petalled, deliciously scented, and with lovely glaucous foliage. 'Madame Plantier' and 'Madame Legras de St Germain' are also white and can be trained to climb a wall or tree as well as develop into shrubs. 'Madame Plantier' is bigger, reaching 4 x 2.5m (12 x 8ft) when fully grown. 'Cuisse de Nymphe' and 'Königin von Dänemark' are both delicately pink, and 'Céleste' is sugar-pink but avoids being too

A corner of the Walled Garden at the very end of July. It is unruly, unkempt, and the roses are past their best, yet it still has that soft, tumbling beauty that the old-fashioned shrub roses invariably give to a border. In a few weeks this will all be cut back hard ready for its second flourish at the end of summer.

sacchariney through its grey foliage.

The Gallicas are almost as robust as the Albas and of as ancient a pedigree. I adore 'Tuscany Superb' and the wonderful flat-top 'Charles de Mills'. 'Scharlachglut' is a Gallica cross and was bred just after the last war, so hardly qualifies as "old", but we have a dozen bushes in the Jewel Garden throwing up a succession of single flowers, varying from scarlet to shocking pink as the sun fades them.

The Centifolias or cabbage roses are as blowsy and opulent as roses know how to be, both in petal and in fragrance. I grow 'Pompon de Bourgogne', which has small, very petalled, pink flowers at the end of May, reddish-purple 'Robert le Diable' which flowers later, and 'Rose de Meaux' which is pink like 'Pompon de Bourgogne' but with larger flowers.

Moss roses are related to Centifolias. At first sight they look as though they are suffering from an infestation of aphids along their stems and buds, but this is, in fact, a moss-like whiskery growth. I grow 'Général Kléber', which has long, mossy stems that almost justify the plant's existence, although the crumpled pink flowers that follow are fabulous. 'Henri Martin' is bright red, very floriferous and quite compact. 'Louis Gimard' is an oddity in that the stems twist curiously as though slightly contorted. The flowers are pink, full and open fairly flat. 'Madame Delaroche-Lambert' has rounder flowers, red leaning towards purple.

The Damasks are tough and very like Gallicas. My favourite is 'Madame Hardy' which is white with a distinctive green "eye". 'Kazanlik' is the archetypal pot-pourri rose, originating from Bulgaria. 'Quatre Saison' is another good Damask although it can promise more than it delivers as the petals crumple a little too loosely to be perfect.

Rose problems

Blackspot

Blackspot is a fungal disease made worse by too much atmospheric moisture, i.e. rain, and there is little that you can do about it. The best policy is to prune well in spring so that each plant has good ventilation, not to crowd the roses with too many leafy herbaceous plants (which is what we tend to do here and which stop air flow and hold water), and to collect up all fallen leaves and burn them so that the fungus does not linger in the soil at the base of the bush. There is some evidence that growing tomatoes near – and even twining through – roses helps ward off blackspot. But it sounds aesthetically challenged...

Balling

Balling is the state where the bud almost opens but the outer petals form a carapace that stops it developing into a flower at the last moment. The result is a ball of petals that rots and eventually drops off. This can be salvaged if you tease apart the outer petals, literally freeing the rose from its bonds. It is caused by prolonged rain at the late bud stage and is especially bad if the rain is sequenced with hot sun, which dries them and forms a crust.

Powdery mildew

Powdery mildew, which takes the form of a pale grey mould on shoots and leaves, is a problem exacerbated by the base of the plant being too dry. The rose gets weakened and becomes more prone to blackspot and other diseases. It often happens in apparently wet summer weather, when the leaves are getting soaked in a lot of gentle moisture but a combination of evaporation and the umbrella effect of foliage means that very little actually reaches the ground. Along with sunshine, roses like plenty of water, so give them a soak if the soil is very dry.

Rust

Rust is another disease that thrives in warm, wet weather. It starts with small orange pustules on the undersides of the leaves and can spread very quickly over the whole plant. These spores turn brown and eventually black, killing the leaves. Remove any leaf that has a trace of rust and burn it. As with all fungal diseases, clean up round the base of the plant scrupulously in autumn so that it cannot overwinter in the ground.

Species roses Species roses are among the toughest plants in the garden and will grow in almost any soil and any position. These are plants that need to sprawl and you need to indulge their laxity. I have planted all mine in borders of various kinds, but they are positioned at the back so they can grow tall and floppy.

The first thing that one notices if you see a selection of species roses in flower is that they are pretty unshowy. No petal-crammed blooms but single flowers, which in turn develop a range of extraordinarily beautiful hips. The thorns vary enormously, from the bristle of *R. pimpinellifolia* to the famously shark's fin thorns of *R. sericea* f. *pteracantha*, or the spiralled interlocking helix of *R. willmottiae*. In Hybrid Teas we endure a hideously ugly bush for the – sometimes – glorious flowers. Fair deal. With Centifolias or some Gallicas we (I do) endure balled flowers, blackspot, and grey mould for the few weeks when the shrub is weighed down with a gorgeously fragrant, subtly voluptuous display, but with species roses you take the plant in its entirety and the flowers are merely the more conventionally all-singing, all-dancing aspect of its performance. The sum of any individual species rose's parts tends to amount to more than the whole. That is their great charm.

One of the less likely parts is the coloured stems. Of the species roses I grow here in this garden, *R. moschata* and *R. complicata* are both green-stemmed, even in winter, but *R. californica* 'Plena' is orange, *R.* x *wintoniensis* red, and *R.* 'Nan of Painswick' a deep alizarin.

Pruning roses is a subject that sends people into a terrible anxiety about how, where, and when to do it.

Shrub roses do not really NEED pruning. Tests have shown that a trim with a hedgecutter is as effective for health and flowering as careful and selective pruning. However, I do prune my roses with secateurs and carefully go over each bush in early spring to give them the best chance for healthy flowering. If you remember the golden rule of pruning – namely, that the harder you cut back the more vigorous the resulting growth, you cannot go far wrong. It means that if a shrub has some weak stems and some vigorous ones, to balance it out you should cut the weak ones back hardest and merely reduce the strong ones by one-third. I also remove any crossing or damaged stems as wounds or abrasions are the point where fungal diseases enter. Climbing roses flower on the current season's growth and are best pruned in autumn, but ramblers should be pruned immediately after flowering as they flower on the previous year's wood and need as long a ripening period as possible. Dead-heading is a form of pruning and both tidies the plant and prolongs flowering. Never just pull off the faded petals but cut back to the next leaf or bud with secateurs.

I have no problem with single flowers and feel no need to apologize for the small size of the flowers on *R. hugonis* or the simplicity of *R. ferreri,* and if *R. moyesii* had any more petals it would explode, so intense is its red.

Species climbers tend to have great vigour and masses of small flowers that appear just the once. In the 1980s and early 1990s, vast quantities of *R. filipes* 'Kiftsgate' were sold to cover a couple of square metres of trellis or wall. *R. filipes* is less powerful but dramatic enough for most gardens. *R. multiflora* has bunches of flowers and will grow as a shrub or climb over a support up to 6m (20ft) high.

Shrubs do not really need much pruning (*see above*) but I cut back weak stems in late winter to induce strong regrowth, and trim over-long stems in autumn to stop the wind rocking the roots. BUT it is important to dead-head if you want to prolong flowering.

Winter shrubs
Winter flowers are few and far between, so winter-flowering shrubs are precious, as are those shrubs providing colour from their leaves, berries, and bark.

Lonicera fragrantissima

There is something forlorn about a lone flowering shrub on a wet winter's day that seems rather futile. Nevertheless, it would be less than optimistically human to abandon the precious few flowers that we do get in midwinter just because they do not quite work in the garden. The few times that I have seen really effective use of winter shrubs, they have been tucked into a corner, or in the lee of a wall or by a door or window. They need to be used as a vignette, not a statement because there is too much sky and, with a few exceptions, the statement is lost in the wind, rain, and muddy grey of a winter's afternoon.

The viburnums are the biggest and best-known group for this. It is such a large and diverse family, ranging from the most familiar of the lot, *V. x bodnantense* 'Dawn', with its floret bubbles of tiny flowers on bare branches that can start appearing in November and last right through to March, to the evergreen *V. tinus* ('Laurustinus'), or the spring-flowering *V. plicatum* 'Mariesii', which looks like an exceptionally lovely hydrangea. *V. farreri* has a good fragrance and is best outside against a warm wall that will trap its scent.

I have been trying to think of ways of making these shrubs work, of improving them, and it cannot be done. The truth is that I think these are dull plants and belong to dull gardening. In the summer, they are hopeless and have to be hidden or absorbed and in winter, for the most part, their flowers are a token, rather like the Christmas present that you do not want. You appreciate the thought but… They stem from a lazy view as garden-as-chore, which breeds the notion that a "good" plant is one that covers most space with least work. Better to fill the body of the garden with shrubs as understorey to a few standard trees – which is what most of them want to do.

I do have a soft spot for wintersweet, *Chimonanthus praecox*. Like many winter-flowering shrubs, it isn't much of a looker but the little primrose-yellow flowers, with their alizarin centres, are fabulously fragrant and make very good cut flowers. The scent stays much longer if kept in a cold room. It can be trained to make a (scrawny) climber on a sheltered, sunny wall, and in many ways it is best grown like this, with a clematis using it for support in the summer.

Although I have been dismissive of these scant winter-flowering shrubs, I do grow a couple of varieties of winter-flowering honeysuckle, *Lonicera fragrantissima* and *L. purpusii*, and the evergreen version, *L. standishii*. This is not out of any particular desire to collect the things but because I somehow acquired them years ago and, tucked away almost entirely out of sight on a north-facing wall in the Spring Garden, they provide the best-scent of all winter flowers. There are usually a few tentative tiny flowers by Christmas and they hit their full stride by the middle of January.

Coloured bark and stems A number of barks shine with jewel-like brilliance in the depth of winter, especially in the month or two between the sap beginning to rise and the first

Taking a breather from stacking up all the brilliantly scarlet-coloured stems of the limes *Tilia platyphyllos* 'Rubra' after pruning the Lime Walk. It is always a wrench to prune these as they look fabulous against a blue winter sky, although skies of that hue are rare enough. When I have finished pruning them all, which takes weeks, the stems are shredded and used as a mulch.

leaf buds emerging. They would be diminished by the brightness of spring, let alone the glare of summer, but are the brightest thing in the landscape on a grey, even wet, January day. Cometh the hour, cometh the plant.

The best known is the dogwood, *Cornus alba*, which has brilliant stems in shades of crimson. It is the new growth that shines the most and, if you coppice them back hard to a stool a few inches from the ground, the smooth, whippy stems grow up thicket-thick like a haze of intense coral. The trick is to cut half of each shrub back each year. All the varieties of *C. alba* grow in almost all conditions (hence their invariable use in municipal and corporate planting), but they thrive in rich, slightly damp soil in full sun.

C. alba 'Sibirica' (sometimes called 'Westonbirt') is the most common, principally, I suspect, because it does not get too big and therefore is better suited to small gardens, but there are a number of *C. alba* varieties, all with red shoots except 'Kesselringii', which has melodramatic, purple-black stems.

C. stolonifera 'Flaviramea' has wonderful shoots that are yellow ochre at the tips and maturing to a rich olive-green at their base. In this garden it seems to produce much denser growth than *C. alba* and shimmers rather than glows. These niceties matter on a bleak January afternoon.

There are some willows that have fabulously bright skins on their branches that can also be cut back hard every year to encourage more vigorous, especially vivid growth. One cannot overstress this point with these shrubs grown for their bark – the harder you cut them back, the more vigorous the resulting growth and the more dynamic the growth, the more intense the colour between December and March.

While the dogwoods will grow anywhere, willows have a distinct preference for damp soil and will struggle on chalk or sand. My favourites are the Golden willow, *Salix alba* subsp. *vitellina*, which has yellow stems veering towards a yolky orange, and *S. daphnoides*, with purple stems coated in cottony bloom.

Although willows and dogwoods look best in groups, there is hardly any need to buy them in bulk unless you are impatient, because they all take very easily as hardwood cuttings, especially the willows. When I cut them back in early March, I always stick a group of 20cm (8in) long stems in a row in a corner of the seedbed, perhaps adding some sharp sand to the narrow trench first. They can be planted out the following autumn.

A few of the ornamental brambles have stems that are covered in a white bloom over winter, which makes them starkly ornate. The problem with these ornate brambles is one of space. I do grow the *Rubus cockburnianus* 'Goldenvale', primarily for its lime-green foliage in spring and summer, but it also has wonderful winter stems, a pinky red dusted liberally with a white bloom. It also takes terribly easily from cuttings and I have found that it will quickly become invasive if you don't keep it cut back, as it roots wherever the arching stems touch the soil, as I suppose you might expect a bramble to do. However, prune it like another bramble, the autumn-fruiting raspberry, and cut the whole thing to the ground each spring, which will stymy any incipient suckers and encourage vibrant new growth, etc. The true *cockburnianus* seems to have a whiter bloom than 'Goldenvale' and is probably a better bet for winter display.

Shrubs with berries There are a number of flowering shrubs that have exceptional fruit, for that is all any berry is, edible or otherwise. To get fruit you must leave the flower to fade into shaggy maturity. Dead-head your roses and you get no hips. And for many gardeners that goes against the puritanical grain of tidiness as well as the more reasonable practice of cutting back faded flowerheads to stimulate more to follow. The fruit needs summer sun to ripen, so shrubs that flower in May and June tend to make for better berriers than the later-flowering plants. Also, shrubs that produce a mass of flowers (ideally high up, well out of tidinesses way) are always going to be a better bet for berries than those with a few choice "blooms".

The most obvious candidates for this harvest of neglect are roses. Not all roses produce hips (just a berry by another name), but most do and some almost more spectacularly than their flowers. In the main, the species roses are more prolific and interesting hip-bearers than hybrid roses. The hips of *R. rugosa* are like tomatoes, *R. moyesii* are like miniature orange bottle gourds, those of *R. pimpinellifolia* are a deep brown, and those on *R. glauca* are bunched like grapes. *R. x wintoniensis* has great clusters of flagon-shaped hips that have a curious purplish bloom.

Hips have an unbreakable link for me with haws, the fruit of the hawthorn, *Crataegus monogyna*. The May blossom is best on untended hedges between fields rather than all the neatly trimmed roadside ones, so anyone not near stretches of wild-hedged fields misses the beauty of haws turning a dark red as they ripen and become irresistibly delicious for the birds.

The oddest of berries are those of *Callicarpa bodinieri* var. *giraldii*, which have a metallic sheen to their purple shanks, as unvegetative as anything growing in the garden. It has taken years for the one bush growing in this garden to get established, and it is still small, although now growing healthily and smothered in small berries, which will stay on long after the leaves fall, growing more metallic as autumn pushes in.

Pyracanthas seem to be regarded as rather lowly plants, but I like them, both for their tiny white summer flowers that smell so intensely sweet, and which bees love so much, and for their fabulous displays of berries. I like their common name, firethorn, as it perfectly describes the way the berries blaze out from the unexceptional matt leaves. At a time of year when light and colour are at a premium, firethorns more than earn their place in any garden. One should be as brash as possible with pyracanthas, and 'Orange Glow' is as brash as they come, although 'Navaho' or 'Golden Charmer' push it hard.

Cotoneasters are slightly more subtle and slightly less dramatic, but still jolly in the kind of way that is *infra dig*. But, like pyracanthas, they will grow in dry shade, train well against a wall or fence, have lovely berries, and there are hundreds of different species to choose from (although I realize that for most people that can be a daunting turn-off. A choice of five good ones would be enough). Most cotoneasters are completely unfussy about where you put them as long as it is not boggy. It is usual to use their adaptability for a very dry spot. Prostrate cotoneasters, such as *C. horizontalis,* are not the most inspired of choices for ground cover, but they can be very useful to hide a septic tank or somesuch, especially in dry shade.

Pyracantha 'Red Cushion'

Rosehips

Berries are the best autumnal colour and some plants, like callicarpas, are grown exclusively for their decorative fruit. Many roses have fabulous hips. The most impressive are rugosas, with their great tomato-like fruit, and many of the species roses. Birds love all berries, but tend to go for red ones first and leave the dark blue and black ones alone.

229

The
Damp
Garden

The Damp Garden

Rather like the Spring Garden, the Damp Garden is an area made in the shadow of the straight lines that I have imposed upon this wavy-edged site and it is all the better for that.

The hornbeam hedges that delineate it have grown wonderfully well here, having the perfect combination of moisture, drainage, and sunshine so that they reached 4m (12ft) in five years. The Damp Garden lies behind this screen, half of it shaded from the midday sun and all of it protected from the wind. It is the first to flood and the last to drain. While it is not permanently wet, the water table is just a little higher and the reservoir of moisture in the soil just a little bigger so that any damp-loving plants get a better chance of flourishing here than anywhere else in the garden.

Because of the regular influx of silt from the river, the soil is as rich as fruitcake and it never truly dries out. It has led an uncertain existence, being happy with massed self-sown angelica, comfrey for a while, and being the main site for compost heaps for two years, but it never quite established an identity until a couple of years ago, when I moved all the hostas and ligularias in the garden down to that spot. The hostas had been mainly in the Spring Garden and the ligularias in the Jewel Garden, and both were unhappy by the end of summer. Funnily enough, the ligularias were suffering most from drought, while hostas simply prefer the wet rather than need it. We have *Ligularia dentata*, *L. przewalskii*, *L.* 'The Rocket' and *L.* 'Desdemona'.

The Damp Garden is so-named because it always floods in winter and occasionally in summer. In the year that this book was written, I dug much of it over and moved many of the plants, giving it a thorough spring clean (*top and bottom right*). These pictures were taken at the beginning of May, when the hostas are emerging and growing inches every day (*bottom left*).

We have, in the way of hostas, *H.* 'Snowden', which has huge leaves with more than a tinge of blue about them, *H.* 'Sum and Substance', which is equally big but yellowish – what Americans call "chartroose"; *H. sieboldiana* var. *elegans* which has wonderful powdery, glaucous leaves, *H.* 'Frances Williams', and others. There are some with white edging, others with white stripes, a few with bluish blazes on a yellow-green background, spear-leaved ones, and others that have leaves like ping-pong bats. Many have been with us for years and I never knew their names at all. Others I have forgotten. But it does not seem to matter with hostas.

To these two wet-lovers I added in the Royal fern *Osmunda regalis*. This has started seeding itself all over the place, much to my pleasure. There is a small quince tree and two bamboos, *Phyllostachys nigra* and *P. aurea*. Self-sown honesty (an escapee from one of the compost heaps that were on the site) has filigreed itself into the area, and it is all set against a backdrop of hornbeam hedges and prolific weeds as the boundary of our garden dips into the water meadows. I am slowly adding primulas, testing what will survive the summer drought and also rather running out of space because of the astonishing vigour of the hostas and ligularias.

The common name of hostas, the **Plantain lily**, *(top)* rightly celebrates their lovely flowers. The unfurling fronds of the Royal fern, **Osmunda regalis**, which loves the damp soil. The seed pods of honesty, **Lunaria annua**, which will become milkily translucent by late summer. The golden spires of **Ligularia przewalskii** are a lot easier to admire than pronounce.

233

Last year we turfed a sort of path along the back of one of the borders, and put a seat there. It was a mistake. No one walked down the path. No one sat on the seat. We make these sort of mistakes all the time, but by their very nature they can be rectified as easily as they were made. So, the grass has all been lifted – having had a year in which to get good and established – the seat has been shunted away, and lovage, some *Stipa gigantea*, and teasels have been planted to add height to the back of the border.

It will always be a difficult area to get right because of the huge influx of weeds that come with every flood and because of the way that the soil veers from submerged to dry over the summer. But when everything is growing lushly in April, May, and June it is one of my favourite secret corners of the garden.

The contorted willow (*facing page*) has a contorted name, *Salix babylonica* var. *pekinensis* 'Pendula'. I took it as a cutting and it is growing well. Teasels, *Dipsacus follonum* (*above*), are biennials that are wonderfully statuesque but self-seed thickly and invariably need thinning. The bistort (*left*), *Polygonum bistorta*, has red spikes of flowers in summer and red-bruised leaves. It will tolerate dry soil but is much happier in damp conditions.

Willow One of the stupidest things I did when we moved here was to take a bundle of willow cuttings from an incredibly vigorous hybrid of the white willow, *Salix alba*, and stick them along the edge of our boundary where it butts up to the water meadow. Like all willows, they rooted in weeks and in the ideal wet conditions grew monstrously. Cutting them back to the ground did no good at all as they respond by throwing up multiple stems with renewed vigour, making 1.8m (6ft) of growth a year. I have calculated that for a month or so in midsummer these monsters grow 2.5cm (1in) a day. This makes them superb material for biomass but hopeless for any kind of garden. The cover that they provided was always thin and now, nearly 10 years later, I am having to try and remove 10m (30ft) trees with trunks 60cm (2ft) across and very extensive roots. So beware the casually planted willow!

Having said that, they are beautiful, especially in spring when the new leaves appear. They are also one of the few trees that are happiest in very wet ground.

A number of years ago I took a cutting from a friend's contorted willow, *Salix babylonica* var. *pekinensis* 'Pendula'. It rooted easily but kept dying back every couple of years. However, in the past three years it has been healthy and is now starting to look like a young tree rather than a rooted cutting, with its curling, corkscrewing branches spilling off a straight stem.

Food from the garden

Vegetables

The vegetable garden

The main vegetable garden was originally intended to be a lawn. The plan – carefully thought through, drawn out, and measured onto the ground with canes and string – was to have an open square of grass, bounded by mixed borders and hornbeam hedges, just near the back door so that the children could play safely and yet feel connected to the house. The vegetables were to be grown further along the site, roughly where the Jewel Garden is now. Indeed, I had already woven fences marking out that area and installed a standpipe and tap to service it. It seemed a perfect arrangement.

Excavating the site Then a local contractor came with an enormous tractor and ploughed the area that was to take lawn, borders, and vegetable garden. But as soon as the vast steel shares bit into the ground and unfurled the soil I knew

that my plans would have to change. The soil was so good – a heavy, rich loam with all the nutritional and moisture-retaining qualities of clay and yet light enough to work and drain – that it would be wasted on grass. The children could play – anywhere, everywhere, but not there. I will admit that they would be the first to say that this has been the prevailing attitude towards the conflicting demands of children and the garden. They have had to fit around it and not vice versa. There are worse childhood traumas to cope with.

So, having changed plans, I shifted the vegetable beds to their current position. It is in full sun, but was very exposed, so I wove a hazel fence around the area and we planted hornbeams inside this. Around the whole perimeter of the vegetable garden are pleached lime trees, which have

adopted their form slowly over the past ten years, but now they provide the desired extra level of shelter without causing too much shade over the vegetable beds.

Then I had to decide how best to arrange the various beds. I knew that there would be borders around the outside and that there must be at least four permanent vegetable beds within these because I wanted central paths to cross in the middle, dividing the garden up into quarters. Each quarter would not be particularly large but would allow some flexibility. Or I could sub-divide them again, creating small, permanent beds.

There is a tendency amongst organic vegetable growers in particular to assume that small, and preferably raised, beds are preferable to open ground. This is not an automatic truth. The advantages of growing vegetables on open ground are many. Open ground gives much greater flexibility than small beds, it makes cultivation easier, especially mechanical cultivation. It makes hoeing easy, it makes irrigation easier, especially with leaky pipes, and it is much better than small raised beds for plants that need to be grown in rows rather than blocks, like beans and potatoes. The disadvantages of growing in large, open beds are that a lot of the work that goes into cultivation is wasted between rows and crops, and the ground becomes compacted from all the inevitable walking on it. It is also aesthetically only attractive when filled with vegetables, looking very bleak in winter.

The aesthetics of growing vegetables has much to do with symmetry and lines. But any vegetable garden must be practical. Brick paths look good but they are there so we can use heavy wheelbarrows in the wettest weather.

Design and layout I decided that I wanted small beds for the vegetables and that they were to be formal and symmetrical, so each quarter was divided into three more beds.

To me the aesthetics of vegetables has much to do with patterns and lines and any vegetable garden is improved if it plays upon that. I also knew that I wanted to edge the beds with low woven hazel fences because this was a medieval system and would relate back to the medieval house that we were still in the process of carefully restoring.

Marking out the beds So I marked out and made the fencing before double-digging all the beds. This was slow, hard work, but when it was done it looked good – and this was before a single seed had been sown. The central paths were made simply by rotovating the ploughed ground and treading them flat. Weeds and grass began to grow soon enough and I cut these every week. By the end of the first summer the grass had almost entirely taken over from the weeds and these were the makings of our current grass paths. Over the years we have substituted paving bricks for much of the grass paths to allow us to wheel heavy barrows in wet weather – which is three quarters of the year.

If I have any regrets about this vegetable garden it is that when I made it I was unaware that the bottom quarter would flood. This is not disastrous, as it always drains quickly, but it does limit what can be grown in this wet

Hard paths mean that access is possible in all conditions and most of the maintenance work can take place without treading on the beds. Each bed was originally edged with woven hazel fences (*left*) which is gradually being replaced by box (*above and far left*).

section and it does bring in weed seeds. The surrounding borders were moved after a couple of years, giving me another 12 beds for vegetables, making 24 in all. If this seems like a lot, I was soon running out of space again and I recently made a new vegetable patch at the far end of the garden, to act as an overspill. There was another reason for the expansion.

The new vegetable patch The original vegetable garden was becoming infested with slugs because of the high component of organic material that had been added to the soil and because global warming has gradually made the climate more congenial to them. Whilst they are self limiting to a degree, the numbers are significantly reduced by not growing crops that they particularly like to eat, like salad crops and dwarf beans. By growing these in another location where there were few slugs, I could use green manure (*see page 45*) more as part of the general rotation as well as to get the crops that we wanted onto our plates. In the medium and long term, slugs are not a great problem and, in the short term, avoidance is often more effective than trying to battle with them head on.

Making raised beds This new vegetable patch is made up of eight conventional raised beds with paths between them made from polypropylene landscaping fabric covered by wood chips made from the previous year's

243

The second vegetable area (*left*) has long raised beds and paths made from wood chips over landscape fabric. Raised beds are best if edged to stop the soil spilling onto paths.

The tightly pruned, leafless espaliered pears (*top right*) are decked with blossom in April. Plastic cloches protect rows of thyme from rain. By mid-July (*bottom right*) the pears have put on a great spurt of new, leafy growth, the garlic has been harvested, and the nearest bed is planted with young celery and celeriac.

Although I always thoroughly water in young plants (*above, top*) they get little irrigation after that. No vegetable material is wasted (*bottom*). What we do not eat goes to the compost heap.

hedge pruning. In time – and when I can afford it – I intend to edge each of these raised beds with boards to stop the edges from collapsing.

When making raised beds there are two essential considerations: the first is to make them narrow enough so that you can comfortably reach the centre from either side – I find 1.5m (5ft) is an absolute maximum width – and the second is to make each bed short enough so that you are not deterred from walking round to work beyond your reach. Ignore either of these and it is certain that sooner or later you will try and step over or directly onto the beds, thereby negating the point of them.

My small beds in the main vegetable garden are designed to make each unit manageable and yet large enough to take a whole crop. The beds look best when planted in monocultures and yet are large enough to take a mix of crops. Psychologically it is also good to have a small area to work on. If I do

not have much time (which is nearly always) it means that I can go out and dig or weed one bed and feel that I have achieved and completed a job. I have a number of scaffolding planks cut to fit the beds that live in the vegetable garden, which I use to stand on and as spacers for planting out. In fact my basic units of measurement for all vegetables are the width of a plank and the span of my hand. It seems to work.

If I were to advise anyone on the making of a new vegetable garden, these are the key points that I would make:
• Have a mains water supply no further than 20m (70ft) from any point, supplied with the largest bore pipe available. Some kind of water tank or reservoir to collect and store rainwater that can be pumped or dipped into would also be useful and energy efficient.
• Spend whatever you can afford on durable paths. Grass looks good but has to be mown and gets very soft in the wet. Good access in all weather saves a lot of time and trouble.

• A nearby point for compost and/or storing animal manure with access to a road is an enormous help. I have to wheel all my materials in and out for at least 50m (160ft), barrow load by barrow load. This is not a hardship, but it does take time.

• At least half the site must have sunlight all day.

• No time, trouble or money spent on making the soil rich, healthy and with a good structure is wasted. Your vegetables are only as good as your soil.

• If there is no existing shelter from wind then plant or build some as soon as possible. Wind is a greater enemy than extremes of temperature.

• Make it beautiful. This is easy to do between summer and autumn but think of the winter. Some kind of permanent structure is advisable.

General principles

The real skill in vegetable gardening is not to grow champion specimens or produce vast harvests but simply to provide a supply of delicious vegetables on any given day.

Start with the soil. A vegetable garden is ideally situated on a south-facing slope with high brick walls to protect it. Failing this paragon (and almost all gardens do) choose a sunny, protected site. Plenty of sunshine is essential but do not underestimate the importance of protecting the site from wind. Walls are wonderful for retaining and reflecting heat but expensive. I made woven fences right around my vegetable garden and planted hornbeam hedges inside this.

It is a good idea to divide the plot up into four equal parts. It does not matter how this is organized, shaped, or subdivided, but it is important to be planning along the lines of a four-part rotation from the outset.

In principle, the soil for vegetables must be very well dug and heavily manured. In practice, these needs vary from crop to crop, but initially all work put into preparing the soil will repay dividends. I cannot stress this too highly. What you put into your soil you *will* get back. It makes no difference if you are planning to use an open bed system, raised beds, or no-dig – the ground must be properly dug and well-manured before you start.

Well-made garden compost (*below and right*) is the best possible addition to the soil. It will nourish both the long-term micro-ecology and the growing plants. And if it is properly made it should smell positively good.

Immediately before planting, I spread compost (*above*) on the previously dug soil and then lightly mix it in with a rotovator. Open ground is best dug and left in clods over winter (*left*) to allow the weather to break it down.

Rotation

You rotate crops primarily to avoid the build up of disease. Rotation also helps break the cycle of certain pests that live in the soil and feed on particular types of vegetable. It also means that the different cultivation demands of different vegetables can be incorporated into an annual cycle. It is therefore an important part of healthy vegetable growing. But my own approach to this is not to be hidebound by it. It is rarely the end of the world if a legume follows a legume or if you grow your onions in the same place for two consecutive years.

There are three main groups of vegetable and the idea when plotting a rotation plan is that no member of any group should follow another in the same group on the same piece of ground. By shuffling everything round at the same time you get a minimum gap of three years between successive same-group crops.

Legumes include all kinds of beans and peas. Tomatoes and peppers get included in this group even though they belong to the same family as potatoes, as do celery, celeriac and squashes. The soil for this group is deeply dug with plenty of added manure or compost.

Brassicas include all types of cabbage, cauliflowers, broccoli, kohlrabi, radishes, mizuna, mibuna, land cress, swedes, turnips, seakale and Chinese cabbage. They follow on from legumes and are usually planted without extra compost being added to the soil; the nitrogen left from the legumes is taken up by the growing brassicas.

Every autumn I sit down and plan the crop rotation for the coming 12 months. This involves two separate plans as very few pieces of ground keep the same crop for an entire year. The plan determines the seeds I order as well as the winter digging programme. I use a computer for this although pencil and paper will do just fine. The hardest thing is to keep symmetry and aesthetic balance with the demands of strict rotation and invariably I bend the rules so that beauty comes before horticultural correctness.

Roots include carrots, parsnips, beetroot, chard, spinach, salsify, scorzonera, onions, leeks, garlic, and potatoes. Some people also include lettuce in this group although I split them between roots and legumes. In practice this is the most diverse and confusing group. Carrots and parsnips, for example, grow best in soil that has no added compost whereas it is important to top up the soil with compost for spinach, lettuce, chard, and potatoes. Common sense prevails. It is important to maintain the direction of the rotation so a legume is followed by a brassica which, in turn, is followed by a root and it is then back to a legume. Parts of the rotation might demand different cultivation but the balance between the crops and the soil is sustained. The solution is to plan it all well in advance so that you know exactly what you intend to grow in each plot together with its winter succession. I stick the plans up in the potting shed – but once made they are there to be broken. You must be flexible.

Rotation of beds Small beds for growing vegetables give more flexibility for winter and summer crop rotation.

Here, I am pulling a crop of sweetcorn and replacing it with garlic. Sweetcorn is a "catch" crop, filling a gap between midsummer and autumn. After digging the ground over, I lightly rotovate in a barrowload of compost and plant the garlic cloves using a board to stand on to avoid compacting the soil and as a straight edge and spacer for the rows. As well as sweetcorn, I sometimes follow garlic with chicory or a green manure.

Weeds

It is very important to keep on top of the weeds in a vegetable garden, regardless of the aesthetic considerations. The very nature of vegetable growing is unnatural insofar that you are forcing a very intensive rate of production from your ground. You are expecting a degree of quantity and uniformity that nature never feels obliged to produce. You are hot-housing vegetables. Therefore any competition will be detrimental. Hoe regularly and keep your vegetables clean of weeds as far as possible as they will take nutrients and moisture from your crops.

I find that a sharp Dutch hoe can work in between growing plants and remove nearly all weeds.

It is important to water in any newly planted out plants, giving them a really good soak. When you are doing any watering, concentrate the flow directly to the roots rather than the leaves of the plants.

Watering

Vegetables need a lot of water to grow and mature. Any vegetable crop will lose more than 5 litres (1 gallon) of water per square metre per sunny day. On a cool, cloudy day it will still lose well over a litre (2 pints) a day. An enormous amount of water passes through the plant but only a tiny percentage remains in it – although that tiny percentage makes up the vast majority of the mature vegetable.

In general, vegetables need more water when flowering and fruiting. A lack of water during this period will irreversibly affect the resulting crop or harvest. The important thing is to water the right amount at the right time.

Different types of vegetable respond differently to different amounts of water at different times. Leafy vegetables, in general, grow more leaves in response to a steady water supply. So lettuce, cabbage, and spinach will all produce a bigger (but not necessarily tastier) harvest if the water is never checked. Roots, on the other hand, will respond in the same way – by growing more leaves. But this does not necessarily mean more root. So you can conscientiously water your parsnips and carrots and see them repay this care with flourishing topknots but actually get no more food as a result than if you watered them less.

With legumes such as peas, broad beans, and French beans, too much water when they are young will harm the crop because energy will go into the plant, producing masses of vegetative growth and fewer pods. In fact, it is recommended that you do not water legumes at all once the seedlings are established, either from sowing or after transplanting (all transplanted vegetables need watering until new growth is visible). However, once they start to flower and produce pods you should give them a good soak.

This is also true of tomatoes, the squash family, and sweetcorn, and will result in more flowers and more and bigger seeds inside the pods. Watering new potatoes as they come into flower will dramatically increase the size of the crop and at the same time help them to mature faster, so you can harvest them earlier. In areas like my own, in Herefordshire, this is of real significance to organic gardeners because we are always in a race against the onset of blight, which invariably hits us some time after the first week of July. If we can use water to bring the crop on by just a few days it can literally save it. On the other hand, if you water onions too late on in their growth you will delay ripening.

I think that this brings us back, as ever, to the soil. If your soil has really good structure and an annual addition of lots of organic matter, either mixed into the soil or as a mulch, then the soil structure will have the right balance between water retention when the roots need it and drainage when conditions are too wet. A good soil structure lets long, healthy roots develop so the plant can grow fast and reach water and mineral reserves deeper down.

As well as saving rainwater, water butts are much quicker to dip a watering can into than filling the can up from the tap.

Sowing seed

Because of the plague of slugs and snails in our vegetable garden I sow almost everything into seedtrays, plugs or soil blocks, raising the seedlings in the greenhouse and cold frames until they are strong enough to withstand slug attack. But if slugs are not such a problem then many seeds can be sown directly into the soil, saving on time and the expense of heating, pots, and compost.

I would recommend buying good quality seeds from an organic supplier like "The Organic Gardening Catalogue" in the UK. Seeds do not last indefinitely so never keep them for more than two seasons. It is better to sow excess fresh seeds and be profligate with

them than to try and keep a half-used seed packet for two or more years.

Sow thinly, especially if you are sowing direct. Thin ruthlessly. When you sow seeds indoors and plant them out as young plants it is natural to leave generous spacing – in my case this is nearly always 22cm (9in), which is the span of my thumb and little finger. Not scientifically arrived at, but it works well – but to do this for emerging seedlings feels crazy. However, most people do not thin hard enough. Commercial growers often sow quite thickly in seedtrays and then transplant the seedlings into plugs where they grow them on before planting out. This makes sowing much quicker and means that they "thin" as they transplant into plugs by discarding the smaller seedlings.

Experiment with potting compost. I like to make my own and to include some soil from the garden in all plugs as the growing seedling acclimatizes to the micro-environment of the soil. For seedlings that are to be pricked out and grown on in trays or pots before being

Sowing seeds individually into plugs is slow but saves time later (*far left*). Cold frames are ideal for raising young plants (*left*), because the amount of protection can be so easily adjusted to allow maximum safe exposure to the weather. Cloches are especially useful in early spring when the weather can vary so much (*bottom right*). A tray of rocket seedlings ready for transplanting into individual plugs (*bottom left*).

planted out this is unnecessary and plain coir works perfectly well.

If you do not have the space or money for a greenhouse then make a cold frame from battens and polythene, with thick polystyrene sheeting to insulate the floor and walls. This makes the raising of tender crops like tomatoes, squashes, French beans, or sweetcorn much easier and means that you can grow on things like lettuce in plugs until ready for transplanting. Anything grown in a greenhouse must be properly hardened off in a sheltered spot outside for at least a week (preferably two) before being planted out. You will gain nothing by attempting to take short-cuts with this.

Finally, respond to the soil and the weather, not the calendar. A sunny day does not mean that the soil has warmed up or that frosts are over. Plants or seeds that go in late often grow faster and catch up earlier sowings. Also most people underestimate the length of the growing season. My vegetable garden can still be very productive right into November.

Planting out chard seedlings in midsummer. The tray in my hand contains individual plants raised under cover in plugs and hardened off outside. Note the board used for standing on so that the soil is not compacted; I also use it to keep the rows straight and even.

Spring shows itself first in tiny details, like the curlews arriving in the water meadows, the first primroses and violets in the coppice, the catkins on the hazel, or the blackthorn blossom in the hedgerows.

Any one of these can promise to deceive, spreading false hope, but when they are strung together they are as thrilling as anything else in the gardening calendar. The days slowly stretch until, at the end of March, the clocks change and we are gifted with an extra hour of daylight in the evenings. Spring here at Ivington is measured on the calendar as the months of March, April and May, although the really important date is February 15th, Sarah's birthday, which is the day when we start seed sowing in earnest. There is a great temptation to sow before then but I have learnt to be patient. The light is increasing daily but heat is a long way off and our heavy soil takes a while to warm up.

The overriding feature of the spring vegetable garden is the variability of the weather. It can range from very warm sun to snow to flooding within the space of a few days and frosts are always likely well into May. Germination is often irregular and even if seedlings do appear and grow vigorously for a week they often then stop growing altogether for another week or more. This is when they are most vulnerable to slugs and it is not unusual to have an entire sowing eaten in a couple of days. Better to wait and let them catch up with the season later.

If I sow too many too soon in the protection of the greenhouse, I accumulate a mass of seedlings that cannot be planted out and which quickly become etiolated due to low light levels. Only tomatoes, broad beans, rocket, land cress, mizuna, mibuna, lettuces, endive, parsley, carrots, beetroot, parsnips, and onions benefit from sowing before April and, of those, only broad beans, parsnips, and carrots can be sown directly into the ground outside.

One of the anomalies of spring is that just at the time when you are busiest in the garden sowing a huge range of

edible crops there is less produce than at any other time of year. The winter crops of cabbages, leeks, parsnips, chard, and chicory are diminishing rapidly and there is very little growing sufficiently quickly outside to take their place. So our leanest months in the garden are April and May. This is where having some cover where you can grow crops becomes a huge help in maintaining the supply of daily fresh vegetables.

However, the fruits of the salad crops that I sowed in January provide a very important supply of fresh leaves from the middle of March right up until the time when the ground in the greenhouse and tunnel has to be cleared so that the tomatoes can be planted out. The broccoli is very much a spring vegetable – although it is fixed more in my mind as a winter crop – and spring greens in April and May are my favourite form of cabbage.

Chicory (*see page 322*) overwinters well in this garden as long as it can be kept dry and will start to grow afresh as the light increases and the days warm up. But the most exciting spring crop is asparagus, which is one of the great culinary treats of the year and our first cuttings are usually made in mid-April.

One of the jobs I look forward to most in spring is the erection of the wigwams for climbing beans and the staking of young peas with pea sticks. The wood for both is cut from hazel and was one of the reasons I planted out my own coppice. It is far too early to plant the beans but I dig compost-filled pits beneath the wigwams and the structures add a dramatic signal that spring is really here and the vegetable garden means business – they also add an architectural element that immediately transforms the garden.

Another marker of spring – regardless of the weather – is the planting of our first early potatoes. There is real urgency to this as the earlier we get them into the ground the more certain we are of harvesting a blight-free crop. However, the actual timing of this varies enormously from year to year, ranging from late February to mid-May. If we do manage to make a very early sowing, the new growth has to be protected from frosts with a layer of fleece or cloches and earthed up a couple of times.

Asparagus is only available to be harvested in this garden from the end of April to the beginning of June, but what its season loses in length it more than makes up for in the pleasure it offers.

Apart from its unmistakable self it tastes to me of tulips, May blossom, rampant weed growth, buttercups, poppies, peonies, lilac, laburnum, clematis, alliums and that astonishing fecund green. Taste cannot hold any more in its mouth. But proper, grown-up indulgence hinges upon denial and to really enjoy the fullness of asparagus you must deny yourself its pleasures out of season. And you must eat it fresh.

This is why it is worth growing asparagus at home, despite it being a bit tricky to establish and quite hard work. You grow it because it gives you a supply of absolutely fresh spears – and also to spit in the eye of the seasonless "food" industry and its joyless inducements of year-round treats. Whatever we can cut in April is a bonus and entirely dependent upon the weather, but May is the fixed month for asparagus with one or two last June cuts and then it must be left to recoup its powers underground, the phallic spears becoming feathery and as succulent as a withered stick.

Growing asparagus I planted our asparagus beds up at the top, in amongst the soft fruit and almost as far from the kitchen as possible. There is no real logic to this, just a combination of available well-drained space and a box of asparagus crowns ('Connover's Colossal') that were left over from a televison shoot and, as with all crowns, needed planting immediately if they were to survive. I had had an abortive attempt a couple of years earlier, putting asparagus in a corner of the vegetable garden that floods. This was a big mistake.

Asparagus roots hate sitting in wet ground. "Crowns", by the way, describe the young plants that are little more than an octopus of straggly roots held together by a central body. From this grow the stems that, immature and fleshy, we eat.

The best time to plant them is March. If you have very well-drained soil then you can more or less bung them in the ground as long as it has been well prepared and is in a sheltered, sunny position. But if you have heavy soil like mine, then an asparagus bed needs special preparation. It involves more preparatory work than planting almost anything else. I will keep it simple but it goes something like this:

• Choose a dry day when the soil is dry. Weed and prepare a good piece of ground as though you were going to plant potatoes or peas.

• Measure out beds 1m (3ft) wide and not more than 10m (30ft) long (otherwise you will be tempted to step across them to get to the other side rather than go all the way round). Leave another 1m (3ft) between the beds.

• Dig out the topsoil from the beds onto the paths. Thoroughly dig over the next layer of soil within the beds.

• Add some mushroom compost and mix well.

• Add masses of grit (I put a 10cm/4in layer right over the base of each of my beds) and rotovate it in. Rake smooth and level.

• Make two ridges about 30cm (1ft) apart running down the length of the bed. The tops of the ridges should be below ground level.

• Drape the crowns over the ridges so that the roots hang down the slopes like inverted

When harvesting asparagus (*facing page*) I use a sharp pruning knife that has a curved, almost hooked blade. The secret is to cut each spear well below ground level so that you get as much of the blanched, tender stem as possible. We only cut enough for one meal at a time and wait until the last possible moment before doing so, since the quality and sweetness start to diminish as soon as it is cut. In a good year the spears grow very fast and they need cutting every few days before they lose their tenderness.

After mid-June the asparagus spears are left to grow into fronds that will nourish the roots for next year's crop. These are cut at ground level as they start to yellow in autumn.

mopheads. Be quick because they must not dry out.

• Shovel the topsoil back over them, making a raised bed as you do so.

• Label, tidy, and reflect that this will not need doing again in your lifetime.

That first May you celebrate the shoots – it means that your crowns are alive and growing – but do not so much as cut a solitary spear. In November you need to cut the feather fronds down to the ground once they yellow. It is important to do this before any ripe berries drop to the ground because only the male plants produce spears and sod's law says that those that drop will be female, germinate and take like a rocket, crowding the bed and thus diminishing the crop. The next spring limit yourself to two cuttings – and only from obviously "good" spears. The year after that you stop cutting on June 1st – allowing plenty of time for regeneration. Then the next year, you cut freely until mid-June.

Harvesting asparagus It is possible to buy special knives for cutting asparagus that have a long curved blade with a serrated inside edge for sawing off the stems below the surface of the soil. But it can be done with any sharp knife, cutting the stems 2.5cm (1in) or so below the ground. If the weather is warm, this will need doing twice a week to stop them becoming lanky and wooden.

Types of asparagus The British tend to grow the green variety of *Asparagus officinalis*, whose green shoots are topped by purple heads and are succulent right down the stem, but asparagus growers on the Continent mainly grow the white type, which is thicker and coarser. It is further blanched by being grown in a deep trench and harvested when only the tips appear above ground. There is also a purple type. There is no great difference between them and the varieties that you are likely to find as plants do not show any great range of characteristics. 'Accell' produces all male seeds, 'Giant Mammoth' is better adapted to heavy soil, and 'Connover's Colossal' is early and heavy cropping when grown on sandy soil. 'Martha Washington' is an American variety that has long spears and is rust resistant, and 'Lucullus' also has long, slim spears.

William Cobbett, that most truculent of eighteenth-century British rural heroes, would have none of this differentiation. "As to the sorts of asparagus of which some people talk, I, for my part, could never discover any difference..." In his time it was a wildly popular vegetable with 105 hectares (260 acres) of asparagus fields in Battersea in south-west London alone, and the asparagus beds in the walled gardens of country houses often taking up a quarter of a hectare (half an acre) – a huge area that would absorb three or four entire gardens now.

To increase production the plants were rested for a month in June and then manured heavily so that they would produce another crop of spears in September. Occasionally, roots were lifted from the bed and taken indoors to be forced on hot beds for November production. Hot beds were made by digging a trench or pit and filling it with 1m (3ft) of fresh horse manure, which was then covered by 60cm (2ft) of soil. The manure

heated up as it decomposed providing powerful underfloor heating. It shows that organic growing can be adapted for forced, almost factory, production without too much problem.

But I am content to let our asparagus arrive, unforced, to be relished almost to the point of surfeit for about six weeks and then wait until the following spring for the asparagus season to return. This way it remains what it always should be – a unique taste that belongs to the soaring fecundity of spring and early summer.

Asparagus cut and ready for cooking. This variety is the green 'Connover's Colossal'. There are three types of asparagus, green, purple, and white. Purple grows mainly underground, with just a few centimetres above the surface, while white asparagus is grown entirely underground. I believe green to have much the best flavour.

Broccoli I like my broccoli small, deep purple before cooking, and racked with flavour. As well as being good on its own, unadorned, it is also the perfect partner for anchovies and chillies.

Purple-sprouting broccoli

These are grown-up tastes, not so good for children or infantilized adult palates. I suppose the "health" industry is so keen to promote broccoli for its undeniable goodness, knowing that it will never win out on the pleasure stakes alone. Wrong of course. You can have your health and eat it. Fresh broccoli is as pleasurable as fresh asparagus or an apple plucked from the tree. It is one of the must-grow vegetables for any gardener with limited space, because although it takes up a lot of space for a long time, the real thing has to be eaten fresh and half a dozen healthy plants will provide plenty of meals if you keep picking the florets, stimulating the plant to produce more and more until they burst into

their yellow flowers faster than you can pick them. You can also underplant them with lettuces, spinach, rocket – any of the fast-growing autumn salad crops that would not compete too much for nutrients and appreciate a bit of shade and shelter.

Like most brassicas, it is a long-haul crop. Its season is surprisingly late – never before the end of March in this garden, and really at its best in April. I always end up clearing away perfectly good plants in May because I need the space, and anyway, by then we are all "broccolied out" in the Don household.

The best time to sow is a year before the peak of harvest, in the first week of April, although you will get a harvest from plants

Purple broccoli sprouts ready for picking (*right*). The sprouts tend to come in a rush, and the more they are picked, the more the plant will produce, until the kitchen cannot keep pace with it. When the shoots develop into yellow (handsome) flowers, the broccoli season is over.

sown at any time up until July. I do mine in plugs in the greenhouse but if you do sow the seed out of doors – and I did so perfectly well for years in a seed bed, along with all the other brassicas, leeks, and wallflowers – sow thinly in the first place and then thin the seedlings early so that they have a 15cm (6in) gap between them. This will seem absurd when they are tiny but broccoli is a large plant and its ability to perform well in a year's time will be strongly influenced by the way that it is treated in its first couple of months.

I usually plant my broccoli a little late and the plants sit in their pots a few weeks too long. This is because I always put them into ground that has been occupied by legumes and the first broad beans are not normally ready for clearing before the beginning of August. If you can get them into the ground by mid-July they will be the better for it. Never add manure to the ground prior to planting as this will only translate into more leaf and fewer spears. Plant them deeply and very firmly leaving at least 60cm (2ft) between each one. The plant will become large and heavy and needs a secure anchor in the ground so might also need staking, especially if the site is exposed. Soak the plants well after planting.

Broccoli is subject to clubroot, which attacks all brassicas, malforming and stunting their roots so the plant cannot develop properly, but sensible rotation and maintaining a sufficiently high pH by adding lime if necessary should avoid this. The biggest enemy to my broccoli comes from the cabbage white caterpillar and either the whole bed must be netted so that the butterflies cannot land on them and lay their eggs or you must pick off the caterpillars every day.

Broccoli is very hardy but not infinitely so. I once lost my entire crop overnight when the temperature touched -14°C (7°F), and this year half a dozen slightly more exposed plants have not survived a night at -12°C (10°F).

You can have your health and eat it. Fresh broccoli is as pleasurable as fresh asparagus or an apple plucked from the tree.

Calabrese is essentially a summer

version of broccoli, and much of what is sold as "broccoli" is in fact calabrese, but it is different enough to make it worth growing if you have the space. You sow calabrese in spring, at the same time as your broccoli, but it will be ready to harvest by late summer, or even earlier if the weather is good. Fast food! You will find that most varieties are more like mini-cauliflowers than broccoli, with large, dirty-yellow curds or florets that do not do a lot for me, especially at a time of year when the garden is bursting with beans, lettuces, carrots, beetroots, and all the rest of the summer harvest. There are exceptions to this – 'Romanesco' is good, with a euphorbia-like yellow-green cast to its florets, and 'Ramoso' (also known as 'De Cicco') has good sideshoots – much nicer than the large central head, which I discard.

Finally, I have grown 'Broccoletto' (also known as 'Cimi di Rapa'), which hovers unconvincingly between broccoli and a turnip. It is very fast indeed – just 8–12 weeks from sowing to the plate – but this is counter-balanced by a lot of waste as you only eat the sweet young leaves and florets, discarding well over half the plant. It grows like a cross between rocket and mini-broccoli, and can be sown direct or in plugs. It is a good, all-round, slightly bitter green vegetable, with none of the bland anodyne quality of bought broccoli.

'Romanesco'

Salad crops are the most important for any modern gardener. All are easy to grow and with a little organization even in a very small garden it is possible to ensure a supply of fresh, healthy leaves all year.

Rocket is easy to grow yet I now

only grow it during the cold months, between September and April. I have fine-tuned this a degree further by only growing it under cover. This is not because it will not grow at other times or unprotected – in fact it is one of the easiest of all plants to grow – but because the quality of the leaves is dramatically affected by heat, water, and light levels, and they also get attacked by flea beetle, leaving thousands of tiny holes in them. This does not make them inedible, but does reduce the quality. In fact young, fresh rocket in March is so superior to

older, later stuff that I would happily forgo this and wait for the rocket season. As the leaves get older they become much hotter and tougher – not altogether unpleasant but nothing like as good as the very fresh, initial leaves.

Rocket is a brassica and should not be grown on ground where there has been clubroot in recent years. If I grow it outside at all, I include it in my salad crop rotation.

There are many variations of rocket, without any named varieties, but the two essentially different types are what is normally sold as

I grow land cress, rocket, mibuna, mizuna, curly endive, and several varieties of cos lettuces in the tunnel to provide generous spring salads.

salad rocket, which has smooth lobes to its leaves, and wild rocket, which is much more finely cut (and superficially similar to mizuna). I much prefer the salad rocket, which also grows better and faster here.

It needs rich soil and huge amounts of water to stop it bolting as soon as the temperature rises. In any event it is a quick crop, taking eight weeks to come to maturity when sown in January and as little as four weeks if sown in spring or summer. I make three or four sowings about 10 days apart to get a succession of fresh young leaves between March and the end of May, and again

between September and December. The seeds will germinate within a couple of days.

I always used to sow directly and then thin, but in line with all other salad crops, I now make all sowings into coir-7s or plugs (the seeds are quite large so this is not as fiddly a job as it is with some lettuce or chicory) and plant them out when they have a decent root system. Rocket grows much better if it has at least 22cm (9in) between plants in each direction, even 24cm (12in) is not excessive. I cut the leaves with a knife, removing all top-growth in one go. This will regrow for at least one and usually two more cuttings.

Rocket seedlings in coir-7s

Land Cress
Land (or American) cress looks remarkably similar to watercress and grows very like rocket, although it is not quite so fast either to grow or to run to seed. It adds a good hot tang to a salad and, if eaten young, the leaves taste very similar to rocket. Although it will grow in any type of soil, it does respond to an almost unlimited amount

of moisture, so it is a good idea to add extra organic material to the ground before planting, to help retain water. The less water the plant receives and the older it becomes, the hotter the flavour of the leaves – and that can mean very hot indeed. I grow it exactly as I do rocket (*see above*), in plugs that are transplanted when the plants have a good root system.

Seedlings ready to plant out

Mibuna
is not a lettuce at all but a brassica and is closely related to mizuna (*see page 337*). It has very long strap-like leaves and a distinctive mustard flavour which, unlike rocket or land cress, does not get stronger as the plant gets older. It is quite a large plant, producing dozens of leaves that can be cut just above ground level and that will regrow very quickly for repeated cropping, so just a few plants provide plenty of salad material. It also cooks well. It is less hardy than mizuna and therefore ideal for a tunnel or greenhouse, but I find it does well outside in autumn, protecting it with cloches as the weather turns colder.

Early Lettuce

Cos seedlings ready for planting out

Lettuce plays such an important part in our diet – I suppose we eat it 300 days a year – that it gets pride of place in the top greenhouse and tunnel in spring. I do not attempt to grow lettuce outside until mid-spring, because March and April can be very cold, and if germination is successful they can sometimes stand without growing for weeks on end. This makes them a sitting target for slugs and snails and I regularly get 90 percent of seedlings wiped out. (Regularly? Yes, every year hope triumphs over experience and I plant out a batch of lettuce seedlings some time in March, thinking that this year they will be fine…) Lettuce are best when grown fast. For this they need plenty of water and an even temperature, preferably constant at around 15–17°C (59–63°F). For a number of years I have used the top greenhouse for our spring lettuce, and have now added the tunnel to add volume and a greater flexibility of succession.

The regime is always the same. Between January 1st and February, I sow a small amount of 'Little Gem', 'Winter Density', 'Tom Thumb', 'Kendo', and 'Rouge d'Hiver' (and any other lettuce that I have not come across that is able to grow at low temperatures) into plugs or blocks, usually in batches two or three weeks apart. Lettuce seed is tiny and a packet will go a long way if sown in this way. These will germinate fast under the mist propagator but the seedlings develop slowly, even in the greenhouse. I plant them out into the top greenhouse and tunnel around mid-February and cover them with fleece. A minimum of 22cm (9in) spacing is best, and although this can seem terribly wide initially, they do grow much stronger and faster as a result.

They are then entirely weather-dependent, and if we get warm days we can be eating the first thinnings a month later. However, they invariably grow fast once they get going and therefore have a good succulent texture and flavour. I will continue harvesting these plants – and replacing some with new seedlings – up until the middle of May, when they have to be cleared to make space for tomato plants.

'Tom Thumb' lettuce growing in the unheated top greenhouse at the end of March. Planted in blocks like this in a raised bed, they quickly fill out to suppress weeds and make the best use of available moisture and nutrients.

Spring greens have a bad press. But fresh spring greens are delicious and eaten in April or May with a rib of beef, boiled potatoes, and fresh horseradish make one of the best food combinations of all.

If you sow seed between July and August and transplant the seedlings into their growing position in October, they will be ready to eat by the following April or May. 'Durham Early', 'Pixie', 'Advantage', 'Prospero' and 'Greensleeves' are all varieties I have grown with success (and pleasure). It is best to sow the seed into a seed tray before pricking the seedlings out into pots and planting them into their final position in October. They do not grow much over winter – instead they look rather puny and carry a frightening whiff of failure about them – but they grow away with a vengeance in spring, and this vigour gives the leaves their extraordinary freshness of taste.

'Prospero'

Sorrel is a herb really, but we grow and use it as a vegetable. It is especially delicious in spring, when it makes a perfect accompaniment to the fresh eggs that the hens are starting to lay with a vengeance.

Sorrel is related to dock, and common sorrel (*Rumex acetosa*) does look distinctly dock-like. It likes a damp spot and all I do is cut off the flowering stem as and when it appears, pulling off lanky, excess growth with my hands. New leaves appear in the extra light. It is astringently bitter but makes an excellent omelette and soup and the juice of a leaf will remove rust, mould and ink stains from linen and silver.

French or buckler-leaved sorrel (*Rumex scutatus*) has very different round, smaller leaves and is less bitter than common sorrel. I think that it would probably be more useful, and I must add it to the vegetable garden.

I grow the sorrel in its own, permanent bed, in a shaded corner, and it is really the least trouble of any plant in the garden, contributing most of its volume directly to the compost heap, but what we do eat is delicious and irreplaceable.

Rhubarb, like the tomato, is a fruit that has somehow been appropriated to the vegetable garden. I think of rhubarb as a fixture – it is as much part of the garden as the lawn or buddleja.

A rhubarb forcer placed over the plant buds as they begin to break in late winter will force and blanch the new shoots to be taller and sweeter and limit leaf growth to a yellow, candle-like flare at the tip. Unforced plants (*shown far right*) grow with much more leaf from the outset.

It is there because it has always been there. But first get your rhubarb. You can grow rhubarb from seed, but it often does not come true to the intended variety. Many people might find the differences between rhubarb varieties too arcane and subtle to worry about, but 'Timperly Early' is probably the most common, 'Valentine' is very flavourful, 'Early Red' (sometimes called 'Early Champagne') has beautiful crimson stalks, and 'Glaskin's Perpetual' is very long cropping. The best and quickest way to start your rhubarb patch is to find someone with a mature plant and some time in winter, after the leaves have died back, get them to lift a plant and chop it up into quarters with a sharp spade. Take a chunk with a couple of clearly visible buds and plant it in soil that you have dug and added plenty of compost or manure to. This bed will be

permanent, and ours is tucked into the south-western corner of the vegetable garden.

The right planting depth should have the buds about 2.5cm (1in) below the surface – but this is not critical. Mulch it thickly with more compost. If you have alkaline soil it is a good idea to mulch each year with farmyard manure, as this tends to be acidic and rhubarb grows best with a pH around 6.0. But it will survive and perform perfectly well on almost any soil as long as it is well manured. Do not pick any stalks for the first year and cut the flowers off as they appear. By the second year you should have a good crop and a really good one two years after planting. It is a good idea – but by no means essential – to repeat this division every four years or so, chucking away the centre of the old plant, as the new exterior pieces grow with much more vigour.

Growing conditions Rhubarb needs temperatures below 5°C (41°F) to break its dormancy and stimulate spring growth and dislikes summer temperatures of more than 30°C (86°F). For this reason, I suggest planting it with shade from the west, which will protect it from the worst summer heat, although it does prefer a sunny site, so do not put it in deep shade. The baby leaves start to peek through the mulch that you should spread thickly around it as soon as the old leaves die back.

Those first tentative rootlings that appear at the same time as the snowdrops come in two guises. If they are in the open they are pink to the point of crimson, topped by a leaf so crinkled that it is almost as deep as it is wide. If you have forced it by placing a bucket, old chimney pot or genuine bespoke terracotta rhubarb forcer over it, then the light-deprived shoots are much paler.

Rhubarb's famous laxative qualities are in fact a simple result of the gut rejecting its unusually high level of oxalic acid, which is the reason it leaves your teeth feeling as though they have been vacuum cleaned. Oxalic acid is a poison, with a fatal dose of around 1500mg (0.05oz). Rhubarb has about 500mg (0.02oz) per 100g (3½oz), so, in theory, a 300g (10oz) helping of rhubarb could be fatal. The chances of dying through eating rhubarb crumble over enthusiastically are remote. But if you eat the leaves you will certainly be ill because the level of oxalic acid is much higher in the leaves than the stalks.

Harvesting rhubarb Do not cut rhubarb stalks but pull them instead, holding each stalk low down near its base giving it a twist as you do so that it tears off. Cutting lets in crown rot, which will manifest itself via spindly stems and damaged buds. There is no real cure for this, so any plants affected should be dug up and burnt. Never take more than half the stalks on any one plant. The remaining half will develop full-sized leaves which, in turn, feed the roots that provide next year's crop.

Summer enters into the vegetable garden through a back door. May is so much the archetypal month of spring that as it ends and June takes over you suddenly realize that summer has come along with it.

The days are long in June and July and there is plenty of light for gardening, from about 4.30am to 10pm. But by August the nights are drawing in, and in early September it is getting dark by 7.30 or 8 o'clock. Every year at the start of the season, I tell myself not to waste a precious moment of summer daylight, yet every year I blithely come to take it for granted.

In fact, there are two quite separate summer seasons here – the end of May through to the first week of July, and then mid-July to the first week of September. There is a real difference between the first week of June, which can be quite chilly, and the middle of August, which has a heavy, solid summeriness to it. The "first" summer season is surprisingly short on crops to harvest, whereas the second is a period of glut, where much of what is grown is gathered to be stored through the winter.

For the vegetable gardener this means that planning has to be careful to get the most out of the ground during this season. It is a question of balancing resources and demands. So new potatoes are wonderful but they take up a lot of ground and lose much in storage; whereas lettuce are essential but can bolt very fast in a hot, dry spell, so a constant succession is needed. Peas and broad beans are important but only if we are prepared and able to keep picking them while they are still young. Plants like celeriac, parsnips, squashes, and tomatoes will not provide anything for most of this time but must have a long growing season and so take up space. So a plan is essential.

Watering can take a lot of time in summer. We are lucky in having a water-retentive soil but nevertheless, all the winter work of digging and adding compost pays dividends in these months. The improved soil structure means that roots can

forage deep for water and nutrients and the compost will hold water much longer. I tend to water everything in very well when it is planted and give certain crops that respond particularly well to watering, like lettuce and celeriac, a really good soak every once in a while. Otherwise everything has to look to its own liquid resources.

As far as pests and diseases go, summer is obviously a time when these can be at their most destructive, for the simple reason that there is most for them to destroy and for problems to feed upon. The rules of hygiene and healthy plants apply more than ever.

But however careful I am, I invariably have more problems with slugs and snails, aphids, birds, fungal diseases, and weather damage (and in this I include drought as well as storms) than at any other time of year. My response to this is always the same: go with it. Organic gardening is not a war waged against nature. Any garden imposes a superabundance of growth on a piece of land and the rest of the natural world responds very quickly to this. If I insist on growing 50 lettuces spaced 22cm (9in) from each other in a block, then

I cannot complain if a thousand slugs join the feast. But I can ensure that each lettuce is growing strongly, with a healthy root system, before I expose them to the depredations of the slugs. And I do.

An important factor in keeping the cornucopia of the summer vegetable garden healthy is to keep weeds to a minimum so that plants can get the maximum available nutrition and moisture from the soil and therefore grow as well as the soil allows. As I explained earlier (*see Introduction, pages 28–31*), this will vary from garden to garden and even within areas of the vegetable patch itself because no two areas of ground are exactly alike. Therefore the healthiest plant might be growing more slowly and be smaller than other, identical plants that are growing faster and bigger but ultimately will be more prone to problems.

As ever, the best defence from attack is from the plants themselves, not the gardener. Our job is to maximize the potential for each plant in each given situation. In return we will receive the biggest, healthiest, tastiest harvests from our vegetables.

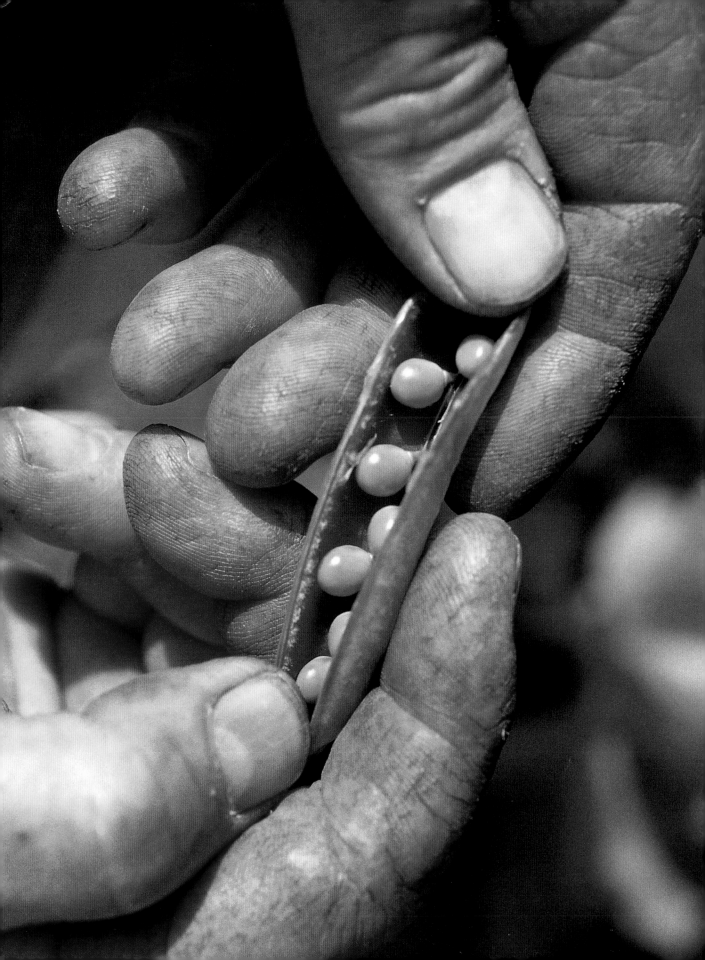

Peas

Everyone likes peas. Every garden with any veg in it at all has to have at least one row of peas, as much as a symbol of freshness and twining productivity as for any practical contribution to the table.

Fresh peas, shovelled from the pod straight into your mouth, are a rolling green absolute. You measure other pleasures by it. If I live to be a hundred, I shall not forget the sight of my daughter, Freya, seen from the bathroom window, her long auburn hair curling in pea-like tendrils, quietly munching her way along a row of peas at 7 o'clock on a sunny July morning. If you have children, it is well worth growing peas – even just half a dozen plants scrambling up a wigwam in a pot – so that the kids can eat them raw and know what peas really taste like.

They have been part of European gardens for thousands of years, primarily for their ability to be stored dried and then cooked to make a nutritious porridge. It seems that the luxury of growing them just to shell and eat straight away was not taken up until the sixteenth century.

To get the best out of peas they must be eaten within hours of picking, before the sugars start to turn to starch. But peas freeze better than almost any other vegetable. This is easy to do at home, although we never freeze peas because commercially frozen ones are so good (they freeze them in the field, as soon as they are harvested) and anyway, we hardly freeze anything in its raw state, preferring whenever possible to eat things fresh as and when they come into season, although when a crop ripens all at once we try to store as much as possible. However, I don't want peas in January any more than I want warm, wet, grey days without break from November right through to March.

Growing conditions Peas need rich soil but not too much water, especially in their first month or so. In the past I have lost dozens of peas sown in pots by overwatering, which, rather than invigorating them, reduces the pea seed to slime. The trick is to sow them into damp compost and leave it unwatered until the shoots appear, and thereafter give them just enough moisture to stop them drying out.

I experimented with sowing peas ('Douce Provence') in coir-7s and soil blocks, but this was a mistake as all legumes have a long first root. This whizzed straight through the coir package and out the other side before any decent rootball had developed, so they all had to be put into pots – which I might as well have done first time round. I wish I could sow them directly outside, but the slug damage is so great that it is not worth it. I can get away with a May outdoor sowing because the plants grow fast enough to outrun the slugs' jaws.

But I do like peas in June, and I often have to wait until the middle or even the end of the month before they are ready. To get early peas you need to sow them around the time of your first broad beans, in November. This must be in the warmest, best drained spot in the vegetable garden, which in this garden means adding extra grit as well as compost to the soil.

If I sow directly outside I give the sown seeds a light watering and then cover them with cloches for the rest of the winter, checking them once a week and only watering if the emergent seedlings are showing visible signs of distress. Traditionally, varieties like 'Feltham First' and 'Meteor' are better at

We like old-fashioned "wrinkled" peas – 'Douce Provence', 'Alderman', and 'Hurst Greenshaft' fit this bill very well. 'Sugar Snap' peas have very slow-developing peas and are without the hard wall to the pod so can be picked before the peas mature; they are eaten pod and all. Mangetout never develop proper peas and are grown specifically for their very sweet pods.

Planting and staking peas

All garden peas crop much better if they are supported, ideally by pea sticks – the brushwood from our hazel coppice offers the perfect solution to our staking needs.

I grow peas in single rows, although they are often sown in double rows. However you space them, pea sticks, ideally from hazel, are the best way to support the growing vines. They should be staked when the peas are just emerging, placing the sticks as a double row either side of the line of plants. The stems need tying onto the stakes for the first 1m (3ft) or so of growth, until their self-clinging tendrils become sufficiently established for the plants to support themselves.

withstanding cold and are therefore suitable for early sowings. But I am more likely to sow the seeds in 7cm (3in) pots, putting three seeds to a pot and removing the weakest after germination, and overwinter these in a cold frame. Again, the potting compost will have extra perlite or grit to ensure good drainage. I also sow 'Douce Provence', 'Alderman', 'Sugar Snap', and some 'Hurst Greenshaft' in March and early May to get a succession throughout summer. Attacks by mice and pigeons are common. Cloches help on early sowings and earthing up – drawing the soil up along the row with a hoe – will make it harder for mice to get to them as well as securing the roots.

All garden peas crop much better if they are supported, ideally by pea sticks – the brushwood from hazel coppicing – if you can get them, or chicken wire supported by canes. But pea sticks are best. They work perfectly, look good, and add much needed vertical structure to the garden.

Pea varieties Modern pea breeding has concentrated on producing short-growing peas to make mechanized harvesting easier. But taller varieties take up no more space in the garden, are likely to ripen better and to crop more vigorously over a longer period. 'Alderman' is a particularly tall variety, reaching over 1.8m (6ft) in rich soil. But this is an advantage because height is always a virtue in the kitchen garden, adding a green texture and form that is much needed.

Mangetout and 'Sugar Snap' peas are eaten whole, pods and all. The former never really develop proper peas and retain flat pods, and the latter do so slowly, which means that if you do not pick them regularly you can harvest the maturing peas and eat them as a normal variety. Both are without the hard wall to the pod which conventional "wrinkled" peas have. There is a lot to be said for growing 'Sugar Snap' peas if you have limited space and perhaps limited patience for the bother of shelling peas. I veer between a nostalgic pleasure at the business of shelling peas around the kitchen table and an impatient desire for the fast-food immediacy of sugar snaps as being the best of both worlds.

Purple-podded peas are hard to get hold of but worth growing if you can find them because they look absolutely lovely – although they do not taste any better than perhaps half a dozen green varieties and the cooked peas are indistinguishable from any other.

Peas are traditionally sown in double rows about 15cm (6in) apart with a gap of about 10cm (4in) between the peas in each row. This works fine but I can see no real advantage over single rows. If I am planting out pot-grown peas I put them 22cm (9in) apart – with a pair of plants at each station. You need room to walk between the rows to pick, which means a minimum of 1m (3ft) and twice that if you can spare the space.

Crop rotation Like all legumes, peas take nitrogen from the air into the soil via warty nodules on their roots. This makes them an essential component in the rotation of vegetables. Traditionally they are grown in newly dug and manured ground and followed by brassica crops like cabbage or purple-sprouting broccoli, which are put into the same plot to use the extra nitrogen the peas have left behind. The following spring the plot is then sown with root crops such as carrots or parsnips, and after these are harvested in the autumn the ground is double dug and heavily manured before sowing with more peas.

They like cool (but not cold), damp weather but hate sitting in wet – hence the need for well-drained but moisture-retentive soil. Their need for coolish conditions means that you cannot really make a successful sowing after the end of May unless there is a sustained cool period. The fastest maturing varieties (like 'Feltham First' and 'Prince Albert') take about 12 weeks to mature and the slowest maincrop varieties (like 'Hurst Greenshaft') can take a month longer – but will go on producing pods for a month.

Saving pea seed You can easily save your own peas for the following year's seed. Leave the pods on the plant for as long as possible, lifting the whole plant just before the pods start to split. Either hang the plant up in a dry shed or store the pods on a tray until they split open and the peas can be collected. Store them in an airtight container or a paper bag in a cool, dry place.

'Sugar Snap' peas

Onions are as central a component of a vegetable garden as daffodils are to spring. You have to deliberately eschew onions for them not to be at the heart of the garden.

'Setton'

'Red Baron'

MY VARIETIES

There are over 500 hundred different varieties of onion, but here are a few selected varieties:

RED ONIONS
'Red Baron'
'Red Brunswick'
'Red Bunching Redbeard'
  (spring onion)
'Rosso di Firenze'
'Southport Red Globe'
'Torpedo'

WHITE ONIONS
'Setton'
'Sturon'
'Stuttgart Giant'
'Turbo'

It is important to keep growing onions (*right*) weed-free if they are to develop good bulbs.

Onions have been an integral part of the cuisine of every nation on earth for as long as recorded time. This is hardly surprising – they are easy to grow, store well, and remain juicy right to the end. They taste good and do you good. The onion has clearly always been one of life's essentials. In the Middle Ages, onions were thought to provoke lust, notwithstanding that everyone, particularly the poor, ate them almost every day. Chaucer's summoner, for example, displayed his lechery openly through his love of "garleek, oynons and eek lekes". The real point is that they were considered robust, common, and unrefined – all of which are precisely the honest onion's chief virtues.

Grow onions as part of your crop rotation to avoid any build up of disease or onion fly, the larvae of which overwinter in the soil. All onions do very well following pumpkins or lettuce, both of which share the same need for rich soil that was manured liberally the previous year, good drainage, and plenty of water, although I gather that people who grow prize onions tend to use the same site year after year. But it is worth bearing in mind that the bigger the onion, the milder – perhaps mild merely means less – they taste.

Growing onions Fast growth is essential to produce good onions, so they need rich soil with plenty of water and no competition from weeds. This means that you must be able to hoe between the plants without damaging them, and your spacing when planting must reflect that, although inevitably you will have to hand weed around the base of growing bulbs.

Onions are grown either from seed or as "sets". Sets are immature bulbs and take 20–24 weeks to mature from planting. Seed takes about a month longer from sowing. To understand their inbuilt timetable properly you have to remember that onions are biennials, which means they seed in summer, germinate and establish small plants, which then grow and flower the following year. Once midsummer comes and the days are getting shorter the spring-sown onions will be increasingly inclined to go to seed, at which point the bulb ceases to have much use for the plant, so it stops investing any strength in it. The best time to harvest is just before they go to seed.

I start off onion sets in coir-7s or blocks, as shown here. This helps to establish the roots quickly and stops them from being tugged at by birds.

I grow autumn sets that establish roots in September and October, then overwinter without much growth before taking off in spring. They are ready to lift in June, bridging the gap between the last in store from the previous season and the first of the summer onions. They do not keep as well as summer onions.

You can sow onion seed in permanent blocks of four – soil blocks are ideal for this as are modules or small pots – and transplant the blocks en masse, 30cm (1ft) apart in each direction. They do not have to be evenly spaced because the growing bulbs gradually push each other apart to allow complete development. The advantages of this system are that the onions are not disturbed from the moment t hey are sown to harvest, so grow faster and stronger, as well as being a very economical use of space.

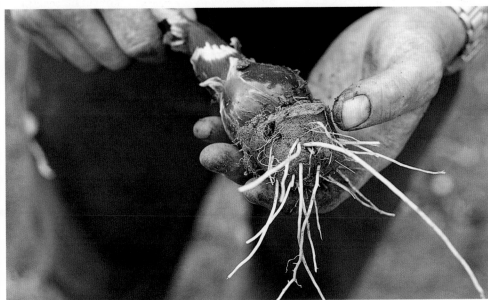

It is best to plant sets as soon as the ground is ready after New Year (although this might well be as late as mid-April) and to sow seed in February and March. At that time of year seed must be sown indoors with some heat, although a windowsill will be fine. I sow into a fairly deep pot so that the seedlings can develop good roots and do not need to be touched until they are ready to transplant to their final growing position out of doors in April. The main drawback of sets is that there is a tiny range of varieties to choose from compared to the wide range of onion seeds available. But they are very easy. They are less likely to get mildew or onion fly, particularly on heavy soil, and less fiddle to deal with. You buy a bag of bulbs, ranging in size from crocus to tulip, and stick them in the ground so that they are two-thirds buried. There is a school of thought that says you should make a hole first so that you do not bruise the growing base that will produce the first delicate roots and another school that says you should prepare the soil sufficiently well so that they go into the ground as easily as a finger into a pile of sieved flour. I belong to the latter tendency, although it is also a good idea to put the sets into drills to stop the growing roots acting as a spring that levers the bulb clear of the ground.

Until the longest day (June 24th), the bulb is putting its energies primarily into leaf growth which, in turn, feeds the bulb and helps it to swell prior to the plant flowering and producing seed. The critical point of harvest is just before the plant runs to seed, so that the bulb is not depleted and will store better. When the leaves start to die back, bend all the tops to the ground to stop growth, and let them shrivel and die. Harvest the bulbs, by lifting them gently with a fork, and leave them on the surface for up to a week to thoroughly dry. The drier they are, the longer they will store.

Storing onions Traditionally, onions are stored tied in ropes, although we always store them on racks. All commercial non-organic onions are treated with a sprout suppressant such as maleic hydrazide to increase storage time, but they are not hard to store at home over winter. Small onions tend to keep longer than large ones and shallots longer than onions.

The key to long and healthy storage is to dry the onions as much as possible before bringing them in to store. A couple of weeks before pulling, stop watering them and bend the tops over. After you have lifted them, leave the leaves attached for as long as they will stay on (they come away when completely dry). This will help stop neck rot. Store them in a cool, dark place, somewhere that air can circulate freely around them.

The important thing is to keep plenty of air around onions or they can go mouldy. Here they are stored in single layers in slatted boxes. Onions will not sprout at 0–5°C (32–41°F) or 24–30°C (75–86°F), so need to be stored within these two ranges. Most onions keep for six to nine months before they start to sprout and soften.

Shallots and spring onions Shallots are onions that form a cluster of small bulbs rather than one big bulb. Spring onions are immature bulb onions grown for their tender stems.

The shallot harvest

SHALLOTS
'Creation'
'Cuisse de Poulet'
'Sante'

Shallots have more flavour and are more tender than many onions. They are also less readily available in your average supermarket, so are perhaps a better bet for the vegetable gardener who is strapped for space.

Hardier than onions, shallots are usually grown from sets that can be planted as early as January for a midsummer harvest. The sets should be given a slightly wider spacing than onions, perhaps as much as 30cm (1ft), to give the cluster room to expand. F1 varieties (and there is hardly any need to grow F1 anything – you are paying over the odds just for some hybrid vigour with no extra taste or keeping qualities) have to be grown from seed however.

Spring onions I know that I am in a curmudgeonly minority but I cannot see the culinary attraction of growing spring onions when herbs like chives and garlic chives produce similar tender green stems to eat raw in salads but have more flavour and are much less trouble to grow. Spring onions are always grown from seed, sown outside direct into drills. Spread the seed thinly, and then thin the seedlings as they grow until they are an even 2.5cm (1in) or so apart. Spring onions will grow fast, and a continuous supply can be maintained from May right through summer by sowing a row or two every couple of weeks.

277

Artichokes are one of the few perennial vegetables, but as they are most productive in their second and third years it is best to add one generation of plants each year and throw one away.

'Violetto Precoce'

'Green Globe'

VARIETIES
'Green Globe'
'Gros Vert De Laon'
'Violetto Precoce'

Artichokes grow very easily from seed if sown with a little gentle heat in spring. They can then be pricked out into individual pots and planted out in midsummer. They grow slowly in the first year. The drawback to growing artichokes from seed is that they do not always come true – so if you sow a seed of a variety such as 'Green Globe' there is no guarantee that the mature plant will be the same variety.

Taking offsets An alternative method of propagation is to take offsets from existing artichoke plants, and in many ways this is a more satisfactory method. Each plant more than a year old will have young growths appearing slightly separate from the main plant. These are attached to the parent root but can be cut off with a knife or sharp spade and replanted and will grow quickly into vigorous plants. They are bound to be exactly the same as the parent and will establish themselves quicker than a plant raised from seed. When you cut them away, they may appear to have too small a root to sustain the

foliage. Don't worry. As long as they have a wisp or two of root, they should develop a healthy root system before sprouting leaves.

Growing conditions Artichokes like a rich, well-drained soil in full sun. They need plenty of water, especially in their first year when they are developing good roots. They are not very frost hardy and I mulch mine with a good layer of straw between November and April. Traditionally, they were mulched with ash, which kept the slugs away as well as adding potash to the soil. If you have a wood fire and there is any ash left over after you have given some to the gooseberries, currants, onions, garlic, and tomatoes – all of which get first call upon the ash in this household – then the artichokes would do well with a liberal sprinkle. I also mulch them well with compost in spring.

Artichokes grown from seed in spring will not produce chokes until September or even October, and it is wise to cut them off when very small to let the plants' energies go into establishing a strong plant rather than big chokes. However, the following spring they will produce artichoke heads from the end of May onwards. In May, you can fry the young, golf-ball sized ones merely split, but from June onwards they develop large chokes the size of onions. Cut them before they get too big, boil till tender, and eat with sea salt and oil or *beurre blanc*.

But if you take offsets from the second year onwards, you will have a constant supply of second- and third-year plants – which will produce the best harvest.

Artichokes are worth growing for the beauty of their leaves alone (*right*). However, the chokes – the unopened flowers – are the prize for the vegetable gardener (*facing page*).

Tomatoes My summer would not be complete without the lines of tomatoes in the greenhouse or tunnel. Supermarket tomatoes are chilled, not fully ripe, and usually a shadow of those grown at home.

'Andine Cornue'

'Beefsteak'

Cordon-trained tomatoes must be staked or trained on a fixed string from the very first. The fruit develop on trusses, starting at the bottom of the plant. Most plants produce four to seven trusses during their ripening period. The tomatoes growing in the picture (*bottom left*) were planted in the polytunnel on newly turned grassland that had not been weeded – hence the landscape fabric. They did very well.

A good tomato should be warm, smell musty and fruity, and dribble seeds and juice when cut or bitten into. My own feeling is that cold, unripe tomatoes are not worth eating. Better to enjoy them in season from July to November, and then eat them as a sauce or chutney.

Tomatoes are an incredibly healthy food. They are high in fibre, potassium, and folic acid, and are also rich in vitamins A and C. They also contain lycopene, which is acknowledged as being an agent in releasing free radicals that help prevent and fight cancers. Tomatoes freeze well, and lycopene is released when the tomatoes are cooked, so, on health grounds alone, there is a strong case for growing enough tomatoes to store for winter use.

Tomato timetable My tomato timetable is this: order seeds in October/November; sow in mid-February; prick out into individual pots in March; plant out into the greenhouse in May; tie up, water, and pinch out sideshoots weekly from June; harvest from the end of July to October. Prepare the soil in December; sow salad crops onto the beds in January, to be cleared ready for tomatoes by mid-May, when an additional light load of compost will be rotovated into the ground.

It is a ritualistic business, growing tomatoes. But I like their special paraphernalia – the twine for tying, the weekly task of pinching out sideshoots, fingers stained first yellow then black and reeking of tomato long after the job is done, watering, removing lower branches – all in the ordered jungle of the cordons. But

given the way that tomato seedlings spring up by the hundred all over the place via the compost heap (I once found a 2.2m/7ft plant loaded with healthy fruit in the Jewel Garden, growing gracefully through a clematis), it is perhaps salutary to let a couple of plants grow untended each year as a reminder that they will grow just fine, thank you, without any help or hindrance from us.

Outside or in? I have grown tomatoes outside deliberately, but in this part of the world they ripen far less successfully than identical ones grown under cover, and are much more susceptible to getting blight from the potatoes, so it hardly seems worth the risk. If you do not have a greenhouse of any kind, then it is probably best to grow tomatoes in a container against a sunny brick wall.

Maintaining cordons There are two basic types, cordon and bush. Cordon tomatoes will go on growing until they die and can – and do – reach 6m (20ft) or more. They are often described as indeterminate. Their fruit ripens over a long period – as much as six months in certain areas – and they need supporting from almost the first. In order to train them to grow upright in a restricted space they have to be constantly pruned – for, by pinching out, you are pruning the tomato plant just as surely as you train an espalier. As a result they are neater, take up far less space, and consequently can be planted much closer together.

This process of pruning is extremely simple. The most important aspect is to remove all

sideshoots growing in the angle between the stem and a leaf. This very vigorous diagonal growth takes up a lot of space and diverts energy away from the main cordon. The easiest way is to snap the sideshoots off with a twist of finger and thumb. This is best done in the morning when the plants are turgid and the risk of tearing or damaging the main stem is much reduced. Any shoots growing up from the base of the plant should be pulled out when removing sideshoots.

The second form of pruning is to remove the lower leaves as the fruits mature. This will allow air and light between the plants and is an important aid to ripening and the avoidance of fungal diseases. I have two criteria for removing leaves:

• If they are directly shading a truss of fruit.
• If they are yellowing (and therefore not contributing to the vitality of the plant anyway).

Another rule is to give the leaf a sharp yank upwards. If it does not come away in your hand then it is probably too soon to remove it. By the time that all the fruit on the plant is turning red the bottom 60–90cm (2–3ft) of the plant can be completely stripped.

As we go into autumn the first frosts will kill all tomato plants and only genuinely hot days will ripen the fruit. So you reduce the number of fruit produced to the maximum that can be reasonably ripened, which is achieved by pinching out the top of the plant. This stops it growing and producing more fruit as it does so. Once stopped, all horticultural attention can be lavished on the fruit that exist rather than producing any more.

Bush tomatoes These are described as "determinate", which means that when they reach their predetermined size, they stop growing. They do not need to have their sideshoots removed, nor staking, although it is a good idea to prop them up to lift the fruits off the soil.

The gap between the first and last fruit ripening is much shorter than it is with cordons – about two weeks to a month. This makes them more suitable to field and commercial production than cordons, but perhaps less useful for the gardener who generally wants as long a supply of ripening fruit as possible.

Increasing the crop Tomatoes are one of the harvests that we want to be as large as possible, because we store the vast majority of the crop by making it into a basic sauce and freezing it. This can be taken out and elaborated upon later. We have never yet managed to grow enough – or anything like enough – to see us through to the following harvest. So I am always eager to maximize the yield.

For this, tomatoes need heat and water and plenty of nutrition. Assuming that you do not have a heated greenhouse, there is little you can do about heat other than to protect them from the cold. Managing their water supply is important. It starts at planting. I plant them deep – burying the stem right up to the bottom leaves. The buried part of the stem will sprout extra roots which will increase access to all available moisture.

I use a leaky pipe irrigation system in the tunnel made from recycled tyres. I do not have the time to hand water the rest more than once a week – when they get a good soak. The secret is to water the plant well but to starve the fruit of water once they turn colour. This will intensify the taste.

To train cordon tomatoes you must pinch out the shoots that grow at 45° angles between the main stem and the leaves. This diagonal growth is very vigorous and puts a lot of the available energy into leaf and stem growth at the expense of fruit. It is best to take out these side shoots when they are still young, and in the morning when the plant shoots are turgid and snap off cleanly.

Tomato pests and diseases
The key to growing healthy tomatoes is plenty of ventilation, good soil, a constant temperature, and a regular supply of water.

Blight

Tomatoes are a member of the Solanaceae family, so are close cousins to potatoes – as well as aubergines and peppers – and suffer the same diseases, especially blight (*Phytophthora infestans*). You should never grow tomatoes in soil that has had potatoes in it for at least two years, and try to keep the two crops as physically far apart as possible within the boundaries of your garden. The risk is greatly reduced if tomatoes are grown in a greenhouse or tunnel, but it is still something to watch out for. The blight manifests itself as pale brown blotches that quickly radiate out on the foliage, often accompanied by a white, downy growth that destroys the leaves. The fungus can also affect the fruit, making it inedible. At first signs of blight, spray plants with Bordeaux mixture (a combination of copper sulphate and lime). I have had outdoor plants with blight that I sprayed and which went on to produce good fruit many weeks later.

Blossom end rot

This manifests itself as a flattened, calloused, hard brown disc at the base of the fruit. It is caused by inadequate water supply which, in turn, stops the plant from taking in enough calcium so that the cells collapse. It is more likely to occur if you are growing tomatoes in peat or very acidic soil. The solution is to water more frequently and, if your soil is naturally very acidic, grow only small-fruited varieties, which are not affected as easily.

Viruses

There are a number of different viruses that afflict tomatoes but most manifest themselves in yellowing, mottled leaves, wilting, and poor setting of fruit. There is not a lot that can be done once a virus has set in, and often the plant will continue to provide fruit, albeit smaller and less of it. Prevention is helped by good hygiene, changing the soil, and – as ever – developing healthy, unforced plants.

Splitting fruit

Fruits sometimes split just before they ripen and the splits often develop a grey, wispy mould. Splitting is caused by an irregular water supply or big variations in temperature, which can often occur in July, August, and September here.

Leaf curl

Leaves sometimes curl up lengthways and look as though they are about to die. This is caused by big variations between day and night temperatures and happened dramatically at the time of writing this, when we had a cool July with cold nights but the daytime temperature inside the greenhouse was very hot. It afflicts older leaves more than young ones, and the solution is to try and balance the temperature as much as possible.

White fly

The adult white fly lays its eggs on the lower leaves of tomato plants. After a nymph stage, the new adult emerges and feeds on the leaves, sucking sap and exuding honeydew on which a fungus grows. The effect is not good at all, damaging plants and restricting the crop. White fly overwinter, especially on perennials, so try not to overwinter plants such as fuchsias in a greenhouse that is to grow tomatoes the following summer. I grow basil with my tomatoes – this seems to work well as a deterrent – and others swear by French marigolds. Planting both basil and marigolds would offer double protection.

Mulching the plants will stop water evaporating although this is more effective for tomatoes grown outside that are exposed to wind as well as sun.

Nutrition is, of course, vital. Tomatoes need a well-dug, rich soil that has had compost or manure added the previous winter. This will ensure a good chance of a decent crop from healthy plants. There are growers who swear by weekly feeds of liquid seaweed or liquid sheeps' manure but as with all plants I am a firm advocate of the plant finding all available nutrition from a healthy soil rather than force-feeding a particular aspect of its nutrition. I do, however, mulch between the plants with comfrey leaves. This adds potash – as well as trace minerals – to the soil and helps develop the fruit rather than the foliage which is all a mulch of compost would do.

Our basic tomato sauce Fill a baking tray with tomatoes so that they are just touching each other. Chop up half a dozen good cloves of garlic and sprinkle over. Add some generous sprigs of thyme, sea salt and splash some olive oil over the lot. Put into a hot oven (the hottest oven in our Aga, gas mark 8 or 230°C/450°F) for about 40 minutes. A lot of water will be lost from the tomatoes, concentrating the flavour.

This is delicious served straight from the oven with some torn basil leaves sprinkled onto it, but it is also the ideal base for a sauce that can be frozen and used later for pasta sauces, soups, and pizzas. Scrape every last piece from the tin and whizz it up in a food processor, put it into a polythene bag or plastic container and freeze.

When I re-use it, I first soften a couple of onions in olive oil, add a whole head of garlic, finely chopped, then add the sauce together with plenty of olive oil and a splash of balsamic vinegar. I cook this for about 20 minutes, stirring all the time. As it cooks, I keep adding olive oil until the sauce reaches the right consistency, and about 10 minutes before serving, I add lots of thyme, oregano, and golden marjoram. How much is lots? It depends on the time of year and how I feel. But usually a very generous handful of each. Add plenty of salt and freshly ground pepper. It will keep for days in the refrigerator.

If you have any tomatoes with green fruits that do not look as though they will ripen before the weather runs out in autumn (*see above*), you can bring the entire plant, roots and all, indoors and hang it upside down in a sheltered, dry spot. Some of the fruit will continue to ripen and the rest can be used for chutney. Alternatively, green tomatoes will continue to ripen stored in a drawer.

Broad beans were an absolute staple of the ancient Mediterranean and north European medieval diet, although their ability to be stored dry made fresh broad beans a rare treat.

Perhaps that is how we should view them, although there are apparently 100 million people worldwide who are unable to eat broad beans at all due to favism, an enzyme deficiency. Broad beans make them very ill. When I was a child, we used to wade dutifully through weeks of leathery, bitter broad beans the size of pebbles until we could thankfully pull up the plants. There is no need for this. Broad beans are best eaten young, while still small and sweet, and will freeze very well in this youthful condition. If they do get large, they can be puréed very successfully.

Growing broad beans To ensure young beans you need to make two or more sowings so that the harvest is spread across the summer. They can be sown as early as October for a crop in May or June, or as late as June for September cropping. I grow our early beans under cover in the largest size of plugs and soil blocks and plant them out as soon as they are 2.5–5cm (1–2in) high. This is partly to speed up germination but mainly to minimize slug damage to the tender shoots. Later sowings go straight outside into the ground because they will grow away fast enough to resist slug

Mature pods

Flowers of broad bean varieties 'Red Epicure' and 'The Sutton'

I grow two or three sowings to spread the supply of tender young broad beans across the year. Here, the central double row is six weeks younger than the outside rows. It is essential to support the plants at an early stage with string and canes, otherwise they are easily blown over in the wind.

Sowing early broad beans

Because broad beans are hardy, I could sow seed in open ground as early as October but I like to give the tender shoots a head start by raising them in the greenhouse before

transplanting them outside. This helps to limit slug damage. I grow our first early beans under cover in the largest size of plugs and soil blocks available. When the seedlings

reach 2.5–5cm (1–2in) high, they are ready to plant out. To produce tender young broad beans, I make the first sowing in October for a crop in May and June.

attack. They can be planted in single rows spaced 1m (3ft) apart, or double rows 30cm (1ft) apart with 1m (3ft) between each pair. Both ways the plant stems will need supporting with canes and strong twine (I use hop twine) before they start to fall and bend.

If sowing early, you need to choose a variety like 'Aquadulce', which came to Britain in the 1850s from Spain. Do not worry if plants seem to stop growing once germinated and visible above ground. They will pick up as soon as the days start to lengthen and warm up, and will have a head start over later crops. But they do not taste any better. I grow 'Bunyards Exhibition' as a very reliable cropper, 'The Sutton' for its excellent taste, and 'Red Epicure', which has wonderful garnet-coloured beans and vermilion flowers. Like all legumes, broad beans fix nitrogen from the air into the soil via their root nodules, thus making them an excellent fertilizer for the following crop, which is traditionally an overwintering root crop, such

as beetroot or autumn carrots, although any salad crop will do well. The other virtue of broad beans is that they develop extraordinary long roots, going down 1.5m (5ft) or more, enabling them to open out a heavy soil and tap into mineral resources that other, more shallow-rooted plants will not reach.

Pest and diseases Broad beans are notoriously prone to blackfly, which are attracted to the soft, sappy growing tip of the plant. If the tips are pinched out after the pods have set it can solve the problem, although more aphids mean more food for ladybirds which in turn will control the level of aphids.

Bean chocolate spot manifests itself as brown splashes on the leaves and is caused by a fungus called *Botrytis fabae*. It can affect yields and even destroy the plant if the infection is bad. Like all fungal infections, it is encouraged by humid, warm weather and tends to afflict later crops rather than earlier overwintering ones.

Lettuce is the single most important vegetable that we grow in this garden. We eat salad from the garden, including fresh lettuce, 365 days a year and, in summer, usually twice a day.

Non-organic lettuce will have had an average of 11 sprayings of insecticides, pesticides, and herbicides, and been given as much water as it can absorb to make it as big as possible. One of my greatest *bêtes noires* is the 'Iceberg' lettuce, which tastes of nothing at all. Yet supermarkets sell more of it than all other kinds of lettuce put together. The truth is that the public get given 'Iceberg' because it is easy and cheap to grow, and because it stays crisp even when shoved between two slices of factory bread and slavered with cheap mayonnaise. It is depressing to consider that in the United States it has been calculated that 'Iceberg' lettuce is consumed at the rate of about 11kg (24lb) per person per year. Yet it is very easy for a small garden to contain half a dozen different types of lettuce to make a fresh, delicious, and healthy salad on any given day of the year.

Growing lettuce To grow a lettuce well you need rich soil, plenty of water, good light levels, and a temperature that does not drop below 10°C (50°F) or rise above 20°C (68°F). This makes it ideal for the British climate from April through to October, provided we do not have a hot, dry summer. Commercially grown, non-organic lettuce is nearly all raised under cover with huge amounts of water – indeed, many are grown hydroponically. This makes them grow very fast and as a result they are tasteless and fail to take up many important minerals.

The greatest skill in lettuce-growing is to maintain a constant supply of a good variety of types without having a glut of any of them. This is best done by sowing a few seeds every 10 days or so from March through to August or, if you have a greenhouse or tunnel, from

'Paris White' cos lettuce ready for harvest. These were raised in plugs and planted out with two plants per plug, making for smaller individual lettuces but providing the same quantity of leaf as if they had been thinned out to a single, more impressive plant.

Preparing the ground prior to planting out (*above*). In the foreground are the blue leaves of the kale 'Cavolo Nero', with a batch of cos lettuce in the middle bed.

Young lettuce seedlings growing in plugs (*facing page, top left*). The principal enemies of lettuce in my garden are slugs and snails (*top right*). Loose-leaf lettuce 'Red Fire', planted alternately with 'Witloof' chicory (*left*). Loose-leaf lettuce 'Aruba' just after planting out (*far left*).

January through to early September. I never sow lettuce directly into the ground because the emerging seedlings are so vulnerable to slug attack in this garden. Instead, seedlings are all sown and raised under cover. Sowing tiny lettuce seeds one or two at a time into plugs or blocks is a fiddle, but it avoids wasting seed, cuts back on handling because there is no thinning to be done, and ensures that each seedling receives maximum water, light, and nutrition from the outset so that it grows healthily. It is also the best way to raise a constant but small supply. It is best to transplant the seedlings outdoors when they have four or five leaves and will grow strongly. I always have to resist the temptation to plant them out earlier, but small seedlings will develop quite slowly for the first three or four weeks before growing away strongly. At this early, slow stage they are very vulnerable

to slugs, and I have often had an entire batch of seedlings eaten over 48 hours.

I always plant out in blocks rather than rows, with 22cm (9in) spacing between plants. These are harvested alternately over a period of four weeks, so that the unharvested lettuces grow out into the vacated space.

Ideally, the growing plants will be watered regularly, but in practice I rarely have time for this and concentrate on watering them very well when first planted out and giving them another really good soak about a week before the first harvest. Anything over and above that is a bonus – or rain.

Varieties of lettuce My favourite types of lettuce are the cos varieties (called "Romaines" in the United States). These were introduced by the Romans from the Greek island of Kos, and have a head made up of upright leaves

291

curved like the hull of a boat. The cos lettuce 'Little Gem' is beautifully crispy and easy to grow, especially in cool weather, as heat and poor soil make it quick to bolt and correspondingly bitter. 'Lobjoit's Green' is much bigger and rather slower to mature, but each leaf has a satisfying bite to it. All in all, 'Lobjoit's' is my perfect lettuce. However, it is only really possible to produce a crop outdoors between June and September. 'Valmaine' is an American variety of cos lettuce, much used for Caesar salad. 'Chicon de Charentes' is a good, tasty, robust variety, 'Paris White' is like 'Lobjoit's Green' but lighter in taste, and 'Rouge d'Hiver' has a rusty tinge to the outer edges of the leaves. These last two will stand for a long time before bolting, which makes them useful for a small household. 'Winter Density', 'Barcarolle' and 'Kendo', are also all cos varieties.

Butterhead or round lettuces have flat, rounded heads and soft leaves. 'Tom Thumb' is a very good butterhead, small (about the size of a tennis ball), sweet, and full of taste. They are not fashionable but the whole point of growing food at home is to have a range and variety that you dip into like a pick'n'mix counter. The seeds are an idiosyncratic black.

Another lettuce with the same qualities is 'Merveille de Quatre Saisons', which is an intense red when exposed to full sunlight. Both varieties have smooth, buttery leaves that melt in the mouth if eaten really fresh. Bear in mind that good lettuce needs to be eaten really fresh. That, of course, is half the battle with good lettuce. Supermarkets may value lettuces that will store for days, and we have got used to the half-eaten lettuce lasting a whole week in the fridge, but I never keep lettuce for more than 24 hours. Beyond that, however carefully

Preparing lettuce for the table. If, as in this case, I lift the entire lettuce plant, I cut off the roots and strip the outer leaves, discarding any that are leathery or badly eaten. The beauty of growing one's own is that you can be profligate with lettuce, eating only the very best.

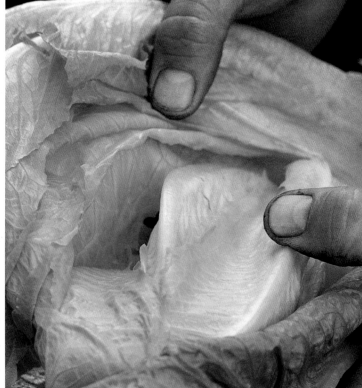

stored, they go past their best and are good only for the compost heap or the chickens (who love them).

'All the Year Round' is, as the name implies, hardy and adaptable enough to crop most of the year, and whilst it is not the best you can grow, it is a lot better than almost anything you can buy, especially in that spring gap, when there is precious little else in the garden. Together with the cos lettuce 'Winter Density', 'All the Year Round' is at the heart of winter salad supplies.

There is a whole range of lettuce that group together under the heading of crisphead or 'Iceberg' lettuces, and it is worth growing one or two to see what they can taste like when they are "chemically clean". 'Mini Green' is another tennis ball-sized lettuce, like 'Tom Thumb' but crisper. 'Webb's Wonderful', the best known crisphead, was bred directly from 'Iceberg', but is not so wonderful. 'Chou de Naples' is the parent of most modern 'Iceberg' lettuces, and has the great virtue of being slow to bolt. 'Iceberg' lettuces were bred from Batavian lettuce introduced into America in 1894 by W. Atlee Burpee & Co, although 'Batavia Blonde' had been grown in Europe since the 1850s. This was – and is, if you can get the seed – quite different from the modern 'Iceberg', having taste and a slight bronzing to the edge of the leaves. The great advantage of all Batavian lettuces is that they will remain standing as mature plants without bolting.

The final type of lettuce is the loose-leaf kind. These have no heart, but consist of a mass of "loose" leaves that can be picked individually, either piecemeal or by cutting the whole lot at once. Either way, they will regrow, and three pickings should be possible if the lettuce gets enough water. The most famous –

and nastiest – is 'Lollo Rossa'. Much better are the 'Salad Bowl' or 'Oak Leaf' types, but they are rather slimy when dressed. Better to eat them with a dribble of oil and lemon juice directly on the plate rather than mixed in the salad bowl.

Red lettuce became trendy with the vogue of the potager, and they are very pretty. This decorative element is important to feed the senses as well as the stomach, but I feel that any space in the garden devoted to food should place taste as the first and foremost criterion of selection. There is another quality to red lettuce that makes them an important addition to my garden, and that is that slugs eat them with much greater reluctance than green lettuce. I grow 'Red Salad Bowl', 'Red Oak Leaf', 'Rosny', 'Red Fire', 'Red Cos', and 'Aruba', all of which have leaves of various intensities of red.

Pest and diseases Slugs and snails are the greatest enemy to lettuce in this garden, and these are much worse in very heavily manured ground. I have found that the best lettuce grows in ground that has been free of manure for two or three years, freshly dug, with a liberal dose of compost rotovated in just before planting. This is not always easy to provide but it is worth bearing in mind.

Lettuce root aphids attack in dry conditions and their effect is dramatic. The plants stop growing and visibly wilt and then die. When pulled up, the roots have a white, powdery, waxy coating, which is discharged by little yellow aphids (*Pemphigus bursarius*) that eat the roots. Hence the wilting. Mine had been allowed to become too dry, which does encourage the aphids. Do not grow lettuces in the same soil for a year after an attack.

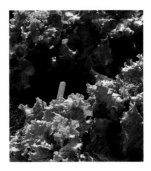
Loose-leaf lettuce

'Red Oak Leaf'

Lettuce are also prone to various diseases. Downy mildew will turn outer leaves yellow and then pale brown, and the undersides of the leaves develop a nasty downy growth. This is a fungal disease caused by *Bremia lactucae*, encouraged by very humid conditions. The only solution is to remove all affected leaves – which might mean pulling the whole plant – and thinning the batch to increase ventilation. Lettuce grey mould is another fungus (*Botrytis cinerea*) and produces a fluffy grey mould on the lettuce leaves. Sometimes this is first noticeable by a slimy brown rot on the stem, and the whole plant collapses. Good ventilation and healthy plants are the best corrective.

Carrots
You have never really tasted a carrot until you have eaten one absolutely fresh, gripping the leaves where they meet the soil and, with a slight twist, eased the tapering orange root from the ground.

The smell – which is such a key component of flavour – is instantly familiar and enticing, but it soon diminishes and is something that can only be experienced by growing your own. One of my favourite dishes of all is pasta primavera, made in midsummer with baby carrots, peas, broad beans, garlic, and good olive oil. It is the most optimistic meal of the year.

Carrots are biennial, establishing decent roots in their first growing season and – if left unpulled – producing an umbel of flowers in the second. Wild carrots have white roots; the familiar orange colour has been bred into them, although they do come in purple, violet, yellow, and white. It was not till the eighteenth century that the Dutch bred the now ubiquitous orange carrot and, since then, breeders have constantly worked on increasing its sweetness. Therefore, this most distinctively "natural" of vegetables is, in fact, a man-made construct.

Carrots can be sown once a month from March through to September (although a late sowing will need protection) for a steady supply of sweet, fresh roots that can be pulled minutes before eating. They like a light, well-drained, alkaline soil. Mine is really too heavy and wet, and the slugs and carrot fly are too predatory for carrots to thrive here. Nevertheless, I do always raise a crop every year, most of which we eat when they are small and tender.

Carrot varieties I have tried many varieties, but I always include 'Amsterdam' types, which are slim, and 'Nantes' varieties, which are more stubby. Both types grow fast and taste sweet. Like any plant with a long tap root, carrots do not like being transplanted, so are normally sown direct in drills about 22cm (9in) apart (although I am experimenting with sowing them in deep plugs to avoid the slug depredations to which the emerging seedlings are prone). However pleasant the weather in early April, resist sowing too early. The soil must be warm to the touch or germination will be poor, and those that do make it will grow slowly and lose much sweetness. One way of helping early sowings is to cover the prepared ground with a layer of fleece or cloches a couple of weeks before sowing, and to keep the seeds covered until the weather warms up.

Sowing seeds Carrot seeds are very small, and so it is difficult to sow them so that they are not too thick. I find mixing the seed with vermiculite helps, and hold a handful of the mix in one hand, pinching it out along the shallow drill with the other. Carrot seeds can also be broadcast. The advantage of this is that they tend to be spread thinner and therefore grow faster, but the disadvantage is that it is harder to weed them. Carrots need careful weeding when they are young. Growth suffers badly from competition but the tiny seedlings are easy to pull up with the weeds.

The ground is best dug but not manured, as fresh compost or manure will encourage the roots to divide and form "fangs". I always add sharp sand to the plot that is to have carrots and parsnips, which directly helps them and also ensures the gradual lightening of the entire vegetable garden.

Common problems Carrot fly can be a problem, especially in early summer, when the flies lay their eggs in the soil around the roots. The maggots hatch and eat their way into the carrots, leaving tell-tale black horizontal gouges that invite disease and infection. These insects can detect fresh carrot up to about 800m (½ mile) away. Thinning the seedlings, bruising the leaves as you do so, throws up the heady aroma of carrot into the air and attracts them. But if you do not thin, the carrots crowd each other out, resulting in a thicket of scrawny veg the thickness of a pencil. So thin you must, carrot fly or not, to 2.5–5cm (1–2in). Then they very quickly grow to full size. The trick is to sow as thinly as possible and grow alliums such as chives, onions, or garlic, which mask the smell, next to the carrots. Some people put up a physical screen around the growing rows, since

the fly travels near to the surface of the ground and cannot rise much above 30cm (1ft) or so. This has always struck me as too aesthetically challenged. Better, if you must, to put fleece over immediately after sowing and leave it there to form a fly-proof barrier. The growing leaves will push it up and it is easily lifted for thinning and harvesting. I do neither, relying on chives, sowing thinly, and thinning in the evening when both scent and fly are less prevalent, removing the thinnings to the compost heap quickly to beat the flies. None of this stops the flies but it does reduce them to a tolerable level.

Potatoes

If you want potatoes to stop hunger you can buy them any time of day or night, raw or cooked. But their quality and taste will usually be at least one step removed from that of the home-grown potato.

Potato foliage, or haulms

Quality and taste are much less of a consideration to the food industry than the size of yield, resistance to disease, and ability to store easily and for a long time. Potatoes that are not grown organically – and many of the fields around my garden are filled with just this crop – are doused with pesticides, fungicides, and herbicides on an almost weekly basis. The farmers deliberately try and "clean" the fields of any insects, weeds, or disease. As a result, they are lifeless, the potatoes growing in a desert of monoculture.

If you want organically grown potatoes as fresh as possible, of a variety exactly suited to the season and method of cooking, then you need to grow them yourself.

Types of potato There are three groups of potatoes, "first earlies", "second earlies", and "maincrop". First earlies mature after about 100 days, second earlies between 110 and 120 days, and maincrop potatoes after 130 days.

I have grown many different varieties of potato over the years but we are restricted by space, the almost inevitable arrival of blight (*Phytophthora infestans*) between early July and late August, and the need for varieties that will store well. I now grow a selection from the list in the box below.

All can be stored unharvested in the ground for at least a month after maturation, but first and second earlies are best lifted and eaten as soon as possible, although first earlies, in particular, are tastier if left in the ground until the last possible moment before cooking. Some of their starch starts to turn to sugar within about an hour of lifting, detracting from the flavour.

Early (or "new") potatoes are best planted as soon as the ground is ready in March or April. I used to try to do this as early as possible but I have learned not to be in a

MY VARIETIES

FIRST EARLIES (harvesting June/July)
'Duke of York'
'Premiere'
'Rocket'

SECOND EARLIES (harvesting July/August)
'Belle de Fontenay'
'Charlotte'
'Kestrel'
'Ratte'

MAIN CROP (harvesting September/October)
'Admiral'
'Cara'
'Maris Piper'
'Romano'
'Roseval'
'Sante'

'Charlotte'

'Santé'

hurry with them. One year the ground was not ready until June 2nd – almost unimaginably late – but we got a decent crop, especially of 'Romano' and 'Sante', despite blight striking in August. You are always warned to plant specially grown seed potatoes that have been raised in "clean" ground and treated (unless stated organic), but we are trying to save and recycle as much seed of our own as possible. However, it is advisable to buy fresh seed at least every three years as viruses will build up in your own stock.

People get very obsessive about how they plant potatoes, as though there was a right or wrong way. There is, but it is not, in my opinion, to do with mere technique. Potato planting is one of those things that has to be done with rhythm and concentration, feeling

Planting potatoes I mark out the rows with string and draw a mattock down the line to make a furrow about 20cm (8in) deep (*left*). Each potato is placed about 30cm (12in) apart (*below*), with all but one or two strong sprouts rubbed off. The earth at the sides of the furrow is then drawn up over the potato seeds to make a low ridge.

297

"Chitting" potatoes
Seed potatoes have to be "chitted". This means exposing them to light so that they develop shoots.

Anyone who has kept potatoes for a week or two in a cupboard or box in spring knows that they sprout long white tentacles, but what the gardener wants are short green sprouts that will initiate fast growth when they are planted. Potatoes can be chitted as soon as the days lengthen after new year, and will take about a month if they are placed on a cool (but frost-free) windowsill. If you have them, egg boxes or trays are ideal for this, but I use seed trays, which also work very well.

Different varieties chit at different speeds, and some can take several months to produce knobbly little sprouts. When it comes to planting out the potatoes, rub off all but one or two large shoots from each seed to ensure larger potatoes in the crop.

Chitting is really just the start of the growth of the potato plant – effectively it is like germinating and growing

seedlings in a propagator before planting out. Potatoes will grow if unchitted – in fact, you cannot stop them – but if you chit them they have a head start once they are planted. This can be important in cold areas because potatoes are not hardy. A late frost can scorch the foliage or even kill them. It is also important in areas prone to blight, because the tubers have maximum chance to develop before blight strikes, which is rarely before July.

the woodiness of the mattock handle and the dry smoothness of potato skin and the exact texture of the soil as the rills are drawn back over. Get those things dead right and the harvest will – with absolute certainty – be the better for it. Perhaps this is the nearest to Zen that the western gardener can attain.

The ritualization of it comes partly because potato seed is so big – no less than a small potato – and partly because it does have a special magic I still find miraculous. How does one potato buried in soil manage to produce up to 20 identical offspring? Even better, a piece of potato peel will produce potatoes in the compost heap. I have learnt the botanical answer to that question but that does nothing to diminish the wonder of it.

Preparing the soil for planting In terms of the planting process, there are those who swear by holes rather than drills, and others who only grow under black plastic, hay, or straw. Each to their own. To get the best crop, the ground should be well dug and richly manured, preferably a few months before planting, and left in large clods for the weather to get in and kill fungi and slugs. A large surface area allows frost to get at the soil and break it down. Just before planting I rotovate the ground and rake it to a fine tilth. Then I mark out rows a pace apart (you need at least 1m/3ft to allow for earthing up and walking between rows for potatoes). I use a mattock to draw deep rills before popping the seed potatoes in at about 30cm (1ft) spacing. I then draw the sides of drill back so that they make a low mound along the line of the seeds.

Earthing up potatoes However you plant them, the top-growth is likely to appear before the last frosts and frost can blacken the leaves exactly as though a blowtorch has been at them. You can avoid this scorching by earthing the potatoes up as soon as all the leaves have appeared and are about 15cm (6in) tall. This is done by drawing soil up with a draw hoe or mattock from between the rows and covering all but the very tops of the green leaves. With first earlies that have been planted in March you may have to do this more than once. Earthing up also ensures that any growing tubers remain covered from light, so stopping them from turning green and poisonous. It also supports the haulms (the top bit) when they are at their floppiest. And lastly, but by no means least, the increased depth of the soil covering works as a protective layer against blight spores being washed from the leaves down into the potatoes.

Potato blight Blight is an airborne fungus that will travel from fields up to 1.6km (1 mile) away. It is especially prevalent in warm, wet weather and needs two consecutive days, each with a minimum of 11 hours where relative humidity is 89 per cent or more and where the minimum temperature is 10°C (50°F). For this reason, it is not usually a problem for earlies. It is recognizable by yellow stains on the leaves which turn pale brown and spread in a concentric circle. As soon as you notice blight, you must cut off all top-growth from the variety that is affected. This can be composted, as a good compost heap will have enough

heat to kill the spores. If your heap is not hot enough, burn the infected plant material on the bonfire. The potatoes can be left in the ground for at least three weeks but will not grow any further. It is best to dig them up on a dry day and then store them in a cool, dark place. I have kept blighted potatoes which I dug in August in good condition right through to May.

These are 'Premiere' – a first early – and this picture was taken in mid-July. They were left to dry in the sun for a few hours before being stored in the dark. Like all early potatoes they should be eaten as quickly as possible.

Beetroot has a better relationship with the gardener than the cook. When I visited a major seed supplier some years ago, I was told, to my astonishment, that beetroot was their best-selling vegetable seed.

Not all beetroot are red. 'Burpees Golden' *(below)* has a very sweet flavour and looks wonderful. The blood red stems of 'Pronto' *(opposite page)* catch the light. The leaves are very good either eaten raw in a salad or cooked like spinach. They have a very high vitamin A content with more iron, calcium, trace minerals, and vitamin C than spinach.

This is despite the fact that, in Britain at any rate, its culinary popularity is limited. Nevertheless, it is a very pleasing and easy vegetable to grow. Traditionally, beets were grown to be eaten cold and doused in vinegar – a waste of a tender and delicious vegetable. The secret of beetroot is to eat the roots when they are small and to grow a succession of crops over the summer so that there is a supply of tender young beets. The best way to prepare them is roasted whole, strewn with thyme and oil and covered with foil so that they do not dry out. Beetroot soup, or borsch, is also delicious. The high oxalic acid content of beetroot means that it can be an irritant, but eaten in small quantities it is easily digestible.

Beetroot comes in all shapes and colours. I particularly like the small 'Pronto' and long 'Carillion', as well as the pink-and-white-ringed 'Chioggia', and 'Burpees Golden', which produces golden leaves and roots.

I sow the seeds in blocks or plugs, putting two or three seeds in each one. Each "seed" is in fact a cluster of seeds bound by a corky membrane. They do not germinate below a temperature of around 7°C (45°F), which means waiting until April for any direct sowings, and if young plants are exposed to temperatures below 10°C (50°F) they are inclined to bolt. Covering an outdoor sowing with fleece helps germination and eventual growth. I do not thin the emerging seedlings but, after hardening them off outside for at least 10 days, plant them out with 22cm (9in) spacing between each cluster. The swelling beets gradually create space for themselves and limit their eventual size without losing any taste. Beetroot is best grown fast in a rich soil with plenty of water and sunshine.

Courgettes – or zucchini – are summer squashes and are really just marrows eaten young, before the fruits mature. The secret is to eat them when they are still small, no more than 22cm (9in) long.

'Alborello di Sarzanna'

If you keep cutting the young fruits, more will grow, and a couple of plants will provide enough for any family to eat courgettes until they can courgette themselves no more. The flowers, of course, are delicious fried in batter.

Summer squashes differ from their winter cousins in having a thin skin that can be eaten, otherwise they share exactly the same horticultural needs. I sow mine in 7cm (3in) pots, two to a pot, in April, putting them to germinate in the propagator. They will not germinate below 13°C (56°F) and do best at around 20°C (68°F). If sowing them outside, this means waiting – in my garden at least – until midsummer for the soil to warm up sufficiently for the seeds to germinate.

They do take up room, but by the same token make superb short-term ground cover and will happily coexist with taller plants like sweetcorn as long as they have rich, deeply dug soil for their roots to get into. The combination of sweetcorn and squashes started as a native American way of deterring racoons from stealing the corn as they did not like the bristly, sticky squash leaves and stems. It seems to work in this garden as the corn is completely racoon-free! We have grown yellow zucchini in among young artichokes and the two seem to cohabit well, the glaucal zigzagged leaves of the artichokes rising up from the dappled squash leaves and the brilliant chrome yellow courgettes zinging up from the ground.

Growing courgettes The ideal site for a squash plant is an old compost heap, which it will hide like a floral tea cosy whilst thriving in the rich, water-retentive growing medium. In open ground plants need at least a square metre (1.2 sq yd) around them and, if you have the space, at least twice that amount.

As with marrows, it is a good idea to dig a pit before planting, adding loads of manure, then refilling and planting in a crater so that water will funnel down to the roots. But courgettes can be grown successfully in pots or even up a wall or trellis, and their spreading season is short – July to October – so they can be fitted around other crops and flowering times. They are ideal for a new garden where one tends to have metres of cultivated ground producing a fine harvest of weeds whilst the perennials, shrubs and hedges get established. Squashes will suppress the weeds, look beautiful, be eminently edible and do no harm to the permanent planting. In general, they justify any space allocated to them.

Cucumbers

I have grown cucumbers very successfully outside, but they need 100 to 140 frost-free days from seed to maturity. As a rule, they do best in my garden when grown in the greenhouse or tunnel.

Outdoors it is best to grow the hardier "ridge" types, such as 'Long Green Maraicher' and 'Boothby's Blonde'. I have also grown 'Crystal Apple' cucumbers – which are small and round – in the vegetable garden without any trouble other than from slugs and snails, which love the texture and taste of their stems.

Indoor varieties tend to have smoother skins. I sow the seed, two to a pot, on the heated propagating mat in late April and, once both seedlings are established, I remove the weaker of the two. The remainder will be repotted into much larger containers in mid-June, when we make space in the propagating greenhouse. I have tried growing cucumbers in beds in the top unheated greenhouse and in grow bags but they like a wetter regime than tomatoes and as much heat as possible, so the propagating greenhouse is ideal during its quiet period in high summer.

Growing cucumbers Cucumbers are very greedy and very thirsty. Planting them in a very rich compost will help satisfy both these demands, but they will need watering much more than tomatoes if they are to produce tasty, fresh cucumbers. Although they need plenty of moisture, they must also have good drainage and the soil texture must be open enough to provide a free root-run. If they are to be planted outside, it is best to dig pits or a trench and add lots of compost.

I train mine up canes, which can be a problem in a container if too many fruits remain unpicked, because the weight will send the whole thing crashing over. The solution is to pick them often, which in turn will stimulate the plant to produce more fruits. But the truth is that there is only so much cucumber a family can eat and they do not store well except as gherkins, which are pickled baby ridge cucumbers. If the cucumbers hang from a trained vine then the fruit will be more or less straight. If they are allowed to sprawl on the ground, they are likely to grow curved. This will not affect the taste.

Traditionally, cucumbers produced male and female flowers. If the male flowers pollinated the female ones, the resulting fruits were bitter, so the male ones (identifiable by the lack of embryonic cucumber swelling behind the base of the flower) had to be pinched off on a daily basis. I still like to grow the old-established variety 'Telegraph', which produces male flowers, but nowadays it is easy to get all-female flowering types, such as 'Cumlaude', 'Carmen', and 'Media', which produce uniformly sweet offspring.

Pest and diseases Cucumbers grown indoors are very susceptible to red spider mite, cucumber mosaic virus, and powdery mildew. I have never had red spider mite, which tends to build up when it is very dry, in my greenhouses. Damping the floor down and watering regularly helps a lot. But I have had trouble with powdery mildew and good ventilation is the best prevention. Cucumber mosaic virus, which is carried by aphids, will yellow and stunt leaves. If noticed, remove and burn the leaves – and, if necessary, the whole plant.

Outdoor ridge cucumber

If you have a very long cucumber, you can harvest half of it while it is still on the plant. The exposed end will callus over, and the remainder of the fruit can be harvested as and when required.

Dwarf French beans The majority of commercial French beans, like those sold all year in supermarkets, are grown in third world countries, involving cheap labour and huge numbers of air miles.

'Golden Sands'

MY VARIETIES
'Annabelle'
'Aramis'
'Golden Sands'
'Hildora' (yellow)
'Maxi'
'Purple Queen'
'Purple Teepee'
'Twiggy'

They are also likely to be subject to the inevitable chemical pollution that non-organic growers resort to. But they are a simple crop to grow at home, taking up little space and freezing well.

The French bean (*Phaseolus vulgaris*) is normally eaten at the immature pod stage, before the beans themselves have developed inside. The next stage, when the beans have grown but are still fresh within the pod, is the flageolet bean. When the pod has fully matured and dried, it becomes the haricot bean. The pods range from quite wide, oval tubes to bootlace "string" beans. Not all are green – I also grow yellow- and purple-podded types.

Every year, I am very tempted (and, I admit, against all experience, often succumb) to plant out the first dwarf French beans in early May during a spell of warm weather, but it is rarely worthwhile. They are not at all frost hardy and will not grow in cold weather. This makes them an ideal target for slugs and snails, which love them, often eating the whole plant so that all that is left are stumpy remnants of the stems. A June planting with another at the beginning of August ensures a supply well into October.

French beans are legumes, so should be part of the same crop rotation as other beans and peas. They require deeply dug and freshly composted soil. If I am sowing direct I sow in double rows 22cm (9in) apart, with 55cm (18in) between each double row and about 10cm (4in) between each bean. If I am planting out indoor-raised seedlings I do so in blocks with 22cm (9in) between each plant. They need plenty of water, so weed assiduously to reduce competition.

I make my first sowing in large plugs in the greenhouse at the beginning of May and harden them off carefully via the cold frames before planting them out in early June. I sow another batch directly in the ground when these are planted out.

Climbing French beans

Climbing beans are essentially the same as Dwarf or French beans. But clearly the fact that some of this family will climb gives the gardener great aesthetic opportunities.

There are certain French climbing beans that have a distinct and delicious taste, and they are much harder to buy than dwarf varieties. I do not grow runner beans as there are many tastier climbing beans. My favourite is 'Burro d'Ingenoli', which has a curiously buttery texture when cooked, pod and all, and tastes wonderful, especially as part of a ratatouille.

All climbing beans grow in exactly the same conditions as their dwarf cousins (*see facing page*). But because they produce so much more growth and foliage, they need extra water and nutrition. I grow mine up wigwams of bean sticks (always made from long, stout hazel poles). Before I put in the supports, I dig a pit and add a barrow-load of compost. An old trick is to line the bottom of the bean trench with newspaper, which acts as a

sponge, but any organic material added to the planting hole will help the soil to hold moisture long enough for the roots to absorb it. Once a week, I leave the hose running at the base of each wigwam for 10–15 minutes to give them a really good soak.

As with dwarf French beans, I sow the seed in blocks or modules in May and raise them under cover, before planting them out in June. I put in one plant to each pole of the wigwam About a quarter of these will get eaten by slugs, but a couple of seeds popped in the ground usually germinate fast and fill any gaps. The wigwams of beans are fabulously decorative, and I am happy to do whatever I can to hasten their arrival. They will continue producing beans until the first frost, which will kill off the plants.

'Blauhilde'

'Borlotto'

MY VARIETIES
'Barlotto Lingua di Fuoco'
'Blauhilde'
'Blue Lake'
'Borlotti'
'Burro d'Ingenoli'

I use coppiced hazel rods tied as wigwams to support my climbing beans. The growing tendrils (which always twist clockwise) need tying in for the first 1m (3ft) or so.

Radishes are perhaps the easiest of all vegetables to grow. They will germinate in fairly cool temperatures, so can be sown in spring, as soon as the soil is workable, and right through summer.

MY VARIETIES
SUMMER RADISHES
'French Breakfast'
'Scarlet Globe'
WINTER RADISHES
'Black Spanish Round'
ORIENTAL RADISHES
'Minowase'

There are varieties that can be sown in summer for autumn and winter use, and Japanese or Asian radishes that can grow as large as parsnips.

The secret of growing radishes is to make sure that they have a constant water supply and never dry out. If they get dry – especially in hot weather – they very quickly bolt and turn woody. They like a well-drained soil that has not been recently manured, since fresh compost will produce lots of leafy top-growth and poor roots. I grow them in the same beds as carrots and parsnips, although radishes are brassicas and if you grow a lot you should include them in the brassica part of your crop rotation. Would anyone grow a lot of radishes? Maybe. It takes all sorts.

Summer types are particularly useful for sowing with parsnips because the latter can be very slow to germinate. If you sow a sprinkling of radish seeds (and they are round and very easy to sow unlike the flat papery discs of the parsnip seed) in the same drill as parsnips they act as a marker for the rows and will germinate, mature, and be picked and eaten before they disturb the developing parsnips. 'French Breakfast' and 'Scarlet Globe' are my favourites – best eaten with butter and salt and served with a glass of dry white wine as an apéritif.

Hardy winter radishes are sown in summer to either stay in the ground over winter in mild areas or be lifted and stored for winter eating. They can come in all shapes and sizes, but all have dark skin. They do not have that sharp freshness that is so central to the summer radish. The only variety of winter radish that I have ever grown is 'Black Spanish'. Asian radishes are sown in July for an autumnal harvest.

Summer radishes like 'French Breakfast' (*right*) grow very quickly when planted out in mid-spring taking 2–8 weeks to mature into rosy cylinder shapes with white tips.

Spinach

The freshness of home-grown spinach in spring is tangible, and no other chemically-grown vegetable contains such high residues of pesticides.

In an American Environmental Protection Agency report on the dietary effect of pesticide residues it came in just behind strawberries.

I love spinach raw in salads or cooked, although you need a surprising quantity of leaves for the latter. Fresh spinach and a fresh poached egg is a wonderful combination. Spinach is, of course, very rich in iron, has a higher protein content than any other leaf vegetable, is rich in vitamin A, and raw spinach has twice the amount of carotenoids that raw carrot has. However, when cooked, the oxalic acid content halts the absorption of the calcium and iron, so if your motive for eating it is entirely for your health, it is better to consume it raw.

Spinach is a cool-season crop and quickly bolts and runs to seed when the temperature rises and daylight hours increase. It is therefore one of the first seeds to be sown in spring, and grows well in late summer and early autumn. It will also overwinter in a tunnel. Spinach beet is more resistant to cold and is longer-lasting than spinach. It makes a perfectly good substitute in winter. You will see "long-day" varieties that are bred to resist the urge to run to seed as the days lengthen and are therefore good for later sowings. I have grown spinach in plugs and transplanted it, but the germination rate can be very poor inside a warm greenhouse. It is better to sow seed *in situ*, thinning it to 15cm (6in) spacing. Unfortunately, slugs and snails are very partial to the young seedlings so it is not an easy crop for us, indoors or out.

The best spinach is eaten young, so I always harvest the whole plant, cutting it with a knife at ground level. It will then produce new leaves for another crop. It is also important to grow the varieties most suited to the season to give yourself a chance of harvesting it before it bolts. 'Monnopa' and 'Viroflay' have less oxalic acid than most so are the most suitable for feeding to very young children. Whatever the variety, spinach needs really rich soil and lots of water. It can be grown before or after any other vegetable crop and makes a good companion for legumes, celeriac, lettuces, or even potatoes, grown as a catch-crop between the rows.

MY VARIETIES
EARLY SEASON
'Avanti' F1
'Bloomsdale'
'Monnopa'
SUMMER
'Matador'
'Viroflay'
LATE SEASON
'Galaxy' F1
'Giant Winter'
'Norfolk'

Autumn is a time of great change. There is a major shift in this garden from early October to the end of November, going from days that feel like late summer to some of the most miserable weather of all.

Fortunately, along the way, we have some lovely golden days with warm, low sunshine. They are made more precious by the knowledge that these are the last shards of summer light.

In autumn the orchard takes centre stage. In winter it can seem a little semi-detached from the rest of the garden, as though there is an absence there, but since the arrival of the blossom in spring it has been an important part of the garden, with the combination of the fruit trees and the long grass beneath them being, at times, as decorative as any of the borders. But in autumn the real business of the place begins. Although there are varieties such as 'Gladstone' or 'Laxton's Early Crimson' that can be eaten at the end of July, my first apples begin to ripen in early September with an unknown (and certainly unordered) cooking variety with very waxy skin and a fluffy texture when cooked. By October I am picking almost daily and by November there are only a few trees still bearing fruit – such as 'Norfolk Beefing' and 'Stoke Edith Pippin'. We store as many apples as possible in the purpose-built apple store to provide us with a supply right through to the following spring. Not all fruits store as well. Pears are really only at their best for a day and I check almost every individual fruit throughout September, picking them as soon as they come away from the tree with gentle upward pressure. But a home-grown ripe pear, eaten on that one day when all the year's growth comes to the fleeting point of perfection, is nicer than anything money can buy.

We have quinces, too, fitting somewhere between apples and pears in appearance but storing better than both. A bowl of quinces on a warm windowsill will fill

the room with their unique and subtle fragrance. The quince leaves turn a wonderful clear yellow in late October, as do the leaves of the hazel in the coppice, reflecting light and giving the air an extraordinary pale buttery tone. The cobnuts are ready for collecting in September and it is always a race to pick them before the squirrels gather their own haul.

The autumn raspberries are the final fruits of the year, still producing luscious berries into November unless we have a really hard frost, which is an increasingly rare autumn event.

There is a great deal happening in the vegetable garden. The last of the tomatoes are still being harvested and chicories, sweetcorn, leeks, squashes and pumpkins are all coming into their peak. The latter are one of the real signifiers of autumn. The fruits of the squashes have been swelling steadily since late summer although until autumn they are mostly hidden by their vast leaves. But when the leaves start to die back they reveal the range of fruits in all their splendour, sitting amongst the decaying

foliage like monstrous eggs. The French beans keep going to the first frosts, as do the late salad crops. However, it is never an easy time because the weather is so variable. Until ten years ago all autumn work was geared towards keeping as much going as possible until the first frosts – which could happen at any time from mid-September onwards, and were inevitable by the beginning of November. But increasingly the pattern is towards very wet, mild autumns. So our biggest task is to try to dig any ground that needs it by the middle of October. Some years it is very wet indeed, with extensive flooding covering a third of the vegetable garden, and we cannot set foot – literally – on any bare soil. Work has to wait. Other years it can be drier and remarkably mild, so everything – including the weeds and grass – keeps growing well past any expected date. But always, inevitably, as the season progresses we fast run out of light, and at the end of October the clocks go back and it is dark by 6pm. This is a bad day. From then on it is sharply downhill to the shortest day on December 21st.

Squashes
I have been a big fan of squashes since I first grew them ten years ago. Until then I had only grown marrows and courgettes and the world of squashes – including pumpkins – remained unexplored.

I had grown marrows and courgettes for many years without thinking of them as summer squashes – which of course they are. But the winter squashes are much nicer, both to eat and to look at. We usually grow more than we can eat, but some – especially the acorn squashes – keep remarkably well and are very decorative.

Squashes are easy to grow but very sensitive to temperature. They hate the cold and you must resist the temptation to sow them too early. The beginning of May is quite soon enough, and midsummer is not too late in these days of globally warmed autumns. It is easy enough to raise them under cover before this, but there is then a period when they sit in the cold frames, not growing much and being attacked by slugs and snails, until the ground is warm enough for them – which is never before the beginning of June – and once they

lose their vigour they never really recover it. Far better to sow them late and plant them out as soon as they have developed true leaves, so that they can do their growing in the ground rather than the pot.

And how they will grow! The more vigorous varieties will stretch for four or five metres or more and produce up to a dozen large fruits. Even if you keep them cut back and pinch off some flowers so that the energy can go into just a few large squashes, you will still need at least one square metre, and preferably two, for each plant.

I sow the seed on edge, two to a 7cm (3in) pot. The compost must be at least 16°C (60°F) for them to germinate, and as soon as both seedlings have developed true leaves I pull the smaller one out and discard it. The survivor must harden off for at least a week before planting out, but if the timing is correct the

'Little Gem'

Harvesting winter squashes before putting them to dry and fully ripen in the autumn sunshine.

MY VARIETIES

'Baby Bear'
'Buttercup'
'Early Butternut'
'Etamples'
'Golden Acorn'
'Golden Delicious'
'Golden Hubbard'
'Jack Be Little'
'Little Gem'
'Turk's Turban'
'Uchiki Kuri'

change in temperature will not be too dramatic.

Squashes like plenty of moisture and really rich soil that does not become waterlogged. I always plant three or four on an old compost heap. This helps the heap by using up moisture that would make it slimy, and is perfect for the squashes. If I am planting just a few in a border, I dig a pit and add plenty of compost, leaving the surface in a shallow bowl to collect water. The plants can be trained up a support but the squashes can get large and very heavy so it needs to be really strong.

A shiny rind is an indication that a squash is not yet ripe. It should have a dull appearance and feel heavy for its size, with a hard, deep-coloured rind free of blemishes and soft or mouldy spots. By the beginning of October our squashes are on borrowed time. Once it gets below about 10°C (50°F) for a week, or there is extended rain, then whatever their size, I bring them all in for storage.

Ideally, harvest consists of cutting all the fruits, piling them into wheelbarrows and putting them out on garden tables to dry. They must be gathered in with a 7–10cm (3–4in) section of stem attached to the fruit, which will stop rot getting in. The more sunshine that they can get after harvesting the longer they will keep, so we leave them outside, covering them with a tarpaulin if it is very wet, for at least a week. This stage hardens the skin and the harder it gets, the longer they keep.

Under proper storage conditions – dark, cool, airy, and dry – acorn squashes will last for 5–8 weeks, and butternut squashes two to three months. 'Turk's Turban' and 'Buttercup' should keep for at least three months. Although they might feel indestructible, try not to pile squashes on top of each other as they will keep much better undamaged.

Celery I am often asked which vegetables are the best to grow organically at home. The obvious answer is all of them, but there is an especially strong argument for growing your own trench celery.

Traditionally grown trench celery is hard to get hold of commercially, for the obvious reason that it is a whole lot more bother to grow. This is, to my mind, justified by its extra succulence and intensity of taste. Anyway, I hate the easy-wipe, painless world of instant anything. Get your hands dirty! Sweat! Ache! Live a little.

Commercial seeds are treated with hormones to make them germinate faster. Then they are usually raised in peat, which should be a no-no for the home grower. Then herbicides are applied to the land before planting and up to five times whilst the crop is growing. Fungicides are used because of the high humidity needed for the crop, and pesticides against leaf miner. The hormone gibberellic acid is sometimes sprayed on to encourage longer stem growth.

From the outset celery needs mollycoddling. It is a tender plant and cannot be sown directly into the soil. I sow the seeds in March and put them on the heated mat to germinate. I broadcast them as thinly as possible into seed trays and then transplant them into 5cm (2in) plugs once they have germinated. I keep them growing under cover until May and harden them off outside for a couple of weeks.

There are two types of celery, trench and self-blanching. Trench celery must be blanched by protecting the growing stems from light whereas self-blanching celery gets all the blanching it needs from its outer layer of stems. Blanching is necessary to make the stems succulent and sweet. I find that trench celery is the better tasting of the two kinds, but it is less hardy and harder to grow. So I grow both. I was brought up to grow celery in a trench which was gradually backfilled as the stems grew. It is the method that I still use although many people wrap a light-excluding layer like black polythene around each plant. This strikes me as a lot of work and fiddle than and is also the perfect home for slugs, so I stick to a simple trench.

I dig the trench when I sow the seeds, adding as much compost as I would for runner beans. It is a hungry crop and the ground's ability to hold water will influence the success of the final harvest. As with any plant, be it edible or decorative, knowledge of its original habitat is the most useful guide as to how best to grow it. Celery occurs in Asia and Europe in marshy, boggy ground and any organic material will help replicate the plant's basic needs. If you dig the trench in March there is time to grow a crop of 'Tom Thumb' or 'Little Gem' lettuce on the ridges made from the trench's spoil, as it will not be needed until July for the first earthing up.

Slugs love celery with a passion to equal my own and it is prone to the various health problems like celery leaf spot and pests such as celery leaf miner and carrot fly.

There are two types of self-blanching celery, the "Standard" which have naturally golden or creamy coloured stems and the American green varieties that genuinely need no blanching. They are germinated as trench celery and then planted out in a block, with about 30cm (12in) space in every

MY VARIETIES
TRENCH CELERY
'Mammoth Pink'
'Solid White'

SELF-BLANCHING CELERY
'Golden Self-Blanching'

Blanching trench celery

As soon as the last frosts are over, I plant the young celery plants into the bottom of the trench in a single row, with about 22cm (9in) between plants. I have tried using double rows before, but the plants do not grow as well and it is hard to dig them up without damaging any adjacent plants. I water them in well and then give them a good soak once a week as they need plenty of water to grow. When the

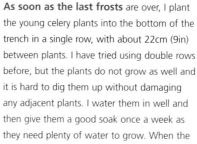

tops of the plants rise above the top of the trench, I take the soil from the ridges and fill in round them so that all that is exposed is a little green leafy top-knot. This is part of the blanching process and has to be repeated at least once more, depending on how vigorously they grow, digging down, if need be, to find the soil to create a kind of earthen clamp around the maturing hearts.

direction. The wider the planting, the bigger the plants. The idea is that each plant shields its neighbour and only the exterior ones need blanching with brown paper wrapped about the stalks and tied with string or straw pushed between them. Blanching is not just cosmetic (although most people apparently find white celery more appealing than pink or green) but also reduces any bitterness. Straw has the added advantage of acting as insulation against the first mild frosts.

Whatever you use will increase the slug-friendliness of the crop, especially if it is a wet year, so watch out for them.

When people refer to celery being "stringy" they are referring to the wisps of tough tissue that lie along the length of the stalk, which can get stuck between the teeth. But the strings are the pathways that carry the nutrients to and from the leaves. This means that so-called "stringless" varieties are likely to be less robust or large than others.

Celeriac *(Apium graveolens* var. *rapaceum)* is, in many ways, easier to grow than celery. The delicious edible "root" is in fact the swollen base of the plant.

Celeriac did not reach Britain until the late 1720s and has never really entered its popular culinary imagination. It is an earthy thing, but delicate and delicious when cooked and very nutritious, unlike celery which, when tough, probably needs more energy to digest than it supplies. It has a taste that is uniquely light and subtle. I like it puréed best (delicious as a left-over, eaten straight from the fridge with a spoon) but it makes a fine soup, chips, roast, or as a component of a good winter stew. A fantastically useful winter vegetable.

Secrets of success I used to find that I could not get the swollen bases to grow into anything like the melon-sized jobs that you find in a greengrocer's. Mine were all knobbly tennis balls or, worse, flattered above ground to deceive whereas in fact they were completely flat below the soil. But I have learnt to give celeriac a long growing season in very rich soil with a constant supply of water.

I start it exactly as celery, sowing in early spring in the greenhouse. The seed is tiny

MY VARIETIES
'Iram'
'President'
'Tellus'

Young celeriac plants are very delicate and slow to grow, so I plant them out into their final position, in blocks about 22cm (9in) apart, about eight weeks after sowing. They need lots of water so a really well enriched, moisture-retentive soil is essential. Every six weeks or so, from midsummer onwards, it is a good idea to remove the side leaves as they start to droop, to focus the plants' growing energy into the swollen edible bases.

Celeriac tastes best when left in the ground and harvested fresh when needed but will need diggging up and storing if there is a chance of hard frosts.

and rather than try to use plugs I broadcast it in seed trays, and then transplant (when they are very small) into plugs or pots before putting them into a cold frame. They grow slowly initially, and might take six weeks before they are large enough to plant out in rows, 22cm (9in) apart and a little more than that between the rows. Unlike celery, the slugs leave them alone once they are established, although they do like a juicy young celeriac plant.

Keep them well weeded and watered and take off the side leaves every six weeks or so, gradually exposing the developing base. Be patient. They take time. Five months from

planting out to the first harvest is about as fast as you can expect.

Harvesting Celeriac are not truly frost-hardy although a light frost does not affect them too much. But if the bulbs themselves freeze they will rot. If you have space they can be dug up in November and stored in boxes in dry straw, shredded newspaper, or coir, or else they can be left in the ground and mulched with straw or covered with a permanent blanket of horticultural fleece. Certainly if they can be kept from freezing they last better, and seem to taste better if they remain in the ground until they are dug for eating.

Aubergines

Aubergines are as exotic as we get here. They are not a staple food for us, unlike tomatoes or basil – which also need protection from our climate – but I usually grow some to contribute to a ratatouille or two.

As their Latin name, *Solanum melongena*, suggests, aubergines are part of the same family as potatoes and tomatoes, although they come from India, on the other side of the world. I sow the seed at the same time as tomatoes and peppers, pricking them out into 7cm (3in) pots and then on into a larger one – usually a size or two larger than the ones for peppers because they can make quite bulky plants. I also stake them, to keep them upright and to ensure that as much sun and air as possible gets around the fruits. They like plenty of moisture and heat so can share the same conditions as cucumbers but are not really compatible with the drier conditions needed for peppers or tomatoes. Having said this I merely make sure they are grown in a rich compost mix and get plenty of water.

These fruits can range from the deepest plum colour to ivory-white, although the cooler the growing conditions the less colour will develop. The secret of success is to give them maximum heat so that the fruits develop fast and can be picked as soon as they are large enough. The longer they are left on the plant, the more bitter they become. A good rule of thumb is to pick when the skin has a bright gloss but the seeds are still white.

MY VARIETIES
'Violetta di Firenze'
'Black Beauty'
'Long Purple'
'Très Hative de Barbentane'

Chilli peppers

Chilli peppers Although I have grown sweet peppers in the greenhouse, I now concentrate on chilli peppers because the return is so much greater from a few fruits that, if dried, will keep for years.

Chillies respond to heat, so they spend their lives in the greenhouse. I sow them in spring, at the same time as tomatoes, in modules, pricking out into 7cm (3in) pots before finally potting on to a 22cm (9in) pot – smaller than those I use for tomatoes, but then these are much smaller, less vigorous plants.

It is best to water them little and often, rather than drenching them once a week. Peppers are prone to fungal diseases, and the best protection against this is to provide enough ventilation – especially at plant height – and to make sure that they go into the evening dry. If possible, the last watering should be no later than around 4.30pm. If we have a cool summer, chilli peppers can be very slow to mature and produce fruit, and we often go into autumn with fruits still forming and ripening. I help them to survive this colder weather by putting them on a heated mat and keeping a constant base heat of about 18°C (65°F). I feed them with liquid seaweed once a week.

The fruits can be picked and used green, or left to ripen to red (or yellow, pink, orange, purple, or black, according to variety). We dry ours in a bowl on a windowsill. That "hit" to which chilli-heads become addicted is produced by capsaicin, an irritant alkaloid that creates the sensation of heat. The hotter the summer, the hotter the fruits will be, especially if picked just after fully turning colour.

MY VARIETIES
There are hundreds of varieties of chilli pepper: I experiment from year to year, most recently with 'De Bresse', a medium hot variety with smallish fruits, and a Cayenne variety with tiny but very hot fruits.

Chard
Swiss Chard is a close relation of beetroot and spinach and is one of the staples of our vegetable garden. It grows spinach-like leaves on strong white stalks, both of which are delicious.

Yellow-stemmed chard

We shred the green leaves from the stalks and cook and use them exactly like spinach – although the leaves do not have such a strong aftertaste – and the stems are very good cooked separately in water or stock and served either with oil and lemon or a béchamel sauce. The leaves and stalks chopped up together make a very good filling for a pie or flan.

We also grow ruby chard, which has bronze leaves and brilliant, intense crimson stems, and rainbow chard, with coloured stems of yellow, orange, pink, and red. But once cooked, all taste remarkably similar and for reliability and taste I would opt for Swiss chard.

The seeds can be sown direct but I sow them in plug trays, one seed to a cell, growing them on and hardening off before planting out at 22cm (9in) spacing. They like a really rich, moisture-retentive soil and will need watering in a hot summer if they are not to go to seed.

If some do start to bolt then I cut the central stem down to the ground. I sow a first batch in spring, and then another in August that will provide plants to overwinter for harvesting the following spring. They are very tough indeed and even though hard winter frost will seemingly reduce the plant to a rotten brown slime (which is best cleared away to avoid rot), new leaves will miraculously appear in early spring.

There are two ways to harvest it – either I cut the whole plant to the ground while the leaves are quite young, or else take a few good leaves from a number of plants. Either way the leaves you pick to eat should be very shiny and obviously healthy. Older, sagging leaves are best cleared away to the compost heap. I take away barrowloads of leaves cut away from the ageing stems so that new, fresh growth can get some light and air.

A bed of chard in October. This will provide two pickings before Christmas and then regrow for a third picking in spring. Ruby chard (*facing page*) is the most decorative of all vegetables, with its crimson stalks and veins.

Florence fennel has evolved – with a lot of help from breeders – from the ordinary herb fennel to a vegetable. The base is swollen and forms an overlapping succession of layers like a bulb.

MY VARIETIES
'Argo'
'Romanesco'

Florence fennel, or *finocchio*, is not an easy vegetable to grow but is well worth the effort as it is delicious, both raw and cooked, stores quite well, and, with its aniseed flavour, is, to me, an essential taste of late summer and early autumn.

The problem with growing Florence fennel lies in its propensity to bolt before the bulbs swell out to any appreciable size, especially if you sow before midsummer, as they are very

sensitive to changing day length. The plant develops a hard core – rather like a bolting leek – leaving just the outer layers of the base as edible. Ideally, one should try and grow it as fast as possible. Any check at any stage in its growth seems to activate a hair trigger and set it bolting. I regularly grow the variety 'Argo' which, because it is fairly resistant to bolting, can be sown earlier in the season.

Growing fennel I raise Florence fennel in plugs in the greenhouse and then pot them on into a rich compost mix in 7cm (3in) pots, leaving them in the cold frame to mature and slowly harden off before planting out once each plant has developed a good root system. (The only way to know this is to very gently check by holding the plant upside-down and easing off the pot. If the compost is held together by the roots, it is ready to go out.) They are usually ready by the beginning of August. I put them into ground that has had beans or peas cleared from it – and is therefore well manured.

I plant them out in rows at 22cm (9in) spacing, watering them in very thoroughly and including them in the watering regime with celeriac and celery, which get a good soak once a week. The bulbs can be left in the ground until the first hard frost rots them.

Fennel as a winter crop I have grown Florence fennel in the tunnel and it overwintered very well, despite no extra protection from quite hard frost and limited watering. The plants lasted right into March while still being edible.

I raise the fennel plants (*left to right*), in the greenhouse, sowing into seed trays and pricking them out into individual 7cm (3in) pots until they have a sufficiently developed root system to be planted out at 22cm (9in) spacing. The secret is to grow them fast so they need rich soil with regular water to develop the delicious fleshy base of the plant.

Chicory The wide range of chicories now available from seed catalogues is a fairly recent – and very exciting – development, and I experiment with new kinds each year.

MY VARIETIES
FOR CHICONS
'Witloof Alba'
'Yellora'

RED CHICORY
'Alouette'
'Palla Rossa'
'Red Treviso' ('Rouge de Trevise')
'Red Verona'
'Variegata di Castelfranco'
'Variegata di Chioggia'

CUTTING CHICORY/ENDIVE
'Grumolo Verde'
'Catalogna Fastagliata'
'Cornet de Bordeaux'
'Coquette'
'Frisée de Ruffec'

The defining characteristic of all chicories is their bitterness. This is much more prevalent in some varieties than others, but it is a quality that can be harnessed to add edge and depth to a dish or meal, and is a welcome exception to the prevailing sweetness of most vegetables.

Chicories are all easy to grow, tough and – especially good – their bitterness deters all but the most determined snail or slug. In short, I like everything about them.

How chicory grows All chicories grow in two stages, initially developing a strong root and producing green leaves, which can be picked for eating raw in salads. In late summer, these leaves undergo a change. Some varieties die right back and then regrow, and others

change colour, turning bright red in response to cold and lower light levels. Some varieties have a kind of self-blanching mechanism where the outer leaves protect the inner ones from light, which results in these being paler and less bitter. As they age, many chicories develop strong leaf stems that are too tough to be eaten raw but cook very well.

Chicories are without doubt an important component of our vegetable garden, particularly as autumn drifts gloomily into winter. They have a long growing season – as much as 10 months – so you have to have the space to give up for them, although I think it more than worth it and anyway, their autumn to spring season covers a period in the vegetable garden when there is least competition for space.

Witloof chicory (*right*) growing in summer. This top-growth will be cut and the roots then forced and blanched to produce the familiar white "chicons".

Spadona chicory before cutting in summer (*far right, above*) and a few days later as fresh growth is produced (*below*). These new shoots are very good in salads.

Clearing green leaves from 'Red Treviso' chicory in late summer to allow light and air to get to the new red leaves that will follow. The earlier green leaves can be eaten but are very bitter and most of mine go straight to the compost heap.

Chicory for chicons Traditionally, Witloof chicory is grown for its blanched regrowth after the initial summer growth of leaves has been cut off flush with the ground. These new leaves, or "chicons" are eaten raw as part of a winter salad. Very good they are too, making an especially good combination with avocado and tomato.

Witloof chicory was "discovered" when a Belgian farmer threw some wild chicory roots into a stable. In this warm, dark environment they quickly grew the characteristic blanched leaves. These are delicious but quite a bother to produce and by no means the best chicory that one can eat.

To get the white chicons you must grow the chicory all summer so that it establishes a strong root system, then cut off the head – which by then looks like a shaggy lettuce. If the weather is mild, the chicory can simply be blanched by placing a flowerpot over it, with straw beneath that to keep the plant from freezing. But the more traditional method is to "force" the chicons: dig up a few roots at a time, trim them, and pot them up in peat or sand; invert a second pot on top to block out any light and put them in a warm dark place so that new white leaves will grow back from the root.

Red chicory Radicchio is a catch-all expression that in Italy is used to describe all red chicories, although we tend to use it to refer to those varieties that grow in a tight ball rather than the more upright leafy red ones.

The red chicories start out life predominantly green, but as autumn sets in the insides of the leaves start to turn red so that they have an extraordinary contrast – green on the outside with burgundy interiors, as sharply and carefully delineated as any livery. These summer leaves die back and are replaced in winter and early spring by new all-red ones that are well worth waiting for. 'Red

Radicchio 'Palla Rossa' gradually changes as the weather gets colder from a green, loose-leaved head to a deep red, tight furl. 'Alouette' is another reliable tight-balled radicchio. The more upright, loose-leafed 'Variegata di Chioggia' and 'Variegata di Castelfranco' both have green leaves speckled with red. 'Red Verona', somewhere between a ball and an upright type, also has lovely red leaves.

Treviso'

in particular has leaves that unfurl like extraordinary cockerel feathers, in the richest, most burnished, alizarin crimson imaginable.

Loose-leaf chicories There are chicories that start out green and remain so for the rest of their growing lives. 'Grumolo Verde' is the toughest of all chicories, surviving any weather and growing almost all year round. It too has two forms, starting out loose-leafed and then slowly developing round, almost spiralled heads.

Catalogna chicory looks quite like a dandelion when growing, with large, deeply serrated leaves. One can grow it as *catalogna brindisina*, or puntarelle, primarily for the stalks that it grows in the spring following planting, or for its stems and leaves, as *catalogna a foglia fastagliata*.

I am particularly fond of oven-roasted Catalogna chicory, each plant lifted whole, quartered, and roasted with a little oil. No other vegetable looks so beautiful as it does when cut, its colour incredibly fresh and bright

and the layers of leaves revealed. Boil them for a few minutes to soften them before roasting or baking in a pan with an inch of water, a couple of cups of white wine, the juice of a lemon, and plenty of pepper. If you roast them without previously boiling them they tend to dry out and be tough.

Endive Another member of the chicory family, although less bitter. The most commonly grown is the curly or frizzled leaf kind, grown in conjunction with lettuce and used in summer salads. However, they are much hardier than lettuce and, if protected by straw, a cloche, or horticultural fleece, can easily last into December. Not only are they constitutionally tougher, but also less tender to eat. This can be remedied by tying the tops of the outer leaves together to blanch the inner ones, which within a few weeks become sweeter and more tender. On the whole, I tend to leave mine unblanched.

The broad-leafed varieties of endive such as 'Cornet de Bordeaux', or hardier curly-leaved endives such as 'Coquette' or 'Frisée de

324

Ruffec', are best suited to winter standing. I sow them in early August, and start to harvest in late September. They will overwinter under a cloche but very quickly bolt in spring.

Winter protection In October, I cover all my chicories with open-ended cloches, to protect the leaves from too much wet rather than the cold and frost which they can withstand. The outer leaves of endives can easily rot and form a brown, soggy carapace around the otherwise healthy plant, ruining it. I also periodically clear away any leaves that are dying back to allow air to reach the inner leaves and new growth. Open-ended cloches also let in a little rain so that the plants do not dry out completely.

Endive 'Cornet de Bordeaux'

Turnips My children are yet to be convinced as to the edibility of a turnip, let alone any more sophisticated culinary appreciation.

But eaten young, golf-ball size, either raw or lightly boiled, they can be very good indeed, and turnip tops (like beetroot tops) make good spring greens and are particularly high in vitamins A, B and C.

Turnips are a brassica, so should be grown as part of the cabbage rotation. They take about 7 to 10 weeks to mature from sowing and need cool weather to germinate, so an August sowing – which ensures cool nights – will produce a crop for October. They need rich soil and plenty of moisture as they are growing.

Slugs love the emerging seedlings so I sow them in plugs or blocks, three or four seeds at a time, and let them mature sufficiently to fend for themselves before planting out. Getting the timing for this right can be tricky but it is vital. I have planted out healthy turnip seedlings and come back the following morning to find every single one grazed to a needle-sized green stump by a herd of snails. Yet if they go out too late they never grow with the proper vigour and the resulting vegetable does not have full flavour or health and is prone to attacks by pests or disease.

Swede Although perhaps the least glamorous of vegetables, I am very fond of swede, mashed and served with plenty of butter and pepper.

Swede is rich in vitamin C, calcium and niacin and a lot more substantial than a turnip. In fact it is a hybrid between the turnip and cabbage, but swedes are hardier than turnips and will overwinter in the soil, and need a longer growing season. They also grow better in a light, well-manured soil. Swedes need at least 20 weeks to mature and I sow them in June, in plugs, although if you have a slug-free garden, it is better to sow them direct and then thin to 22cm (9in) spacing. However much you like swedes, they are large root vegetables and no one family needs a huge amount. I have found that they can be successfully intercropped with purple-sprouting broccoli, which is slow to mature and needs wide spacing. By the time that the broccoli is ready for harvesting in March, the swedes have all been lifted.

Sweetcorn I always grow sweetcorn, and we have about half a dozen meals in which we eat it with relish, yet in most years, half the crop goes to the hens.

MY VARIETIES
'Doux Miner'
'Golden Sweet F1'

Like asparagus, fresh sweetcorn tastes so much better than anything that you can buy. I do not cut the cobs until the water in which they are to be cooked is on a rolling boil and take them straight from garden to stove. Because they are so special when eaten directly from the plant, we do not store any, which means that in a good year, when the couple of dozen plants I grow might produce 50 good cobs, we will eat no more than half. But nothing is wasted, as the rest go to the chickens over the course of the winter, and they pick the dried cobs clean. It is also a very decorative crop, and it is hard to think of late summer and autumn without a small bed of the tall corn.

The seeds are sown in May in 7cm (3in) pots and planted out in July. There is no need to be earlier than this as they need hot days and warm nights to grow well. I often underplant them with courgettes. They must be planted in a block, spaced about 45–60cm (18in–2ft) in each direction, rather than in rows, as they are wind-pollinated and if planted in a straight line the wind can merely blow all the pollen away!

The cobs tend to be ready to pick when the tassels at the end of them turn dark brown but I test to see if they are ripe by carefully folding back the surrounding sheaths and squeezing the corn. If they secrete a milky juice then they are ripe and can be picked. The stems are too woody to be composted immediately so we shred them before adding them to the compost heap.

My most recent crop, of 'Doux Miner', was grown from organic seed from France although I have grown an F1 variety, 'Golden Sweet', that has performed well.

I sow my sweetcorn in late April, in large plugs or small individual pots, germinating them in the greenhouse and then growing them on in a cold frame. I then harden them off for a couple of weeks before planting out in early July. They are planted about 60cm (2ft) apart, in a block to aid pollination. I use the beds where either broad beans or garlic have been cleared. I often underplant the corn with courgettes.

Winter The most beautiful thing about winter in the vegetable garden is frost, icing the crinkled leaves of cabbages and box hedges.

Occasionally we get a hard hoar frost and every twig and stem is rimed in pink ice as it reflects the dawn light. This is becoming increasingly rare, especially in December. Far more often cloud covers the sky for days on end. This cloud cover brings rain on most days and always very low light levels. The ground never dries out and although it is usually fairly mild, little grows at this time of year.

Winter has two distinct halves. This first half, ending with the arrival of the New Year, is by far the worst and has to be endured. It does not get light until after 8am in the morning and is too dark to work outside beyond 4.30pm in the afternoon.

Gradually, the leaves all fall from the pleached limes surrounding the vegetable garden and the espaliered pears are exposed to their bare bones. Only the brick paths that we put into this area at huge expense and effort make any kind of access possible. It was money and time very well spent.

I love the gap between Christmas and New Year, and treat it as a kind of horticultural retreat that I look forward to for months. If the weather is bad, there are gardening books to catch up on and garden plans to be made for the coming year. When everything in the month or two leading up to Christmas has been a downward slide, once the days start to lengthen there is suddenly something that seems incredibly positive about working outside until dark, even if it is just pacing things out and really, really looking, and then working on in the evening at the drawing board on the same project. I use these plans as a kind of list of resolutions for the coming year. It never all happens, of course, but it is a fine way of linking mind-gardening and the dirty-handed stuff.

It is not just plants and their health that need a good long cold snap. Cold ground means dry, workable soil. If it gets

really cold, and freezes hard, then it means that cultivated soil will break down to a lovely, friable tilth. Best of all, dry, cold weather kills off all the fungal spores and moulds that thrive in wet warmth – the blights, blackspots, and the sooty, grey, and white moulds that fur plants like the inside of a kettle. Aphids die off and slugs and snails suffer. A month of sustained cold in the garden is like a purge, cleansing it and purifying it from all the accumulated waste of fecund summer.

There is, of course, a price to pay for this. Not all plants like it – artichokes, for example, cannot survive unprotected if the temperature falls much below -5°C (41°F) and need to be given a thick mulch of straw. But other plants, such as garlic, need a cold period in order to trigger their spring growth or germination. People think of extreme cold as a big problem, but when living in the countryside frozen weather can make life much easier. It is the only time in the winter months that there is no mud and for a few deluded days we walk outside in our shoes and push loaded wheelbarrows across the grass without sinking down to the axle in mud. The cold weather passes, of course, and it is soon back to the slither and slide of winter gardening.

But as soon as the New Year begins everything seems to get better. The weather tends to get colder and drier and the days start to get longer. At first this happens by moments, but these accumulate, and by the end of February it is light at 6.30am in the morning and stays light until after 6am in the evening. February is one of my favourite months, even though the weather can be at its most hostile. This last gasp of winter is buoyant with hope. It only delivers titbits but promises everything. Every year my excitement mounts thoughout the month like a child approaching Christmas. There are seeds to be sown, a lot of pruning to be done, ground to be prepared, and the last of the deciduous planting to be finished. Spring is just around the corner.

Cabbages
It would take a very small garden or the most dedicated brassicophile to fill a winter garden with cabbages, but from the range available, it is surely worth growing one or two kinds.

Cabbages are delicious and simple enough to grow. Although summer cabbages, such as 'Greyhound', are appreciably faster-maturing than their winter counterparts, such as 'January King', all cabbages need quite a long growing season. It is a factor that needs some planning to fit them into the garden scheme of things but which is of great virtue in winter, as it carries the corollary that they stand ready and waiting for eating all winter if need be.

Growing conditions
Brassicas – the family to which all types of cabbage belong, as do cauliflower, radish, swede, turnip, and kohl rabi – all share the same preference for well-drained, well-manured soil in an open position. The manure should not be fresh, nor the site recently dug, so it is usual to grow cabbages on a piece of ground that was previously used for legumes and should have been freshly manured before these were sown. The legumes will have left nitrogen in the soil via the nodules in their roots. Peas and broad beans tend to get cleared in mid- to late summer, which is when my winter cabbages are planted out.

Winter cabbage varieties
Winter cabbages come in a number of shapes and forms. We do not grow anything like a comprehensive selection but I do like to have some (and there are hundreds of different varieties available) of each of the following:
• Savoys are recognized by their crinkly, bluish leaves. They are hardy and very good to eat.

• January King have a slightly purple tinge to their leaves, and again are hardy and have a very good flavour.
• Red cabbages are very hardy, with thicker leaves, and are relatively untroubled by cabbage butterflies or slugs. As well as being good to eat (especially with game), I grow them unashamedly for their decorative virtues.

January King-type cabbage

Kale
I have grown purple curly kale, which looks wonderful, but we found it remarkably undigestible. However, the black kale 'Cavolo Nero', also known as black Tuscan cabbage (which is very similar to palm tree cabbage), is an essential part of our winter diet. It is hardy (although it has been killed in this garden when temperatures dropped below -12°C/54°F), withstands long cooking, and is delicious.

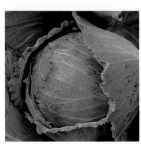
Red cabbage

Growing from seed
I sow seed of all types in April and May into plugs, blocks, or seed trays and prick them out into individual pots or plugs, which is more labour intensive than sowing direct but much easier to protect against slug damage and less wasteful on seed. They are ready for planting out by late June, or whenever the peas and beans have been cleared to make room for them. I have found it makes a huge difference to their development if they can be planted out as soon as they have a reasonable root system, and a crude form of succession can be created by planting out half a dozen plants a week throughout summer so that they mature gradually during autumn and winter.

'Cavolo Nero'

Planting out 'Cavolo Nero'

I sow the seeds in a tray, germinating it on the propagating bench before pricking them out into plugs or small pots. I let them develop a good root system before planting them into ground that has just been cleared of a legume crop. If given space, 'Cavolo Nero' will develop into large plants, but I plant quite closely – about 22cm (9in) – because I want more smaller plants for a constant supply of fresh young leaves.

Tender young 'Cavolo Nero' leaves

Before planting out, the soil should be treaded firm – as though preparing a lawn – before raking over. The cabbage head makes the plant very top-heavy and the roots, which are strong enough to grow through the compaction, must be anchored as firmly as possible. If you plant out in blocks at 45cm (18in) spacing, they soon cover the ground. This makes smaller cabbages but looks better and stops weeds.

Common problems The soft growth of young plants is easy meat for slugs but they soon get too tough for them if they are healthy plants. But there are some more virulent potential disasters waiting for every cabbage, however tough. The first is likely to happen just after planting out and comes in the pretty, shaky flutter of a cabbage white butterfly. In fact, there are two species of butterfly that do the damage, the large white and the small

white. The large white lays its eggs on the leaves. These hatch after about a week and the yellow and black caterpillars cover them by the hundred, stripping the young plants to a skeleton. We pick them off by hand but spraying with salt water works well.

The small cabbage white butterfly lays eggs deeper into the plant and its green caterpillars do their dastardly work less conspicuously but to just as noxious effect. However, plants can recover from attack. I have known 'Cavolo Nero' to be stripped bare of all but the tiniest leaves, grow back and provide meals for the family right through until March.

The only real protection for the cabbages from these two butterflies is to cover the plants with a fine-mesh netting as soon as they have been planted outside.

Both butterflies have the curious ability to taste the quantity of mustard in a plant, the principle being the stronger the taste the better the host for their eggs. The curiosity factor in this is that the plant developed the mustard taste as a defence against insects rather than an attraction. The butterflies take on the mustard taste in their own tissues, which works effectively against predation by birds.

Biological control There is a micro-biological spray called *Bacillus thuringiensis*, which is widely used commercially to control cabbage butterflies. It is designed so that it only kills caterpillars when they eat it via the leaves. It has been genetically engineered into commercial crops but is still under investigation as to its effect on the broader butterfly population – especially the monarch butterfly. While it is preferable to pyrethrum or derris, which are both organically acceptable

but not selective in their killing, I do not feel happy using it.

Clubroot is always pronounced as the worst thing that can happen to a cabbage (other than being cooked at a rolling boil for 20 minutes) but I have yet to experience it. It is a fungal disease that swells and misshapes the roots. In consequence, the plants limp along in a pointless fashion. The fungus stays in the soil after the affected plants are removed, so it is important never to grow cabbages on the same site in consecutive years, and the normal advice is to have all brassicas as part of a three- or four-year rotation with legumes, root crops, and onions. Like all fungi, clubroot does best in badly ventilated, badly drained conditions and is also more prevalent in acidic soil.

The caterpillars of cabbage white butterflies are a constant summer problem for all brassicas. The best cure is prevention, and a fine net (*below*) will keep butterflies from laying their eggs on the growing cabbages.

Leeks are an essential element of this garden and, as they were a staple of the medieval diet, are almost certain to have been grown on this site for at least the last thousand years.

Planting leeks (*below left to right*). Standing on a board to avoid compacting the soil, I make planting holes about 15cm (6in) deep with a dibber. The roots have to be disentangled before each leek is popped into its hole. This is then backfilled with water, not soil.

They are a handsome vegetable, unaffected by weather and standing right through winter into spring. In fact, I often leave them to form their round seedheads on tall stems – looking as good as many an allium grown in a border solely for its decorative qualities.

I sow my leeks in pots, sprinkling the black seeds thinly onto the compost and germinating them on gentle heat in the greenhouse. Once they have all germinated I move them to a cold frame. By sowing in pots, the roots and young stems have a chance to develop and do not need pricking out or disturbing until they are ready to plant out into their final position

in the garden, which can be anything from June to late August. When it comes to planting, I remove the pot and gently separate the long roots of each seedling. Leeks can be sown in a seedbed outside, but the soil must be at least 7°C (45°F) before they will germinate, and when they are very young slugs and snails will overcome their distaste for alliums and graze them.

Leeks like a well-manured and well-drained soil in a sunny position, and they make a good follow-on crop to new potatoes, early broad beans, or peas. Ideally, I like to rotovate in a thin layer of compost immediately before

planting out to give the plants an extra boost of nitrogen.

Leeks must be blanched to make the stems white and tender. You can either do this by planting them in a shallow trench and drawing the soil up around the growing stems – as with celery (*see page 313*), or plant the seedlings into individual holes, which is what I do. This is where a dibber becomes essential. I keep all broken wooden spade handles for a second life as a dibber, shaping the shaft into a smoothly rounded point. I dib the holes about 15cm (6in) deep and slip the seedlings in without refilling.

I always plant leeks in a block, 22 x 22cm (9 x 9in) apart. The wider the spacing, the larger each leek will grow. I find that a 22cm (9in) spacing is plenty. You can get a crop of very tasty, slim leeks grown in rows with each seedling set 8–10cm (3–4in) apart. Once the seedlings are all in their holes, I fill each hole with water from a watering can. This washes the soil down around the roots as well as giving them liquid.

Gradually, they grow to fill their holes and are securely anchored, although in the first week or so, before the roots lock into the soil, birds do occasionally tug them up and they have to be replanted.

If the leeks start to throw up a thin, central stem with a little minaret of bud, this should be cut off and the leek harvested immediately as it is a sign that the leek has started to bolt.

I grow 'Alora' for early harvesting and 'Musselburgh' and 'Alvito', which mature later.

Leeks that are left to bolt look beautiful but develop a hard, woody core and are inedible.

Parsnips have been grown in Britain since the Romans introduced them and were very widely eaten before the potato became the staple starchy vegetable.

They are currently undervalued, perhaps because they are not quick and instant. They are a Sunday vegetable, perfect baked or roasted with a joint of meat. They belong exclusively to winter, needing a frost to intensify the sugars in them. They will withstand any amount of foul weather, and will stand unharmed in the ground until you want to eat them, unlike carrots, which need to be lifted soon after the first frosts. Parsnips wait for you in the ground and there is something immensely satisfying about digging along a row, perhaps marked only by a few wisps of leaves after a winter of rain and frost, and to extract half a dozen muddy cones tapering to a long tail.

They are not at all difficult to grow but need a long growing season, so are best sown in April on a piece of ground that will not be needed for a year. The soil must be dug to a good depth if the roots are to develop to any size, and I add grit or sharp sand to the ground when I dig it to facilitate a good root run.

The flat seeds germinate very slowly – sometimes taking up to five or six weeks to appear – so I always sow a sprinkling of radish in the drill at the same time as the parsnips. These will germinate quickly and mark the row and help space the parsnips out. They get pulled and eaten before the "host" crop gets properly underway.

Winter salads I like to boast (mostly to myself) that I can provide the ingredients for a salad from this garden 365 days of the year. Not always the biggest salad, but a salad nevertheless.

Author displaying wares in rare winter sunshine.

But it is not always easy. If the weather is really harsh, even the toughest lettuce needs protection. I use cloches outside, and inside the tunnel, where I raise salad crops in autumn for winter consumption, I will cover beds with fleece in freezing weather. I have found that hardiness is improved by keeping the soil drier than normal. The combination of cold and damp is much worse than cold and dry.

I sow the main ingredients for winter salads in August, in plugs or seed trays in the greenhouse so that they are ready to plant out in their final growing position by September. I try and include as wide a variety as possible, partly for the sake of the dining table but also to increase the chances of something – anything – being harvestable in the middle of winter. So I will sow, in no particular order of preference, the following for eating right through from October until March:

• Lamb's lettuce or corn salad. This is a great favourite in this household, although we grow it with varying success. When it does well it is triumphant, providing fresh leaves with a unique melting texture. But it grows slowly and we rarely pick it before November, taking another couple of cuttings before it irrevocably runs to seed in spring. Slugs love the young seedlings, which are particularly vulnerable because they grow slowly at first, so I only plant them out when they are growing strongly in their plugs.

• Mizuna has finely serrated leaves that taste mustardy and not unlike rocket. It is a robust, large plant. I cut it regularly throughout winter.

• Mibuna like mizuna, is another Japanese brassica but with very long, rounded, strap-like leaves. It has a distinctive although mild mustard taste to it and makes a productive winter and spring cut-and-come again salad vegetable. If the weather is mild, it will regrow within just a couple of weeks but it is not terribly hardy – anything below -5°C (23°F) can kill it. For this reason, I protect it with a cloche from November onwards.

• Of the winter lettuces, 'All the Year Round', 'Valdor', and 'Arctic King' are good butterheads; 'Marvel of Four Seasons' is a red semi-hearting lettuce and looks good in the garden on the plate; 'Rouge d'Hiver' and 'Winter Density' are cos types that grow to a good size and are hardy, and 'Little Gem' (also a cos) is much smaller and less hardy but very sweet to eat. 'Catalogna' is a good loose-leaf lettuce.

• We eat young chicory leaves of all kinds raw in salads throughout the winter. If it can be kept from rotting through the combination of cold and wet, radicchio 'Palla Rossa' will regrow with varying degrees of enthusiasm depending on the weather, and will usually limp on into early spring with the protection of cloches.

• I have tried on a number of occasions to grow claytonia or winter purslane as it is a useful, if slightly bland, addition to the range of winter salads, but it is not at all happy on our wet, heavy soil. But if you have well-drained, light soil it will grow well and develop diamond-shaped leaves on succulent stems. It stops growing in the middle of winter but comes again as the days lengthen, quickly going to seed.

Watering young salad crops growing in February in the unheated greenhouse (*left*) and 'Lobjoits Green' cos growing in late October before the first frosts (*below*). These will be eaten throughout winter.

Herbs

The herb garden

Our herb garden started life in the walled garden, around the other side of the house. The walled garden was the first part of the whole garden to be cultivated and we planted it with 40-odd roses transported in pots from our previous garden, a few herbaceous plants and herbs. Herbs and roses have a natural affinity and make good bedfellows. For the first year or two we were more than happy to see the lemon-balm, yarrow, fennel, feverfew and lovage spread with such vigour as they filled the rather empty ground and hid the alarming amount of horseradish and bindweed that was endemic to the garden. But gathering herbs meant going out of the kitchen, down the hall, out the front door, across a lawn into the walled garden and then a rather scattered process of harvesting amongst the flowers. This was perfectly acceptable – even charming – when not in a hurry but more often than not we wanted to nip out, grab a handful of chives, thyme or whatever and nip straight back to the kitchen. Taking in the roses on the way was not really an option.

The time for change was finally driven by the soil. When I made this part of the garden, I did not put enough time and care into preparation, and although I dug the soil over and rotovated it, I had not broken up the pan of compacted earth created by the bulldozer which was brought in to clear the building rubble. This pan formed a solid band, like a seam of rock. Roots could not penetrate it and in winter water pooled on its surface but – crucially – all this was hidden to the eye. While Mediterranean herbs will survive cold weather and a degree of wetness, they were having to sit for weeks or months at a time in cold wet conditions, and there is nothing that they hate more. So it was all dug up, providing the perfect opportunity to relocate the herbs.

The new site was on the other side of the house and therefore much closer to the kitchen. The site was not ideal as the surface was cobbled over, but the location made gathering herbs for culinary use easy. We decided to make a formal herb garden with four small beds set within a square and edged in box. To do this we had to excavate the local red sandstone just below the cobbled surface of what had been an old yard. Whilst this did not offer much in the way of nutrition for growing plants, it did ensure very good drainage. We dug down 30cm (12in) and made raised beds constrained by 15cm (6in) oak boards, filling them with topsoil robbed from the rest of the garden, horticultural grit and mushroom compost. Although shallow, this was enough soil but we made the mistake of not taking into consideration the angle of the sun on the beds for half the year. In summer it was fine, but between April and October the sun did not rise above the roof of the house, casting the herb garden in shade until mid-afternoon – just as it was getting dark.

So a couple of years later we made the herb garden twice as big by removing a large slab of concreted area and moving our oil tank. It sounds unpromising but this new herb extension was – is – a completely sunny site. It is remarkable what a pneumatic drill, willing hands and some ingenuity can do in the pursuit of a garden.

We have left some mature rosemary in the four original, shadier, herb beds, but as we are increasingly growing annual herbs in the vegetable garden this has created some space which provided us with a paved seating area in the centre that is perfect for a drink in the evening sun. It is only sunny enough to sit out there for half the year – and for half that time only in the evening – but what was too restrictive for sun-hungry herbs suits our human needs just fine.

Our herb garden has shifted twice in the past ten years although now it has come to rest just beyond the back door so that you can nip out of the kitchen, get a handful of herbs and be back at the stove within a minute.

Herbs in the home
Herbs are somehow much more domesticated than vegetables. A pot of herbs by the back door makes complete sense whereas a pot of vegetables is an act of defiance.

There are obvious reasons for this. There is scarcely a savoury dish that cannot be improved by the addition of some herbs. Herbs add an instant freshness to what might otherwise be a plain dish. Two eggs cooked and eaten with bread is fine, but an omelette made with fresh chives, parsley and a little marjoram accompanied by good bread and butter is one of the best meals that a spring evening has to offer.

The second is that for millennia, the herb garden was the household's pharmacy. The range of "herbs" that we use for medicinal purposes is tiny compared to that of our quite recent ancestors. The old lady we bought this house from in 1991 had lived here all her life, and she told us that her mother's chemist was "the hedge" meaning that she gathered wild herbs and plants for all her needs, including, amongst many others, elderflowers for shampoo and soap, nettles for purifying the blood, dandelion for kidney disorders and comfrey for bruises and sprains. A small supply of essential herbs growing in the garden or knowledge of those in the hedgerows was considered as indispensable as the modern first-aid kit.

Herbs for medicinal use We use very few herbs medicinally. This is through ignorance and laziness as much as choice because, like everyone else in the Western world, we have grown up trusting our cures if they come from a pill or bottle rather than a plant growing without any corruption

or processing by man. Odd. But I find myself increasingly inclined to use herbs instead of pharmaceuticals and any garden can supply some basic medicines. The process of learning will continue.

We do use mint a great deal as a digestive. Whilst no variety of mint will do any harm, peppermint (*Mentha* x *piperita*) is by far the most effective, and we grow this solely for use as a tea. Just pick a handful of leaves and infuse in boiling water. A cafetiere is ideal. If I have an upset tummy I drink warm peppermint tea until it is better – and the healing effect kicks in very quickly. It helps that the tea is delicious and makes a very good after-meal digestive. Chewing on a handful of fresh fennel seeds is another good aid to digestion.

Herbs in cooking We only grow what we use: rosemary with potatoes and lamb; mint with new potatoes, salads, couscous and yoghurt sauces; basil, thyme and marjoram

whenever we eat tomato in any form; parsley and garlic with almost everything; chives with salads and eggs; lovage in stocks and soups; we collect fennel seeds in autumn and store them in an airtight jar for cooking with pork – a perfect combination; dill with fish; tarragon with chicken; sage with pasta and potatoes; horseradish with beef – and that is a list just off the top of my head. It is not an ambitious range but we always have masses of the herbs that we cook with on a daily basis. To me the real luxury of a herb garden is not being able to have a collection of rare and unusual herbs, but to have an abundance of the ones that I like to use fresh for cooking. Quantity is as important as quality. There is something generous and luxurious about gathering a whole basketful of parsley or a big bunch of rosemary rather than eking out little sachets or jars which are a poor substitute for the real thing. Herbs should never have to be rationed when they are in season.

Annual herbs

We grow almost all our annual herbs in the vegetable garden, although any spare plants may be dotted into the herb garden if we run out of space elsewhere.

The reason for this is twofold. First, we tend to use a great deal of the annual herbs and there is just not the space for them in the herb garden. Far easier to incorporate them into the vegetable crop rotation. The second reason is that we have found most of them suffer badly from shading when grown in the hurly-burly of a herb garden. Shrubby plants like sage, hyssop, rosemary and the more voracious herbaceous perennials like lovage and horseradish will swamp the annuals. They need plenty of light and air to develop into vigorous plants with plenty of soft growth.

It all goes back to the virtue of quantity in the herb garden. For most of the herbs that we use on a regular basis we want to have a continuous and unlimited supply. In practice this is difficult and involves storing many herbs in some form or another, but where fresh

One of the best things about growing herbs in beds from seed rather than growing herb plants in pots is that you can produce large quantities for a generous harvest *(above)*. Regular cutting back and clearing the herb beds will ensure a continuous supply of fresh leaves *(opposite)*.

herbs are a possibility I try and make them a certainty.

Each year I prepare one of the sunniest vegetable beds by adding sharpsand and mushroom compost. Not too much of the latter, but enough to add some 'beef' to the soil. The sharpsand is to help drainage and root run and most herbs appreciate an enormous amount of it. Grit would be better but ruinously expensive. Basil, thyme, dill, coriander and chervil all get sown in this mix. I also grow more basil, coriander and chervil in the polytunnel and greenhouse. Garlic is given its own bed as part of the general vegetable crop rotation and I grow parsley as an edging to onions – the strong odour of the onions gives the parsley some protection from attack by carrot fly. Of our annual herbs, garlic, basil and parsley are by far the most important to us.

Garlic

is a very important crop for us. It is an antiseptic and boosts the immune system. Whenever I feel a cold coming on I eat extra garlic and we try to grow enough to last us until late spring.

As its Latin name (*Allium sativum*) suggests, garlic is a member of the onion family and, does best in rich, well-drained soils. It is wrong to think of garlic as a Mediterranean herb – in fact it originated in Central Asia – and is unknown in the wild. It will grow very well in the far North of Europe, although it does need rich, well-drained soil and as much summer sun as possible.

In an ideal world I sow my garlic as soon after mid-October as possible. In practice this

means any available time at the end of the year. I often make two or even three sowings because the main problem at this very wet time of year is getting the soil into a suitable state for planting. Garlic needs plenty of compost added to the ground and this must be thoroughly worked in. I often sow garlic to follow carrots, as the garlic likes the extra sharpsand the carrots have received and in the rotation, the soil is now ready for some serious beefing up with compost.

MAGIC AND MEDICINE

Garlic has always been powerful magic. From the ancient Egyptians and first-century Hindus to the present day, garlic has been used to keep the insides clean, alleviate heart disease, and ward off terrors in the night.

Sowing garlic bulbs I use last summer's crop of garlic bulbs for seed, selecting the fattest bulbs and breaking them open – biggest cloves in one basket, small ones, which will go to the kitchen, in another.

As a rule, the bigger the seed clove the bigger the garlic bulb it will produce *(left)*. The reason for sowing garlic in autumn is to let the roots develop before the cold weather sets in. In practice, with the development of global warming the weather is often very mild right into the New Year and a sowing of garlic as late as February can grow and ripen perfectly well, although an earlier sowing increases the chances of success.

I sow in rows measured by a plank *(right)* that I tread on, which means that each plant gets equal space around it. It is important to keep the rows or blocks evenly spaced because you will have to keep them well weeded and it is almost impossible to hoe down irregular lines. There are people who recommend dibbing a hole for each clove but I find that too laborious, so I push them in, pointed-end up, as far as my fingers will reach into the sticky but loose earth *(far right)*. I also think that dibbers compact the soil around the initial growing roots. As for the spacing between individual cloves, I always give them plenty, measuring a span of my hand between each clove – about 22.5cm (9in) between each plant.

Once the roots have established – and the tops have appeared *(left)* like green wisps of flame above the ground – garlic needs one month with the temperature below 10°C (50°F). If it fails to get this then the cloves tend to develop into one small bulb without dividing into separate cloves. If this happens, keep these "rounds" and use them as seed for next year's garlic sowing. As with all onions, garlic needs to be kept weed-free and watered whilst growing. If any of the plants develop seedheads, cut them off as they appear.

Fresh garlic straight from the ground is wonderful, with its sheath of leaf covering the whole bulb and the cloves hardly separated and as shiny and white as an unripe conker.

Storing garlic bulbs Not all species of garlic can be stored for longer than six months. Short dormancy bulbs, such as the very early 'Sprint' or later 'Thermidrome' will only last from the summer harvest until the end of that same year. Longer dormancy bulbs, such as 'Cristo' and the Spanish 'Moraluz' will keep well into spring, and I now mainly grow the latter variety to extend the garlic season.

Crop rotation Garlic cleanses the ground and is an excellent crop to precede brassicas. The cabbages seem to benefit from the allium residue once the garlic is cleared, and the ground is ready at exactly the time the spring-sown brassicas are ready for planting out.

Lifting and storing We start lifting garlic in dribs and drabs from the end of May when it is mild enough to eat raw, but the main crop is usually ready in the first few weeks of July, around the same time as the new potatoes. Garlic needs to be harvested as soon as it is ready otherwise the bulbs start to shrivel and their storing capacity reduces. Leave them in the ground until the leaves have yellowed and then dig them up on a clear sunny day so that they can be left on the ground to dry. Failing that, take them into a dry, well-ventilated place and let them dry for a few weeks, leaves and all. This is when their storage capacity is established. Once they are truly dry, cut off the leaves and roots and strip the very dry outer skin before storing them. We store them in a basket in our potting shed, which is very cool and dark but never freezes. This seems to suit the garlic bulbs perfectly. I have tried using the leaves to plait them into ropes but they do not keep any better for this. The essential ingredients of storage is a good airflow, dark and a constant cool temperature. Any trace of dampness will induce rotting and fungal trouble.

Basil is another important herb for us, but primarily for one simple use, making pesto sauce. As a family we love pesto with pasta, or just on bread. But to make it you have to grow a lot of basil.

Fresh basil leaves make the perfect accompaniment to tomato, especially when both are eaten raw.

There are many types of basil and over the years I have grown quite a few of them but we always come back to the common sweet basil (*Ocimum basilicum*) as it makes the best pesto. And pesto rules.

Basil and tomatoes share identical cultural requirements and I tend to grow the two together wherever possible. Both plants need rich soil, plenty of water and lots of heat and sunshine. The most variable commodities are the last two and on the whole basil fares much better grown in a greenhouse or polytunnel than outside – although that does not stop us filling whole beds with it.

I start sowing basil in February, and make another three or four sowings before the end of spring. The deadline to beat is the first frost, which will kill every plant. Basil takes about eight weeks to mature sufficiently to harvest so the latest we can sow is the end of May, beginning of June. Basil is not tolerant of temperatures below 5°C (41°F) and in September, and just occasionally at the end of August, night-time temperatures normally drop to this level.

Sowing basil seed Ideally the tiny black basil seeds are sown in plugs or soil blocks,

Making pesto

The secret of good pesto is to make it whilst the basil leaves are absolutely fresh. We harvest the leaves and immediately strip them from the stem and chop them up (a food mixer is best for anything other than very small quantities) with olive oil, garlic and pine nuts. If it is to be frozen – and the majority of our pesto is stored this way – we omit the parmesan cheese as it does not freeze well.

where they can remain until transplanted to their final position, but because we grow so many plants I find it easier to broadcast the seed thinly onto compost in seed trays. I then place the seed trays on a heated mat rather than covering them. Once the basil seeds have germinated, the trick is to grow them on as fast as possible at every stage. Towards this end, I prick out the seeds into plugs, or transfer them into a larger seed tray as soon as they develop two true leaves. When the young plants are about 5cm (2in) tall, they can be transplanted to the greenhouse but they need to be bigger than this if they are going outside. I add extra mushroom compost to their planting site – which will also have been manured in the autumn – as basil responds to very rich soil. The plants are potentially large and bushy, and need plenty of space to grow fast. I give them between 22cm (9in) and 30cm (1ft) of space in each direction. Cold weather will check their growth and the leaves become tough and chlorotic. They can still be eaten, but are not so good. Water the plants frequently.

Harvesting basil leaves In early summer we harvest the larger leaves of the plant, pinching out the tops and taking perhaps three quarters of the foliage from each plant, filling a basket at a time. But until late summer we always have far more basil than we can possibly eat on an ad hoc basis. However, the harvest proper is yet to come. Later in the summer, before the first frosts, we take all the basil plants grown outside in the vegetable garden and pull them up, filling barrowloads. We then immediately convert the fresh leaves into pesto sauce (*see opposite*, Making Pesto) and freeze most of it in bags. When the sauce is defrosted, sometimes almost a year later, it tastes as fresh as the hour that it was made.

Basil is best grown very fast which means giving it uninterrupted heat, water and goodness. In our climate this is difficult out of doors and it will invariably flower and set seed sooner than indoor basil which diminishes the leaf flavour. To prevent this, I cut off the flowerheads as they appear.

Coriander looks just like a rather delicate parsley but its smell is distinctive and pungent, even from very tiny seedlings. It is one of the most ancient of all cultivated herbs.

I grow coriander in exactly the same way as parsley, sowing the seed in plugs and then transplanting the seedlings to their growing place. I make the first sowing in January and grow the plants on in the greenhouse. By the middle of May they will be bolting uncontrollably and I pull them up and replace them with tomato plants. The second sowing of coriander is made in April and the seedlings are planted outside in a shady corner of the vegetable garden.

The problem with raising coriander is how to delay it going to seed, or prevent it from bolting. In both instances, the leaves grow rapidly and they change from widely splayed (*see right*) to very finely cut in appearance, like fennel leaves. You can, of course, harvest coriander seeds for grinding up and using in curries and chutneys, and make a virtue of letting the plant go to seed. But for me the plant ceases to have a function at that point. I just aim to keep coriander well-watered and cool – which gets increasingly difficult after May. The plain *Coriandrum sativum* is the least likely to bolt, whereas *C. sativum* 'Morocco' is best for seed.

Young coriander leaves are used in cooking. After flowering the leaves appear very finely cut.

349

Parsley is one of the most useful all-round herbs that we grow. We use flat-leaf parsley a lot, including making a pesto from it, using the leaves instead of basil and substituting walnuts for pine nuts.

French or flat-leaf parsley

Parsley is a biennial and will run to seed if left to grow beyond its initial growing season. But this process can be delayed if you cut the entire plant close to its base with a sharp knife *(below)* whilst it is still young. It will respond by producing a fresh set of leaves and this process can be repeated at least twice and often up to four times before the plant irreversibly runs to seed.

Parsley is a fairly hardy plant, surviving quite a few degrees of frost but the cold does kill off the top growth so some kind of protection is necessary for plants raised outside. Parsley likes rich soil with good drainage and plenty of water, although in my garden it fares best of all when grown in raised beds in the polytunnel, where the air is dry and the roots are watered. It will also happily grow in partial shade.

We only grow French or flat-leaf parsley (*Petroselinum crispum* var *neapolitanum*) as it is infinitely better in the kitchen than its curly cousin. Parsley is a biennial and a member of the carrot family, which means that its small umbellifer flowers will develop in its second growing season. As soon as parsley develops a strong, hollow central stalk, the leaves become much coarser – this is the time to replace the plant with a young one.

Like carrots and parsnips, parsley is prone to attack by carrot fly. To avoid attack, I always aim to plant it near onions or garlic as their powerful scent helps to confuse the fly. Parsley also makes a good edging plant in the vegetable garden and I will often line a path with it, making it easy to pick.

Sowing parsley seed To keep up the supply of young, fresh leaves I make three sowings: early spring, for harvesting in summer and autumn; the second in late spring for harvest in autumn and early winter and the third in late summer, which should keep us supplied until the next year's spring sowing is ready.

I always used to sow parsley where it was to grow and then thin it heavily, but young plants can be prey to slug attack. I now prefer to sow seed in plugs and transplant the seedlings when they are a couple of inches tall. Sowing in seed trays is a bad idea because the roots dislike being disturbed. For good results, the temperature of the soil or growing medium must be warm. If it is cold to the touch then the seeds will not germinate.

Dill (*Anethum graveolens*)

Dill is certainly worth growing in any garden for aesthetic pleasure alone. It is an exceptionally beautiful herb with feathery fronds for leaves and a wonderful lemon-yellow starburst flowerhead.

We also grow dill partly for the way that it can enhance the flavours of fish or lamb, and because it is a good umbellifer that attracts hoverflies to the vegetable garden and the nymphs of these will eat aphids.

It is best to sow dill seed in plugs or soil blocks rather than seed trays, as it resents being transplanted. Whenever you read that a plant dislikes being moved or transplanted, what is meant is that the roots are very sensitive to any movement and will usually react by going into emergency survival mode. For most annuals this means setting seed as soon as possible. The great advantage of sowing in plugs or blocks is that the young plant can be moved out of the greenhouse to the vegetable bed without the roots being unduly disturbed.

Dill is tender and I plant out the seedlings as soon as the risk of frost has passed. Dill grows best on very well drained, poor soil and needs plenty of sun, so is a good bedfellow for thyme, rosemary or any of the other Mediterranean herbs. Plants have a tendency to blow over so will need some kind of support.

Dill (*Anethum graveolens*)

Borage (*Borago officinalis*)

No plant is easier to grow than borage – once you have planted it in your garden it will seed itself with the promiscuity of a forget-me-not. Borage will flower from midsummer until the first frosts, although occasionally it will behave like a biennial and start flowering in April. In general it likes hot sun and poor, well-drained soil, to the extent that it will grow in every cranny of a stone path, but it is not fussy and will make itself at home in a well-dug bed alongside any herbaceous plant. The hairy leaves are rich in mineral salts and are good with savoury dairy foods, such as cream cheese. Much nonsense is written about the efficacy of borage's non-flatulent role as a cucumber substitute but it exists in its own right as an essential ingredient of a glass of Pimms. No other qualification is necessary. Borage does have, as a great bonus, beautiful blue flowers, and as long as it is kept under control by extensive weeding and thinning, it is a really welcome addition to our walled garden.

Angelica (*Angelica archangelica*)

Angelica is a prolific self-seeder but the seed does not spread far. The clumps remain in the same place, giving the impression that it is the same perennial plant that returns each year, whereas in fact it is a biennial. The seed ripens and falls in July and August and immediately germinates, establishing small plants that overwinter beneath the shade of their parent before growing strongly the following spring when the parent plant has died back. And strongly it does grow too – a healthy plant produces wonderful giant umbels of flower as big as footballs on strong stems.

It loves our heavy, damp soil and is best when growing in some shade. As a rule of thumb it is unlikely ever to grow well wherever Mediterranean herbs like rosemary or thyme are thriving and vice versa.

An essential in any garden for its appearance alone, angelica was traditionally eaten as a confectionery – the stems were candied – but it is also good added to stewed rhubarb.

Borage (*Borago officinalis*)

Korean angelica (*Angelica gigas*)

Perennial Mediterranean herbs

The thing to bear in mind about all the Mediterranean herbs is that they like a bit of rough, and our soil is as rich and fat as best butter.

It is always salutary to go and see plants growing in their natural habitat, and with so-called "Mediterranean" plants there are two things that invariably strike me. The first is just how extreme conditions are. A dry, sun-baked hillside is a desperately harsh place. Our holiday-centred experiences tend to lock into coastal countryside softened by human pampering but take a walk across inland Provence or the Atlas mountains and you are way out of the comfort zone.

The second thing is that plants that we are accustomed to in our gardens are always twice the size of the "wild" originals, which have adapted to survive and multiply and so waste little energy on surplus growth. The only job is to set seed and set seed fast, bypassing the niceties of form and foliage, if necessary.

But the gardener has to strike a balance. We cannot reconstruct a Mediterranean hillside in our gardens to suit the occasional Mediterranean herb. Anybody with an ounce of sensibility wants rosemary to be bushy and fresh-shooted and flowering against a sunny wall for as long as possible before it makes its procreative way into seed. And everybody wants a fulsome lavender bush throwing up floral spikes like a flowery pin cushion. In other words, we do not want the plant to replicate its natural behaviour. We want an

unnatural lushness that only comes from unnaturally mild conditions.

Growing conditions

But it is terribly easy to err on the side of softness when growing all the Mediterranean herbs. Given our absence of Mediterranean heat and drought, you really cannot overdo the coarsening of the ground for rosemary and its ilk. This means diluting the topsoil as much as possible with grit (ideal) or sharpsand (pretty good), and avoiding any kind of organic material (too nutritious). If you have a deep, water-retentive soil it is a good idea to barrow some of it away and replace it with hardcore, leaving your thinned-down topsoil as a layer no deeper than 15cm (6in) over this. If these growing conditions seem absurdly hostile then you will have got it just right.

All the Mediterranean herbs also love chalk. But lavender and rosemary will grow very well in containers as long as they have enough space for a root-run. In other words, just because some herbs like poor soil and dry conditions, don't fall into the trap of allowing them to get pot-bound and unable to take in any water at all. Any plant that has evolved to live in drought conditions will have roots that want to range freely to seek out moisture.

The Mediterranean herbs like dry conditions and poor soil. My garden, with its high level of rainfall and very rich, water-retentive soil is not ideal, yet we do manage to grow the herbs that we need. Here, oregano is flowering and needs cutting back and teasels – which do best in moist conditions – are allowed to remain amongst the herbs simply because they look good.

Rosemary (top) will flower from late winter until June. **Thyme**, also in flower, needs light and air to thrive. **Sage** tolerates our wet weather better than most herbs, although purple sage suffers more than common sage. **Bay** is very sensitive to cold weather. We grow it in pots and overwinter it in the greenhouse.

Rosemary
Every time I pass a rosemary bush – which is at least a dozen times a day – I dabble my hands in the leaves as I brush past, releasing a breath of Mediterranean sunshine.

Rosemary softwood cuttings

The herb garden in spring with the rosemary bushes in flower. Tulips and rosemary make good bedfellows as they share they same need for sun and good drainage.

The leaves – simultaneously dry and sticky – reek exotically of southern sun. Essential for lamb and very good with potatoes, I would grow rosemary even if I never ate it at all.

But I must have lost two dozen good rosemary bushes over the past ten years through poor drainage coupled with winter wet. They hate sitting in wet ground and show their displeasure by dying back, first one branch turning brown and black-tipped and then always inexorably followed by the whole damn thing. Young plants seem to be more prone to decline but it could just be because they have smaller root-systems.

You can – and should – make the drainage around the plant roots as free as possible. I plant any new rosemary bushes into a bucketful of pure grit, but beware of creating a sump into which all the surrounding water drains. The only long-term solution is to create an area that is exceptionally well-drained and keep your rosemary limited to it.

I have seen rosemary grown as a climber and espaliered in rather stringy layers, and the upright form 'Miss Jessop's Upright' is very popular, but I like rosemary bushes that sprawl and buckle under the weight of their own gnarled branches. Given sunshine, shelter and drainage, a rosemary bush can live for a generation, although it will lose its youthful vigour after about five years. Occasionally, I prune one of the two whopping bushes we have and chuck the prunings on the fire to fill the room in midwinter with fabulously evocative scent – a whole southern hillside breathing into our Herefordshire house.

Thyme
For years we had problems growing thyme until I eventually worked out that it could not tolerate shade of any kind and that it was not suited to the hurly-burly of the herb garden.

At first, I planted thyme in the same herb beds as rosemary, with good drainage and lots of sunshine, and the plants would start out well and grow strongly. But by midsummer the leaves would blacken and die off and by autumn all that would be left were a few sad leaves at the end of lanky, woody branches. Not good. Since then I have grown thyme in open beds in the vegetable garden and it has never looked back.

There are dozens of different kinds of thyme but we only grow two sorts, common thyme (*Thymus vulgaris*) and lemon thyme (*Thymus* x *citriodorus*) which is especially good for cooking. I grow the common thyme from seed, broadcasting it onto a seed tray and then pricking out the tiny seedlings into plugs or at a wider spacing in another tray once they

are large enough to handle. They grow slowly but are large enough to plant out by midsummer, although I may leave them to overwinter in a cold frame for planting out the following spring.

All thymes can be grown from cuttings, which take very easily from new soft growth sometime between May and July. I take a few dozen softwood cuttings, each a couple of inches (5cm) long, and stick them at one inch spacings around the edge of a pot. They take a few weeks to root and can then be planted out into a very sunny spot (very widely spaced so that they do not become shaded) or potted up and grown on before planting out in late summer. For cooking, it is much easier to keep a supply of young, tightly-cropped thymes, so I replace the plants completely every two years and harvest the leaves by cutting the whole

Thymus vulgaris

Thymus x *citriodorus* 'Silver Queen'

Cutting thyme in the vegetable garden. Thyme grown in the herb beds becomes shaded by other plants and grows lanky so we grow our main supply in open beds in the vegetable garden.

Thyme will grow in almost totally dry conditions and easily becomes waterlogged in our wet winters so I keep it covered with cloches from October until April. This is to protect it from the rain rather than the cold and I leave the cloche ends open for ventilation.

plant right down to the ground, whilst the stems are still very soft. This avoids all the twiggy bits and the bother of stripping the thyme leaves from the stems.

I also keep thyme permanently under cloches through the winter months or whenever it is particularly wet during the year. Thyme plants seem to be perfectly happy in almost total dryness and never get too hot. Growing thyme under cloches prevents mildew developing and also stops the foliage from getting sodden and falling on neighbouring plants, which would shade them and cause die-back.

Lavender
It seems curious that lavender, which in reality is a pretty but unexceptional shrub, should have such a strong hold on our senses. Few plants evoke so many things so powerfully.

Cutting back lavender in late summer

Lavender labels and defines a colour, even though on inspection, the plant comes in lots of shades from dark purple to white. It evokes a whole mood or atmosphere of gentle, if not genteel, refinement and prettiness, and, most powerfully of all, the scent of a few tiny flowers crumbled between your careless fingers will trigger a chain of evocations that can be provoked by nothing else.

It is a healing plant 'of especial use' as one Tudor writer noted, 'for all the griefes and pains of the head and heart'. It is supposed to be one of the most ancient of all manufactured perfumes, with lavender water mentioned in twelfth century literature. We know that the Romans added it to their baths, giving it the name "Lavandula", from *lavare* (to wash). Certainly, a few drops of lavender oil added to your bath seem to induce an extra restfulness and ease. Lavender in gardens tends to be

grown either as a loose hedge or as a single plant whose softness is part of an almost archetypal prettiness. My granny would cut the flowers on their long stems and dry them in the airing cupboard before putting the dried flowers – which fell apart and looked like seeds – in little muslin bags, stitched together with lavender-coloured cotton. She then put the bags in amongst her drawer full of billowing directoire knickers. I could not bring myself to enquire what they actually did, but there you have the essence of English garden lavender – beautiful, useful, sanitising and a little-old-ladyish.

Growing lavender It is curious how this most Mediterranean of plants has become so English, so perfectly suited to tea on the Edwardian lawn and a hazy patrician charm. Some of this is simply the glaucal shimmer of its tiny leaves matched with the fuzz of flowers hovering on their spikes that associates well with any pastel colour. It is also a robust and very tolerant plant. It likes full sun, plenty of air around it, alkaline soil and good drainage. But lavender will struggle on whereas more temperamental rosemary will give up the ghost, even though both plants have the same origins. The important point is winter drainage. Lavender, like rosemary, hates sitting dormant in cold water. In summer it will respond to some watering and I have lost plants in pots through under-watering.

Lavender lives for ages, its flowers sparser and sparser in proportion to the woody growth. The secret of keeping a lavender bush in good shape is to clip it to shape in spring, but try to avoid cutting into the old wood, which will not always regenerate. If you crop the entire plant back to old wood it can mean big trouble. Lavender is evergreen, which means that it keeps – and needs – its leaves all winter. If you cut into the old wood, which does not have any leaves, and new leaves do not grow, then it will not survive the winter. Then, after it has flowered, cut back to the leaves with perhaps a third trim in autumn to keep the shape. With this treatment the plant will hold a tight pebble shape well.

Lavender will grow from seed as well as take easily from cuttings. Seed should be sown in autumn and the seedlings overwintered before pricking out in spring and planting in early summer. They grow on fast. Cuttings are best taken either from non-flowering stems as softwood cuttings in May, or as semi-hardwood cuttings in late summer from new growth. Overwinter the rooted cuttings under cover and plant out the following spring.

Types of lavender There are many different types, varieties and colours to choose or confuse. Here are just a few. *Lavandula angustifolia* is common or English lavender. It has the familiar mauve flower spikes and will grow to a height and spread of about 1m (3ft). The two most common varieties are *L. angustifolia* 'Munstead' and *L. a.* 'Hidcote'. Ironically, both are named after large gardens institutionalised into the horticultural aspirational psyche and yet both are always sold as "suitable" for small gardens. Well, they are a bit smaller than standard lavender but not significantly. I suspect that this is a harmless marketing trick and, like almost all plants in garden centres, they are cheap and easy to produce. 'Hidcote' is a deeper mauve and a bit more vigorous than the paler, bluer, faster-growing 'Munstead'. Both make good hedging plants, where hedge and edge combine to make a gentle demarcation line. There is a white form, *L. angustifolia* 'Alba', which does not grow quite so tall, and *L. a.* 'Nana Alba' which, like all plants with 'nana' and 'alba' in their name, is white and very small. *L. a.* 'Rosea' has pink flowers as does *L. a.* 'Jean Davis'. But pink lavender is like white chocolate, perfectly nice but somehow not perfectly right.

Lavandula lanata makes a dome of soft woolly leaves, with long spikes twice as high again, topped with purple flowers. *Lavandula stoechas*, or French lavender, has unusual mauve bracts on top of the flower spikes and very narrow leaves that grow markedly up the stems. *L. stoechas* will grow well in acidic soil, unlike all other lavenders. *L. dentata,* which is not entirely hardy, has leaves that are prettily crimped and the flower spikes are topped with bracts of pale blue.

Lavandula angustifolia 'Hidcote'

Lavandula 'Sawyers'

Lavandula 'Helmsdale'

Lavandula dentata var. *candicans*

357

Sage I grow sage in three colours – green, purple and variegated. As well as the normal broad-leaved sage, I have the narrow-leaved version which is much the best for culinary use.

Narrow-leaved sage (*Salvia lavandulifolia*) grows just as easily as other types, which is to say that once started you can hardly stop it performing year after year. If there was room for only one sage in my garden, this is the one that I would grow. At the end of a cold winter it can look like a straggly refugee but, cut back hard in March, it soon sprouts new leaves of exuberant freshness. Then come the flowers, a mass of violet and purple spikes with the typical protruding lower lipped petal and raised hooded arch above. Even if you dislike the taste or smell of the plant, the flowers make its place in the garden essential. But I love the taste and instantly distinctive scent. Just the words make me hungry. I am writing this at lunchtime and crave potatoes cooked in a hot oven with oil, parmesan and lots of sage. A delicious and ridiculously simple meal is also to be made by mixing a handful of fresh sage leaves in with pasta and olive oil or butter.

Sage also has very powerful healing and antiseptic properties and was used to preserve meat. In fact the more one researches into the curative properties of this herb, the more it appears to have been considered a cure-all, and regular consumption the best way of promoting good health.

Purple sage (*Salvia purpurea*) grows slower and smaller than its green cousin and seems to like our non-Mediterranean winters less, but as long as good drainage is maintained, it always restores itself by mid-spring.

It is important to prune sage hard as it can become very lank and bow down under the weight of its branches, thus shading all interior and lower leaves. I always used to prune sage in early spring but now do it after flowering in late summer, so that we get the best possible show from the flowers and yet there is time for the new shoots to harden off before the winter frosts.

There is a price to pay for flowers, however, as the energy they use up means significantly fewer leaves which have a milder taste. To produce sage leaves with the most intense flavour for cooking, it is best to prune the plant before flowering in spring. The one sage that avoids the dilemma between flowers and foliage is the variegated leaf form *Salvia*

The different varieties of sage that I grow are shown below from left to right: common sage *(Salvia officinalis)*; purple sage *(Salvia purpurea)*; and narrow-leaved sage *(Salvia lavandulifolia)*.

officinalis 'Icterina' which virtually never flowers.

However judiciously you prune sage, it will increasingly become woody and produce fewer leaves, so it is a generally a good idea to renew plants every four or five years. Sage cuttings take pretty easily, either from softwood cuttings in spring or semi-ripe cuttings in autumn. Cover freshly planted softwood cuttings with a polythene bag to keep the humidity high until they root, which should be after 10 days or so. Semi-ripe cuttings taken in late summer or autumn will not need this treatment but are best planted into a very free-draining mix and overwintered in a cold frame before planting out in spring.

Marjoram It is easy to get confused between oregano and marjoram, but, for the record, wild marjoram and Mediterranean oregano are one and the same plant.

In Britain wild marjoram, *Origanum vulgare*, is much less aromatic than its Mediterranean counterpart, oregano. Pot marjoram is *Origanum onites*, and *Origanum majorana* is Sweet marjoram, which comes from North Africa and has the best flavour.

The herb grows in low mounds and by cutting boldly into the mounds when you need supplies for the table, you can prevent it from becoming straggly and woody. If marjoram is growing quicker than you can use it – which it invariably seems to do – be brutal and give it a hard prune. The new growth will return incredibly quickly. Bees adore the flowers and for this reason alone it is worth leaving at least one patch to flower on all summer without cropping the plant back.

Marjoram is another Mediterranean herb with powerful antiseptic qualities and it is used for digestive and respiratory problems. It was also one of the essential "strewing herbs" – those plants that were cut and spread on the earthen or stone floors of medieval houses to absorb the dirt and sweeten the air. In fact in Britian it seems to have been used much more extensively for its health-giving properties than as a flavouring, possibly because local wild marjoram, which grows quite freely on chalk downland, does not have the intense flavour of its Mediterranean cousin.

We use golden marjoram (*Origanum vulgare* 'Aureum' and *O. v* 'Gold Tip') mostly for cooking, because in our damp, mild climate it has a better flavour than the Greek oregano – although in its natural Mediterranean home, the Greek version has a stronger and more aromatic flavour. I would not dream of making a tomato sauce without marjoram, although between December and February I am scratching around for enough good leaves to make it worthwhile collecting. I also suspect that we stick with the golden and variegated marjorams because both grow strongly and the yellow leaves add a good touch of colour to both garden and plate.

Although marjoram grows easily from seed, it often does not come true so I take cuttings. As with thyme, put perhaps half a dozen around the edge of a pot of compost with extra grit or perlite and place them under the mist propagator where they root easily. Pot them on and plant out the following spring.

Oregano vulgare 'Aureum'

Origanum x onites

Hyssopus officinalis

Hyssopus officinalis f. roseus

Laurus nobilis

Rosemary (facing page top left) in late summer growing in the herb garden showing strong new growth. This is the ideal material and time for taking cuttings. **Lovage** (top right) in the walled garden where it is grown purely for decorative effect. **Marjoram** (bottom right) in flower. The bees love this. **Fennel** (bottom left) in flower. We value the seeds highly as the best accompaniment to roast pork.

Hyssop

Hyssopus officinalis is a beautiful shrub with intense violet-blue flowers. There is also white hyssop (*H. o. f. albus*) and pink-flowering hyssop, *H. o. f. roseus*). Hyssop flowers attract butterflies and bees and, in researching this book, I also found out that hyssop is good for diverting cabbage white butterflies, which is something I wish that I had known years ago. The flowers are good to eat in salads, whilst the leaves are an aid to digestion, particularly of fatty foods, and are traditionally used with game.

Hyssop is easy to germinate from seed, even when it is sown directly into the ground. When given favourable growing conditions, hyssop makes an excellent edging hedge for a herb garden. I tried growing a hedge of hyssop in our walled garden when it was still the herb garden. This failed dismally because – like all edging hedges here – it became suffocated by the plants that it was supposed to be bordering. Hyssop – as with all the Mediterranean plants – needs plenty of space, light and air to thrive.

To be honest I have never grown hyssop well – it seems to need exceptionally dry, sunny conditions and because it is rather a marginal herb for us it tends not to get pride of Mediterranean place.

To maintain hyssop, I trim it back lightly in autumn and then again hard in spring after the worst of the weather. It is important to keep the stems trimmed if the plant is not to become a very woody bush.

Bay

Fresh bay leaves are useful for adding a distinctive rich, aromatic flavour to soups and stews but it is difficult for us to grow bay well. In ten years, we have never managed to overwinter a bay without at least a third of it being killed off by cold weather. Bay is not designed for cold, wet winters and, like most evergreens, it is prone to desiccation in very cold winter winds. Shallow roots also make the plant more susceptible to hard ground frosts.

All in all, our battle to keep bay trees seems to contradict my basic rule of never forcing a plant to grow in sites where it is made to behave unnaturally. But bays are tough trees and usually recover from what might seem a hopeless situation. If they do die back I cut them back to green growth – which might be the base – and they usually re-grow. For the same reasons that we cannot grow rosemary without losses, we have long given up trying to grow bay planted in the ground. The combination of winter wet, icy winds and air temperatures below -12°C (14°F) is too much for them. So we grow small plants in pots and bring the pots into the greenhouse from November until March. But up until May I keep some horticultural fleece near each outdoor plant to drape over the bush for protection if it is a cold night.

Other than its hatred of cold, wet winters, bay is remarkably easy to grow. It hardly ever needs watering and you should never feed it. I change its potting compost every two or three years, moving it into a slightly larger pot each time (but only slightly – it is a mistake to increase the pot size of any plant too radically) and make sure you add a lot of extra grit or perlite to the compost.

Occasionally bay is attacked by scale insects, especially if grown indoors alongside citrus plants, but these are easily tackled by wiping each leaf with vegetable soap and water or with white spirit. However, the latter does little to improve the flavour of the leaves.

Lovage

Levisticum officinale

Lovage is an unlikely Mediterranean herb as it grows very happily in rich, damp soil and seems to be wholly unaffected by the worst of British winter weather. However it originates from the Middle East and was brought to Britain by the Romans, becoming an essential element in monastic herb gardens. Its main uses are as an aid to digestion but it was also valued as an aphrodisiac (perhaps simply on the basis that one was more likely to be a lover without belly ache) and as a deodorant and antiseptic. In the kitchen, lovage makes a very useful addition to sauces, soups, stews or anything that needs a celery-flavour with an added hint of aniseed.

We grow lovage extensively, finding it valuable as a foliage plant as the slightly chalky leaves are the perfect foil for any flowers with softer colours – and especially roses. Lovage will grow from seed but I find that the best method of propagation is by division. Dig up the very fleshy root in autumn or spring (I always do this in spring) and chop off pieces with a spade. As long as each section of root has a visible bud it can be replanted to make a separate plant. By its second year it will be well established and after 3 or 4 years very substantial indeed, growing to 6 feet (1.8m) on rich soil.

The real secret of growing lovage is to be ruthless about cutting it down. Let the umbels of tiny, almost green flowers develop for their beauty and the way that they attract hoverflies (and perhaps their seeds) and then cut the plant down to the ground. It will re-grow vigorously and the young leaves are much nicer to eat than the old. In rich soil each plant can take two or even three such prunings a year.

Fennel

Foeniculum vulgare

Fennel Wherever it can bask in full sunshine, fennel grows in our garden like a weed, liking our rich soil and yet able to grow in seemingly soil-free cracks in paving stones or even walls. We love it, both to eat but especially to look at, so we only pull up those plants that are spoiling the desired aesthetic effect. We use the feathery foliage with fish and the fresh seeds are a wonderful addition to roast pork. We pound up fennel seeds, garlic, olive oil and salt in a mortar and spread the resulting paste over the meat, which is sitting on chopped Florence fennel bulb (which is eaten like a vegetable). This is then roasted slowly for three hours so that the meat is cut through with the flavour of fennel. Munching fresh fennel seeds is a very good way of settling a dodgy stomach and I often grab a handful as I pass the plant between August and October.

Given a good soil that it can get its deep roots into, fennel will make a really substantial and handsome tall plant. We grow it in the walled garden for its foliage and the bronze version (*Foeniculum vulgare purpureum*) in the Jewel Garden. Bronze fennel is less robust than its green cousin, both in size and resistance to the cold and wet, although it is seldom actually killed off by bad weather. It just looks thoroughly defeated.

Fennel is very easy to grow from seed and mature plants can be lifted and divided by root division in autumn or early spring. I find it best either to transplant self-sown seedlings in spring or to lift a mature plant, take off the young sections of root and throw away the older core – the plant does not perform very well after three or four years of growth.

Lemon balm

This is one of the more thuggish herbs, edging its way sideways with brutal determination. But it has many saving graces, being bright of leaf, easy to grow and deliciously lemony when eaten raw in salads, with cheese or drunk as a tea. But it is horrid when cooked.

We grow two types of lemon balm, the standard green-leaved *Melissa officinalis* and the variegated *M. o.* 'Aurea'. Both will grow almost anywhere, their roots spreading out into otherwise inhospitable corners. But they really thrive in a deep, rich soil – like ours. I have found that the only way to control lemon balm plants is to chop out at least half every year and throw away (or replant elsewhere) the innermost section, leaving the healthier outside part. The flowers are very popular with bees so the plant is useful to have on that account alone. However, the flowers grow on long stems and can look rather dry. Once the novelty of the flowers has worn off (after about three days), I leave a few flowering plants for the bees and cut the rest right back. They quickly re-grow with fresh leaves.

Melissa officinalis 'Aurea'

Tarragon

Tarragon did not enter the English herb garden until the Tudor period and still seems distinctly foreign, even exotic. Part of this is down to its excellence as a culinary herb, particularly with chicken and eggs, and partly because it can be tricky to grow. In fact, it is as comfortable in my garden as any of the other Mediterranean herbs, which is to say, not entirely. There are two kinds of tarragon, French (*Artemisia drancunculus*) and Russian (*Artemisia dracunculoides*), and unfortunately the French, which is by far the best for cooking, is more difficult to grow in this garden. It hates the cold and the wet whereas Russian tarragon, which is able to put its roots down in any soil or conditions, is not really worth its space in the garden. So there is no easy solution, but I maintain a supply of tarragon by replacing the plants every few years with new stock taken from softwood cuttings which root fairly well under the mist propagator in the greenhouse. This is not a bad idea however suitable the growing conditions in your garden, because the leaves of young plants have the best flavour.

Feverfew

(*Chrysanthemum parthenium*) started out in the Mediterranean, but has adapted so well to northern life that it is easy to think of it as indigenous. Feverfew is completely hardy and will grow anywhere that it is not too wet nor too shaded. The golden form *Chrysanthemum parthenium* 'Aureum' pops up all over this garden lasting most of the year and it is welcome, its bright yellow flowers adding an important zing to the borders. It produces little daisy-like flowers that are individually unremarkable but make a good massed effect, and then it becomes tiresome and needs radical weeding. However, feverfew self-seeds profusely and it will always return with a vengeance.

Feverfew is used as a treatment for migraine and headaches and just eating a few leaves (which are best harvested before the plant flowers) can be helpful – although they are very bitter to the taste so it is best to disguise them with something more sweetly palatable. It is important not to overdo this remedy – half a dozen leaves a day is more than enough.

Artemisia drancunculus

Chrysanthemum parthenium

Perennial non-Mediterranean herbs

To most modern, post-Elizabeth-David people, herbs have become synonymous with heat, strong sunshine and the oily, resinous aromas of the Mediterranean.

But the range of herbs that originate or will grow happily in a more northern temperate climate is very large. We tend to grow and use only a very limited range of herbs but until recently this garden would have provided a wide range of indigenous plants that the owners would have used for medicinal, cosmetic and culinary purposes. I was in the Republic of Ireland recently, visiting a herbalist, and he told me that his healing skills were based upon the belief that local plants healed local ailments. So, if a region was known to be damp and cold, causing respiratory or rheumatic problems, then the herbalist would go to a local damp, shaded site and find the plants that he needed to cure that ailment. There is a great deal of practical sense in this – as well as a certain degree of simplistic association. In practice, the organic gardener should also try and use indigenous plants for herbal purposes, rather than seeing herbs as something to add a touch of sunshine to a dish.

Of course our predecessors would have had a very much broader definition of what a herb actually was. Herbs were simply "useful" plants, and whilst we have reduced the

category down to a small group of leaves, flowers and roots, they would have included barks, woods and berries, and plants that we now consider weeds. Having turned our backs on the vast majority of traditional herbs as "old-fashioned" or even – that ultimate of twentieth-century put-downs – "unscientific" – there is now in the twenty-first century a huge resurgence in herbal usage. This is the key. A herb is defined and appreciated by the way that we use it. Otherwise it becomes another flower, leaf or even weed. From the pharmaceutical giants that scour the globe looking for new plants from which to derive medicines, to the increase in cosmetics based on plant extracts and "nutriceuticals" (therapeutic foods containing herb extracts), herbs of all kinds are becoming more highly valued as we re-learn just how much they can benefit us.

I know that we in this household are guilty of ignoring the full range of plant resources growing under our noses. Nevertheless, the few perennial non-Mediterranean herbs we grow are all important on decorative, culinary, medicinal and environmental levels.

Carrying a basket of horseradish root to the kitchen *(facing page)*. Horseradish has enormously deep roots and was a troublesome weed in the walled garden so now it is relegated to a rough edge of the drive where it seems happy and cannot overrun the flower borders.

Mint *(top)* flowering in the coppice where it is grown decoratively. **Chives** flowering in the vegetable garden where they serve primarily to combat carrot fly. A patch of **horseradish** in rough ground and **comfrey** flowering in the damp garden where it is grown not only to suppress weeds but also for its important contribution to the compost heap.

Mint

When I was growing up you would find mint in every kitchen garden, although it was rarely used except for the inevitable sauce (chopped and doused with malt vinegar) to accompany roast lamb.

Mint is ubiquitous, probably because it is one of the easiest herbs to grow and once established will need almost no care and lasts indefinitely. But in this facility also lies its downside for the gardener, especially one with limited space. It is terribly invasive. Put a couple of small plants in the corner of a border and in five years the mint will have taken over the whole thing. There are two solutions to this. Either plant it in an old bucket or bucket-sized pot with the bottom removed, which imprisons it and has the added advantage of needing no cultivation (mint likes a rich, slightly moist soil but will grow anywhere, anyhow). Or confine mint to containers. We do both. We grow spearmint in an old cattle trough, apple mint in a cast-iron oven and peppermint beneath a fig tree in the corner of the yard with areas of brick and two walls between it and the next available patch of soil to invade.

Types of mint There are 25 species of mint but we only grow three types. Apple mint (*Mentha suaveolens*) is the ideal accompaniment for potatoes – especially if they are new and simply boiled. The leaves are rounded and very soft and thick, the undersides felted with woolly hairs. The scent of apples is very subtle – or even remote – but with new potatoes its refinement is a virtue.

Mentha spicata is spearmint, the mint that ran riot in the gardens of my childhood. The leaves are pointed and the fragrance instantly recognisable from a billion toothpaste tubes and chewing gum packets. But it is not a modern taste. It has long been associated with oral hygiene: the ancient Greeks made use of it, while in Chaucer's time (fourteenth century) it was rubbed onto the teeth and gums as a cleanser. Spearmint can be used to flavour anything, from puddings to sauces and drinks, although we use the slightly stronger

Left to right: Spearmint *(Mentha spicata)*, Apple mint *(Mentha suaveolens)*, and peppermint *(Mentha piperata)*.

At the end of autumn, the mint plants become straggly so I cut them back hard. In spring, I clean out the metal containers and top up with fresh compost to give the new shoots a boost.

peppermint (*Mentha piperata*) for the latter. This has a dark stem and the underside of the rounded leaves are blushed with purple. Peppermint offers the best cure for a troubled digestion, as well as being a delicious drink, either hot or cold. Just pick a few leaves, pour boiled water over them, infuse for a minute or two (not too long as it becomes bitter) and drink. We do not use peppermint for cooking as the strong flavour tends to swamp everything else. Spearmint is not as pungent as peppermint and although less efficient as a digestive, it is easier to balance with other flavours in the kitchen.

Maintaining mint Once the mints start to flower the leaves become faded and coarse in texture and it is best to cut them right back to the ground. Clearly if you do this to all the mints at the same time it will result in a period of mintlessness, so I do half at a time, waiting until any new leaves are growing strongly before cutting back the remaining half.

It is a good idea to take a section of root from any of these mints at the end of summer, pot it into good compost and keep it in the greenhouse or on the windowsill. It will grow throughout winter, not producing a vast amount of leaves, but at least providing a fresh taste when needed.

Propagating mint All species of mint can be grown from seed but new plants take so easily from root cuttings that it is hardly worth the bother. Dig up some roots and cut these into sections, each with a visible node or shoot. Place each in a pot or seed tray of potting compost and keep in a sheltered place. Shoots are inevitably produced and can be planted out after about four weeks.

Peppermint tea is deliciously refreshing and the very best cure for any kind of disturbed digestion or colic. You can make it in a jug, mug, or as I usually do, in a cafetiere, simply by pouring boiled water over a handful of fresh leaves and leaving them to infuse for a few minutes.

Comfrey

Comfrey grows very well here and can become an intrusive weed in the wetter parts of the garden. But it is handsome in full fig, up to six feet tall and carrying pink and purple-tinged white flowers.

I grow a row of comfrey which I use mainly as a green mulch beneath my tomatoes. Comfrey leaves rot down very fast providing the tomatoes with an intensive potash feed as well as helping the soil to retain moisture and suppressing weeds.

Wheeling a load of freshly cut leaves for mulching. This amount of plant material will have come from perhaps only four plants. Each plant will provide three or four harvests between April and October.

One of the problems of growing comfrey (*Symphytum officinale*) in amongst other plants is that it is very prone to falling over in wind or heavy rain, swamping any plants beneath it. It is best to treat comfrey plants rather like broad beans and either stake each plant well or grow them in rows, supported by string and canes.

For centuries the mucilaginous leaves (which make good-ish fritters) have been used to heal bruises and broken bones but the comfrey liquid feed produced by the leaves is now an essential weapon in the armoury of the organic gardener.

But I grow comfrey, quite a lot of comfrey, just for the compost heap and as a nutritious mulch. The only reason that I do not make a comfrey liquid is that it is used primarily as a source of potassium, which I have in almost limitless supply as wood ash from our indoor fireplaces. Given that it takes around four weeks to make comfrey liquid, and it stinks of decomposing proteins (comfrey leaves are about 3.5% protein), it loses some of its appeal. But for those prepared to make comfrey liquid and for those without a good source of fresh wood ash, it is excellent.

We grow a "crop" of comfrey in a bed alongside the polytunnel so that there is easy access to its leaves, but I also harvest comfrey leaves from the plants that we have growing all over the garden for the compost heap.

Harvesting comfrey leaves For the first harvest of the year (when the plant stalks are long) I cut the whole plant to the ground, chop up the plant material and mix it into the compost heap, where it works as an activator, speeding up the composting process of other materials on the heap. Comfrey also has a high carbon content that is invaluable at a time of year when fresh foliage with a high percentage of nitrogen tends to dominate the compost heap. At the same time, all the trace minerals that comfrey is so good at extracting from the soil go back into the compost. For subsequent harvests, which tend to be leafier, I use the leaves like a poultice around the base of tomatoes, gooseberries, beans and onions, and the potassium quickly leaches into the growing roots.

Comfrey is easy to divide in autumn or spring to make new plants, or it can be grown from root cuttings – which is a fancy way of saying that any piece of comfrey root popped into the ground will develop into a plant.

Horseradish is another of our favoured weeds. I would not be without it but for a while it was the bane of this garden, appearing in flower borders and beds despite continuous weeding.

Armoracia rusticana

Horseradish *(Armoracia rusticana)* is NOT a plant for the herb garden. It spreads very vigourously and lifting it once it has taken hold is no easy business as it has an enormously long and robust tap root. The only way to control its spread is by digging out every scrap of root that grows anywhere other than in your designated horseradish area. We grow ours in the weedy verge of the drive and in the coppice – although it is surprisingly slow to take hold there – probably because the young trees take too much moisture from the soil for the horseradish to be vigorously happy.

Like mint, horseradish needs its own separate area, but unlike mint, the length of its root makes it unsuitable for all but the largest container. It is said to help potatoes resist disease but as I rotate my potatoes and horseradish needs a permanent bed their association and its benefits must perforce be temporary and occasional.

Throughout the year we harvest the roots to make horseradish sauce – the perfect accompaniment to a rib of beef (which is quite the best cut of beef, organically reared of course, eaten in spring with plain boiled potatoes and fresh spring greens). Horseradish sauce is also good with trout and pike – which we occasionally catch in the river that runs at the bottom of the garden. The root becomes stronger and stronger in flavour as the year progresses, with spring roots almost subtle but Christmas roots blisteringly powerful, one sniff of which can reduce grown men to tears. I speak from sobbing experience.

The best way to propagate horseradish is to take a piece of root with a crown attached and simply plant it where you want it to grow. Nothing will stop it.

Cleaning and peeling horseradish roots. Fresh horseradish can be astonishingly powerful but it is fairly mild in summer and autumn. By the end of the year the flavour is certainly stronger than anything you can buy.

Chives

I grow chives (*Allium schoenoprasum*) in the vegetable garden, partly because there is more space there to grow the kind of quantity that we like to use, but also because chives are a useful weapon against carrot fly. A few chives seems a contradiction in terms – they need to be plentiful, gathered in bunches rather than wisps. When it comes to the carrot fly, I always line the bed that I grow carrots in with a "hedge" of chives: the intention is to confuse the visiting fly with their strong onion smell. I have no evidence to what extent this works, if at all, as we still suffer from carrot fly attacks to a greater or lesser extent each year, but it certainly does no harm.

Chives look good with their grassy tubes of leaf and look even better in flower, their purple bobbles balancing on stalks indistinguishable from the leaves. Unlike many herbs, they taste as good in flower as before, and the flowers are delicious in salads. Bees also like them.

Before chives start to set seed, I cut the plants down to the ground, filling a barrow with the rank tang of onion, and they re-grow anew. In a good year this new growth can be repeated four or five times.

Chives are easily grown from seed and it is worth remembering that each of the tiny wisps of seedling will make a substantial plant in a few years time. But once you have successfully propagated a few plants from seed, it is much easier to divide up clumps of existing plants in future years. As I move mine each year, I divide them as soon as they show the first flush of growth in spring, chopping each plant into as many as four sections, throwing away old plants that are getting tired and creating new from the divisions.

Chive flowers are both decorative and tasty.

Tansy

I was prepared to overlook tansy (*Tanacetum vulgare*) as a "proper" herb, although it does make up part of our herb garden as well as growing in both the Jewel and Walled gardens. We only use it for one purpose and that is to deter flies in the home. It is a powerful insect repellent and was a traditionally used as a strewing herb. Tansy was taken for driving away wind after eating peas and beans in Lent, and was also part of the preparations for embalming corpses to deter worms. The leaves are distinctive and a good foil for other more spectacular plants. The button-headed flowers, which come in late summer, are a cheerful golden yellow. It is hard to think ill of tansy, unless you find its invasive tendency too much to accomodate. But it pulls up very easily.

Tanacetum vulgare

Fruit

The Orchard

When I first came to Ivington and planned the transformation from field to garden, I knew that I wanted an orchard to be part of it. Not just a collection of fruit trees, but a billowing orchard that had its own identity, almost independent of the rest of the garden.

My previous house had a large mature orchard that was clearly marked on the 1832 tithe map and was probably much older still. It covered two hectares (five acres), which was more than twice the size of this entire garden and produced tons of apples, the vast majority of which we could not collect, let alone eat, but I valued every inch of it, loving the way it had its own unique mixture of purpose and natural balance.

An orchard is more than the sum of its trees. It is a place complete and integral in its own right and cannot be made just by planting two or more fruit trees. There has to be a sense of arrival and permanence. Gardeners have known this for centuries, and from early medieval times through to the nineteenth century orchards were valued more highly than any other part of the garden as a place for contemplation and relaxation as well as their supply of fruit.

This sense of place – which has to do with structure and enclosure – can be created only by using standard or half-standard trees. The development and mass adoption of bush, spindlebush, dwarf bush, and dwarf pyramid trees in the twentieth century thwarts the whole concept of an orchard as anything but an area of the garden given over to the production of fruit, removing the magic and reducing it to an open-air version of a fruit cage. This is fine (up to a point) for commercial purposes, and is obviously useful for people with limited space, but an orchard it is not.

All fruit trees are grown on rootstocks that differ from the tree itself, and these rootstocks are categorized according to the type and vigour of the growth that they will support. Standards are trees grafted onto an M111 or M2 rootstock and must have a trunk at least 1.8m (6ft) or more. A half-standard uses an M106 or M111 rootstock and its trunk, by definition, must be 1.4m (4½ft) high. This means that there is room for people to walk beneath standards and for sheep to graze beneath half-standards. Grass – and for that matter a whole range of plants – has enough light to grow well between the trees which in turn support a range of bird and insect life. Grazed orchards are a strong feature of the countryside around this garden, although far too many have been grubbed out by greedy farmers and replaced with soulless rows of much smaller, tightly packed trees maintained by a harsh chemical regime. In these modern fruit factories, you can have as many as five thousand trees to 0.4 hectares (one acre), while in a proper orchard a hundred trees per acre is plenty. The trees have to be spaced sufficiently far apart to allow light and air to them in maturity; generally, this means leaving 5–6m (15–20ft) spacing in each direction.

It is debatable how many trees you need before you can call them an orchard, but I would suggest that six is a minimum and a dozen strains the concept less. So, even the most modest orchard needs space. I had plenty of that. I had an open, unplanted 0.8 hectares (two acres). There was surely space enough there to make a small orchard. It seems to me that the combination of this kind of large space with the human proportion of a small field filled with apple trees growing as wide as they are high, is the perfect summation of cultivated land.

An orchard is more than the sum of its trees. It is a place complete and integral in its own right and cannot be made just by planting two or more fruit trees. There has to be a sense of arrival and permanence. Gardeners have known this for centuries...

Planning the orchard I wanted a good cross-section of apples, pears, plums, damsons, and greengages, but I knew that apples had to take the dominant role.

Herefordshire is apple country. Until well after World War II, every farm made its own cider from orchards of cider apples and perry pears, as well as growing at least enough dessert and culinary apples to keep the household. The grass beneath the trees would be grazed by sheep in spring and midwinter, providing important grazing and controlling the grass length. Even now, there are enough remaining orchards in Herefordshire for the roads in late October to be choked for days with tractors pulling trailers piled with apples to the cider maker in Hereford. So, apple orchards are part of the fabric of this countryside and my orchard has grown from that tradition.

Making an orchard Of course, my vision of an orchard was based upon the full-blown mature thing, at least 30 years old and perhaps three times that.

I paced out five good steps between planting positions and marked them with bamboo canes and the canes seemed absurdly insignificant. However, I knew that they were just ciphers for trees and it did not dint the dream. But when the 50-odd bare-root trees arrived they made two bundles that I could easily carry in each hand. When planted, they scarcely troubled the skyline more than the bamboo canes. That first summer, the grass grew halfway up their stems. My orchard was planted, but it still existed mainly in my head.

However, with a little faith, careful planting, thick mulching, and the passing of a few years, the trees establish fast. Now, five years on, the orchard is beginning to take shape. The trees,

although still less than half their mature size, are now clearly trees. The spaces between them are defined by the planting rather than engulfing it. The fruit is increasing and is now in proportion to the branches, whereas for the first couple of years the apples, in particular, seem wildly outsized because the branches that bear them are so relatively slender and short. The chickens live there and scratch about in the piece we keep mown for them and around the bases of the trees. When you go there, you arrive at a distinct place rather than just another side of the garden.

I confess that I did rearrange the orchard a few years ago, as a result of my insatiable demand for more growing areas. I moved a dozen trees to fill the interstices between others, making a kind of quincunx pattern (sort of – I can never measure anything straight, so none of them properly line up with each other). This set the moved trees back about three years, which I find is a good rule of thumb for recovery of any tree that is moved unless it is very tiny – one year to recover from the trauma of the move, one to start gently growing again, and another to take off from the point that it had reached before it was moved. The moral of the story is to think twice before transplanting. If you must move a tree, do so with the largest root ball that you can manage and treat the tree as an invalid for a full 12 months afterwards.

This extra density of planting will result in overcrowding, but not for a generation, and there are few arboreal problems that a good saw will not solve.

Our chickens scavenge beneath the growing fruit trees in the orchard (*top*). They manure the ground, raise the fertility, and eat most potential pests. However, they also scratch up any mulch, which can be infuriating. These apples (*bottom right*) are ripening well but probably could have done with a bit more thinning. After midsummer, the grass beneath the trees is kept mown short (*bottom left*).

I cut the orchard grass soon after midsummer using a powerful rotary mower, which chops it up and makes it easier to compost.

I have also used a scythe to cut the orchard grass, which is energy-efficient and very satisfying to use, but takes skill and a great deal of hard work and makes hay rather than compost.

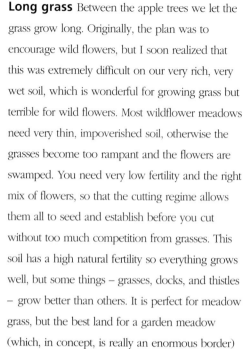

Long grass Between the apple trees we let the grass grow long. Originally, the plan was to encourage wild flowers, but I soon realized that this was extremely difficult on our very rich, very wet soil, which is wonderful for growing grass but terrible for wild flowers. Most wildflower meadows need very thin, impoverished soil, otherwise the grasses become too rampant and the flowers are swamped. You need very low fertility and the right mix of flowers, so that the cutting regime allows them all to seed and establish before you cut without too much competition from grasses. This soil has a high natural fertility so everything grows well, but some things – grasses, docks, and thistles – grow better than others. It is perfect for meadow grass, but the best land for a garden meadow (which, in concept, is really an enormous border) is probably very thin soil over chalk.

However, the grasses themselves are very beautiful, and we have common bent (*Agrostis castellana*), which has loose fronds of widely spaced seed heads, each seed visible within its transparent casing. There is the violet plume of Yorkshire fog (*Holcus lanatus*) mixed with red fescue (*Festuca rubra*), which is much more delicate but equally pink and the whole field shimmers with a pink haze that sits a couple of feet above the ground, balanced on the end of stalks, billowing pollen at the slightest touch. The crested dog's tail (*Cynosurus cristatus*) is everywhere in its quiet way. Cocksfoot (*Dactylis glomerata*) is more visible and is constructed with widely spaced "branches" looking as though they are soldered onto the main stem and carrying tufts of flowerheads. Smooth meadow grass (*Poa pratensis*) has a tucked-in, neatness to it, despite its tufty heads.

By the second week of June, the grass creates waves lapping about each tree. Buttercups, meadow geraniums, clover, sorrel, plantains, and

trefoil – not to mention docks, thistles, burdock, and hemlock – grow beneath the surface of this grassy lake. I never cut it before midsummer's day – June 24th – and try to do so as soon as possible after this date. In practice, this can be any time in July. Cutting and raking it up is slow, hard work, whatever tool I use. I have done it with a scythe, which is efficient and fun, even though I am not very good at scything or – most importantly – keeping a good edge on the blade. I have used a strimmer with a blade attachment, which is very good if the grass is matted and growing through itself in a tangle, as it often is by mid-July. But in recent years I have used a powerful rotary mower, designed for cutting difficult areas of long grass. This does the job with astonishing efficiency.

But however you cut it, it has to be raked up and, in my experience, immediately cut and raked again because the first cut never gets all the grass that is lying flat. So it is a big job and one that takes a day to cut and at least a day to rake. At the end of it, we are left with a large heap of grass cuttings. The secret of composting this is to soak it really thoroughly as you pile it up. We put in a layer and drench it before adding another layer. Only if all the grass is sodden will it compost. Otherwise, the outer layer is amazingly efficient at insulating and protecting the rest of the heap from all weathers and it will take anything up to three years to turn into useable compost. There will be a lot of grass seeds in amongst the heap, so it must get really hot to kill these off. I maintain the cooking process by turning it every month or so for the first four months before letting it sit – still very wet – all winter. I have found that the best way to use it is to mix it in with the growing compost heap the following spring. This adds bulk and lots more brandlings that are very abundant in the grass heap. I think this is because it is exactly the combination of wet and aerated dry material that they like best.

If the cut grass is left on the ground it will nourish the soil as it decomposes, raising the nitrogen content, which will make the grass grow stronger and reduce flowering. This is a general rule of all gardening: if the nitrogen level in the soil is too high, the result will be lush, green growth. This will mean more insect damage and more fungal problems, and fewer flowers as the plant's energy will be diverted into leaves and foliage. If the grass is long, it will also take time to decompose and cause short-term browning, and even death, of all plants beneath it – including the grass.

If the grass is cut with a scythe or non-rotary mower you end up with hay, which is much slower to compost but has its uses. The obvious one is as a feed if you have livestock. But it also makes a good mulch for fruit trees, although it is invariably full of grass and weed seeds, so must be topped up before these have a chance to grow. You can also spread the hay over a patch of heavy and bare soil, wet it thoroughly for about a month, and then sow seeds onto this or plant through it. As long as it stays moist, it will rot down into the soil and encourage extra worm activity that will help break up the heavy ground. Once the grass is all gathered, the orchard is kept mown so that the apples fall onto shortish grass and the chickens extend their range out into the orchard.

We have kept mown a narrow path through the long grasses that grow beneath the field maples in early June. Our soil is too rich and wet for most wild flowers, but the grasses themselves are very beautiful.

Orchard fruit
Horticultural jargon designates all fruit that grows on trees with the ugly term of "top fruit", as opposed to "soft fruit", which grows on bushes or, like strawberries, on plants.

For the gardener, the differences are practical and aesthetic. You can protect and cage soft fruit, but not top fruit. In the case of a very old pear or walnut, these can be very large trees indeed. One has to think more in terms of a flowering wood than a fruit cage. There is a relationship, like no other in the garden, between the increasing permanence of the tree and the seasonal transience of its fruit. I think that this depends upon size. Somehow, the cut-down, shrunken trees that are widely promoted as being "suitable for small gardens" destroy the magic of orchard fruit. It is, after all, hardly a practical relationship. We live in an age of industrial food produced like widgets and shipped to any corner of the globe without respect for locality, season, or variety. Uniformity and availability is all. One big tree producing a random harvest of fruit for a few weeks in the year is not efficient. Which is all the more reason why we should celebrate and plant them in every garden. For apples and pears, the answer lies in the choice of varieties that are deemed unsuitable for mass production.

Any garden is transformed by a mature fruit tree. Even a small garden could revolve around a good-sized apple tree, which would provide the light shade for the mixed woodland planting that does so well in the northern hemisphere. Fruit, of course, also means flowers, and some of the most gorgeous flowering trees are orchard trees. Pears provide some of the best and earliest fruit blossom, and apples and quinces are as good as many roses.

I confess to a mild infatuation with apples and pears. This goes beyond a love of the trees and the taste of the fruit. I am also fascinated by the enormous range of varieties of both and the way that they have been bred and cultivated for centuries as the archetypal orchard fruit. In my own orchard, I have 36 different types of apple, some very common but

many providing us with fruit unobtainable from any shop.

Not all my top fruit is in the orchard. I have an avenue of espalier pears in the vegetable garden that, in a good year, produce a huge and sumptuous harvest. Another pear is trained against a south-facing wall. There are hazelnuts in the coppice that we gather and keep until Christmas. In the damp garden we have quinces, young as yet but I have just made our first *membrillo* – the Spanish quince preserve that has a firm, jellied texture allied to a wonderfully smoky, delicate taste. This part of the world is famous for its damsons, and we have a number of short, scrubby trees growing in both the orchard and our hedgerows which produce a constant supply of the intense, dark plums. We also have "proper" plum trees, which we use mainly to make jam.

But I have had my failures. For a number of years, I coaxed a pair of medlars along, although they were afflicted very early on by fireblight, which is a particular hazard of all the rose family (which includes apples, pears, hawthorns, and medlars). The fruit are an acquired taste, as they should really be eaten "bletted", or rotten, but they make a good jelly to accompany

meat. In the end I gave up and burned them, although I am tempted to have another attempt soon as medlars are ancient and pretty much unimproved over the last millennium, which seems to me to add to their virtues. They can still be found growing wild in hedgerows and woodland, with their large white flowers as fine as any fruit blossom in spring. Figs are the most exotic fruit that we grow. I do not believe in struggling to raise a few scrawny peaches, apricots, or other delicious, non-indigenous fruits when the tree is desperate for a warmer, drier climate. As with all organic gardening, the secret of success with fruit is to go with the flow. Even our figs struggle to produce a regular crop in our climate, but they always look magnificent and in late summer yield a small but delicious harvest.

My main aims are to create an orchard that is a beautiful place and a supply of organic fruit that will give this household the variety of fresh, seasonal fruit that is so hard to obtain in any shop. And if I am honest, even if they were easy to buy and very cheap, I would still grow lots of orchard trees because the marvel of a tree producing the annual miracle of fruit never fails to delight me.

Apples
I love to eat apples in every conceivable form. I adore the trees, their blossom, even the smell of the wood on a fire. But some apples are very much better than others.

Some apples – most of the rubbish sold in supermarkets – are a tasteless, unpleasant disgrace. An apple should have an identity. Its taste, texture, shape, colour, and aroma must be distinctive. But whatever your choice of variety, any apple is best left on the tree until ripe and stored carefully – two things that commercial production cannot cater for because it is entirely driven by considerations of longevity of storage, ability to withstand handling, and appearance over and above taste. So bland, indistinctive apples are the unfortunate norm.

Planning my orchard When it comes to choosing varieties of apple, it is rather like planning a wine cellar. You are laying down fruit for the future. Some will take a while to mature, while others will provide plenty of fruit after just a few years. Some varieties grow into sizeable trees, whereas others, regardless of rootstock, never attain more than a scruffy maturity. A good apple tree should last for at least a hundred years.

You should have a mix of apples where each reflects a distinct character. That character must be of the locality as well as the owner. So when I planned my orchard, I looked around. Certainly, there were apples growing everywhere, so it was not a folly to be planting more, but on the face of it this is not ideal apple-growing countryside. What apples like best is rich, well-drained soil, warm, dry summers, and mild, damp winters. Northern France and the South-east of England fit this bill exactly, but here in the extreme West of

England, right on the Welsh border, we have (in theory) too much rain, overly heavy soil, and frosts in May, which can wipe out the flowers of early varieties.

The truth is that many apples are surprisingly tricky to grow healthily. They dislike wind; need plenty of sun, good drainage, and good soil; grow much better in sites that are no more than 150m (500ft) above sea level; and do not like too much wet, which can cause scab, mildew, and canker. Spring frosts can also destroy the buds from which the apples stem. Yet the apple is ubiquitous in Herefordshire. The County Council has adopted an apple as its logo. The country's largest cider maker is in Hereford. Despite the ravages of the bulldozer, and rapacious farmers grubbing for easy money, orchards are everywhere. So clearly, some varieties were better suited to growing in this area than others.

Evolution of apple varieties Apples are able to adapt to an amazing breadth and variety of growing environments. If you throw an apple core into a hedgerow, and if its seeds germinate, the "wilding" apple tree that results will not produce a fruit exactly the same as the apple that you so nonchalantly threw aside. This is because they do not grow true from seed. Every apple contains the genetic material, in its seeds, for a brand new apple variety that would, astonishingly, bear very little resemblance to either parent tree. This "heterozygosity" accounts for the ability of apples to grow in such a range of locations

I store my apples on slatted shelves and purpose-built stacking, keeping the different varieties apart. When storing apples, it is vital to reject any that are not perfect, because they will not keep and will spread rot to the other, healthy apples.

around the world. Given the permutations of "appleness" that each tree can potentially produce, sooner or later every tree will generate a seedling that is adapted to whatever environment the tree finds itself in. So, varieties have evolved and died out throughout recorded history. It is reckoned that over six thousand different apples have been bred over the past two millennia, and two-thirds of those have died out.

Because most apples are extremely bitter, and are only good for making into cider (which until the nineteenth century was by far the most common way of consuming apples), those that are sweet enough to eat have been jealously preserved. In consequence, apples, like roses, are now always grown grafted onto rootstocks because vegetative reproduction is always true. Normally, vegetative reproduction involves taking cuttings, but since most apple cultivars are unwilling to root from cuttings, each is grafted onto the roots of another compatible tree, which is always a type of crab apple. (Pears, on the other hand, are always grafted onto quince rootstocks.)

Apples have always attracted plant breeders, and Herefordshire and the neighbouring country of Worcestershire have had their apple obsessives, from Thomas Andrew Knight in the eighteenth century, to gardeners such as William Crump at Madresfield Court in the early twentieth century. Inspired by them, I wanted to encourage local, rare varieties, and decided to include as many apples as possible that had originated in this part of the world in my orchard, as well as the ones that I knew from experience I liked to eat. I also wanted to have as wide a selection of apples as possible, with a range of characteristics that covered as long a season as possible.

When collecting windfalls, to avoid mixing up varieties, I collect my apples either by single variety or two varieties at a time that have very different skins.

In this last respect I do not think that I succeeded very well, and were I to plant another orchard I would have fewer early varieties, which keep very badly, and more later-ripening cultivars, chosen for their keeping qualities to provide us with apples in early spring.

Early-fruiting varieties, such as 'Discovery' or 'Tydeman's Early Worcester', can be ripe in August, whereas later ones such as 'Sturmer Pippin' will not be properly ripe until the middle of November.

Pollination of apple trees If you want to have a spread of ripening times you will also have a spread of blossom, and because no apple is reliably self-fertile, each tree will need a pollinator. It is best to make sure that every tree is accompanied by another apple from the same group so that they can cross-pollinate each other (*see page 390*).

What this means in practice is that an 'Egremont Russet' (Group 2) is unlikely to cross-pollinate with 'King of the Pippins' (Group 5). But it will do fine in conjunction with 'Ribston Pippin', 'Reverend W. Wilks', 'George Cave', and 'Lord Lambourne', among others from Group 2. Likewise, the 'King of the Pippins' will pollinate happily with 'Newton Wonder', 'William Crump', or 'Mother' from Group 5.

There is no need to be overly restrictive about this, because trees from neighbouring groups tend to pollinate each other. A good rule of thumb is that if there is another apple tree within 30m (100ft) in flower at the same time as yours for at least three days, then you should get fruit.

But not every year. Many apples are biennial, which in practice means that they

VARIETIES IN MY ORCHARD

DESSERT APPLES

'Autumn Pearmain' (1)
'Chivers Delight'
'Crimson Queening'
'Egremont Russet'
'James Grieve'
'Jupiter'
'King of the Pippins'
'Lamb Abbey Pearmain'
'Laxton's Superb'
'Laxton's Fortune' (2)

'Madresfield Court'
'Mondial Gala'
'Peasgood's Nonsuch'
'Ribston Pippin'
'Rosemary Russet'
'Spartan'
'Stoke Edith Pippin'
'Strawberry Pippin'
'Tydeman's Early Worcester'
'Worcester Pearmain'

CULINARY APPLES

'Arthur Turner' (3)
'Blenheim Orange'
'Bramley's Seedling'
'Devonshire Buckland'
'Doctor Hare's'
'Glory of England'
'Grenadier'
'Hambledon Deux Ans'
'Herefordshire Beefing'
'Lane's Prince Albert'

'Newton Wonder'
'Norfolk Beefing' (4)
'Reverend W. Wilks'
'Tillington Court'
'Tom Putt'
'William Crump'

alternate between good and bad crops. There are always good and bad years anyway, biennial or not. Some crops will be scabby, others may have bitterpit, and the earwigs, wasps, and moths will have their day. But, in line with the whole ethos of organic growing, I do not see apple-growing as a war to be waged against nature. Even the bad years are good enough.

I have 40 apple trees in the orchard, with two each of four varieties ('Blenheim Orange', 'Worcester Pearmain', 'Herefordshire Beefing', and 'Bramley's Seedling'). That is 36 different varieties (*see above*), of which about a dozen are quite rare and very specific to this area.

I do not spray my apples but I do try and keep them weeded and mulched (with mixed success – it is one of those jobs that keeps getting pushed down the list). I also prune them each January (*see page 389*) with some care.

Rootstocks and grafting The starting point of selecting any apple tree is to choose the right rootstock. This is really important because it will determine the size and vigour of the tree. I wanted an orchard of standards and half-standards, so that determined the rootstocks for me.

The process of "creating" an apple variety is simple: you merely graft a bud from a named variety, which will dictate the fruit that is produced, onto different roots chosen for the desired size and vigour of the mature tree. The resulting fruit will always be of the graft (trunk and branches) rather than the stock (roots). Grafting can take place with maiden trees in the nursery, or with mature trees in the orchard. The process, and the result, are identical.

When the graft has "taken", the top-growth above the graft is cut off, leaving the grafted bud growing on the roots (stock) of the crab

TIP-BEARERS

'Irish Peach'
'Lady Sudeley'
'Worcester Pearmain'

TIP- AND SPUR-BEARERS

'Autumn Pearmain'
'Blenheim Orange'
'Bramley's Seedling'
'Discovery'
'Gladstone'
'Hambledon Deux Ans'
'Laxton's Early Crimson'
'Tydeman's Early Worcester'

This apple tree branch has snapped off under the weight of its fruit. It is important to thin fruit ruthlessly from young trees in June, until the branches are strong enough to bear the load of fully grown apples.

apple. The join between the two trees is visible as a knobbly lump at the bottom of the trunk, which must always be kept above soil level when planting.

The reason for using different rootstocks is that apples have enormously varying growth habits. Bramleys, for example, are very vigorous, whereas 'Worcester Pearmain' grows slowly. If you grew trees on their own roots, they would need to be much more widely spaced so most garden orchards would have room for only one variety. This is true if you grow apples from seed or cuttings – the variety is assured but the vigour would be completely unknowable.

Until World War I, trees were produced on "paradise stock", which was originally a dwarfing rootstock from France, but there was no control or classification. Paradise stock from one nursery could be – and often was – quite different from an identically named rootstock from another supplier nearby. Because of this confusion, the East Malling Research Station set about classifying rootstocks. The first they produced was called Malling Type 1, which became shortened to M1. Eventually they got up to M27, although only about ten are in use and of these only four are common.

To confuse matters, another research station, the John Innes Horticultural Institution, based at Merton, also worked on rootstocks, collaborating with East Malling. The results of this work produced stocks that were named Malling Merton, or MM. So that they would not be confused with the M types, they were numbered from 100 up, hence the rootstocks MM106 and MM111.

Characteristics of common rootstocks

• **M27** Very dwarfing – ideal for containers;

needs rich soil and support throughout its life.

• **M9** Dwarfing – makes for a small tree that comes into bearing early. The fruit tends to be large and ripens earlier than identical varieties on bigger trees. Has brittle roots so needs permanent staking. It is good for cordons and containers, but needs a rich soil.

• **M26** Semi-dwarfing – used a lot in commercial orchards because it stays small but produces early, large fruit. It will tolerate poorer soil than M9, but is a slow starter. It can be used for espaliers and cordons on very good soils, and needs permanent staking.

• **MM106** Semi-dwarfing – medium-sized tree that grows and crops well on poor soil. Suitable for a half-standard (with a clear trunk of 1.2m/4ft), or a large, bush-shaped tree. Crops heavily on good soils. Best for espaliers or cordons on poorish soils.

• **MM111** Vigorous – ideal for standard or half-standard trees. It can resist potash deficiency in the soil and is notably drought-resistant.

• **M25** Very vigorous – suitable for large standards. It is capable of producing up to 180kg (400lb) of fruit on a large mature tree.

How to plant an apple tree Plant any tree into a generous hole, thoroughly loosening the subsoil and adding some compost or manure.

Position the tree in the hole and place the stake on the side of the prevailing wind, remove the tree (keeping the roots covered and preferably wet) and bang in the stake firmly. Standards should have a stake with 1.8m (6ft) above ground level, whereas smaller trees do well with a shorter stake angled against the wind. Plant the tree, carefully working the soil around all the roots and

Pruning I was taught that an apple grows best if there is room for a pigeon to fly straight through the centre of the tree.

The only considerations when pruning are to control size and shape, to improve light and ventilation, and to improve fruiting.

I start in the new year by removing any branches that are crossing or rubbing, then thin any crowding shoots, trying to maintain the balance and shape of the tree. It is an easy and rewarding job, especially if it is done every year or so and the tree has not become a tangle of branches. However, the pruning should not be extensive every year and, in fact, hard winter pruning stimulates growth. The main concern is to remove unwanted branches. If you have espaliered trees that need encouraging to grow more vigorously in a particular direction, hard winter pruning would achieve that end faster than merely leaving them to grow untouched.

Having "cleared" the tree, I then prune to improve fruiting. In spur-bearing trees (which includes most varieties), the idea is to build up a framework of knobbly "spurs" growing at regular intervals along each branch. These will bear the coming year's fruit, which will develop on last year's wood. The idea is to develop these spurs along the length of each branch, pruning

each one back to just a couple of buds each year (*see bottom left*). I do my summer pruning in late July.

There are also tip-bearing varieties (*see facing page*), which produce most of their fruit from the terminal fruit buds of shoots made the previous summer. Cut these off and you will have no fruit! You can easily tell in a tree more than three or four years old as the spurs will be very obvious. However, to confuse the issue some varieties are both tip- and spur-bearers. If in doubt, simply do not prune except to remove crossing or diseased wood. Of my apples (*see page 385*), only 'Worcester Pearmain' is a tip-bearer, while 'Autumn Pearmain', 'Blenheim Orange', 'Bramley's Seedling', 'Hambledon Deux Ans', and 'Tydeman's Early Worcester' are both tip- and spur-bearers and pruned as for spur-bearers.

Summer pruning is done to restrict growth by reducing the supply of carbohydrates to the roots. I do not do this as I want my apple trees to grow as large as possible, but it is necessary if you grow restricted forms like espaliers, fans, or cordons, or if you have a bush tree that is outgrowing its available space.

firming it down properly. Tie the tree to the stake using a flexible tree tie.

Water well. Leave a wide area at least a metre (3ft) in diameter clear of growth and mulch it thickly with compost. Check each stake after strong winds, as they often snap underground, appearing secure but leaving the tree vulnerable to damage at the next storm.

When securing staked trees, make sure that the tie is not too tight. Stretchable ties are best, otherwise, as is evident here, the growing trunk can very quickly be damaged.

Pollination The best apples need another apple from the same group (or an adjacent one) to pollinate them.

Apple varieties are divided into groups, according to flowering times, with Group 1 being the earliest to flower and Group 7 the last. If apples are to cross-pollinate, the pollen must be carried by a bee from flower to flower, so the two trees must be flowering simultaneously. The greatest chance of pollination comes with trees in the same group, but since there will be a flowering overlap with the groups on either side these can also successfully act as cross-pollinators.

As a rule of thumb, any apple tree within 30m (100ft) of another will pollinate it if it is suitable. So, if there is not another apple tree in sight, always plant more than one tree from each group in your garden.

There are some apples that will set a crop without a pollinator – but not nearly so reliably. The following varieties come into this category:

'Beauty of Bath'
'Charles Ross'
'Chiver's Delight'
'Crawley Beauty'
'Ellison's Orange'
'Emneth Early'
'Greensleeves'
'James Grieve'
'Keswick Codlin'
'Lord Derby'
'Newton Wonder'
'Sunset'
'Worcester Pearmain'

Damsons and plums

When we first came here, there were damson and plum trees growing in the shelter of the curved wall, among the building rubble of what was to become the walled garden.

The southern boundary of this piece of garden was made up of a hedge of damsons, and there were various plum suckers growing in the field. Other than the large hazel beyond the back door, these were the only indicators of "gardening" that survived the last occupant. However, I found out that the walled garden had once been the vegetable patch for the farm, and clearly damsons (and to some extent plums) had at one time been highly prized.

Damsons, greengages, bullaces *(below)*, and myrobalans are really just forms of plum, although they tend to be treated separately. While plums get a good press, damsons are not widely grown enough and if I could have just one tree, I would choose damson over any plum every time. This part of England, along the border with Wales, has a long tradition of damson-growing, and 65km (40 miles) or so east, in the Vale of Evesham, is the major plum-growing region of the country. All members of the plum family like our rich, heavy soil, but only damsons, which are by far the toughest of them, really relish our strong winds and very cold snaps of winter weather.

Plums

Damsons The damson is one of the first fruit trees to come into blossom, following on just after the blackthorn in late March. There is a twisting main road near us that is flanked by

'Farleigh Prolific'

Damson cheese, which has nothing to do with dairy products and everything to do with a delicious, extra-thick conserve made from damsons.

damson trees in the hedgerows. The repeated effect of delicate blossom – no blowsy voluptuousness here like the apple trees to follow, just a dainty sprinkle like powder snow – builds a rhythmic beauty as you go past, a kind of visual clattering of a stick along railings. Yet the damson is a scrubby, untidy tree, hardly worth its place in the garden on aesthetic grounds – it is the massed effect of trees planted every 5m (15ft) or so in a hedgerow that works so well. The leaves turn an amazing yellow in September, but are the first to fall.

Damson jam is the richest and best, and damsons also work well in pies and crumbles, as well as being delicious on their own or stewed. They are one of the few fruits better preserved in a kilner jar than frozen, and a jar of rich red fruits swimming in crimson liqueur is an ornament in its own right. But we collect the fruit from our trees primarily to make damson cheese. For the uninitiated, this has nothing to do with any dairy product, but is a very thick, extremely intense conserve. It is the best accompaniment to game of any kind, superb with lamb, and ironically is also very good with a strong cheese. It is certainly the most intense liquid the kitchen can conjure.

The intense juice of damsons was used to make commercial dye for wool and leather; indeed, in the nineteenth century, when every well-dressed woman had a pair of leather gloves, dyeing leather with damson juice was an important small rural industry in these parts.

Damsons are not difficult to grow. They will come true from a stone (thus a stone from a 'Bradley's King' will produce a 'Bradley's King' tree) and will yield fruit within 15 years. Alternatively, you can buy a tree grafted onto a rootstock that will control the amount of

growth. 'Pixy' is a dwarfing rootstock, described as "a real space-saver", which would, I suppose, mean that it could be grown in a container. 'St Julien A' (which is also used for peaches and apricots) is a larger rootstock, making a tree up to 4m (12ft) tall. 'Brompton' is vigorous and used for standards and half-standards, as is 'Myrobalan'.

Because it comes true from seed, the damson has quietly carried on down through the years so that the fruit you eat from your slightly scruffy tree in the garden tastes the same as the fruit the crusaders brought back from Damascus. You need not worry about cross-pollination with most damsons.

Of the self-pollinating varieties, 'Merryweather' produces the biggest of all damson fruits and is a heavy cropper, the fruit lasting well into autumn on the tree. 'Bradley's King' was first recorded just over a hundred years ago, and its fruit, which is covered in bloom when ripe from mid-September on, is sweet enough to be eaten raw. I have planted 'Farleigh Prolific' and 'Merryweather' in the walled garden against the hedge of natural damsons, to add to their mass.

In fact, damsons are much more variable in their fruiting than plums, bearing, on average, a good crop every three years, a moderate one every three years, and none at all every three years. For this reason, we gather as many as we can and turn them into as much damson cheese as possible, knowing that it may have to last for well over a year at a time.

Plums The plums burst into blossom just after the damsons, overlapping by a few days, the baton passing from hedgerow to orchard. Plum blossom sits on the trees thinly, measured as much by the sky between the flowers as the

massing of the blooms themselves. Indeed, a spring sky never looks so pure a blue as it does when seen between these aerial flowers.

We inherited three scrawny plum trees, but I have never established what variety they are. All ripen in August, attracting wasps by the dozen and tasting rather watery and bland when eaten raw, although they are delicious stewed or made into jam. I planted 'Shropshire Prune' in the orchard, and already it is growing into a handsome tree with dark blue, almost black, fruit with real intensity of taste. This is – I think – a local plum, although you will find it listed by suppliers as a damson – and it is damson-like in the smallness and darkness of its oval fruit, but is very sweet and plum-like to eat when ripe.

The fact that there is such doubt or debate merely shows the close relationship between damsons and plums. Whatever you like to call it, it is a variety known since the sixteenth century, and is perhaps the nearest taste we can experience to the fruit of the Tudor dining table.

Caring for damsons and plums

Plums are all liable to a handful of annoying – but not serious – diseases and attacks, such as silver leaf, brown rot, the plum leaf-curling aphid, and the plum fruit moth. Do I care about these? Not a jot. I leave them to sort themselves out without any help or hindrance from me. Damsons simply take no notice, and the plums look out of sorts but continue to produce fruit every year.

The only rule that is worth observing is to prune plum and damson trees only during the growing season to avoid the cuts being infected with silver leaf or canker, and to prune only to thin or correct a tangled growth. If in doubt, the trees are best left well alone.

Plums growing in the walled garden. I do not know what variety this is, but it is insipid to eat raw yet makes excellent jam. The appearance of both the leaves and the fruit is less than perfect – partly because I give them no attention at all. But the jam still tastes very good …

Figs The way that figs change from a bony framework of stubby, pointed branches to soft layers of idiosyncratic leaves is one of the most dramatic transformations in the garden.

The tiny, pea-sized fruit overwinter before growing and ripening in late summer.

A perfectly ripe 'Brown Turkey' fig (*top, opposite*); two fruits in midsummer (*bottom left*) – the large one will ripen but the tiny fruits will have to be removed as they will not ripen or survive winter; the dramatic leaves of figs look very good set against a stone wall (*bottom right*).

Even when leafless, figs are striking. They have a curious grey bark that wrinkles and gathers when branches bend or twist, like a pair of tights negotiating a knee. Left to their own devices, and with sufficient heat, figs will make a good-sized, spreading tree. They will suffer any amount of hard pruning. A south- or west-facing wall is the only seriously viable way of producing ripe figs in Britain – I have half a dozen trained against the south-facing stone wall of the walled garden.

There is a myth that you must plant figs in very poor soil. In fact, it is best to provide figs with the same soil as any fruit tree – a good loam with some manure or compost. They also need regular watering. However, it is essential to provide good drainage, and restricting their roots after they have become established stops the development of too much non-fruiting wood. I have found that if you plant figs quite tight up against a wall it provides a natural inhibitor to root growth and sucks up any extra moisture.

Figs can also be grown successfully in containers. I have had four figs in large pots waiting for a permanent home for the past seven years, and they are perfectly healthy, although much smaller than their kin that were planted out. They need watering and a certain amount of feeding with an annual mulch of compost and liquid seaweed every month in the growing season.

Figs bear two fruit crops a year, but in Britain only one of these has any chance of ripening. The successful fruits are formed at the end of summer and overwinter as tiny pea-sized buds near the tips of shoots. Any new fruits that develop and grow in spring or summer will not have time to grow and ripen before winter so should be picked off at the end of October. This feels a bit drastic but is necessary so that the tree's energies can be channelled into developing next year's fruit.

Pruning Most figs will suffer damage from frost, mainly at the tips of shoots, and this should be cut out after the worst frosts are over (usually mid-April). Whilst you are doing this, thin the branches so that there is 30cm (12in) or so between each one, trying to cut shoots that do not have fruit buds on them, taking them back to one bud. Around midsummer, after the figs have grown their leaves, I always prune back any outward-growing shoots, to stop them shading the ripening fruit, and to develop the lateral growth over the wall. I also prune non-fruiting branches to encourage more new shoots, which in turn will bear more figs. It is important to do this second pruning operation before the end of July, so the new growth it will provoke has a chance to ripen before serious frosts come along.

Fig cultivars 'Brown Turkey' is the toughest and most reliable cropper in northern Europe. 'Brunswick' has exceptionally big fruit on large, tough and often ancient trees but takes a few years to develop fruit and will ripen only in good summers. 'Black Ischia' crops in September right through to October.

Hazel nuts There were only two trees in the overgrown paddock behind the house where I wanted to move our garden. One was a large hazel by the back door. I realized at once the tree was a treasure.

The hazel produces a mass of hazelnuts each autumn and, judging from the hollow, uncoppiced trunk at the centre of its stool, has done so for a couple of hundred years. Growing nuts for deliberate harvest is rare in modern gardens, but until this century they were a much valued crop. A nuttery is a kind of nutty orchard and a lovely notion, with its own flora of plants adapted to the cycle of coppicing. Hazels were one of the staples of prehistoric people, especially the Celts, and were an emblem of wisdom. The expressions "in a nutshell" and "sweet as a nut" surely emanate from hazels. It is not only humans who value them for food. For most of early autumn, our terrier sits beneath the nut tree gazing wistfully at the branches above her in the hope of not a nut but a squirrel falling off the tree into her mouth.

The wild hazel of woodland is *Corylus avellana*, commonly known as the cob. As Geoffrey Grigson points out in *The Englishman's Flora* "It is decidedly pagan". To make it Christian, the tree was given the name of St Philibert, a seventh-century Benedictine, and later shortened to "filbert". Confusingly, we now classify *Corylus maxima* as a filbert and differentiate it from a cob by the way that the husk completely envelops the nut, which in turn is rather longer than the more rounded cob.

Even more confusingly, one variety of filbert, the Lambert filbert, introduced in about 1830, is also called the Kentish cob. Other varieties include the frizzled filbert and the Cosford nut. The Victorians evidently took their hazels seriously, and regarded the slow luxury of cracking the shells and extracting the kernels to the accompaniment of a glass of port as a rich pleasure. So do I.

The nuts should be allowed to ripen on the tree and be gathered as soon as they fall, but the temptation to collect them from the branches is usually too great. Hazelnuts will store until Christmas if kept in their husks, which stops them from drying out too fast. If collected whilst still green, leave them in a dry place and they will ripen by about November.

Walnuts If the hazel is the most common of nuts, then the walnut is certainly the most majestic. Unlike the hazel tree, the walnut makes a distinctive and regal tree up to 45m (150ft) tall. We don't have one in this garden at the time of writing, but I don't know why. We all love to eat walnuts and they make superb trees. It is an omission. I grew up with a large walnut tree in the garden and had two superb ones in my last garden. By the time you read these words, one may well be slowly growing outside this window. (It is the gardener's constant complaint: so many plants and so little space.)

The common walnut (*Juglans regia*) was introduced to Britain by the Romans. There was a burst of walnut-planting at the end of the eighteenth century in this part of Herefordshire, with the idea of making walnut "orchards", but too many trees failed for the idea to materialize. However, there is still the happy residue of lines of walnuts in fields across the county.

Walnuts are picked – knocked down – with

their sticky, green peel still on them. This has to be removed and the nuts dried, after which they will store for up to a year. Pickled walnuts – which are delicious – are picked "green", whilst the kernel is still soft.

The American walnut (*Juglans nigra*) grows bigger than the English version, although without the latter's silvery cast to the bark. The fruit looks like a small, white-flecked apple, which splits as it ripens to reveal the kernel – what we call the walnut – inside.

Walnuts like heavy, moist ground and grow slowly. They resent intensely being transplanted, so need careful positioning. They need to be either put in the ground when very small, or grown in pots for the first few years and then put into their final positions. Either way, they cannot be expected to produce any fruit for at least ten years. They pollinate erratically, so it is best always to plant two together. The American walnut exudes a kind of self-protective poison from its roots. This particularly affects apples, so do not plant walnuts in an orchard.

Our large – and very old – hazel growing in the Spring Garden in early May, just as this section of the garden is coming to the end of its performance. All the planting is based upon the woodland pattern of almost total winter and early spring light followed by almost complete summer shade.

397

Sweet chestnuts The sweet chestnut (*Castanea sativa*) is not only edible but historically an important source of nutrition. I would like to grow it here – indeed I would love to plant a coppice of them. It is extremely fast-growing, and responsive to hard pruning, so it tends to be interchangeable with hazel as the primary coppice tree.

Large swathes of Kent are covered with chestnut coppices that produce straight poles for fencing. The sweet chestnut identifies the geology of an area as surely as a rhododendron. It likes a light, well-drained, acidic soil, and where it will grow, it does so with exuberance, yet where it feels uncomfortable, it simply refuses to take up residence. Nevertheless, I include it here because, like the walnut, I am tempted to try it. There are some wonderful, enormously ancient, sweet chestnuts growing just 8km (5 miles) away. The nearest chestnut coppice is on the Malvern Hills, 48km (30 miles) away.

The casings of the kernels are as prickly as hedgehogs, and they decorate the autumnal tree like lime-green Christmas baubles. Although we used to feast off the raw nuts to the point of sickness when I was at school, they are best roasted.

The nuts are produced much more prolifically in a hot summer and become edible after the first frosts, but you have to watch them because birds and squirrels love them. Once harvested, they must be kept cool and dry and will store for a year.

A bowl of cobs. We gather these in September and early October, let them dry for a week or so, and then slip the nuts free of their husks. They will then keep well until Christmas.

Quinces

Quinces fall almost exactly between apples and pears – in perception, if not botanically. It is not just because of the fruit, although that would be reason enough, but the tree itself.

The quince does not make an impressive tree in any accepted sense. Tending to be straggly, it can often appear to be in a permanent state of buffeting, as though it is wincing before an expected blow. The growth differs from variety to variety and many are fine enough, but none matches a mature apple or a fine old pear. In fact, its relative weediness is used by growers to tame pears, as nearly all pears are grafted onto quince rootstocks to stop the trees from getting too big.

However, the quince "package", when fully assembled into its component parts of flower, fruit, and tree, is irresistible. I am, of course, talking about *Cydonia oblonga*, the culinary quince. The decorative quince, *Chaenomeles japonica*, does produce edible fruit, but they are not as good as that of the culinary quince, so chaenomeles are mainly grown for their exceptionally hardy and beautiful flowers that provide invaluable cheer in late winter.

The cydonia's flowers are simple, with four basic, soft pink petals, yet they have a bone-china elegance and refinement that makes them as lovely as any rose. The comparison is apt, because quinces, like apples, hawthorns, and rowans, amongst others, are members of the rose family. They also have the most delicious, almost edible fragrance. Some flowers are like perfume, but quinces have a bouquet. You drink the scent.

I bought four quinces four years ago on the basis that the four slight variations gave me four times the chances of growing a decent quince. This has proved a successful, if trifle extravagant, way to go about things. The varieties that I ended up with were 'Lescovac', 'Portugal', 'Vranja', and 'Champion'. If there had been six varieties available I would have bought six. At that time it was all one to me. I wanted the essential quinceness, the central mysterious element that defined their similarities, rather than the details that made up their differences. All quinces are self-fertile so, unlike apples and pears, you do not need more than one tree to get fruit.

The history of the quince I read that the Tradescants brought 'Portugal' into the country in the seventeenth century, but knew that quinces were cultivated by the Romans and thereafter by every European gardener who had an orchard. Orchards were, of course, highly prized in medieval and Tudor England, and fruit of all kinds was precious and much valued. We think of fruit as being synonymous

'Lescovac'

Quince blossom has an elegance and refinement that makes the trees as decorative as any other fruiting trees. They flower quite late, in mid-May, and are self-fertile.

Quinces make small but neat trees that need no pruning. This one is 'Lescovac'.

with freshness, and are therefore inclined to eat it raw if possible, but this is a modern trend. Back in the reign of Elizabeth I, when the most modern part of this house was built, fruit was nearly always eaten cooked. Raw fruit was considered to be bad for you. This meant that a fruit like quince, which is rock hard and practically inedible when raw (and therefore not quick, easy, or convenient for the modern cook) was placed on a par with apples and pears, and needed no more preparation than they did. So quinces were baked into pies, made into wine, and into a preserve named *marmelo* by the Portuguese.

From this, via a substitution of Seville oranges for quinces, we have marmalade. A tenuous connection to this is that my great, great grandmother introduced marmalade to Britain on a commercial scale via a shipload of unwanted Seville oranges in Dundee. But that is another, long story. It seems that until the seventeenth century, quinces had equal billing with any other fruit in a well-stocked orchard.

In the seventeenth century, people scraped the soft down from the skin of the fruit and the leaves, mixed the scrapings with honey, and used it as a hair restorer. The resulting sticky, downy poultice on a shiny pate is a happy image. I could also have rubbed my spleen with quince juice to cure dropsy or my lungs to control asthma, or put it on my inflamed eyes and skin ulcers if I happened to be plagued by these things. The seeds, when boiled, apparently produce a mucilage that was used as a kind of hair gel.

The "usefulness" of quince was based on reverence. In Jewish mythology, the forbidden fruit in the garden of Eden was not an apple, but a quince, the quintessential fruit of good and evil. They were considered an emblem of love and dedicated to Venus. To me, this is entirely explicable, with the combination of fulsome but flowing curves, exquisite colour, taste, and scent all combining to make it as sexy a fruit as can be grown. In Mediterranean countries, brides would eat one before retiring to the bridal bed, properly fortified for the nuptial rites.

Quinces at Ivington I wanted quinces growing in my garden, partly as a Tudor fruit that was appropriate to a Tudor garden, and partly to add depth and subtlety to the orchard. However, by the time I had planted all my apples, there was no room left for quinces. Part of the problem is that quinces like wet ground, whereas apples and pears prefer well-drained soil. They do not readily share the same space.

Although we have a huge amount of rain here, the only truly wet ground is in a piece of the garden that regularly floods. It had lived through various half-hearted incarnations until I realized that it made sense to stop fighting the regular flooding and use it for our wet-loving plants (this is not as obvious as it might seem, because it gets a great deal of sunlight and can become hot and baked in summer).

However, we cleared it, and moved in all our hostas and ligularias, as well as the best-shaped quince – which happens to be 'Lescovac'. The tree responded to its new home with four fine fruit. They were like fat pears, as yellow as an autumn leaf in the sun and covered in the same peachy down as a newborn baby's head.

There were not enough to make jelly – which, to my mind, is the best thing to make with them – so they ended up adding flavour to an apple pie, which was fine, but somehow

A basket of quinces heading for the kitchen. They will store for a long time and can be kept in a bowl in a room to act as a fragrant pomander. Most of mine are made into *marmelo*, the jellied preserve that is good with cheese and meat.

did not feel celebratory enough. I suppose we could have left them in their bowl to be a pomander, as the fruit have a fragrance as delicious as the flowers. In fact, it is very flowery, not really fruity at all. This year, as I write, there are at least 40 fruits on the tree, so we shall have quince jelly to last all year, as well as quince with apple and a roast chicken stuffed with a whole quince – one of the most delicious ways to use quince in my opinion.

Caring for quinces In general, quinces are hardy and trouble-free, and do not need any pruning, other than to remove any dead or crossing branches. They certainly do not respond well to shaping in any way, obstinately returning to the tangle of branches that is their natural growth. The fruit needs sunshine to ripen, so always plant the trees in a sheltered, sunny location. Remember that they need much more water than most fruit trees, so if they are not in a naturally wet (but not boggy) spot, such as the edge of a pond, where their roots can reach the water, they may need a regular soaking.

Because quinces are members of the rose family, they are prone to fireblight, which causes a dying-back and browning of shoots and leaves. However, they are less susceptible to this than many other members of the family (I have recently dug up and burned a pair of medlars because they were irredeemably smitten by fireblight).

Quinces can get a fungal disease of the leaves, known as quince leaf blight, which is caused by the fungus *Diplocarpon mespili* and results in brown spots and even leaf drop. This seems to vary from year to year and, like all fungal problems, is not helped by the effects of global warming that makes for warmer, wetter winters and summers. The fungal spores overwinter on infected shoots, so prune and burn any visibly affected ones and pray for a series of really hard frosts.

Pears
Pear trees can be fantastically long-lived and hardy, if grown on their own roots, although modern trees are usually grown on a quince rootstock, which produces a smaller, earlier-fruiting tree.

Even in early spring, the fruiting spurs of the espalier pears are very evident (*top left*). Pear blossom (*top right*) is early, so prone to frost damage. The pears have to be harvested carefully, and before they fully ripen. Here (*bottom*) are 'Williams' Bon Chrétien, an early variety.

The pears in midsummer, before summer pruning. Celeriac and celery can be seen growing in the background.

Of the rootstocks onto which pears are most commonly grafted, Quince A is moderately vigorous and Quince C is more dwarfing. For a standard or half-standard, you will need a tree grafted onto a special stock, as neither of these two rootstocks are man enough for the job.

Pear trees become regal with age, with beautiful pinky grey bark cracked into a thousand square platelets on a really big, old tree. In this part of the world, there are still old pear orchards, with trees 18m (60ft) tall. These were planted in the early 1700s, dating back to the heyday of perry pear production, when the heavy Herefordshire soil was considered less suitable for apples, and perry was more widely drunk than it is today. To reach this size, a pear tree must be grown as a standard on its own roots, with no intention of seeing it mature in your lifetime. Do not build up the expectations of your children either. A standard pear grows slow and long. Planting it is like planting an oak or at least a beech. It belongs to bigger time than people.

Whatever the size of the tree that bears the fruit, pears *have* to be eaten ripe to get anything like the full range of their taste and texture. Practically all supermarket pears are pale travesties of the real thing, which has a combination of slippery, honeyed sweetness and a tight, close-grained texture of the flesh. The problem is that pears only reach that point of perfection for about a day. So, if ever there was a fruit to grow at home to use as a gastronomic yardstick, it is the pear. As such, it is worth treating them as the most precious of treats, with the same reverence you offer caviar, truffles, or the best wine.

Growing pears at Ivington For a number of years, I have struggled to grow pears well in this garden. I began by planting an avenue of 18 pears that I bought as a job lot in an auction. They were all labelled 'Doyenné du Comice', but in fact four of them are 'Williams' Bon Chrétien'. It took me years to establish this. For the first three years, I intended to grow them as standards, but then decided to espalier them. By this time they had grown beyond the best stage for training and I had to cut them back radically. About six years ago, I noticed that all had developed canker. Every year since is

Pruning Fruit trees trained as espaliers, fans, or cordons need pruning in summer and winter to create and maintain their shape and yield the best fruit.

Whilst summer pruning will restrict and curtail growth of espaliers, winter pruning, done whilst the tree is dormant, will stimulate lateral growth of the espalier tiers, resulting in vigorous new growth in the following spring.

But in summer, sometime between the middle of July and the middle of August I reduce all the vertical growth (*right*) to create the spurs for next year's fruit. I also cut out any wayward or crossing branches or obviously damaged or diseased wood. This also removes a lot of foliage that is blocking sun from the ripening fruit, and maintains the shape of the tree (*bottom right*).

So to summarize: cut lateral growth in winter to make it grow more strongly, and cut vertical growth in summer to restrict it and to create fruiting spurs.

meant to have been their last as I resolve to dig them up and burn them, perhaps replacing them with espalier apples, which would do much better. But every year they bear lovely blossom in April, followed by fruit that we harvest in September. The trees are blighted and riddled irretrievably with canker, but they have each become like an old dog with a limp: not much use for catching rabbits but much loved. I had planted an extra 'Doyenné du Comice' from this job lot in the orchard with the apples and paired it with 'Black Worcester', which dates back to 1575 and is supposed to produce "large, round" fruit, but has so far produced only tiny, rock-hard pears. It is a culinary tree, so the fruit are inedible raw, but I like to eat pears poached and stewed. The 'Doyenné du Comice' refused to fruit at all.

Dealing with canker Canker is noticeable in pears when the bark starts to split and crack and shrivel around lesions, and stems shrivel and die back. Canker is caused by a fungus, *Nectria galligena*, which enters through wounds caused by frost damage, pruning cuts, scab infection, or even woolly aphid. These wounds are almost impossible to prevent, and there are only two ways of countering it, one preventative and the other reactive.

You are supposed to react by removing all trace of the canker, cutting branches back to healthy wood behind the site of the fungal attack, and burning the infected prunings.

You counter it by growing healthy trees on a well-drained site, by adding lime to the planting hole (I wish I had known this when I was planting mine!), and by making sure that there is good ventilation without over-exposure to wind. Trees grown slowly without too much nitrogen are less susceptible to the disease. It

may be worth growing varieties that are not so susceptible. 'Doyenné du Comice' is not one of these. A canker infection means that it is impossible for an espalier to establish a really strong framework of branches from which you can create decent fruiting spurs. It is a disaster.

I really wanted a bumper harvest of pears each autumn, and given my reluctance to uproot the espaliered pears in the vegetable garden, I planted another ten trees in the orchard in an attempt to do better. I chose four 'Doyenné du Comice' – because they are undoubtedly the best dessert pear and I did not know then that they were susceptible to most pear problems – two 'Conference' pears, two 'Williams' Bon Chrétien', and two of 'Concorde', which is a cross between 'Williams' Bon Chrétien' and 'Doyenné du Comice' and makes a beautifully healthy, archetypally pear-shaped fruit.

I planted them with the care of a father bathing his newborn baby for the first time. I regularly whispered sweet nothings to them, and provided everything that a pear could want for in this world. Of these ten, only the 'Concorde' trees thrived – and are still doing well. It is an excellent variety for an organic grower in hostile pear country, growing strongly and producing beautifully healthy fruit (albeit shyly). I have dug up the rest and they are sitting in large containers, without a home to go to. I should choose the healthiest and grow it against the south side of the house, but the whole area around our buildings is either bedrock or archaeology – there has been a building on this site for at least a thousand years, and I am loath to destroy any of that for the sake of a pear. The only solution is to make a large enough container, as pears grow perfectly well in pots.

All my pears are afflicted with canker. This disease can be fatal, and you should prune back to unaffected wood at the first sign of it. Good drainage and ventilation are the best methods of prevention.

'Doyenné du Comice'

'Williams' Bon Chrétien'

The avenue of espaliered pears in the vegetable garden in mid-July, before summer pruning. From this angle, the espalier shape is almost completely hidden behind the volume of new vertical growth. If this was not pruned back before winter it would grow back the following year with twice the vigour and the espalier shape would soon be lost.

Not knowing much about pear-growing, I assumed for a long time that the canker was a result of poor technique on my part. However, I recently learned that this is a very difficult area for pears. It is too wet, too cold, too windy, and the soil is too heavy. Conventional wisdom is that pears are tougher and more tolerant than apples, but only up to a point.

A favourite fruit Pears have attracted breeders and collectors for centuries. There were extensive pear orchards in Britain by 1200, and by the mid-seventeenth century over 50 different varieties were grown, of which only one, 'Jargonelle', is now still common. By the 1840s, this had exploded to over 700 different varieties. Pears were (and still are) considered the connoisseur's fruit, and were thought to be much better and more sophisticated than the apple. But there are far

fewer varieties of pear to choose from nowadays and, compared to apples, not nearly as many have been developed to adapt to potentially hostile conditions.

But every farmhouse in the vicinity has at least one pear, invariably trained against the side of the building where it will catch most sun. It is very often a 'Conference', which is reliably self-pollinating. 'Conference' is primarily a culinary pear – although it is very good as a dessert fruit when eaten perfectly ripe – and this means that it can be stored more easily, usually in jars.

Enjoying the harvest Storing dessert pears is impossible without refrigeration, which ruins their taste. They must be eaten when ripe, and the season spans just a few autumnal weeks, so there is no point in having too many trees for domestic use.

From the beginning of September, I go round each of our 24 trees testing each individual fruit, cupping the bulb in my hand and gently twisting and lifting it. As the month progresses, more and more come away from the tree. They are not fully ripe at this stage, and are not likely to be ready to eat. Instead, being careful not to bruise them, I lay them out individually on a sunny windowsill in an unheated room. It is light more than heat that they need, although supermarkets store them below a certain temperature to delay ripening. Over the course of the following week or so, they accumulate a yellow flush, tinged in some varieties with orange as the ripeness washes through them. I turn their hippy bodies sunwards once, to get the process even.

It is no use prodding and pushing a pear to test for ripeness because all you will do is bruise the flesh, leaving a mushy wound beneath the skin. Pears ripen from the inside out, so the flesh immediately beneath the skin is the last to be ready. You must be gentle. If I press my thumb at the base of the pear there will be a slight yielding. Not a soft squidginess, but just a bit of gentle give. You want to eat it as soon as there is any softness to it at all. And never bite into a pear like you do an apple. That is barbaric.

Sit. Get a clean plate and, if possible, a beautiful knife. Consider and admire the pear before you cut it into quarters, always peel it (this is not for the sake of your health, but because the tough skin detracts from the perfect texture), slither the core away, and enjoy the firm juiciness. I rarely eat a dessert pear for the rest of the year, and if I do it merely confirms the mistake.

'Williams' Bon Chrétien' pears being picked (*above*). Those on the ground are not windfalls, but are placed there so I don't drop them! The same pears (*below*) ready to ripen in the sun, which will take a few weeks.

Soft fruit There is almost nothing in the garden that is so rewarding to cultivate as soft fruit. It is (quite) easy to grow, stores well, and the large volumes of fruit produced are never less than a treat.

Let me first define what I mean by soft fruit: it is fruit that does not grow on trees and includes, in this garden, strawberries, raspberries, gooseberries, redcurrants, whitecurrants, and blackcurrants. The plants and forms that these fruits appear on vary from the low, herbaceous, leafy mounds of strawberry plants, and the various bushes of currants, to raspberries grown on canes in cordons.

Once established, most soft fruit needs very little time or attention and is one of the first things that I would recommend the owner of a new garden should plant. Even if you have very little space, nothing beats summer pudding made from fresh blackcurrants, redcurrants, and raspberries, although chasing it hard for the top culinary spot are fresh raspberries, gooseberry fool, strawberry and raspberry jam, gooseberry ice cream, and redcurrant jelly.

All soft fruit is very short-lived and at its most delicious when eaten ripe and freshly picked. This means that its season is relatively short, and when it is over, it is gone for another ten months or so. If there are those who see this as a disadvantage, then they will probably not be an organic gardener, or even a grower of food in the garden, because this seasonality seems to me to be the essence of good food, and soft fruits exemplify this.

However, with the exception of strawberries, all soft fruit freezes very well. Indeed, a good-sized crop can be eaten throughout the year, albeit without the magic that is always lost in the process of storing fruit.

All soft fruit shares a liking for rich, well-drained soil, although gooseberries are very hardy, blackcurrants will tolerate more wet (and use any amount of richness in the

soil) than most, and raspberries grow well on a sandy, slightly acidic soil. But in general they can all share the same site.

Settling in my soft fruit plants I tried integrating soft fruit into the vegetable garden, but ran out of space. In old cottage gardens in particular, you will see (if you ever come across an old cottage garden, which is rapidly becoming a very rare sight) a couple of gooseberry bushes and perhaps a redcurrant, growing happily in amongst the cabbages and hollyhocks and providing enough fruit in season for a few pies as well as jams and jellies to last into winter. In a very different way, the potagers of France also incorporated soft fruit with vegetables, maximizing their structural and aesthetic value. But there is much to be said for growing soft fruit all in a separate area, not least because you can put a net over it as it ripens because birds will strip a fruit bush overnight as soon as the fruit starts to colour.

Our soft fruit area evolved by default, and has involved moving currants and berries rather more than any text book would advise. I rather like this haphazard scheme of things, and had I planned it at all the only change I would have made would have been not to have positioned the asparagus beds slap in the middle of the currant bushes! It is the site of the old rickyard of the farm, where the corn was built into stacks, or ricks, to stand until needed for threshing. Half the area had a layer of cobbles about a foot below the surface, which had to be broken through for planting, but the soil, as everywhere in this garden, is a rich loam.

Soft fruit needs sun and shelter. Our fruit-growing area is open to the sun except in the very early morning, which is a good thing, because it reduces the chances of damage to buds and flowers from very late frosts. It is also naturally protected from the wind on all but the northern side. I have planted a hawthorn hedge to remedy this, but most of our wind comes from the west and rather than being cold is gusty and wet. I have used the natural barriers of the raspberries and cordon gooseberries across the line of this wind to act as further shelter for the currants.

Raspberries
It seems strange to us now but raspberries used to be considered a useful wild fruit, whereas the bramble was a delicacy to be carefully cultivated.

In Tudor times "raspis", as they were known, were used more as a gargle for a sore throat than for eating, whilst a dish of blackberries was considered fit for a king. Today, blackberries (*Rubus fruticosa*) grow in the hedgerows like weeds and raspberries (*Rubus idaeus*) are a dish fit for any man.

All raspberries are better than almost any other fruit, but a good raspberry is my favourite of all the fruit in my garden. I love the dollops of juiciness beneath the taut skin and their just-enough toughness that survives careful picking but easily explodes inside the mouth. I would not want to eat them every day, and indeed probably only do so a couple of dozen times a year, but each of those times – even when idly standing between the rows of canes, gently pulling the pink fruits off their bleached cones of stalk before popping them into my mouth, reaching instantly for another, holds firm in the memory with the intensity of a wonderful meal. Like all soft fruit, they must be eaten perfectly ripe to be appreciated for what they are, and they are only in this state for a day or so at the most. You *need* them growing at home.

There are two kinds of raspberry: summer and autumn-fruiting. Summer-fruiting varieties ripen in this garden between the end of June and August, and grow on canes that grew the previous year. They need permanent support. Autumn-fruiting ones start to ripen in August and can continue into November and fruit on the current year's growth. This means that they are cut back each year; the only support that they require is to stop them toppling onto the path. Autumn-fruiting ones are often a better bet if you live in an area of low rainfall, or with quick-draining soil, as the fruits are likely to have cooler conditions and more rain in September than June and July, when the summer-fruiting ones most need it. Our heavy rainfall also suits them well, although they prefer a much lighter, better-draining soil. I grow 'Malling Jewel' and 'Glen Ample' for summer, and 'Autumn Bliss' for autumn.

'Glen Ample'

Growing raspberries Raspberries require an infrastructure but, once established, they are easy enough. The first important thing to know about them is that they have a mass of very shallow, fibrous roots. This means that they gain most of their moisture and nutrients from the top 15cm (6in) of the soil and that it is almost impossible to hoe them once planted. Their cultivation requirements follow from this.

Before you plant, it is a good idea to construct a solid support system for the canes – full-grown raspberries in leaf are heavy and can catch the wind like a sail. I put in posts every 30m (10ft) and stapled horizontal wires between them 60cm (2ft), 1.2m (4ft), and 1.8m (6ft) above the ground, that the canes are tied to with soft twine. It probably would have been better to have drilled through the posts and bolted them at the ends, so that the wires could be tensioned.

The time to plant raspberries is between October and March. Dig the ground very well and weed fastidiously. They prefer a slightly acidic soil, so do not add any mushroom compost (which is alkaline), either when preparing the ground or mulching the mature plants. Garden compost is ideal. Prepare a trench a spit (spade's depth) deep and 1m (3ft) wide, and add plenty of well-rotted manure into the bottom. Backfill, adding a generous amount of garden compost mixed in with the topsoil. This is only ever done once, so do it well. I added a lot of sharp sand, as though I was preparing an asparagus bed, and planted the roots level with the surface, mounding the soil over them – all to improve drainage and avoid the fatal risk of the plants standing in a puddle of water.

Set the canes in the ground vertically, and cut back to 22cm (9in). As soon as vigorous new growth appears, prune the original cane to ground level. This means that there will be no fruit in the first year from summer raspberries. I protect the shallow roots and suppress weeds by mulching them thickly with garden compost each March. In November, I rake the mulch to one side to let the birds eat the pupae of raspberry beetles.

Maintaining raspberries Pruning raspberries has to be done correctly but it is not difficult and is one of those jobs that marks the season for me – I do it as soon as possible in September on summer-fruiting raspberries. There is something about converting the vigorous tangle of brambly shoots into a couple of rows of neatly spaced, pale green rods, each tied with green twine and slightly fanned from the base, that makes me feel that summer's work is completed and the garden is prepared for winter.

I start by cutting out the brown stems that bore the fruit, taking them off right down by the soil. It is best to do a length of about 1.8m (6ft) at a time, otherwise there is too much to clear and you cannot see what you are doing. This leaves the young green shoots that will produce next year's crop. Each plant will have between two and ten of these shoots and they need thinning, ideally to four or five per plant. The important thing is to preserve the strong, healthy ones and keep an even spacing, removing all the rest right to the base. Fan out the survivors evenly, to 7–10cm (3–4in) apart, tying each cane to the three levels of wire. The best way to do this is to secure a long piece of twine to the wire and weave it around each cane, like an open wicker basket. It is a deeply satisfying process.

Autumn-fruiting raspberries should be pruned in the New Year, cutting all canes right back. I remove any suckers outside the row as I do this (they pull up easily), and have another pulling and thinning session in June, leaving the strongest growth to fruit. I have suffered in the past by neglecting this second prune, with the result that there was an enormous volume of growth that became very wet and the fruit suffered as a result. They do not need tying in, although I wrap them with heavy twine as they grow in exactly the same way that I support broad beans (*see pages 285–288*).

It is said that you should not grow potatoes near raspberries as the potatoes will become more prone to blight. The raspberries do not seem to suffer any ill-consequences from the association. In the average-sized garden, this advice is irrelevant as all plants are grown close together anyway. Birds can be a real problem, and netting is the only solution, even if it is just a temporary affair thrown over the canes for a month or so.

Pruning summer-fruiting raspberries. It is best to do a short section at a time. The first job is to remove all of the previous year's growth (*top left*), cutting the plant down to the ground. These have brown canes, whilst the new growth – which are for next year's fruit – are a beautiful pale blue-green (*top right*).

I then reduce the new growth to about six strong canes on each plant. The selected canes are evenly spaced and tied to supporting wires with soft twine (*bottom left*) – the wires need to be strong as midsummer raspberries loaded with fruit and leaves are heavy. The easiest way to do this is with a continuous thread, interweaving between the canes. This is about as fiddly as my clumsy fingers can manage. The last job is to trim back or tie in the loose tops growing above the top wire (*bottom right*).

Strawberries can be delicious, but they are ridiculously over-hyped. For the past 30 years, the market has been saturated by tasteless, mass-produced, watery mush masquerading as strawberries.

Alpine strawberry

'Royal Sovereign'

Types of strawberry The tiny fruits of alpine strawberries (*top*) are produced from midsummer right through to the first autumn frosts. They nearly always have a better, more intense flavour than the more familiar, large-fruited maincrop strawberries. These only fruit for a month or so in midsummer (although they can produce a few more fruits in late summer).

No other soft fruit varies so dramatically in quality – from the divine to the frankly disgusting – and if you want to eat strawberries that taste as good as folk- and marketing lore perversely persist, you must grow your own, wait until June and eat them as they should be eaten, still warm from the sun. Certainly a strawberry should never venture into the chilly depths of a refrigerator if it is not to be ruined forever.

All strawberries are herbaceous plants, dying down in the winter. They are self-fertile, propagating from runners – plantlets that grow on long, horizontal stems. Modern large-fruited strawberries are a cross between American *Fragaria virginiana*, which arrived in Europe in 1556, and *F. chiloensis*, which did not hit England until early in the eighteenth century.

The tiny native wild strawberry, *F. vesca*, which can still be found in hedgerows and woodland verges, is closely related to the small but especially delicious alpine strawberry, *F. alpina*, which fruits constantly from June through to October. The latter is easily grown from seed and makes a good decorative edging, although it can become an invasive – albeit tasty – weed. "Perpetual" varieties are a cross between wild and modern strawberries, bearing a succession of fruits that ripen between July and October, whereas the modern maincrop strawberry, characteristically larger, bears all of its crop in June–July.

Easy to grow Luckily, all strawberries are very easy to grow. They like rich soil, with lots of compost and good drainage and as much sunshine as possible. It is important to weed the site very well as strawberries are awkward to weed once established.

The best time to put in new plants is late summer, which will give them time to establish so that they will produce a crop the following June. There are those that advocate removing these first fruits in order to let the plant develop strongly and to encourage an even bigger harvest the following year, but this is denial taken too far – unless the plants only went in that spring, in which case it is a good idea. Space them 45–60cm (18–24in) apart in rows or blocks with the base of the central crown at soil level. This gap between plants will seem terribly wide, but they need room to spread and the crop will justify the extra nutrients that each plant will get as a result.

Strawberry plants are only really worth keeping for four years, so it is best to dig up plants after their third harvest and put them onto the compost heap. There are two reasons for keeping your strawberry stock refreshed. The first is diminishing fruiting after the third year, and the second is that strawberries are very prone to viral diseases, which tend to linger in the soil. For this reason, you should never replace old plants with new on the same site. Let it rest for at least three years before going back to strawberries again.

Renewing your plants is no hardship, as once you have established plants they will produce a mass of runners after fruiting, each one of which is a potential new plant. I have got into the habit of taking plenty of runners and I now have four separate groups of plants,

Potting up strawberry runners Established plants will make a mass of new plants on long stems that grow after fruiting.

You should only take runners from young, vigorous plants, as most strawberries develop viruses as they grow older. This affects fruiting and general plant health, and is one of the reasons for discarding any plants more than four years old.

Taking runners is easy. The simplest way is just to peg down the tendril into the soil on either side of the plantlet. I use home-made wire staples, but large fencing staples will also do very well. About a month later, cut the runner either side of the pegs, and lift the rooted plant. A slightly more sophisticated method, which I use, is to sink a small pot in the ground (*top left*), fill it with potting compost, and peg the runner into this. The structure of the potting compost encourages better rooting, and by the time you cut the connecting stem the plant is already potted up and growing happily.

Using this "potting" method, it is also easier to store the little plants until you are ready to plant them into their final position on a new site. The only problem I find is that I am always forgetting to gather them all up, and find myself digging up root-bound, potted strawberries a year or two later.

each a year older than the next, grown in a long bed so that the whole lot shuffles up and down it with the oldest being chucked onto the compost heap. I overwinter the vacated ground with grazing rye as a green manure and then use it as a nursery bed for a couple of years before the slow march of the strawberries returns. This seems to work fine.

Caring for the crop In March I put a cloche over a dozen mature plants to encourage them to fruit a little earlier than the others, partly to jump the gun and partly to provide ripe fruit over a longer period. I leave the end of the cloche open to provide ventilation and water them every few weeks. Water all young plants well as they are growing, but be careful not to get the fruits wet once they start to colour. In a wet summer (like the one in which I am writing) botrytis – which manifests itself as a grey mould on the fruits – is a real problem. Too much water will also dilute the taste of the fruit, reducing the intensity of the sweetness.

417

My varieties I confess that I do not know what variety my strawberries are! They were originally given to me in the shape of half a dozen plants wrapped in damp newspaper and I have taken stock from them ever since. 'Royal Sovereign' is said to be very good (if you can get hold of it) 'Elvira' has good flavour and good mildew resistatance, 'Cambridge Favourite' is another good taster and is pretty disease-resistant. Avoid any variety that claims to be good for freezing.

If there is a sustained spell of very wet weather I put more cloches over ripening fruit to act as umbrellas.

The fruits should be kept off the ground to avoid slugs and rotting, so tuck straw or a mat around each plant. If the blackbirds are not to take the lions share of the crop you will have to net them before the fruit start to turn red (birds seem to ignore all green fruits) and I do this at the same as I straw them. The problem, of course, is to provide protection that allows you to get easily at them without getting tangled in netting. But it is worth taking trouble over this.

Once the last strawberries have been collected, cut the foliage off about 7cm (3in) above the crown (being careful not to damage it) and rake up every scrap of leaf to reduce the risk of disease or infection. The sooner the leaves are cut back, the better next year's crop will be as a result. I do not feed my plants as I do not want them to outgrow the resources of the soil and there is no evidence that it produces tastier fruit – which is the sole reason for the strawberry's existence. But I do mulch in spring with mushroom compost.

Soil Your soil is likely to be the determining factor for the taste of your strawberries. A light, sandy soil is likely to give an earlier crop, but the richer and heavier the soil the better the flavour. According to the books strawberries do not grow terribly well on chalk, although I was bought up in a chalky garden and we seemed to grow strawberries well enough. If your soil is chalky do not be put off, but bung in plenty of manure or compost.

I cover some of my strawberries with open-ended cloches from spring onwards to encourage earlier ripening and to keep them dry, which helps minimise fungal diseases.

Gooseberries

I love gooseberries. I love the balance of tart acidity with honey sweetness and their combination of firm, almost crisp skin and the sweet, seedy, pulpy juiciness that it contains.

These gooseberries are nearly ready for picking. When fully ripe, they acquire an almost translucent quality.

Gooseberry fool, gooseberry ice-cream, gooseberry crumble, gooseberry jam, gooseberry pie – they are all wonderfully good. But until very recently I thought that I was not terribly good at growing gooseberries. They always either got defoliated by sawfly or the fruit became heavily coated in grey mould. However I now know that there were two quite separate problems happening, one of which was my "fault" and the other quite beyond my control.

But in principle, gooseberry bushes are as tough as oak. Ancient, gnarled specimens continue to produce a fine crop of fruit for decades. They like rich soil with plenty of moisture – which we have in abundance – and lots of potash. I mulch each bush with a shovel of wood ash from the fire every spring.

Problems Sawfly are an ever-present liability with gooseberries, and also redcurrants. There are three species, the common gooseberry sawfly (*Nematus ribesii*) the lesser gooseberry sawfly (*Nematus leucotrochus*) and the pale gooseberry sawfly (*Pristiphora pallipes*), but the niceties of type are low on my list of priorities when sawflies attack. All of them lay their eggs at the base of the bush, as near to the centre as possible. When the caterpillar-like larvae hatch they then proceed to eat as many of the leaves as possible, stripping them back to the midribs so that ghostly tatters are all that remain. As they munch – with astonishing hunger, stripping a good-sized bush in 24 hours – from the inside out, the first signs of them are usually after they have reached the outer parts of the bush and most of the damage has already been done.

The overwintering pupae hatch in April and lay eggs on the young leaves, placing them in rows parallel to the main vein. If you can spot these and knock the eggs off then you are ahead of the game already. If not, the eggs will hatch and the young larvae do their worst for about a month, then pupate and emerge three weeks later, and so the cycle continues until all gooseberries (and redcurrants) are completely stripped, or winter comes. There

Gooseberries are particularly responsive to potash, which encourages fruit rather than lush, leafy growth. A good organic source of this is wood ash. I keep all our ash from the indoor fireplaces and sprinkle it liberally around the plants in spring. It then leaches very quickly into the roots.

are usually about three cycles in a summer. The larvae can be knocked or shaken off the bushes, and *in extremis*, you can – and I have – use derris or pyrethrum powder which will kill them. But I don't like doing this. Derris and pyrethrum are chemical poisons, albeit sanctioned for organic use, and go against my basic principle of not using anything on food growing in the garden that would harm me if I were to ingest it in any quantity.

The other vital weapon in the war against sawfly is wind. Bushes should be exposed and well pruned so that air can ruffle readily through them. I have found that since we cleared some of the shelter from ours, the sawfly problem has lessened. I prune the bushes so that they stand off the ground on a "leg" – a short stem – and prune the centres

very hard so that the bushes form the shape of an open goblet. This helps.

I also grow gooseberries as cordons (*see overleaf*) and, very slowly, these are getting established and doing well, so far resisting sawfly attention and any form of mould (*see below*). The disadvantage of cordons is that each plant will bear a lot less fruit than a healthy bush. The advantage – other than health, is that they take up much less space. Swings and roundabouts.

Mould and mildew American gooseberry mildew presents itself as an ashy mould covering the fruit and crumpling the leaves. The fruit are still perfectly edible, but turn to mush when cooked so can only be used for jam. It is a fungus encouraged by the

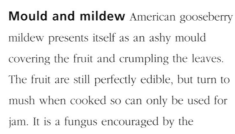

combination of dry air and poor drainage, and I now suspect that the recurring problem on some bushes and not others was due to very local drainage problems. I also think that it is endemic to certain plants and the secret – as ever – is to be ruthless and to get rid of any chronically under-performing plants. I was given three old bushes and took cuttings from these three and all have suffered from mildew. All will now go through the shredder and the healthy plants – 'Invicta' and 'Whitesmith', both bush and cordon – can carry the mantle.

Bush-whacked Finally, I wrote about my gooseberry problems in my weekly column for *The Observer*, and got an email from a reader who said that she never had any trouble from sawfly. Her grandmother used to chuck a bucket of wood ashes over the bushes as she passed (must have made the berries a bit gritty) and never saw a sawfly in her life. I was being too kind on the bushes, she said. I should stop pruning and mollycoddling them and let them have a bit of competition from weeds and a good dose of neglect. I suspect that she is right. All gardeners have the tendency to see their efforts as a battle against nature instead of an easy co-existence. But it is galling to see gooseberries grow and ripen, swelling into pickable perfection, and then find that a bird, insect, or disease has got to them first. You feel robbed.

Gooseberry cordons I had problems growing gooseberries because the plants were attacked first by sawflies and then by mould. But I then experimented with growing cordons.

Cordons are essentially a single stem grown vertically or trained diagonally. Their severely restricted form, which reduces foliage and branches to the minimum, allows a much greater exposure to air and light to the woody stem. This deters the sawflies, reduces the risk of the fungal infections that cause mould because any moisture evaporates more quickly, and gives the fruits the maximum sunshine in which to ripen. You can create your own cordons from hardwood cuttings taken in autumn, although most fruit nurseries will supply cordons ready trained. Half of mine were originally bushes that I pruned radically to just one leading shoot. This shoot is tied to a cane which, in turn, is supported by wires. For maximum ventilation it is best to grow cordons in open space but they can also be trained up a wall or fence. Let one sideshoot develop every 7–10cm (3–4in) and keep

these pruned back to two or three buds, removing any other sideshoots as they appear. The gooseberries grow on fruiting spurs and these should be reduced to half their length immediately after fruiting and pruned again in late winter to 2–3cm (about 1in).

Blackcurrants

Given the right conditions, blackcurrants are terribly easy to grow. They make wonderful puddings, sorbets, sponge puddings, jelly, and – most importantly of all – summer pudding.

It is almost impossible to buy a really good summer pudding, and extremely rare to find one in a restaurant, as almost invariably they are over-elaborated. The secret is in its sublime simplicity. As everyone (should) know, the essential ingredient for a summer pudding is blackcurrants. There is no other incentive needed to grow them.

Summer pudding Here is our recipe:

400g (14oz) raspberries

300g (10oz) blackcurrants

300g (10oz) redcurrants

125g (4–5oz) caster sugar

8 slices of day-old white bread

Do not be fooled by the proportions of the fruit – it is the blackcurrants that matter most. And never, never add strawberries. They will ruin it completely.

Put the raspberries in a large bowl. Top and tail the currants. To release their juices, cook the black and redcurrants, in separate saucepans with half the sugar in each, and just enough water to prevent them burning. Simmer for 2 minutes. Add the hot currants to the raspberries and mix them together.

Use a 1.5 litre (2½ pint) pudding bowl. Cut a circle of bread for the bottom and line the sides by overlapping the slices to cover completely. Pack the bowl with fruit and juice, keeping back a little of the juice. Put another circle of bread on to cover the top. Cover with a plate with a weight on top, and leave in the refrigerator for 24 hours.

Turn out onto a plate and pour the reserved juice onto any white patches of bread.

Varieties Blackcurrants are widely grown as a commercial crop around my part of Herefordshire, loving our rich soil and wet climate. It is a mistake to lump them in with other currants as they prosper only in really rich, fertile conditions, so dig in plenty of organic matter well before planting in early winter so that it rots well in. They like sunshine, but will happily tolerate a bit of shade. If you live in an area which is cold or prone to late frosts, try a later-flowering variety like 'Ben Lomond' or 'Ben More'. These will, of course, produce their fruit a bit later too.

Blackcurrants should be planted deeply, at least 1m (3ft) apart and preferably twice that for larger varieties like 'Ben Lomond'. 'Ben Sarek', which I also grow, is appreciably smaller so might be better for a small garden.

Once they are in the ground and heavily mulched you can pretty much forget about them until you harvest the great mass of glossy black berries, like caviar on steroids, attached to their "strigs" (the dangly bit that links fruit and wood). But if you do not net them as they ripen the birds will strip the entire crop.

Pruning As with all pruning, once you understand the growth and flowering pattern of the plant, everything is a matter of common sense. Blackcurrants fruit best on one-year-old wood. In practice this means that the best fruit is gained two years after pruning. The regime is to prune immediately after the fruit has been collected, which is by the end of July in this garden – or, even simpler, prune with the fruit still on and take whole branches indoors to

'Ben Sarek'

423

pick at the kitchen table. Although pruning can be left well into autumn without blowing the whole operation, doing it promptly gives the new wood the longest possible growing season. The bush will grow new shoots almost immediately which will bear some fruit the next year but burst into swags of currants the year after that.

There are two methods of pruning. In the simplest, which takes a few years to really get up and running well, you cut one in three bushes completely to the ground after fruiting, and then keep doing this in rotation every year. Thus in each summer one-third of the bushes (the ones pruned the previous year) will have young stems bearing a little fruit;

one-third (pruned two summers ago) will be positively groaning under the weight of the crop, and in the last, oldest third, fruiting will be slightly diminishing, and the bush thus ready for pruning. If you do this it follows that some of your bushes will be only minimally productive each year, so this method does depend on your having at least twice as many blackcurrant bushes as you need.

The second method is to prune one in three of the main branches from each bush each year. If you have fewer than six bushes this is the better approach. Take out the oldest ones, right to the base, as well as any crossing or awkward branches, leaving plenty of air and light for the new growth.

Mulching Blackcurrants are prodigiously hungry plants and will bear fruit in almost direct proportion to the amount of goodness that they are fed. The best way to feed them is to mulch generously every year, after pruning.

A mulch will also reduce competition for water and nutrients by suppressing weeds. A thick layer of organic matter will do this, as will landscape fabric, which lets moisture through but blocks light so that nothing will grow or germinate beneath it. I lay a strip of this fabric between rows and cut it back around each plant to allow space to pile on garden compost, in as thick a layer as possible. When it comes to blackcurrants, you cannot be too generous.

Whichever blackcurrant pruning method you choose – cutting back one in three bushes, or one in three stems on each bush – you should cut growth right back, close to the ground. You will almost certainly need loppers for old, thick branches. Whatever time you choose to prune, the wood will smell deliciously of the fruit as you cut.

Redcurrants and whitecurrants Whereas blackcurrants are quite different from redcurrants, redcurrants and whitecurrants are the same thing, but in different colours.

You can do different things with them in the kitchen, but as far as the grower is concerned they require identical treatment.

Redcurrants are remarkably undemanding to grow, and will quietly continue producing beautiful swags of translucent red berries for year after year. Redcurrant jelly – what my children call "lamb jam" – is very good with lamb or any game, and redcurrants are one of the essential components of summer pudding (*see* Blackcurrants, *previous page*). The juice is good as a setting agent for any jam and especially useful for raspberry jam as this has a tendency to be extra runny.

The main use of the slightly sharper whitecurrants used to be as "verjuice", before lemons were readily available. As the juice was clear it could be added without staining the rest of a liquid or dish.

Planting Plant these currants at at least the same spacing as blackcurrants, although they can be kept smaller with hard pruning. I grow red 'Laxton's No 1' which fruits early (which, in practice means early July) and 'Junifer' which is a new variety and also early but has the feature of producing fruit on one-year-old wood as well as the more usual two. Despite their reputation as one of the easiest fruits, I initially had great problems with my red- and whitecurrants and they suffered terribly from sawfly (*see* Gooseberries) which stripped the leaves and stunted growth – although it takes more than a sawfly to set back the bushes too much. But then I moved them to a more open and sunnier site, and they have never looked back. They will in fact live for years, often still growing in the overgrown ruins of a cottage garden, long after the cottage itself has fallen

Whitecurrants (these are 'White Versailles') differ from redcurrants only in their colour. They have a very acidic, clear juice, which before the availability of lemons was very useful in the kitchen.

into hopeless decay. But you will rarely see them hanging with great festoons of jewelly fruit as you would in a fruit cage, because the birds will have them as sure as night follows day. All currant-eating birds love a redcurrant above all others, so you have to provide some kind of protection for them whilst they are fruiting. We put up a fruit cage in June and take it down immediately after harvesting the currants, as our cats regard the trapped birds with the same greed as the birds do the fruit.

The bed we planted our currants in had previously been used for pumpkins and then artichokes, so it was well dug and manured, but all the evidence is that they will bear fruit perfectly well in poor soil and in almost total shade. They need room to grow and have plenty of air so a minimum of 1.5m (5ft)

Redcurrants are an essential component of summer pudding – indisputably the best dessert known to mankind – and make very good jelly, which is excellent with lamb or game as well as on bread and butter.

between each plant is needed. You can train currants into loose bushes, goblets, cordons, and even espaliers but I grow mine as open goblets (*see facing page*). This is mainly to improve ventilation, which in turn makes life uncomfortable for sawflies, but it also lets the sun into the bush and helps ripening.

Plant problems In rich soil and with fairly wide plant spacing, there will inevitably be a weed problem. It is said that nettles benefit currants, but this is not an experiment that I am eager to try. I get stung by enough nettles as it is without encouraging the blighters. The flowering annual *Limnanthes* (poached egg plant) is also said to help, both attracting pollinators and suppressing weeds, and I have thought of broadcasting seed beneath the bushes. As it is I hoe every ten days or so which is no great labour. An alternative would be to mulch with landscape fabric, as I do the blackcurrants, but as they are in a more prominent position I am resisting this utilitarian but aesthetically challenged solution.

The leaves often develop purple blisters that look disastrous but in fact have no influence on either the crop or the bush. They are the result of the currant blister aphid (*Cryptomyzus ribis*) at its work. I do nothing to deter it.

Pruning These currant bushes need summer pruning, rather like apples and pears, immediately after picking, but not too drastically – just to remove some of the surplus, soft new wood and encourage the remainder to ripen and harden. Cut the new shoots back by perhaps a third, then harder in winter to form a strong spur. The idea is to develop a strong permanent framework of branches with fruiting spurs growing off it.

Pruning redcurrants

Redcurrants fruit on short spurs growing from old wood, and pruning is necessary to shape them and to restrict new growth.

I like to grow my bushes on a "leg" – a short trunk that lifts the bush off the ground. I also try to create a goblet shape, with the outer branches cupping an empty space inside them. This allows for maximum ventilation and light, and makes the fruit much easier to pick. Once the shape is established, which takes a couple of years, all that is necessary is, in late winter or spring, to cut out all new growth that does not fit this shape, remove any damaged growth and shoots that cross each other or the centre of the bush, and shorten each side branch from the main framework by about 15cm (6in) – this encourages the buds that remain to grow into fruiting spurs.

Index

Page numbers in *italic* refer to the illustrations

a

Acacia 20
Acanthus 21, 197
 A. spinosa 198
Acer 24
 A. campestre 107
  A.c. 'Postelense' 107
  A.c. 'Schwerinii' 107
 A. griseum 107
 A. palmatum 107
  A.p. 'Dissectum Atropurpureum' 107
 A. platanoides 107
 A. saccharinum 107
 A. saccharum 107
Achillea 21, 169, 207
acid-loving plants 30–1
acid rain 22
acid soils 14–15, 31
aconites 143, 144, 144
Aconitum 'Newry Blue' 172
acorn squashes 311
African blue lily 21
Agapanthus 21, 72, 197
Agrostemma 25
Agrostis castellana 378
Ajuga 207
 A. reptans 24, 206
Alcea rosea 185
Alchemilla mollis 108, 109, 204, 204, 207
alder 106, 106, 139
algae, in ponds 22
Algerian iris 147
alkaline soils 14, 30–1
Allium 155, 170, 197
 A. aflatunense 155
 A. christophii 155
 A. giganteum 155, 163
 A. 'Purple Sensation' 154, 155, 168
 A. schoenoprasum 371, 371
 A. schubertii 154, 155
 A. sphaerocephalon 154, 155

Alnus cordata 106, 106
 A. glutinosa 106
alpine strawberries 416, 416
Alstroemeria 21, 207
altitude, temperature and 25–6
American gooseberry mildew 421–2
American walnut 397
anchusa 172
Anemone 143
 A. blanda 143
 A. x hybrida 207
 A. nemorosa 112
Anethum graveolens 351, 351
Angelica 233, 351, 351
 A. archangelica 351, 351
 A. gigas 170
animal manure 46–53
annual weeds 76, 77
annuals 176–87
 climbers 186
 for damp soil 184
 hardiness 24, 25
 scent 187
 in shade 187
 sowing 178–9
 tall annuals 185
Anthemis 207
aphids 76
 companion planting 17
 honeydew 110
 lettuce root aphids 293
 predators 82
apple mint 366, 366
apples 308, 377, 380–1, 382–90, 383–90
 orchards 375, 376, 383
 planting 388–90
 pollination 384–5, 390
 pruning 389
 rootstocks 384, 385–8
 staking 390
 storing 383
 varieties 383–4, 385, 388
apricots 381
Aquilegia 141
 A. vulgaris 207

Armoracia rusticana 370, 370
arrow bamboo 193
Artemisia 20, 21, 207
 A. dracunculoides 363
 A. dracunculus 363, 363
 A. schmidtiana 207
artichokes 163, 164, 278, 278–9, 329
artificial mulches 54, 56–7
Arundinaria japonica 193
ash, as natural fertilizer 57, 61
ash trees 24, 106–7, 106, 113, 139
asparagus 255, 256, 257–9, 258–9
aspect 19–20
Aster 16
 A. novi-belgii 203
Astilbe 206
 A. rivularis 206
Astrantia 207
 A. major 206
Atriplex hortensis 179, 184
aubergines 67, 73, 317, 317
autumn
 autumn colour 104
 vegetables 308–27
azaleas 31

b

Bacillus thuringiensis 84
bacteria, in soil 28
balling, roses 224
bamboos 193, 201, 204, 217, 233
bark, coloured 226–8
bark, crushed 66
basil 17, 70, 71, 343, 345, 348–9, 348–9
Batavian lettuces 293
"batter", hedges 114
bay trees 24, 353, 360, 360
bean chocolate spot 288
beans
 crop rotation 248
 sowing 67
  see also individual types of bean
bearded irises 156
bear's breeches 21

bedding plants 21
beds and borders 134–5
 box hedging around 120
 digging 32
 herbaceous perennials 200–7
 planning 93
 raised beds 35, 243–4, 244
 vegetable gardens 241, 243–4
beech 24, 116, 119
beetles 83
beetroot 249, 254, 300, 300–1
Bellis perennis 206
bells-of-Ireland 176
berries 229
Betula 24
Bidens 207
biennials 176–87
 for damp soil 184
 hardiness 24, 25
 scent 187
 in shade 187
 tall biennials 185
biological pest control 333
birch trees 24
birds 80, 134, 419, 428
black-eyed Susan 185
black kale 'Cavolo Nero' 331, 331, 332, 332
black pine 24
blackberries 413
blackcurrants 410–11, 423–4, 423–5
blackfly 80, 288
blackspot 224
blanching celery 313, 314
blight
 potato 15, 251, 296, 299, 414
 tomato 15, 283
blood, dried 59
blood, fish and bone 60
blossom 380, 392–3, 404
blossom end rot 58, 283
bluebells 112, 139, 207
bog plants 205, 206
bonemeal 59
borage 61, 196, 351, 351
Borago officinalis 351, 351
borders see beds and borders
boron, natural fertilizers 58

botrytis 417

box
in containers 27, 74
cuttings 67, *68*, 72, *121*
hedges 24, *115*, 120–2, 164, 172
soil 31
topiary *124*, 126–7, *126*, *127*

box psyllids 127

Brachyglottis 'Sunshine' 20

Brachyscome iberidifolia 21

brandlings 43, *43*

brassicas
crop rotation 248
pests 84
*see also individual types of
brassica*

brick
paths *95*, 96, 97, *97*
walls 98–9, *99*

broad beans 268, 285–8, *285–8*
growing conditions 285–8
pests and diseases 80, 288
sowing 254
watering 251

broccoli 248, 255, 260–1, *260*

bronze fennel 172, *172*, 362

broom 20

brown rot 393

brugmansia 69

Brunnera 207

buckler-leaved sorrel 265

Buddleja 217
B. davidii 20, 24

bugle 24

bulbs 142–61
hardiness, 25
planting 142–3
potting compost 67
spring bulbs 149–53
summer bulbs 155–61
winter bulbs 144–7

bullaces 391, *391*

busy lizzies 176

butterfly bush 20, 24

butterhead lettuces 292

Buxus sempervirens 120
B.s. 'Aureovariegata' 120
B.s. 'Elegantissima' 120
B.s. 'Gold Tip' 120

B.s. 'Handsworthiensis' *115*, 120
B.s. 'Latifolia Maculata' 120
B.s. 'Suffruticosa' 120

C

cabbage white butterfly 17, 84,
84, *85*, 261, 332–3, *333*, 360

cabbages 255, *330–3*, 331–3, 347
crop rotation 248
diseases 333
growing conditions 331
growing from seed 331
pests 332–3
planting 331–2, *332*
watering 250
winter cabbage 331

cacti 69

calabrese 261, *261*

calcium 31, 58

Calendula 179
C. officinalis 183, 184, *184*

Callicarpa bodinieri var. *giraldii*
229

Camellia 24, 31, 210, 212, 217

Campanula lactiflora 206

canary creeper *186*

candytuft 21

canker 393, 405, 407–8, *407*

carbon, in compost heaps 44

cardboard, in compost heaps 44

cardoons 24, 163, *164*, 169, 190,
200

Carex buchananii 190
C. comans 171
C.c. 'Bronze Form' 190, *190*
C. flagellifera 171, 190
C. hachijoensis 'Evergold' 190
C. kaloides 171

carpet, as mulches 57

carrot fly 17, 87, 295, 350, 371

carrots 294–5, *294–5*, 345
crop rotation 249
pests 295
sowing 254, 295
varieties 294
watering 251

Castanea sativa 400

Catalogna chicory 324

"catch" crops *249*

caterpillars 23, 84, 261, 332–3,
333

catmint 21

cattle manure 46–8

cauliflowers 248

Ceanothus 210
C. 'Autumnal Blue' 210
C. 'Gloire de Versailles' 217
C. impressus 210

cedars 24, 103

celeriac 245, 268, 315–16, *315–16*
crop rotation 248
sowing 67, 315–16
watering 73, 269

celery 245, 313–14, *313*
blanching 313, *314*
crop rotation 248
sowing 67

Centaurea cyanus 25

Cerinthe 177
C. major 'Purpurascens' 172

Chaenomeles 211
C. japonica 401

chalky soil 30–1, 353

chard *173*, 249, *253*, 255, 318,
318–19

Cheiranthus 'Blood Red' 21, 163,
165 (see *Erysimum*)

cherries 209, 211
flowering cherries 103, 199
wild cherries *102*

chervil 345

chestnut, horse *105*

chestnut, sweet 113, 400

chestnut fences 100, *101*

chicken 49–53, *172*, 377

chicken manure 49, *51*

chicory 67, *85*, 255, *290*, 322–5,
322–5, 337

chilli peppers 317, *317*

Chimonanthus praecox 210,
226
C.p. 'Luteus' 210

Chinese cabbage, crop rotation
248

"chitting" potatoes *298*

chives 17, 343, *365*, 371, *371*

chocolate cosmos 170

Choisya ternata 217

Chrysanthemum parthenium
363, *363*
C.p. 'Aureum' 363

Cirsium rivulare 206

citrus trees 69

clay soil 21, 30

claytonia 337

Clematis 31, 171, 209, 212,
213–15
C. alpina 141, *209*, 213, *213*
C.a. 'Albiflora' 213
C.a. 'Burford White' 213
C.a. 'Constance' 213
C.a. 'Jacqueline du Pré' 213
C.a. 'Pamela Jackman' 213
C.a. 'Ruby' 213
C. armandii 210
C. cirrhosa 210
C. 'Etoile Violette' 170, 215
C. 'Gypsy Queen' 213
C. 'Honora' 213, *214*
C. 'Jackmanii' 170, 210, 215
C. 'Jackmanii Superba' 213,
215
C. macropetala 197, 211, 213,
213
C. 'Madame Julia Correvon'
210, 215
C. montana 211
C.m. var. *rubens* 'Elizabeth'
213
C. 'Moonlight' 211
C. 'Niobe' *208*, 215
C. 'Perle d'Azur' 170, 213
C. viticella 25, 189, *208*, 215
C.v. 'Purpurea Plena
Elegans' 170, 215

clematis wilt 215

climbers 209–15
annuals 186
caring for 209
choosing 210–12
clematis 213–15
French beans 305, *305*
hardiness, 25

cloches *252*, 417–19, *419*

clubroot 58, 261, 333

cob nuts 309, 396, *400*

Cobbett, William 259

cobble paths 96, *96*
cocksfoot 378
cocoa shell mulches 55, *55*
coir 65
coir-7s 65, *66*, *178*
colchicums 143
cold frames *70*, *72*, *252*, 253
cold weather *see* frost
colours
  autumn colour *104*
  Jewel Garden 135, 169–72
  sun and 20
  Walled Garden 135
  winter shrubs 226–8
comfrey 61, 233, *365*, 369, *369*
common bent 378
companion planting 17, *17*, 81–2
compost 42–4, *246–7*
  animal manure 46–8
  comfrey leaves 369
  compost bins 42–3, *42*
  grass cuttings 41, 378–9
  as a mulch 54
  as potting compost 66
  weeds in 76
compost mixes 64–5
  coir 65–6
  for cuttings 67
  for vegetables 252–3
concrete paths 98
containers
  herbs in 353
  lilies in *158*
  wind protection 74
contorted willow 235, *235*
coppices *112*, 113, 135
cordons
  gooseberries 421, *422*
  tomatoes 280–2, *281*, *282*
coriander 345, 349, *349*
Coriandrum sativum 349
  C.s. 'Morocco' 349
corms 143
corn cockle 25, 176
corn marigolds 176
corn salad 336–7
cornflowers 25, 172, 176, 179
Cornus 217
  C. alba 228

C.a. 'Kesselringii' 228
  C.a. 'Sibirica' 228
  C. stolonifera 'Flaviramea' 228
corydalis 143
Corylopsis 217
Corylus avellana 217, 396
  C. maxima 396
cos lettuces *289*, 291–2, *291*, 337, *337*
Cosmos 176, 177, *178*
  C. atrosanguineus 170
  C. bipinnatus 185, *185*
    C.b. 'Purity' 185, *196*, *197*
Cotinus coggygria 20
Cotoneaster 20, 211, 229
  C. horizontalis 229
cotton lavender 20
courgettes 302, *302*
cow parsley 82
cowslips *139*, 153
crab apples 384
crambe 197
cranesbills 21, 24
Crataegus 24
  C. monogyna 123, 229
crested dog's tail 378
crisphead lettuces 293
Crocosmia 16, 155, 159, 170, 183
  C. 'Emily Mackenzie' 159
  C. 'Lucifer' 159, *159*, *173*
  C. masoniorum 159
  C. paniculata 159
Crocus 25, 141, 143, 146, *146*
  C. laevigatus 146, *146*
  C. tommasinianus 139
crop rotation 248–9, *248–9*, 273, 347
crown imperial 153, *153*
Crump, William 384
cucumber mosaic virus 303
cucumbers 65, 69, 303, *303*
cultivation 32–5, *33–5*
currant blister aphid 428
cutting tools 40–1
cuttings 67–8, *121*
Cyclamen 143
Cydonia oblonga 401
Cynara cardunculus 207

Cynosurus cristatus 378

d

Dactylis glomerata 378
daffodils 139, 142, 143, 149
Dahlia 16, 68, 143, 155, 160–1, *161*, 183
  D. 'Arabian Night' 160–1
  D. 'Bishop of Llandaff' 160–1, *168*, *173*
Damp Garden 133, 135, 230–5, *230–5*
damp soil, annuals and biennials 184
damping off, seedlings 67
damson cheese 392, *392*
damsons 139, 199, 381, 391–2, *392*
Daphne 217
  D. laureola 217
  D. mezereum 217
dead nettle 24
Delphinium 68, 172, 189
  D. 'Black Knight' *205*
  D. 'King Arthur' *205*
derris 84, 421
Deschampsia flexuosa 190
design 90–3
  vegetable gardens 242–5
Dianthus 21
  D. barbatus 21, 170
Dicentra spectabilis 207
digging *29*, 32–5, *33–4*, 202
Digitalis 207
  D. ferruginea 171, 189
  D. purpurea alba 109
    D.p. f. *albiflora* 177, 187, *187*
dill 82, 343, 345, 351, *351*
Dipsacus fullonum 234
  D. sativus 184
diseases 16
  broad beans 288
  cabbages 333
  crop rotation 248
  cucumbers 303
  lettuces 294
  roses 224
  tomatoes 283, *283*
  vegetables 269

division, perennials 202
dock 77, 265
dog violets *112*
dogwood 228
dolomitic lime 60
doors *95*
downy mildew 294
drainage 21, 22
  grass paths 96, 97–8
  yew hedges 122–3
drought 20, 21, 27, 74, 207
dry areas, plants for 20, 21, 207
ducks 53
Dutch hoes 78, *79*, *250*
dwarf French beans 304, *304*

e

early potatoes 296–7
earthing up
  leeks 335
  potatoes 299
earthworms 30, 80, 86, 134
earwigs 161
east-facing walls 20, 211–12
Eccremocarpus scaber 210
Echinacea 16, *169*, 189
  E. purpurea 203, *204*
Echinops 21, 207
  E. ritro 24, *197*
eggs, keeping poultry 49–51
Elaeagnus 20, 217
elder, golden 217, *217*
electricity, in greenhouses 72
endive 71, 254, 324–5, *325*
English lavender 357
Eranthis 143
  E. hyemalis 25, 144, *144*
eremurus 197
Erigeron 206
Eryngium 21, 207
Erysimum 'Blood Red' 21, 163, *165*
  (see *Cheiranthus*)
Escallonia 'Iveyi' 210
eschscholzia 179
espaliers *245*, *404*, *406*, *408*
Eucalyptus 20
Euonymus 20, 24
  E. fortunei var. *radicans* 211
Eupatorium purpureum 206

Euphorbia 21, *138*, 141
  E. characias 207
  E. griffithii 'Fireglow' *173*
  E. palustris 206
  E. polychroma *203*
  E. robbiae 207
evening primrose 21, 81–2, 184, 187, *187*
evergreens
  climbers 210
  hardiness 24
  hedges 116
  trees 103
  wind damage 27

f

Fagus 24
farmyard manure 46–9
Fatsia 217
fences *95*, 100–1, *100–1*, 113
fennel *168*, 197, *361*, 362, *362*
  beneficial insects and 17, 82
  bronze 172, *172*, 362
  seeds 343
  see also Florence fennel
fertilizers 81
  natural fertilizers 57–61
fescue, red 378
Festuca glauca 170, 190, 192
  F.g. 'Blue Fox' 192
  F. rubra 378
feverfew 363, *363*
Ficus 20, 210
figs 20, *196*, 199, 209, 381, 394, *394–5*
filberts 396
Filipendula 204
  F. rubra 206
fireblight 381, 403
firethorn 229
flame-guns, weeding with *77*
flea beetle 262, *263*
flooding 135, 139, 233, 242–3
Florence fennel 320–1, *320–1*, 362
flowers 130–235
  annuals and biennials 176–87
  bulbs 142–61
  organic gardening 16–17

Foeniculum 207
  F. vulgare 362, *362*
    F.v. purpureum 362
foliage
  autumn colour *104*
  dried by winds 27
  drought-tolerant plants 207
forcing rhubarb *266*
forget-me-nots 81–2, 141, 177, *184*, 187, 197
forks 38, *38*
formers, topiary 124
Forsythia suspensa 211
fountain grass 192
foxes 50
foxgloves 109, 171, 177, 187, *187*, 189
foxtail lilies *158*
Fragaria alpina 416
  F. chiloensis 416
  F. vesca 416
  F. virginiana 416
Fraxinus 24
  F. angustifolia 'Raywood' 106, *106*
  F. excelsior 106
freezing vegetables 271
French beans 309
  climbing beans 305, *305*
  in cold frames 253
  dwarf beans 304, *304*
  seedlings 67
  watering 251
French lavender 357
French sorrel 265
French tarragon 363, *363*
Fritillaria imperialis 153, *153*
  F.i. 'Rubra' 153
  F. meleagris 153, *153*
fritillaries *139*, 141, 143, 153
frost 18, 22–5, 27, 212, 328–9
fruit 372–429
  orchard fruit 380–409
  rootstocks 375, 384, 385–8
  soft fruit 410–29
  see also individual types of fruit
Fuchsia 217

g

gages 209
Galanthus 25
  G. nivalis 144, *144*
garlic *245*, 329, 343, 345–7, *346–7*
  companion planting 17
  crop rotation 249
  planting *346*
  storing 347, *347*
Garrya elliptica 211, 217
Genista 20
Gentiana 206
Geranium 21, 72, *138*, 141
  G. 'Ann Folkard' *173*, 189
  G. endressii 24
  G. phaeum 207
  G. sanguineum 24
Geum 'Borisii' 206
  G. 'Mrs Bradshaw' 170
Ginkgo biloba 24
gladioli 143, 155, 160, *160*
gladiolus thrip 160
Gleditsia 20
globe artichokes 278, *278–9*, 329
globe thistles 21, 24
glyphosate 75
golden marjoram 359
golden willow 228
gooseberries 410, 411, 420–2, *420–2*
  American gooseberry mildew 421–2
  cordons 421, *422*
  pests 84, 420–1, 422
gooseberry sawfly 420–1
grafting, apples 385–8
grape hyacinths 25
grass
  composting 41, 43, 44, 378–9
  cutting tools 40–1
  digging up grassland 32–5
  lawns 94–6, 199
  mowing 41
  in orchards 375, 376, *377–9*, 378–9
  ornamental grasses 170, 171, *188–93*, 189–93
  paths 94–6, *94*, 242

planting bulbs in 142
temperature and 23
gravel mulches 56
green manures 45, 243
greengages 391
greenhouses 68–72, *69–71*, 73
grit, improving soil 30
guinea fowl 53
gum trees 20
gunnera 205

h

half-hardy plants 24, 176–7
Hamamelis mollis 217
hardening off *178*, 253
hardiness 24–5
hardwood cuttings 68
haricot beans 304
hawthorn 24
  berries 229
  hedges 116, 123, *123*
  topiary 126
hay 379
hazel
  coppices 113, 139
  fences *95*, 113, 242, *243*
  hurdles 27, 100–1, *100*
  nuts 381, 396, *396–9*
heathers 31
Hebe 20
Hedera 211
hedge-cutters 41, 114, *116*, 127–8
hedgehogs 83
hedges 114–23
  cutting 114–16, *116*
  "hedges-on-stilts" 119
  planning 92–3
  planting 116, *117*
  snow damage 26
  weeds in 75
  as windbreaks 26
  woven fences and 113
Helenium *169*, 189, 206
  H. 'Moerheim Beauty' 171, *203*
Helianthus 177, 179, 183
  H. annuus 185
    H.a. 'Lemon Queen' 185
    H.a. 'Russian Giant' 185

H.a. 'Velvet Queen' 185, *185*
Helictotrichon sempervirens 170
Helleborus 24, *138*, 139, *146*, 201
  H. argutifolius 141
  H. corsicus 207
  H. foetidus 140–1, 207
  H. niger 140
  H. nigercors 141
  H. orientalis *139*, 140, 141, 207
  H. viridis 141
Hemerocallis 206
henhouses *51*, 52
Henry Doubleday Research
  Association 61
herb Robert 139
herbaceous perennials 16, 24,
  200–7
herbs 197, 339–71
  annual herbs 345–51
  cooking with 343
  growing conditions 353
  medicinal uses 342–3, 365
  perennial Mediterranean herbs
    352–63, 353–63
  perennial non-Mediterranean
    herbs 365–71
  see also individual herbs
Hesperis matronalis 25, 187
Het Loo, Holland 119
Heuchera 206
Hidcote, Gloucestershire 119
hips, rose 224, 229, *229*
hoeing weeds 78, *79*, 250
hoes 39, *39*
Holcus lanatus 378
holly 24, 103, 139
  in containers 27
  hedges 116, 123
  topiary 126, 164
hollyhocks 185, 189
honesty 187, 233, *233*
honeydew 110
honeysuckle 25, *208*, 209, 226
hoof and horn 60
hormone rooting powder 68
hornbeam hedges *115*, 116, *116*,
  118, 119–20, 141, 169, 172, 233
horse manure 49
horseradish 343, 345, *364*, *365*,

370, *370*
Hosta 16, 74, 206, 207, *232*, 233,
  233
  H. 'Frances Williams' 233
  H. sieboldiana var. *elegans* 233
  H. 'Snowden' 233
  H. 'Sum and Substance' 233
hot beds 259
hoverflies 17, 76, 82
hurdles 27, 100–1, *100*
Hyacinthoides non-scripta 112
Hydrangea macrophylla 'Lanarth
  White' *216*
  H. petiolaris 25, 211, *211*
Hypericum 20, 217
hyssop 345, 360, *360*
Hyssopus officinalis 360, *360*
  H.o. f. *albus* 360
  H.o. f. *roseus* 360, *360*

i

Iberis umbellata 21
'Iceberg' lettuces 289, 293
Ilex 24
  I. aquifolium 123
Impatiens 187
Imperata cylindrica 'Rubra' 190,
  192
insects, beneficial 17, 76, 82
  see also pests
insulation
  cold frames 72
  greenhouses 72
Inula 204
  I. magnifica 206
Ipomoea tricolor (morning
  glory) *186*
Iris 143
  I. 'Cantab' 147
  I. chrysographes 156
  I. clarkei 156
  I. 'Eternal Waltz' *157*
  I. forrestii 156
  I. 'Gingerbread Man' *157*
  I. histrioides 156
  I. 'Kent Pride' *157*
  I. reticulata 147, *147*, 156
  I. sibirica 24, 156, *156*
  I. unguicularis 25, 147

I.u. 'Mary Barnard' *147*
I. 'Wild Ginger' 172
Irish yew 123
iron, natural fertilizers 58
irrigation *73*, 74
Italian alder 106, *106*
ivy 211

j

Jasminum (jasmine) 24
  J. beesianum 210
  J. nudiflorum 24, 211, 217
  J. officinale 210
  J. polyanthum 210
Jerusalem artichokes 26
Jewel Garden 132–3, 135,
  166–75, *167–74*
Juglans nigra 397
  J. regia 396

k

kale 331
Kerria japonica 24, 217
kirpi *39*
Knautia macedonica 170, 206
Kniphofia 21, 189, 207
knives 40
kohlrabi 248
Korean angelica *351*

l

labels, sowing seeds 67
laburnum *168*, 169
lambs' ears 207
lamb's lettuce 336–7
Lamium 207
  L. maculatum 24
land cress 71, 248, 254, 263, *263*
landscape fabric, under paths
  244, *244*
Lathyrus latifolius 211
  L. odoratus 186, *186*
Laurus nobilis 360, *360*
laurustinus 226
Lavandula (lavender) 20, 31, 353,
  356–7, *356–7*
  L. angustifolia 357
    L.a. 'Alba' 357
    L.a. 'Hidcote' 357, *357*

L.a. 'Jean Davis' 357
  L.a. 'Munstead' 357
  L.a. 'Nana Alba' 357
  L.a. 'Rosea' 357
  L. dentata 357
    L.d. var. *candicans 357*
    L.d. var. *candicans* 'Helmsdale'
      357
  L. lanata 357
  L. 'Sawyers' *357*
  L. stoechas 357
lawns *see* grass
leaching, nutrients 31
leaf curl, tomatoes 283, *283*
leafmould 55, *55*, *56*, *103*, 207
leeks 249, 255, 334–5, *334–5*
legumes
  crop rotation 248
  green manures 45
  nitrogen-fixing 45, 57
  watering 251
lemon balm 363, *363*
lemon thyme 355
lemon verbena 187
Leonotis 16, 171, 177, 185, *185*
lettuce grey mould 294
lettuce root aphids 293
lettuces 268, 289–94, *289–93*
  in cold frames 253
  crop rotation 249
  early lettuces 264, *264*
  in greenhouses 71, *71*
  growing conditions 289–91
  pests and diseases 81, 269,
    293–4
  preparing for table *292*
  sowing 67, 254
  varieties 291–3
  watering *71*, 73, 250, 269
  winter lettuces 337
Leucojum 143
Levisticum officinale 362, *362*
Leymus arenarius 190
light 132
Ligularia 74, 171, 233
  L. dentata 206, 233
    L. d. 'Desdemona' 233
  L. przewalskii 206, 233, *233*
  L. 'The Rocket' 233

Lilium (lilies) 31, 65, 143, 156–8, 169, 197
  L. candidum 158
  L. martagon 158
  L. 'Red Night' *158*
  L. regale 25, *156*, 158, *198*
lily-of-the-valley 143
lime, adding to soil 31, 60
lime trees 24, 141
  pleaching 110–11, *110–11*, 163, 172, 240–1
Lime Walk *108*, 109
Limnanthes 428
  L. douglasii 21, 184
Lippia citriodora 187
liquid fertilizers 61
loam 28–9
Lobelia 206
Long Garden *162*, 163–4, *164–5*
Lonicera 217
  L. x americana 211
  L. fragrantissima 210, 211, 217, 226, *226*
  L. nitida 126
  L. periclymenum 25, 210
    L.p. 'Belgica' 210
    L.p. 'Graham Thomas' 211
    L.p. 'Serotina' 210
    L. purpusii 226
    L. standishii 226
  L. x tellmanniana 211
loose-leaf lettuces 293, *293*
lovage *198*, 234, 343, 345, *361*, 362, *362*
love-in-a-mist 25
Lunaria annua 187, *233*
lungwort 24
lupins 31, 201, 204
Lychnis chalcedonica 206
  L. coronaria 171, *173*
Lyme grass 190
Lysichiton americanus 205
Lysimachia 206, 207
Lythrum 189, 206
  L. salicaria 206

m
machetes *39*
Macleaya 16, 170, 190

M. cordata 204
Madonna lilies 158
magnesium, natural fertilizers 58
Magnolia 210, 217
  M. grandiflora 210
Mahonia 24, 217
  M. japonica 217
maidenhair trees 24
Malcolmia maritima 21
mangetout 273
manure 46–53
maples 24, *102*, 107, 139
marigolds *168*, *169*, 179, *179*, *180*, 183, 184
marjoram 343, 359, *359*, *361*
marmalade 402
marrows 302
Matthiola incana 187
meadows 40–1, 189, 378
mechanical tools 41
medicinal uses, herbs 342–3, 365
Mediterranean herbs *352–63*, 353–63
medlars 381
melianthus 24, 72, 170, 190
Melica altissima 'Atropurpurea' 192
Melissa officinalis 363
  M.o. 'Aurea' 363, *363*
melons 67
Mentha x piperita 343, *366*, 367
  M. spicata 366–7, *366*
  M. suaveolens 366, *366*
mibuna 71, 248, 254, 263, *263*, 337
mice 86
micro-climates 21
micro-organisms, in soil 28, 29
mildew
  American gooseberry mildew 421–2
  downy mildew 294
  powdery mildew 224, 303
Mimulus 184, 187
minerals
  fertilizers 57–60
  in weeds 76
mint 343, *365*, 366–7, *366–7*
Miscanthus nepalensis 190

M. var. purpurascens 191
M. sinensis 'Goldfeder' 190
  M.s. malpartus 190
  M.s. 'Morning Light' 190
  M.s. 'Silberfeder' 190, *191*
  M.s. 'Strictus' 190
  M.s. 'Zebrinus' 190, *191*
mist propagators 67, 68
mizuna 71, 248, 254, 337
mock orange 20, 24
moles 84–6
monarda 189
monkey flower 187
monoculture 15, 17, 81, 244
Morello cherries 211
morning glory *186*
mortar, walls 98, 99
mosaic leaf virus, on tomatoes *283*
mowers 41
mulches 54–7, *54–6*
  for blackcurrants *424*
  hedges 116
  perennials 202, *202*
  watering and 74
  weed control 77–8, *79*
mulleins 21, 189, *197*
Muscari 25
mushroom compost, mulches 55
Myosotis 184, 187
myrobalans 391

n
Narcissus bulbocodium 149, *149*
  N. cyclamineus 143, *148*, 149
  N. jonquilla 149
  N. 'Lemon Glow' 149
  N. minor 149
  N. 'Portrush' 149
  N. 'Rip van Winkle' 149
  N. 'Rockall' 149
  N. 'Sweetness' 149
  N. 'Tête-à-tête' 149, *149*
  N. 'Trevithian' 149
  N. 'Tutankhamun' 149
nasturtiums 177, 179–81, *180*
nematodes 84
Nepeta 197
  N. x faassenii 21

netting, over strawberries 419
nettles 61, *61*, 76, 428
Nicotiana 176, 177, 187
  N. alata 21, 187
  N. sylvestris 109
Nigella 25, 172, 176, 179
nitrogen 379
  animal manure 48, 49
  in compost heaps 44
  crop rotation 248
  green manures 45
  natural fertilizers 57–8
  in rainfall 22
north-facing walls 211
Norway maple 107
Norway spruce 24
nurseries 64
nuts 396–400, *396–400*

o
oak trees 20, 24, 103, 105, *105*, 113
Ocimum basilicum 348
Oenothera 21
  O. biennis 187, *187*
offsets, artichokes 278
onion fly 275
onions 274–7, *275–7*
  crop rotation 249
  growing conditions 274–5
  sets 275, *275*
  sowing 254
  storing 277, *277*
  watering 251
Onopordum 177, 190, *198*
  O. acanthium 185
Ophiopogon planiscapus 'Nigrescens' 173, *190*
orache, purple *168*, *169*, 170, *175*, 179, *180*, 181, *182*, 183, 184
orange trees *196*
orchards 375, 380–409
  grass in 375, 376, *377–9*, 378–9
orchids 143
organic matter, improving soil 29
Origanum majorana 359
  O. onites 359, *359*

O. vulgare 359
  O.v. 'Aureum' 359, *359*
  O.v. 'Gold Tip' 359
Osmanthus 217
  O. decorus 217
Osmunda regalis 233, *233*
overcrowding 17
oxalic acid, in rhubarb 267

p

Pacific Coast irises 156
Panicum miliaceum 'Violaceum' 192
  P. virgatum 188
  P.v. 'Hänse Herms' 192
Papaver orientale 21
  P.o. 'Ladybird' *183*
  P.o. 'Patty's Plum' 171, *183*
  P. rhoeas 25
  P. somniferum 182–3
paperbark maple 107
parsley 254, 343, 345, 350, *350*
parsnips 255, 268, 336, *336*
  crop rotation 249
  sowing 254
  watering 251
Parthenocissus quinquefolia 211
paths
  brick paths *95*, 96, 97, *97*
  cobble paths 96, *96*
  grass paths 94–6, *94*, 242, *379*
  planning 92, 93, 94–8
  Spring Garden 139–40, *140*
  stone paths 96, *96*, 98
  in vegetable gardens 241, 242, *243*, 244
  wood chip paths 244–5, *244*
pea sticks 255, 272, *272*
peaches 381
pears 308, 380, 381, *404–9*, *405–9*
  canker 405, 407–8, *407*
  espaliers *245*, *404*, 408
  rootstocks 405
  storing 408–9
  weeping pears 169, *205*
peas 268, *270–3*, 271–3
  crop rotation 248, 273
  growing conditions 271–2

saving seed 273
sowing 67
supporting 272, *272*
varieties 273
watering 251
peat 63–4
peat soil 31
pebble mulches 56
pelargoniums 65
penknives 40
Pennisetum alopecuroides
  'Hameln' 192
Penstemon 21, 24
  P. 'Garnet' 170
peonies 201
peppermint 343, 366, *366*, 367
peppers 65, 69, 248
  chilli peppers 317, *317*
perennial weeds 77, 78
perennials 200–7
  division 202
  dry soil 207
  hardiness 24
  shade 207
  supports 204
  wet conditions 206
Perovskia 20
pesto, recipe *348*, 349
pests 16, 80–7, 269
  biological control 333
  broad beans, 288
  cabbages, 332–3
  carrots, 295
  companion planting 17
  crop rotation 248
  cucumbers, 303
  lettuces, 293
  predators 80–1
  tomatoes, 283
Petroselinum crispum var. neapolitanum 350
pH values
  acid rain 22
  soil 31, 60, 76
phacelia 179
pheasant grass 189, *191*
Philadelphus 20, 24
phlox 204
Phormium tenax 206

phosphates (phosphorus)
  animal manure 48, 49
  natural fertilizers 58
Phyllostachys aurea 233
  P. aureosulcata 193, *193*
  P. bambusoides 193
  P. nigra 193, *193*, 233
Picea abies 24
pine trees 24, 103
Pinus nigra 24
planning gardens 90–3
  vegetable gardens 242–5
plantain lily *233*
planting
  apple trees 388–90
  bulbs 142–3
  cabbages 331–2, *332*
  clematis 215
  climbers 209
  garlic *346*
  hedges 116, *117*
  potatoes 297–8, *297*
  raspberries 413–14
  trees 104
pleaching
  hornbeam 119
  limes 110–11, *110–11*, 163, 172, 240–1
Pleioblastus 'Gauntlettii' 193
  P. pygmaeus 193
plug plants, coir-7s 65, *66*
plum fruit moth 393
plum leaf-curling aphid 393
plums 199, 209, 381, 391, *391*, 392–3, *393*
Poa pratensis 378
poached egg plant 21, 184, 428
pollination, apples 384–5, *390*
Polygonum bistorta 234
polypropylene mulches *54*, 56–7
poppies 81–2, *168*, 170, *170*, *173*, 176, 179
  opium poppies 176, 179, *179*, *180*, 182–3, *183*, 197
  oriental poppies 21, *174*, *183*, 204
  Shirley poppies 25
potash (potassium)
  animal manure 48, 49

comfrey liquid 369
natural fertilizers 58
potatoes 268, 296–9, *296–9*
  blight 15, 251, 296, 299, 414
  "chitting" *298*
  crop rotation 249
  early potatoes 255
  earthing up 299
  planting 297–8, *297*
  preparing soil 298–9
  varieties 296–7
  watering 251
Potentilla 169
  P. fruticosa 20
potting composts *see* compost mixes
potting sheds *62*, 63
poultry 49–53
powdery mildew 224, 303
primroses 24, *112*, *138*, 139, 141, 207
Primula 206, 233
  P. vulgaris 24, *112*
privet, topiary 126
propagation 63–8
  cuttings 67–8
  division 202
  potting composts 63–6, 67
  sowing seeds 66–7
pruning
  apple trees *389*
  blackcurrants 423–4, *425*
  coppices 113
  damsons and plums 393
  espaliers *406*
  figs 394
  pleaching limes 110–11, *110–11*, 163, 172, 240–1
  raspberries 414, *415*
  redcurrants 428, *429*
  roses *225*
  shredding prunings 56
  shrubs 217
  topiary 124–8, *127*, *128*
Prunus 'Taihaku' 199, *199*
Pulmonaria *138*, 141, 207
  P. saccharata 24
purslane, winter 337
Pyracantha 211, 217, 229

P. coccinea 211, *211*
P. 'Golden Charmer' 229
P. 'Navaho' 229
P. 'Orange Glow' 229
P. 'Red Cushion' *229*
pyrethrum 84, 421
Pyrus salicifolia 'Pendula' *205*

q

Quercus 20, 24
  Q. robur 103, *105*
quince leaf blight 403
quinces 308–9, 380, 381, 401–3,
  401–3

r

radicchio 321–2, *321*
radishes 248, 306, *306*
rainfall 20–2, 73
raised beds 35, 243–4, *244*
rakes *38*, 39
raspberries 309, 410, 411,
  412–13, 413–14, *415*
  planting 413–14
  pruning 414, *415*
  summer pudding recipe 423
  supports 413
rats 52, 86
red cabbages 331, *331*
red chicory 321–2, *321*
red hot poker 21
red lettuce 293, *293*
red spider mite 303
redcurrants 410, 411, 425–9,
  426–9
  pests 84
  pruning 428, *429*
  summer pudding recipe 423
"Redgra" paths 98
Rheum palmatum 206
rhizomes 143
rhododendrons 31
rhubarb 266–7, *266–7*
Ribes alpinum 217
Robinia 169
  R. pseudoacacia 20
rock dusts 60
rocket 71, *252*, 254, 262–3
Rodgersia 206

roof gardens 27, 74
root vegetables
  crop rotation 249
  watering 250–1
  *see also individual types of
    vegetable*
rootstocks, fruit trees 375, 384,
  385–8, 405
Rosa 210, 217
  R. 'Alba Semiplena' 199, 222
  R. *banksiae* 'Lutea' 210
  R. *californica* 'Plena' 224–5
  R. 'Cantabrigiensis' 141, *220*,
    221
  R. 'Cardinal de Richelieu' 199,
    220, 222
  R. 'Céleste' *220*, 222–3
  R. 'Chapeau de Napoléon' *219*,
    220
  R. 'Charles de Mills' *219*, *220*,
    223
  R. 'Complicata' 224–5
  R. cuisse de nymphe 222
  R. *farreri* 225
  R. *filipes* 'Kiftsgate' 225
  R. 'Frühlingsgold' 221
  R. 'Général Kléber' 223
  R. *glauca* 229
  R. 'Henri Martin' 223
  R. *hugonis* 141, 221, 225
  R. 'Kazanlik' 223
  R. 'Königin von Dänemark' *198*,
    222
  R. 'Louis Gimard' 223
  R. 'Madame Delaroche-
    Lambert' 223
  R. 'Madame Hardy' 223
  R. 'Madame Legras de St
    Germain' 222
  R. 'Madame Plantier' 222
  R. *moschata* 224–5
  R. *moyesii* *220*, 225, 229
  R. *multiflora* 225
  R. 'Nan of Painswick' 224–5
  R. 'Nevada' *219*, *220*, 221
  R. 'Paul's Himalayan Musk' 209
  R. *pimpinellifolia* 221, 224, 229
    R.p. 'Double Yellow' 221
    R.p. 'Glory of Edzell' 221

R. 'Pompon de Bourgogne'
  223
R. quatre saisons 223
R. 'Robert le Diable' 223
R. 'Rose de Meaux' 223
R. *rugosa* 229
  R.r. 'Alba' *219*
R. 'Scharlachglut' 171, *214*, *216*,
  223
R. *sericea* 221
  R.s. f. *pteracantha* 224–5
R. 'Souvenir de la Malmaison'
  210
R. 'Souvenir du Docteur
  Jamain' 209, 211, *219*, *220*
R. 'Tuscany' *219*
R. 'Tuscany Superb' *220*, 222,
  223
R. *willmottiae* 224–5
R. x *wintoniensis* 224–5, 229
rosemary 31, 197, 343, 345, *353*,
  353, 354, *354*, 361
roses *138*, 197, 199, 212, 218–25,
  341
  companion planting 17
  cuttings 68
  diseases 224
  early roses 221
  hardiness 24
  hips 224, 229, *229*
  midsummer roses 222–3
  pruning *225*
  species roses 224–5
rotary mowers 41, 378, *378*
rotation *see* crop rotation
rotovators 41
royal fern 233, *233*
Rubus cockburnianus 217
  R.c. 'Goldenvale' 228
  R. *fruticosus* 413
  R. *idaeus* 413
ruby chard *173*, 318, *319*
Rudbeckia 177, 204, 206
  R. *fulgida* 185, 206
rue 20, 207
runner beans 26
runners, strawberries *417*
rushes 193
Russian sage 20

Russian tarragon 363
rust, roses 224
Ruta graveolens 20
rye, Hungarian grazing 45, *45*

s

sage 343, 345, *353*, 358–9, *358*
salad crops 69, 71, 255, 262–4,
  262
  winter salads 336–7, *336–7*
Salix 24
  S. *alba* 235
    S.a. subsp. *vitellina* 228
  S. *babylonica* var. *pekinensis*
    'Pendula' 235, *235*
  S. *daphnoides* 217, 228
  S. *fragilis* 15
salsify 249
Salvia 16, 24, 69, 72, 177, 189
  S. *guaranitica* 170, 172
  S. *lavandulifolia* 358, *358*
  S. *officinalis* 358
    S.o. 'Icterina' 358–9
  S. *patens* 172
  S. *purpurea* 358, *358*
Sambucus 217
  S. *racemosa* 'Sutherland Gold'
    217
sandy soil 21, 31
Santolina 20
Sasa 193
Savoy cabbages 331
sawfly 84, 420–1, *422*
scale insects 360
scalpings, paths 97–8
scent
  annuals and biennials 187
  shrubs 217
Scilla 25, 143
scorzonera 249
scythes 40, 378, *378*, 379
sea holly 21
seakale 248
seaweed meal 58, 60
secateurs 40
sedges 193
Sedum 204, 207
  S. *spectabile* 204
seedlings 67, 73, 252

...ds, saving 182, *182*, 273
  see also sowing
seep hose *73*, 74
semi-ripe cuttings 68
shade
  annuals and biennials 187
  east-facing walls 212
  perennials 207
  shrubs for 217
shallots 277, *277*
shears 114, 128
Shirley poppies 25
shredders 56
shreddings, mulches 56
shrubs 217–29
  cuttings 67, 68
  for dry areas 20
  hardy plants 24
  roses 218–25
  winter shrubs 226–9
Siberian irises 156
silver leaf 393
silver maple 107
sitting areas 20
Skimmia 217
slugs 23, 69, 82–3, *85*, 243, 251, 254, 269
small gardens, shrubs for 217
smoke bush 20
smooth meadow grass 378
snails 69, 82–3, *84*, 251
snakeshead fritillary 153, *153*
snapdragons 176, 177
snow 26
snowdrops 25, *138*, 139, 141, 142–3, 144, *144*
snowflake, summer 143
soft fruit 410–29
softwood cuttings 67–8
soil 28–31
  acid soils 14–15
  alkaline soils 14
  in borders 134
  compaction 21
  digging *29*, 32–5, *33–4*, 202
  drainage 21, 22
  herb gardens 345, 353
  layers 28–9
  mulches 54–7

natural fertilizers 57–61
  for perennials 202
  pH values 31, 60, 76
  rainfall and 22
  for strawberries 419
  structure 29
  testing 29–30, *30*
  tilth 35, *35*
  types of 30–1
  vegetable gardens 245, 246, *246*
  wildflower meadows 378
Soil Association 65
soil blocks 66
Solomon's seal *139*, 141
Sorbus 24, 103
sorrel 265, *265*
south-facing walls 20, 210
sowing seed 66–7
  annuals 178–9
  basil 348–9
  carrots 295
  parsley 350
  vegetables 251–3, *252*, 254
spades 32, 37–8, *37*
spearmint 366–7, *366*
spinach 249, 250, 307, *307*
Spiraea thunbergii 24
splitting fruit, tomatoes 283
spring
  bulbs 149–53
  vegetables 254–67
Spring Garden 132, 135, 136–41
spring greens 255, 265, *265*
spring onions 277
sprinklers 74
spruce, Norway 24
spurge 21
squashes 163, 268, 309, *310–12*, 311–12
  in cold frames 253
  crop rotation 248
  sowing 67
  watering 73, 251
Stachys 207
  S. byzantina 170, 207
staking *see* supports
standards
  in coppices 113

fruit trees 375
stems, coloured 226–8
Stipa 189–90
  S. arundinacea 189, *191*
  S. gigantea *188*, 189, *189*, 190, *192*, 234
  S. tenuissima 190
stock, night-scented 187
stone
  paths 96, *96*, 98
  walls 98–9
storage
  apples *383*
  freezing vegetables 271
  garlic 347, *347*
  onions 277, *277*
  pears 408–9
straw
  in chicken manure *51*, 52
  in compost heaps 44, *44*
strawberries 410, 416–19, *416–19*
  caring for the crop 417–19
  growing conditions 416–17
  potting up runners *417*
  soil 419
strimmers 41
subsoil 28
sugar maple 25, 107
sugar snap peas 273
summer
  bulbs 155–61
  vegetables 268–307
summer pudding recipe 423
sun 19–20
sunflowers *62*, 172, *175*, 176, 177, *178*, 184, 185
supports
  apple trees *390*
  clematis *213*
  climbers 209, *209*
  new hedges 116
  peas 272, *272*
  perennials *174*, 204
  raspberries 413
Swan river daisy 21
swedes 248, 325
sweet peas 16, *162*, 163–4, *163*, 171, 177, *178*, 184, 186, 209
sweet rocket 25, 187

sweet William 21
sweetcorn *249*, 251, 253, 326, *326–7*
Swiss chard 318, *318*
switch grass *188*, 192
Symphytum officinale 369
Syringa 217

t
Tanacetum vulgare 371, *371*
tansy 371, *371*
tarragon 343, 363, *363*
Taxus baccata 122
  T.b. 'Fastigiata' 123
teasels 177, 184, *184*, 185, 234, *234*
temperature
  and altitude 25–6
  cold weather 22–5
  plant hardiness 24–5
  rainfall and 21–2
tender plants 24
terraces 197, *199*
Thalictrum 169, 190
  T. delavayi 206
  T. speciosissimum 206
thinning seedlings 252
Thuja occidentalis 24
thyme 31, *245*, 343, 345, *353*, 355–6, *355–6*
Thymus x citriodorus 355
  T. x citriodorus 'Silver Queen' 355
  T. vulgaris 355, *355*
Tilia 24
  T. cordata 110, 111
  T. x europaea 110–11
  T. platyphyllos 'Aurea' 111
    T.p. 'Rubra' 111, *227*
tilth 35, *35*
tithonia 171, 177
toads 83
tobacco plants 21, 187
tomatoes 268, 280–4, *280–4*, 348
  blight 15, 283
  bush tomatoes 282
  in cold frames 253
  companion planting 17
  cordons 280–2, *281*, *282*
  crop rotation 248

in greenhouses 69, *70*, 71
increasing the crop 282–4
pests and diseases 283, *283*
sowing 254
tomato sauce recipe 284
watering 74, 251
tools *36–9*, *37–41*
topiary 26, 114, 124–8, *124–9*
topsoil 28–9
trace elements, natural fertilizers 58
training topiary 124–8
trees 15, *102*, 103–9
  autumn colour *104*
  coppices *112*, 113
  cuttings 67, 68
  for dry areas 20
  hardiness 24
  moving *105*
  planning 92–3
  planting 104
  pleaching limes 110–11, *110–11*, 163, 172, 240–1
  standards 113
trellis 27
Trollius 206
Tropaeolum peregrinum 'Canary Creeper' *186*
trowels 40
tubers 143
tulip fire disease 143
Tulipa (tulips) 109, *138*, 141, 143, 150–2, 164, 172
  T. 'Abu Hassan' 150
  T. 'Black Parrot' *151*, 152
  T. 'Blue Parrot' 150–2
  T. 'Carnaval de Nice' 150, *151*
  T. 'General de Wet' 152
  T. 'Negrita' 150, *151*
  T. 'Orange Artist' 152
  T. 'Orange Favourite' *150*, *151*, 152, *173*
  T. 'Queen of Sheba' 150
  T. 'Queen of the Night' 150, *152*
  T. 'Rococo' 152
  T. 'Spring Green' 150
  T. sylvestris 143, 150

  T. 'West Point' 150
  T. 'White Triumphator' *109*, *139*, 150
tunnels *70*, 71, 73
turf, stacking 32
turnips 248, 325, *325*

V

vegetables 239–337
  autumn vegetables 308–27
  companion planting 17, 81–2
  freezing 271
  paths in vegetable gardens 97, *97*
  pests and diseases 269
  rotation 248–9, *248–9*
  soil 245, 246, *246*
  sowing 251–3, *252*, 254
  spring vegetables 254–67
  summer vegetables 268–307
  watering 73, 244, *244*, 250–1, *250*, 268–9
  winter vegetables 328–37
  see also individual vegetables
ventilation 27, 72
Verbascum 21
Verbena 21, 177
  V. bonariensis 168, 170, *188*, 189, 207
veronica 20
Viburnum 24, 217, 226
  V. x *bodnantense* 217
    V. x *bodnantense* 'Dawn' 226
  V. davidii 217
  V. farreri 217, 226
  V. plicatum 216
    V.p. 'Mariesii 226
  V. tinus 217, 226
Viola 82, 170, 187, 206
  V. reichenbachiana 112
  V. riviniana 112
  V. tricolor 187
violets *112*, 139, 207
Virginia creeper 211
Virginian stock 21
virus diseases, tomatoes 283, *283*
Vitis coignetiae 211
voles 86–7

W

Walled Garden 133, 135, 194–9, *194–9*
wallflowers 21, 163, 164, *165*, 187
walls 98–9, *99*
  climbers 209, 210–12
  sun and shade 20
  vegetable gardens 246
walnuts 396–7
wasps 76
  parasitic wasps 17, 87
water, rainfall 20–2
water butts 22, *251*
watering 73–4, *73*
  greenhouses 72, 73
  new hedges 116
  roof gardens 74
  standpipes 92
  trees 104
  vegetables 73, 244, *244*, 250–1, *250*, 268–9
wattle trees 20
wavy hair grass 190
weather 14, 18–27, 328–9
weeds 75–9
  in animal manure 48
  in compost heaps 43–4
  edible weeds 76
  green manures 45
  in vegetable gardens 250, 269
  weedkillers 75, 76
Weigela 217
west-facing walls 20, 210
wheat, as a windbreak 26
white cedar 24
white willow 235
whitecurrants 410, 425, *425*
whitefly 17, 87, 283
wigwams *208*, 209, *209*, 255, 305, *305*
wildflowers 40–1, 189, 378
willow 15, *102*, 139, 235
  coloured stems 228
  cuttings 67
  hardiness 24
  hurdles 27, 101
wind 26–7
  drying plants out 74

plant stress 27
walls and 99
windbreaks 26–7, 245
winter
  bulbs 144–7
  shrubs 217, 226–9
  vegetables 328–37
  weather 328–9
winter aconite 25
winter jasmine 24
winter squashes *310–12*, 311–12
wintersweet 226
Wisteria floribunda 25
  W. sinensis 210
Witloof chicory 320, *321*
wood anemone *112*
wood ash, natural fertilizers *57*, 61
wood chip paths 244–5, *244*
woodland
  coppices *112*, 113, 135
  plants 207
worms, in compost heaps 43, *43*
wormwood 20, 21
woven fences 113

y

yarrow 21
yew 103
  hedges 116, 122–3, 197
  soil 31
  topiary *125*, 126–7, *128–9*, 164

z

zinc, natural fertilizers 58
zinnias 176, 177, 179

Acknowledgements

AUTHOR'S ACKNOWLEDGEMENTS

This book has been a long time in the making and has taken an enormous amount of work from many people to bring to completion.

I would especially like to thank David Lamb and Anna Kruger at Dorling Kindersley for their constant encouragement and for nurturing the project through some sticky times. Bella Pringle was also a great help with the photoshoots.

Behind the scenes at my end I owe many thanks to Ian Bloom, and also to Araminta Whitley and Celia Hayley. Leigh Hughes was, and is, an invaluable source of calmness, efficiency and order.

For over a year I spent far more time writing about this garden than actually gardening. So the help of Gareth Lorman and his replacements, Norman and Jayne Groves, was invaluable. Without them I would have been desperate.

Especial thanks to Ari Ashley for a year of wonderful photographs. Thanks also to Nick Meers and Peter Anderson.

But by far the biggest burden of gratitude is owed to my wife and children. Our home and garden is just that – a family home, and they endured it becoming the location for countless photoshoots as well as my obsession with 'the (bloody) book' that meant my almost total withdrawal from family life for over a year. Without Sarah the garden would not be the same. It is a genuine collaboration and any credit that is owed is due to her as much as to me. Any mistakes or misjudgements are, of course, entirely my own.

The following companies were very generous and I would like to thank them for their assistance: Honda for rotary tillers and a mower; Countax for a ride-on mower; Fort for wheelbarrows; Habitat for deckchairs; The Organic Gardening Catalogue and Thompson & Morgan for quantities of seeds; Unwins for Coir Jiffy 7's.

PUBLISHER'S ACKNOWLEDGEMENTS

Dorling Kindersley would like to thank Louise Abbott, Zia Allaway, Pamela Brown, and Annelise Evans for editorial work, Alison Donovan for design assistance, Hilary Bird for the index and Mel Watson for picture research.

PICTURE CREDITS
(t = top, b = bottom, r = right, l = left, c = centre)

All photographs by **Ari Ashley** except:

Peter Anderson: 1, 6, 14b, 16, 17, 29tr, 44cl, 51, 88–89, 91tr, 93, 94, 96tl, 102br, 104, 118tr, 119tr, 126, 164, 166, 168b, 173tr, 184br, 188tr, 191br, 229br, 243bc, 246tr/br, 249 tc/bl/br, 268br, 281bl, 284tr, 309bl, 315, 316bl, 327tr/bl/br, 337br, 338, 342tr, 343br, 346tl/ct/c/cr, 349tr, 361bl, 377bl/br, 380tl/bl, 382tr/bl/br, 385tl/cl/tr, 388, 390tl, 407br, 409tr, 410tl, 411br, 415 all, 425tl/tc

DK Picture Library: 186cl, 220cl/tr/bc, 325b, 351br, 355cr, 356cl, 357 all, 358br, 359tr, 360tl/cl, 363tr

Garden Picture Library: 187tr, 220c/br

Garden Picture Library and: Bjorn Forsberg 105br, Jacqui Hurst 144tl, Michael Howes 147b, Howard Rice 147tr/148, Mark Bolton 157tl, Howard Rice 193br, Philippe Bonduel 211tl, Neil Holmes 226tl, Clive Boursnell 351tr, David Cavagnaro 363cr

Jerry Harpur: 157tr

Marcus Harpur: 149t/b, 156tl, 157bl/br, 193tr, 229tr

Nick Irvin: 374t/b

Nick Meers: 14tl, 91tr, 97, 132–133, 134tr, 136, 138tr/b, 140, 159tl, 169t, 170tl, 181, 198br, 214, 222–223, 240–241, 246bl, 328tl, 397

Sea Spring Photos: 329bl, 349br

Sea Spring Photos/Joy Michaud: 261, 265tr, 306, 331tr/cr, 336tl, 358bl

ACKNOWLEDGEMENTS